A Chinese Melting Pot

All MP3 audio files in the book can be downloaded at
https://www.hkupress.hku.hk/+extras/1681audio/ .

A Chinese Melting Pot

Original People and Immigrants in Hong Kong's First 'New Town'

Elizabeth Lominska Johnson and Graham E. Johnson

Roy + Cathy in
friendship.

Betsy   and Graham

HKU
PRESS
香港大學出版社

Hong Kong University Press
The University of Hong Kong
Pokfulam Road
Hong Kong
https://hkupress.hku.hk

ISBN 978-988-8455-89-8 (*Hardback*)

British Library Cataloguing-in-Publication Data
A catalogue record for this book is available from the British Library.

10 9 8 7 6 5 4 3 2 1

Printed and bound by Hang Tai Printing Co. Ltd., Hong Kong, China

Contents

Illustrations

Tables

Preface

Why Tsuen Wan?

When we explain our long-term fascination with Tsuen Wan, we are sometimes met with expressions of surprise, ignorance, or polite indifference, even on the part of people who are otherwise familiar with contemporary Hong Kong. Some may remember it as a place from which they went on hill walks or visited monasteries, but others wonder why we are excited about, and loyal to, a place that superficially appears to be simply another urban development, and the terminus of one branch of the Mass Transit Railway. Furthermore, it is not just the general public that often has been indifferent. Despite its important contributions to the economic and political development of Hong Kong, and its value for the comparative study of social organization and change in south China, Tsuen Wan has attracted minimal attention from anthropologists and sociologists like ourselves.

Tsuen Wan now looks and feels like many other parts of urban Hong Kong, with its shopping malls, public housing, and high-rise middle-class housing complexes. Judging by outward appearances, few could imagine the distinctive phases of its development, or believe that when we first saw it, in the late 1960s, Tsuen Wan was a burgeoning, but chaotic, industrial city.

Until the early twentieth century, Tsuen Wan was a separate district within the area that became the Southern District of the New Territories after British rule was established in 1898, located in a spectacular and rugged setting on the foothills of Tai Mo Shan and land reclaimed from the sea. It was unique in that all of its more than 20 villages were inhabited by Hakka people, a sub-ethnic group within the Han Chinese population, speaking a distinct variant of Chinese, although using the common written language. Its many small lineages lived together in relative peace, managing their own affairs and wresting a difficult livelihood from the land and sea by farming the limited amount of land that was available and doing in-shore fishing. In the late nineteenth and early twentieth century, many men resorted to temporary emigration in the hope of economic betterment. Those with some means engaged in business, both in its coastal daily market town and on Hong Kong Island, which was readily accessible by water. After 1917, Castle Peak Road provided a land link to Kowloon. The district's location made possible the development of some small industries and a major oil depot even before the Japanese occupation of 1941–1945. These developments, together with government dam-building projects, offered wage labour opportunities.

In the early post-war period, Tsuen Wan began to industrialize at a remarkable rate. Its development was made possible by its proximity and relatively easy access to Hong Kong and Kowloon, its abundance of fresh water, and the availability of land and labour. These attracted industrialists from the Shanghai region, who were relocating in advance of the establishment of the People's Republic of China, bringing capital investments, machinery, and skilled workers. Its development followed an entirely different trajectory from those of other districts of Hong Kong's New Territories, making Tsuen Wan special, and in its own way, exciting. In much of the New Territories in the 1950s, the indigenous people, the descendants of those who were resident property owners when the British assumed control, were giving up rice agriculture. The response of many of working age was to emigrate from Hong Kong to Britain, to which they had free access, where they could make a living in Chinese restaurants. They often rented out their land to immigrant vegetable farmers from China.

In Tsuen Wan, the indigenous population, by contrast, rapidly became engaged in the new economy. They no longer needed to emigrate. Waves of newcomers, who rapidly came to outnumber the original inhabitants, developed their own ways of coping with the stress of change and the unfamiliar environment, forming associations based on various commonalities that offered mutual support. By the late 1960s, Tsuen Wan was a booming industrial town with a population of over 250,000, primarily immigrants. The principal industries were those producing textiles, with related treatments, such as dyeing, resulting in pollution of both air and water. The whole town had a grimy, makeshift appearance, with tenements and squatter housing crammed in wherever space permitted. Grey concrete predominated and there were few green areas.

This was Tsuen Wan when we first saw it in 1968, as two young students hoping to conduct our doctoral research in a place characterized by rapid change. It was a very different place than it is now. The initial result of Tsuen Wan's economic transformation was, frankly speaking, a mess. The industrial township that, largely uncontrolled, had grown up in the early post-war years of massive immigration was expanding rapidly, but under a government that was overwhelmed, and needed resources and time to engage in adequate planning. In 1961, government officials realized that something must be done to bring some order to the near-chaos that existed, and in 1961 designated Tsuen Wan the first 'satellite city', a 'new town', following the British model, and began to implement urban planning, albeit somewhat retroactively, with an anticipated eventual population of one million. Scattered through and around the town were the original villages that had been guaranteed their land rights by the terms of the Peking Convention of 1898, thus complicating any planning that was to be undertaken.

Once we had learned enough about this situation to define our projects, we plunged into our research. Graham, the sociologist, concentrated on the town as a whole, and the immigrants from other parts of China who lived and worked there, although he also interviewed indigenous leaders, while Elizabeth, an anthropologist, focussed primarily on Kwan Mun Hau, one of the villages that had been part of the territory when it came under British rule in 1898. As our work progressed, we became more and more fascinated by what we were learning; and now, almost 50 years later, armed with considerable additional information gained over the intervening years, we continue to be excited by the insights we gain as we pore over our material.

The industrial world of the 1960s has now passed. Tsuen Wan is now fully integrated with the modern and affluent territory that Hong Kong has become, no longer colonial, and a special administrative entity of the People's Republic of China. The descendants of the original inhabitants, now only a tiny fragment of the population, remain, as do their villages, although many have moved to new locations. Their cultural distinctiveness has faded but still remains.

Our observations of the changes in Tsuen Wan deepen our commitment to creating a record of social relations in this distinctive area of the New Territories before it is too late, fulfilling our obligation to preserve the knowledge that its people entrusted to us, in the hope that others will come to appreciate its special characteristics.

Acknowledgements

We owe an enormous debt to so many, a debt which has grown over the more than four decades that we have been involved with Tsuen Wan. Without question our deepest debt is to James Hayes, who drew attention to Tsuen Wan through his significant publications based on his long-term experience with both the district and the town. These were written from his perspectives as an historian and senior government officer with responsibility for Tsuen Wan during its most tumultuous times, with genuine concern for its people. We are grateful to him for demonstrating his usual generosity in encouraging us to write a book that is based on our own experience. He has given his ongoing support to our work, patiently offering information and advice whenever we have asked, and urging us on.

James L. Watson also supported us in this project, knowing that many fruitful comparisons can be made with the large and powerful Cantonese-speaking lineage villages that he and Rubie S. Watson have studied for an equally long time, but also with other forms of social organization that existed in the New Territories and in the adjacent Pearl River delta region. He has regularly badgered us about 'writing the book'.

We sincerely appreciate the kindness, acceptance, and help we have received from the people of Tsuen Wan, past and present. We owe a debt of gratitude to the leaders, both native and immigrant, whom we interviewed. Without their help and cooperation large portions of this study would have been impossible. In the 1990s, Ho Wing-kwong, community leader and local historian, spent many hours sharing his knowledge of Tsuen Wan's past, gathered during his lifetime of study. Chan Lau-fong was also generous with his time and knowledge.

We are deeply grateful for the kindness and the friendship of the residents of Kwan Mun Hau over the years. They welcomed our family into their village, talked with us, hosted us at meals of delicious Hakka food, and invited us to their ceremonies. They have been polite, helpful, and patient with our questions.

In particular, we wish to thank Yau Shui-cheung, his wife Yau Chan Shek-ying, and their children for helping us in innumerable ways and sharing their knowledge of Hakka culture. It was Yau Chan Shek-ying, with her remarkable memory, who sang almost all of the mountain songs and laments reproduced here, and encouraged Elizabeth to record them. She also shared her knowledge of their meanings, thus giving us a window into another world, the world of her youth. Her family has agreed that the recordings should be donated to two Canadian libraries and archives (see Chapter 2, footnote 72), where they are available to the public.

Their daughter Miriam Yuk-kuen Yau, who is fluent in Hakka, Cantonese, and English, has been more than an interpreter. She has been a research associate and a friend, offering sensitive guidance and significant insights. Her oldest brother, Mark Yau Yan-loi, gave us a much-improved understanding of their mother's songs and laments, as well as his advice, unfailing support, and friendship.

We thank Paul Siu-kwong Yau for many discussions about the functioning of the Yau lineage of Kwan Mun Hau and Hoi Pa. He took time to meet with us on many occasions from 1968 until the present, sharing with us important lineage documents, both historical and contemporary.

Our first next-door neighbours in Kwan Mun Hau were Kwok Yung-hing and his wife, Kwok Fung Yin-ha. No ethnographer could have had better neighbours. They always have been willing to discuss our queries, thoughtfully sharing their deep knowledge of Tsuen Wan. In 1970 they agreed that we might adopt their youngest child as our goddaughter in the traditional Chinese sense, thereby cementing our relationship over the years.

Numerous colleagues, friends, and advisers in Hong Kong, the United States, Canada, Germany, and the United Kingdom have given their help and advice. To all, we express our thanks. Graham Barnes, district officer during our first stay in Tsuen Wan, was extremely important in providing access to government documentation, and finding us housing on two occasions. The late Marjorie Topley was an insightful sounding board for our ideas. Howard and Janet Nelson gave us valuable support during our early months in Hong Kong.

We could not have written this book without the information and support given to us by all of these people. Those errors that remain are our responsibility.

Stanley Sheung-yan Wong was one of our principal research assistants from 1968 to 1970, and unfailingly polite and resourceful in any situation. Others who gave significant help with Elizabeth's research include Grace Yan-chi Chu and Jennifer Chi-yee Wun, both of whom understood Hakka and had a genuine and respectful interest in learning from the people we interviewed. Dr Philip Clart, University of Leipzig, and the late Wang Ji-ming provided Elizabeth with authoritative translations of genealogies and official publications, without which her understanding would have been much more limited.

Dr George C. S. Lin, professor of geography at Hong Kong University, expertly prepared the maps. Marilyn MacLean Denton was kind enough to read our manuscript and gave us invaluable comments. We have benefitted more than we can say from her years of experience as a writer, and her keen eye.

We were fortunate in obtaining research funding from many sources. We initially had fellowships from the London-Cornell Project for East and Southeast Asian Studies (Graham) and the Population Council (Elizabeth). We held research grants from Canada Council, later the Social Sciences and Humanities Research Council of Canada (Graham), The Joint Centre on Modern East Asia University of Toronto-York University, the University of British Columbia Museum of Anthropology (Elizabeth), faculty research grants from the University of British Columbia, and a fellowship from City University of Hong Kong (Graham).

We are deeply grateful to the editors of Hong Kong University Press. They have been supportive of our efforts, insightful in their comments, and a pleasure to work with throughout the project.

A Note on Romanization

Chinese terms are, in general, romanized according to the Hanyu Pinyin system. The most prevalent version of spoken Chinese in Hong Kong is Cantonese, and we have chosen to romanize distinctive terms into Cantonese using the Yale system. Chinese characters are included in the first occurrence. We worked almost entirely in Cantonese, although we provide a few Hakka terms, and one in Hokkien.

We have used the British colonial government romanization system for place names, following *A Gazetteer of Place Names in Hong Kong, Kowloon and the New Territories* (Hong Kong: Government Printer, 1960). We romanize place names and personal names in China using Hanyu Pinyin. The names of Hong Kong–based individuals are romanized according to local practice. Some terms also reflect historical usage; thus, the Cantonese groupings in the New Territories are designated 'Punti' (Pinyin: *bendi*), the other indigenous land-based speech group as 'Hakka' (Pinyin: *kejia*), and people from northeast Guangdong as 'Teochiu' (Pinyin: *Chaozhou*). Deities worshipped throughout the Chinese culture area are romanized into Pinyin, while those which are highly localized are romanized into Cantonese. This is especially significant for village gods, whose names may also reflect Hakka cultural influence.

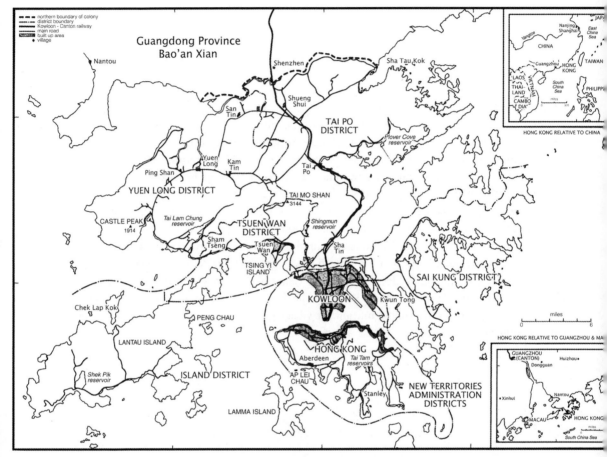

Map 1: Map of Hong Kong, Kowloon, and the New Territories, 1969

1

Getting Started

On 19 April 1968, we approached Hong Kong by air carrying our four-month-old son. The clouds suddenly parted, we glimpsed Hong Kong, and experienced the drama of the tight approach to Kai Tak Airport. Our plane banked sharply, just over a densely packed area of tenements, and landed. We were graduate students from an American university, bound for Asia for the first time, hoping to complete our research projects, write book-length theses, and receive our degrees. We had research funding for two years and some general ideas of what we hoped to accomplish. We were blissfully ignorant of how much work lay ahead, and how exciting and full our lives would be.

Our Hopes and Plans

It was customary that after taking course work and discussing our disciplinary interests with our teachers and fellow doctoral students, we should define research topics and strategies. Ideally, in anthropology (Elizabeth's field) or sociology (Graham's), students should conduct 'field work'. This meant choosing a setting (a 'culture', a 'society') and becoming immersed in a part of it (a 'village', a 'town'), as a way to comprehend it and carry out research on agreed-on themes (i.e., 'developing and writing a thesis'). The two disciplines had slightly different approaches, which we were to follow, but overall these differences were not crucial.

We had met during our studies at Cornell University, in the United States. Elizabeth's interests included social organization and change, and population studies. Graham had previously done his undergraduate studies in sociology and economics in England, where his tutor had suggested China as his area of future specialty. Once we had married, Elizabeth followed suit. Graham had been introduced to Maurice Freedman, professor of anthropology at the London School of Economics, who was ushering in 'a Chinese phase in social anthropology',[1] and had recently published an important volume on Chinese kinship,[2] building on his earlier studies of Chinese families in Singapore. Graham was also fortunate enough to meet Barbara Ward who, in the 1950s, had begun her important field research with fishing people, which over time had extended to other aspects of social and cultural life in Hong Kong.[3]

Hong Kong had gradually emerged as the location of our field research. Fortunately, Cornell offered superb instruction in Chinese languages, and we both had the opportunity to study Cantonese

---

1. Maurice Freedman, 'A Chinese Phase in Social Anthropology', *The British Journal of Sociology* 14, no. 1 (March 1963): 1–19.
2. Maurice Freedman, *Lineage Organization in Southeastern China* (London: Athlone Press, 1958).
3. Barbara E. Ward, *Through Other Eyes: Essays in Understanding 'Conscious Models'* (Hong Kong: Chinese University Press, 1985), includes some, but not all, of her important contributions.

Plate 1: View of Tsuen Wan with Tai Mo Shan behind, as seen across the bay near Tsing Yi Island, c. 1968. Oil tank of Texaco depot on right, Fuk Loi Tsuen low-cost housing estate on left.

to the extent that we could carry out basic conversations when we arrived in Hong Kong, where we continued language study.

Why did we choose Hong Kong, and more specifically Tsuen Wan, as our research site? Until the 1970s, China was closed to foreign researchers, which meant that social scientists went either to do research in Taiwan; to do 'China watching' from Hong Kong, for those interested in the People's Republic of China; or to do research on Hong Kong itself. Hong Kong as a British colony was accessible, it was affordable, and the colonial government in general supported foreign researchers. There had been considerable political conflict in the year immediately preceding our arrival and while this conflict continued, although less violently, Hong Kong still offered relative stability.

Our choice of Tsuen Wan as a research site resulted from our interest in studying the social effects of economic transformation, albeit from our somewhat different disciplinary perspectives. In retrospect, we believe that our complementary disciplines led to a much richer understanding of Tsuen Wan. Hong Kong government reports indicated that this rapidly growing town seemed to be a prime example of intense economic and social change, although it was otherwise questionable that we, a couple with a small baby, should choose what appeared to be a most unattractive and disorganized place to do our kinds of social science research. These include actually living in the research site, learning by observing and taking part in ongoing social activities, and conducting more formal interviews.

From the moment we arrived in Tsuen Wan, only two weeks after our arrival in Hong Kong, it was sink or swim. To the best of our knowledge, we were the only Western family living there immersed in a wholly Chinese context. We had to speak Cantonese, the Chinese language most commonly spoken, if we were to manage and form social relationships. There were some British families among the police, who led a very separate existence, and a few missionaries dedicated to their work. However, they were not particularly visible. We were conspicuous, and even suspect in the volatile political climate of the time.

Orientation

During our first two weeks, we stayed in Kowloon and attempted to become oriented to the vibrancy and complexity of Hong Kong. On our first day, a fellow anthropologist gave us a tour of the New Territories.[4] We were impressed by the rural villages and the extent of cultivation that we saw, the rice paddies and plots of vegetables and flowers, a great contrast to the intense urban environment of crowded Kowloon.

This period included a series of conversations. We met with government officials, who were open and frank, and generous with their time. They included James Hayes, who had served as district officer in the Southern District, and who was developing a significant reputation as a local historian. He had been instrumental in the resiting of the Shek Pik villagers, many of whom had moved from Lantau Island to Tsuen Wan, making way for reservoir construction.

We also interacted with the other social scientists who were in Hong Kong at the time, benefitting from their experience and advice. We had discussions with the most knowledgeable anthropologists working in Hong Kong, Marjorie Topley and Barbara Ward, who suggested studying one of the Tsuen Wan villages. Maurice Berkowitz, a visiting scholar at the Chinese University, who was studying the social impact of moving villagers to flats in Tai Po because of reservoir construction,[5] thought that if we were to consider Tsuen Wan, we should include a study of a village or villages, factories, power relations, and religious practices.

Ten days after our arrival, we made our first trip to Tsuen Wan to see Graham Barnes, the district officer. It was a cordial visit in his office, located in a factory area, facing a hillside covered with squatter structures. We first discussed housing. We learned that there were the original villages, some bearing the brunt of urban and industrial development, including several that had been resited to locations outside the central development area. In contrast, others had been resited to flats in Tsuen Wan, because of reservoir development. There were low-rise tenements, some dating from the late 1930s, and others on land reclaimed from the foreshore in the 1950s and 1960s. Government resettlement estates had first been constructed in 1957 to rehouse squatters, although many squatters remained. A Housing Authority estate, Fuk Loi Tsuen, rehoused people whose income levels met authority requirements.

We discussed how the government saw its role in the process of development in the rural and agricultural New Territories, where industrial Tsuen Wan was the exception. Our conversation turned to land and in particular the Crown Land Resumption Ordinance. Under it, land could be resumed for public purposes such as roads, bridges, reservoirs, or, as in Tsuen Wan, for resiting entire villages that lay within the growing urban centre and whose houses and lands stood in the way of planned development of the industrial town that had grown haphazardly. Resumption was not outright seizure. Rather, compensation was arrived at through a process of negotiation. Indigenous ownership of land and property was enshrined in the governance of the New Territories shortly after the British lease in 1898. It was established after a thorough cadastral survey, in which land uses, for housing or agriculture, for example, had different values for tax purposes. In negotiations concerning compensation for resumed land and property, government policy provided for no increases in the value of land classified

---

4. The British colony of Hong Kong grew in stages. Hong Kong island was ceded 'in perpetuity' to the British Crown in 1841, as was much of the Kowloon peninsula in 1859. A much larger area, the 'New Territories', was leased to Britain for 99 years in 1898 through the Peking Convention. The area north of the Kowloon peninsula and bounded by the Kowloon hills became known as New Kowloon. Its villagers did not enjoy the rights accorded to others in the leased area.

5. Morris L. Berkowitz, 'Plover Cove Village to Taipo Market: A Study in Forced Migration', *Journal of the Hong Kong Branch Royal Asiatic Society* 8 (1968): 96–108.

as agricultural, regardless of current use. Further transactions in resumed land were part of a planned series of development steps, which should not, therefore, involve the original owner directly.

The solution was land exchange. Land was surrendered, and the former owner obtained new land and building rights within Tsuen Wan at a fixed premium. This was a policy specific to the New Territories. Elsewhere, building land could be obtained only by attending an auction of Crown land. Land in Hong Kong was deemed to be owned by the Crown, and even the ancestral holdings of New Territories inhabitants were considered to be Crown leases. Indigenous villagers hardly saw it that way and granting them building rights was an indirect way of recognizing actual land values. Even so, there was not enough building land available for all claimants to use. Instead, the government issued 'Letters of Exchange', titles to develop land as it became available. These became part of a market of negotiable instruments which developers could use and, as their values increased, from which villagers benefitted. The benefits could be realized in several different ways. A typical arrangement was partnership with a building company, which would provide the capital to develop land, with the completed project split between the building company and owners of the Letters of Exchange.[6]

The biggest challenge, from Graham Barnes' perspective, was the appreciation in value of agricultural land which lay within the layout plan that had been formulated for central Tsuen Wan. Of the older villages, three had been resited in 1964 and moved from high density locations to an area on the outskirts of the growing town, receiving agreed-on compensation for houses and their lots, and for agricultural land.

In the wake of various political problems, spillovers from the Cultural Revolution in China, the stock market and real estate values had crashed. In 1968, villagers opposed agreements that had been painstakingly negotiated over several years, although conditions were becoming intolerable because of crowding and summer floods. The political situation in Tsuen Wan was complex. Some people were sympathetic to the left-wing politics of China, and they were hedging in dealing with the government through their village representatives, who, as members of the Tsuen Wan Rural Committee, were part of the consultative process whereby the district officer interacted with the indigenous population.

Much of our conversation focussed on this indigenous population, with whom the consultative process was firmly established. However, Tsuen Wan was unique within the New Territories, as it was highly industrial and had a largely immigrant population. The textile industry, the core of Tsuen Wan's economy, was dominated by entrepreneurs from the Shanghai region. There were also business leaders from Huizhou and the Chaozhou area, both situated in Guangdong but speaking different versions of Chinese. The complex array of speech groups apparently formed discrete communities, about which we had much to learn. Oddly, there were no company offices, although much manufacturing, and no automatic telephone service. Tsuen Wan seemed isolated from Hong Kong's business district.

Our Move to Tsuen Wan

We concluded that Tsuen Wan would be appropriate for our research, and the more we learned, the more intrigued we became. We were given free access to the District Office and provided desk space in a corner of the land registry, with its volumes of records of land ownership and use from the 1904 survey. Graham Barnes was also kind enough to locate a flat that we rented, following our decision to make Tsuen Wan our home for the duration of our research. This would enable us to learn about the place through direct observation and participation in social life.

Our arrival, two weeks after we landed in Hong Kong, must have been highly entertaining to any of the inhabitants who happened to see it. Our spacious flat was on the eighth floor of Waldorf

---

6. For a detailed scholarly account, see Roger Nissim, *Land Administration and Practice in Hong Kong*, 3rd ed. (Hong Kong: Hong Kong University Press, 2012).

Mansions, a new building just outside central Tsuen Wan. We hired a lorry to collect the second-hand furniture we had purchased, then rode from Kowloon to Tsuen Wan sitting in the back on a rattan couch, holding our baby amidst the furniture we had bought—a most unusual way to travel to such an unlikely destination for a Western family.

From the vantage point of our new accommodation, we could look down on the disorder of the town, with its factories, tenements, early resettlement blocks, its first low-cost housing estate, and, if one knew where to look, some of the original villages. We faced the challenge of formulating specific research proposals, then planning strategies to implement them. This was daunting. We could not just remain in our flat overlooking the town, we needed to find ways to get down to street level and carry out the research that would help us make sense of a place that was undergoing such extraordinary change.

For seven months we lived in Waldorf Mansions, improving our Cantonese, exploring the town and its surroundings, and entering into relationships with local people, such as vendors in the market where we made our daily purchases, and restaurant staff. Life in our flat seemed increasingly rarefied. We worked desperately to find a research location and to delineate research proposals that would be appropriate to Tsuen Wan and acceptable to our advisers.

Early Decision-Making

Elizabeth had determined that her research would focus primarily on kinship and the demographic aspect of her training, particularly with respect to family formation and structure. She hoped to learn about people's attitudes regarding the size and structure of their families and the number of children they had or hoped to have. It seemed likely that Tsuen Wan in the late 1960s was undergoing what is called 'the demographic transition', which is associated with the processes of urbanization and indus-trialization.[7] During the demographic transition, mortality rates fall due to improved medical care, public health measures, and food quality and supply. In response to lower childhood mortality, birth rates decline if couples wish to limit the number of children they have and have the means to do so. Information available in the late 1960s indicated that in Hong Kong birth rates were falling, in part because of the work of the Hong Kong Family Planning Association. Estimates were that 42% of all married women aged 25 to 45 were practicing some form of contraception in 1967.[8] Furthermore, the age at marriage was rising, which would contribute to a declining birth rate. As a result, one would predict that family size was decreasing. The literature also suggested that complex households composed of several generations or families of several brothers living together would be unlikely to continue to exist.[9]

In 1968, the process of urbanization in Tsuen Wan was in full force, and medical and family plan-ning services were readily available. It seemed to offer an ideal setting for study. The question, however, was where within this complex and apparently unstructured town could such research be conducted.

Graham Barnes discussed various possibilities with Elizabeth, as did other knowledgeable people. One that we seriously considered was that we live in a room in a resettlement block. We decided against this, however, because it would be obvious that we did not meet the eligibility requirements, and because household structure within them was controlled. Elizabeth's research would be meaningless.

---

7. J. C. Caldwell, 'Toward a Restatement of Demographic Transition Theory', *Population and Development Review* 2, no. 3/4 *(September–December, 1976)*: 321–66.
8. D. Podmore, 'The Population of Hong Kong', in *Hong Kong: The Industrial Colony: A Political, Social and Economic Survey*, ed. Keith Hopkins (Hong Kong: Oxford University Press, 1971), 35.
9. This literal biological basis of kinship studies now has been expanded to include socially created kinship. Likewise, the theory that complex kin relationships might not survive in contemporary urban contexts is being reconsidered. See Linda Stone, *Kinship and Gender: An Introduction* (Boulder, CO: Westview Press, 2014), 22–24, 292–95.

Interviewing clients at family planning clinics or social work offices was another possibility, but she had used this method previously and had learned that it did not provide sufficient depth of information. There were also ethical concerns because such clients could not refuse to cooperate without fearing that they might risk losing the services they had come to obtain. What was needed was a residential unit where she could learn both by living among its members and observing daily life, and by doing interviews.

Living in a middle-class residential building in Tsuen Wan was far from what we had in mind, although determining what we had in mind took time to work out. Nonetheless, we were in Tsuen Wan and began to appreciate both its complexity and its unexpected charm, as we explored it to the full. Our explorations helped us determine where we might live and where Elizabeth might do her research.

Exploring Tsuen Wan

From our flat we had good views of our surroundings. Across from us was the Far East Bank Building, then the tallest building in Tsuen Wan, although largely devoid of tenants. Behind it was the entrance to the crowded and cluttered village of Upper Hoi Pa. To the left was an amusement park at the junction of Texaco Road, which led out to a peninsula on which the Texaco Oil Depot was located. To the east were the stark and crowded six-storey blocks of Tai Wo Hau, Tsuen Wan's first resettlement estate. In the distance were the harbour and Tsing Yi Island, and a view of the typhoon shelter. Typhoons were dramatic when viewed from the eighth floor and heightened further by weather reports on the radio. It was impressive seeing fishing boats come in for shelter, and equally so as they left in a long

Plate 2: One block of the Tai Wo Hau resettlement estate with 'park' in foreground. Tai Wo Hau Kaifong Welfare Association can be seen on the ground floor, c. 1969.

Plate 3: The upper market and shophouses that were built in the 1930s, as seen in the late 1960s.

line after the winds had died down. From the rear, we were able to look down onto Sam Tung Uk, an original Hakka compound village, with its ancestral hall facing our building.

We explored the town and found much of interest at ground level. It was a veritable hotchpotch. Chung On Street was the major thoroughfare, and between the Castle Peak Road junction and the original waterfront, just beyond Castle Peak Road, there was a series of shophouses from the 1930s. Ground-level business activity was diverse, and much was unfamiliar to us. On the higher floors there were different kinds of activities, among which seemed to be clubhouses for people from different parts of China, athletic associations, practitioners of Chinese medicine, business associations and trade unions, and the offices of the Tsuen Wan Rural Committee and the Tsuen Wan Sports Association.

The market included butchers' stalls, selling largely beef and pork, and others selling live fish, live chickens, bean curd, vegetables, and fruit. Beyond Market Street there were butchers selling roast pork, barbecued pork, roast chicken, and roast goose. We found shops selling tea, condiments, gold, cloth of all kinds, electrical goods, and cakes. There were rice shops with big wooden bins of different kinds of rice from China, Southeast Asia, and the very best, and most expensive, from Hong Kong itself—the paddy fields around Yuen Long. On the east side of the street there was a bazaar selling bamboo products, brushes, soap, washboards, dust pans and tin boxes made from beer cans, all kinds of kitchen utensils, knives, and with a photographer's studio crammed in. There were also several cinemas, with enormous hand-painted posters depicting current attractions. On the side streets were small restaurants featuring different regional cuisines. Prominent were Hakka and Shanghai-style restaurants, which gave clues to the ethnic composition of the population, as did the sometimes-pungent odours of street-side snacks such as freshly fried Shanghai fermented bean curd.

A smaller market close to the ferry pier on Yeung Uk Road had a large number of water-dwellers selling shellfish and fish. This street became an evening market, including street-side food stalls (大排檔) selling cheap but delicious foods. Chuen Lung Street, from the waterfront to Sha Tsui Road, had

Plate 4: Fishing boats in the harbour. The boat-dwellers' extremely limited living quarters and possessions can be seen, together with their fishing gear, c. 1969.

a market selling garments, many probably produced in Tsuen Wan's factories. It ended with a China products store, the town's only department store, a five-storey building selling cheap and useful, if not fashionable, goods. As one of the few air-conditioned shops, it was a place to escape the heat and humidity of Hong Kong from April until November. Some of the larger China products stores in Hong Kong and Kowloon sold luxury goods, but Tsuen Wan was a working-class town in 1968 and there was little demand for these. That said, when the cold northern winds blew at the onset of winter, it was the place to buy quilts, padded jackets, and long underwear.

The factory area was to the west of the town centre, beyond Fuk Loi Chuen, the post office, the terribly polluted *nullah* (drainage ditch), the fire station, and the District Office. Here there were modern textile factories employing the bulk of the labour force, but also factories that made Thermos bottles, enamelware, furniture, and foodstuffs. There were also many small factories, each employing only a handful of workers. Especially notable were the so-called 'flatted factories', government buildings like resettlement blocks housing diverse small enterprises which likely had been relocated from squatter areas. These remained in the hills above Castle Peak Road, extending up to Route Twisk, linking Tsuen Wan to Shek Kong, a military camp, on the other side of Tai Mo Shan. There were a few small villages on the mountainside. The most significant was Chuen Lung, half way up the mountain road, notable for some excellent teahouses.

Beyond the factory area, Castle Peak Road followed the coast, through the small village of Ting Kau, with some modern villas and a beach; Tsing Lung Tau, with a substantial water-dwelling population in the bay; and on to Sham Tseng, a large indigenous village surrounded by squatters and known for its roast goose. The settlement contained a brewery, an industrial bakery, a cotton mill, and the dock for the Ma Wan local ferry (街渡).

Plate 5: Factories in western Tsuen Wan, c. 1969. Their height suggests that they were spinning or weaving mills. The China Dyeing Works is on the left, and squatter areas behind.

The islands of Tsing Yi and Ma Wan were linked to the mainland only by ferry. There was a group of farming villages on Tsing Yi, a small market centre, a substantial water-dwelling population in the harbour, and ship repair yards on the northwest coast. Ma Wan had a major village and some small hamlets. It had been the location of the Imperial 'Kowloon Customs'. Its Tianhou (天后) temple displayed memorial boards presented by imperial officials who had served there.

On the landward side of Castle Peak Road in central Tsuen Wan there were several villages. The upper storeys of the old houses of Muk Min Ha were level with the road. It was crowded and run-down, with many small industries, and was surrounded by squatter settlements that merged into the old villages of Sai Lau Kok and San Tsuen. Some fields remained, growing vegetables rather than rice, which were skirted by two paths that led up Lo Wai and through extensive squatter areas to several religious establishments in the foothills of Tai Mo Shan. The easterly path flanked Sam Tung Uk, to the east of which there were silk weaving mills, simple wooden sheds using Jacquard looms to produce brocades—their punched cards creating elegant patterns. To the north of the village was the Tianhou temple, a distinguished building with a wealth of historical information on stone tablets, lintels, and a bell dating to 1743. Tablets recorded a series of restorations, the most extensive occurring in 1897. There was a school in one side hall, and a shrine to a group of local martyrs in the other.

Beyond the temple there was a bean curd factory, a glass factory,[10] a number of religious institutions, and a huge squatter area, the majority of the occupants of which, we were to learn, were Teochiu immigrants. It was dominated by a most remarkable squatter structure, a temple made of ferroconcrete formed into an enormous red bottle gourd in front of a mountain with a giant monkey's head, and

10. See Barbara E. Ward, 'A Small Factory in Hong Kong: Some Aspects of Its Internal Organization', in *Economic Organization in Chinese Society*, ed. W. E. Willmott (Stanford: Stanford University Press, 1972), 353–86.

Plate 6: Muk Min Ha village as seen from Castle Peak Road in the late 1960s, with a Shanghai tailor selling clothing and monastic robes in the centre.

depicting three-dimensional life-sized scenes from the famous Chinese novel *Journey to the West* (西遊記). When we first encountered this on one of our early walks we were dumbfounded and had no idea what it might be.

A series of valleys ran down the mountain. Shing Mun valley ran from the Shing Mun or Jubilee Reservoir and was intensively cultivated by vegetable farmers, many of whom lived in huts by their fields, running to market twice a day with freshly cut vegetables on carrying poles. Immediately to the east were the three resited villages of Kwan Mun Hau, Yeung Uk, and Ho Pui, fronted by the newly built and heavily fortified police station, overlooking Tai Wo Hau resettlement estate. Beyond the three villages was the Kwai Chung valley. Sheung Kwai Chung was tucked in a verdant hollow to the north, along with some other smaller villages. Chung Kwai Chung was close to the main road and contained a number of factories, and nearby were the villages of Lei Muk Shue and Shek Lei, whose fields were about to give way to resettlement estates. The valley dropped down to the village of Ha Kwai Chung, resited in 1964, with its pleasant little Tianhou temple on the shore of Gin Drinkers Bay. Further east, up to the boundary with New Kowloon, accessible only along Castle Peak Road, was the sizeable village of Kau Wa Keng and the post-war settlement of Kau Wa New Village.

This large and complex district was to be at the centre of our lives for the following two years. We continued to visit the outlying parts, but most of our focus was directed towards the town centre and its development.

Focusing Our Research

Tsuen Wan had a number of advantages for Graham's work. Living in the town and becoming familiar with its complexities helped to determine the kinds of questions that he might ask. Initially working in the District Office, talking to staff responsible for creating plans to deal with the district and its issues, and having the opportunity to read files and documents, were all fundamentally important. Graham found much of interest, starting with the land records from the 1904 survey. It was fascinating to understand the emerging industrial and densely populated landscape in the context of its former agricultural character. Infrastructural improvements were urgently needed. There were major challenges, and the indigenous land owners seemed important to their resolution if town planning was to be effective and a 'new town'[11] created.

Yet the bulk of the rapidly expanding population was not indigenous. They were immigrants to Hong Kong. We wished to learn how migrants from diverse origins participated in Tsuen Wan's industrial development and adjusted to their new lives. The extent to which immigrants had developed support systems and a degree of social cohesion increasingly became the focus of Graham's work, in comparison with the indigenous population and its response to fundamental change. He was helped by the information he found in the District Office files. They revealed unpublished information about planning decisions, the structure of economic activity, the many organizations that had been formed as the population had grown and become more diverse, and the complex political decisions that had been made in a colonial structure that had been created to deal primarily with an agricultural population in the New Territories.

China was a society firmly based on agriculture, yet it was also highly urbanized and contained some of the world's greatest and largest cities. Such cities were characterized by immigrant populations who had coped with the disruptive effects of migration by creating associations based on the same place of origin, occupation, or surname. When Chinese people went abroad in large numbers, especially after the mid-nineteenth century, they too created such organizations for mutual support in alien and often hostile social contexts. These associations and their leaders gave them stability in their new environments, whether these were cities in China, or mines, plantations, or cities overseas.

The District Office files suggested that associations were significantly increasing in numbers as the population grew. They might well provide important clues as to how the huge numbers of newcomers were coping with the wrenching changes in their lives. Associations, their leaders, and leadership began to emerge as the central issues of Graham's research.

The question still remained as to where Elizabeth should do her research and where, therefore, we should live. Finally, Graham Barnes, in discussions with us, came to the conclusion that the only suitable location would be one of the original villages. These were, and are, meaningful social units, composed of people with kinship relations of long standing. As villages and lineages that had resided in the New Territories prior to the British lease of 1898, they had special rights guaranteed by the Peking Convention. These rights included access to the government through representative bodies, the right to bury their dead on the mountainsides, and special land rights that they held as descendants of the original owners, which allowed them to remain together in their villages despite the fact that they might have to be relocated for urban development or government infrastructure projects. They came to be called 'original inhabitants' (原居民).[12]

In Tsuen Wan, resiting of villages had begun as plans for the town proceeded. Graham Barnes suggested Kwan Mun Hau village as a possible location for Elizabeth's research, because the District

---

11. These challenges had been discussed in a 1959 study group. See Gerald Moore, ed., *Tsuen Wan Township: Study Group Report on Its Development* (Hong Kong: Hong Kong University Press, 1959).

12. When we first lived in Tsuen Wan, this term was not in common use. Instead, the local people, who were Hakka, called themselves 'original people' (本土人), to distinguish themselves from Punti (本地人), the term used for Cantonese people. They spoke mutually unintelligible Chinese languages. The Hakka, generally, were later arrivals. The 'painstaking Hong Kong Colony Census' of 1911 found 47,990 Cantonese and 36,070 Hakka people. See James Hayes, 'A Mixed Community of Cantonese and Hakka on Lantau Island', in *Aspects of Social Organization in the New Territories* (Royal Asiatic Society Hong Kong Branch Weekend Symposium 9th–10th May, 1964), 21.

Office had been in frequent communication with its leaders in recent years. Kwan Mun Hau was the first of the Tsuen Wan villages to negotiate an agreement to move to a new site after requesting this in 1959 because of intolerable conditions in their old village.[13] The move had been successful, and they had been resited for four years when the District Officer put forward our request to them in 1968.

We will never know why the leaders of Kwan Mun Hau agreed to having us live among them, given that the reasons must have been very hard for them to understand. Research on their community conducted by adults who were still students was not part of their experience. Furthermore, even then, relations between Western expatriates and the local Chinese people were quite distant, with many differences of lifestyle, residence, and wealth.[14] In addition, our connection to the colonial government was commonly known, as we had been introduced by the district officer. Despite their satisfaction with the new village, relations between their leaders and the colonial government were tense. Political divisions in Tsuen Wan, and elsewhere in Hong Kong, were deep, with tension between the pro-China left-wing and those with right-wing views. Those who were left-wing were critical of the colonial government. Although the indigenous people had special access to the government through the system of village representatives who participated in a rural committee, and, above this, a New Territories–wide body, the Heung Yee Kuk (鄉議局), two of the three village representatives of Kwan Mun Hau were left-wing in the 1960s (the third had died), and one had been obliged to step down from his positions as village representative and chair of the Tsuen Wan Rural Committee after he had spoken against the government in the Heung Yee Kuk. The villagers had not yet agreed on how to fill his position, and many still referred to him as 'our village head'. To this day we do not know why we were able to rent a floor of a village house belonging to an ancestral trust of one of the lineages, when our motives must have been suspect.

In general, we believe we were made more acceptable to the people of Tsuen Wan by our small son. The fact that we were a family made us appear normal, and this blond, blue-eyed, mischievous boy was both a curiosity and a source of amusement—and someone to be indulged. Furthermore, our lifestyle was different from many of the expatriates we observed, in that we spoke Cantonese to the best of our ability and tried to dress modestly, eventually, for Elizabeth, in Chinese-style clothes. She carried our baby on her back in the cloth square with four straps (孭帶) used by local Chinese women, a method that was extremely convenient when walking in the crowded streets of the town.

Settling In

Kwan Mun Hau village became our home for eighteen months, where we were happy and worked hard. That we were both carrying out virtually full-time research, whether formal or informal, and trying to give adequate care to a small and very active child made for a busy life. Furthermore, living in Tsuen Wan was very demanding due to the air pollution, the deficiencies in infrastructure, and the climate, which at that time was unmitigated by air-conditioning. It was wet in the spring, so the laundry would not dry, shoes grew mouldy, and the walls ran with moisture; very hot and humid in summer; then clear and cold in the winter when the north wind blew, allowing villagers to make special wind-dried pork (風肉).

Still, we were very fortunate that air-conditioning had only just arrived, and people made do instead with electric fans in their homes. In the evenings, while people sat outdoors and conversed, we could walk around with our baby and talk with them. Although the indigenous people of Kwan Mun Hau were Hakka, all except the oldest women also spoke Cantonese, often quite accented, which they had learned either in school or through their interaction with Cantonese-speaking immigrants.

---

13. James Hayes, *Tsuen Wan: Growth of a 'New Town' and Its People* (Hong Kong: Oxford University Press, 1993), 67.
14. James Hayes, *Friends and Teachers: Hong Kong and Its People 1953–87* (Hong Kong: Hong Kong University Press, 1996), 11–13.

Plate 7: This fruit vendor came through the village every evening with his heavy load and, like so many other local people, was very kind to our child. His missing tooth suggests poverty.

We were fortunate, also, that television had only just become available, although by the end of our stay many more families owned a television, which increasingly became an impediment to research. Furthermore, women often did putting-out work from factories, assembling plastic flowers and ornaments, or finishing mops by rolling the threads on their thighs. This work was generally done outdoors, sometimes in groups. In addition, there were the happy sounds of children playing games after school, as they were less burdened by homework than they are now.

At that time, immigrants were desperate to find ways to earn a living, and some used their skills to become hawkers. Many, both men and women, came through the village in the course of a day, all with their distinctive calls. They sold prepared foods such as rice with salt pork wrapped in bamboo leaves (粽), a bean curd dessert (豆腐花), other popular snacks, and cooked meats such as sausage and chicken feet. A kindly older man sold fruit in the evenings, with his heavy baskets on a carrying pole. Others had special skills and trades, such as castrating cats and chickens, dyeing cloth, or sharpening knives. Their calls added to the liveliness of the village and attracted villagers who wanted their products and services.

Another set of distinctive sounds came from directly below our second-floor home. We lived above the Country Village Store (鄉村商店), which sold bread and biscuits, some canned goods, soft drinks, and beer—but it was primarily a mah-jong parlour, catering to the indigenous men of the village. Living there, we quickly became accustomed to the sound of clattering tiles. The store also served as a gathering place for village men, and we sometimes heard animated discussions. When carrying out these discussions they normally spoke Hakka, which meant they could be conducted in privacy. At that time, even the younger and middle-aged villagers could speak or at least understand Hakka, so this was comfortable for them and reinforced their unity.

One of our special memories is of an evening during the winter of 1968–1969, when a large group of native men gathered around the tables in the shop to enjoy a special winter treat, stewed dog meat. To our great surprise, one of them came upstairs to our home and brought a bowl of it for us. We have to think that this was a sign of their growing acceptance of us, because the consumption of dog meat was illegal in this British colony.[15]

Research Themes

Having moved into the village in November 1968, Elizabeth began to adapt her research proposal to this setting. We learned that Kwan Mun Hau was comprised of indigenous people of three surnames: Yau, Chan, and Fan. While the Fan lineage included only a few households who no longer had an ancestral hall, the presence of the larger Yau and Chan lineages was apparent in their ancestral halls, rebuilt when the village moved. The Yau hall is located on the third terrace and includes important elements from its predecessor in old Kwan Mun Hau: granite door frames and sills, and stone paving. The Chan hall is on the highest terrace of the village. Their original hall, and some members' homes, had been located in an adjacent village, Ham Tin, evidence that the lineages had not been confined to Kwan Mun Hau.

The fact that the original population of Kwan Mun Hau was organized into lineages added potential richness to Elizabeth's research, because she could now hope to learn about the impact of rapid urbanization and industrialization upon lineages as well as their constituent households. Based on research that had been done on urbanization, one would anticipate that lineages would not be able to maintain their traditional structures and functions in this new context, but she needed to investigate this.

There was another social feature of Kwan Mun Hau which made it an especially significant place for her to do research. This was the fact that its indigenous people, like all of those in Tsuen Wan, were Hakka. At that time, most of the anthropological studies being done in the New Territories of Hong Kong concerned Cantonese people, primarily those in large single-lineage villages.[16] Jean Pratt had conducted one study of a Hakka village in the New Territories.[17] In 1968 it was the only source.[18] Important research on Hakka people was being done in Taiwan by Myron Cohen,[19] but was not available to us until later.

Elizabeth's research method, both then and on return visits to Tsuen Wan, was to use what are called semi-structured interviews, in addition to participant observation. These consisted of lists of questions that she hoped to discuss with individuals, both men and women. The goal was to try to ensure that the person was at ease and speaking in a conversational style, while also giving her the information and opinions she was seeking. As such, she did not ask the questions in rigid order, but rather by following the direction of the conversation.

---

15. Dogs and Cats Ordinance, January 1950.
16. Most of our understanding of Chinese society came from research done in pre-revolutionary China or in overseas Chinese contexts. Anthropological research was just beginning in Taiwan but was not yet published. Jarvie stated in 1969: 'Sociology and anthropology [in Hong Kong] have hardly begun'. See 'Introduction', in *Hong Kong: A Society in Transition Contributions to the Study of Hong Kong Society*, ed. Ian Jarvie and Joseph Agassi (London: Routledge, 1969), xv.
17. Jean Pratt, 'Emigration and Unilineal Descent Groups: A Study of Marriage in a Hakka Village in the New Territories of Hong Kong', *The Eastern Anthropologist* 13, no. 4 (June–August 1960): 147–58.
18. See our bibliography for later publications on Hakka people, including J. W. Hayes, 'A Chinese Village on Hong Kong Island Fifty Years Ago – Tai Tam Tuk, Village Under the Water', in *Hong Kong: A Society in Transition Contributions to the Study of Hong Kong Society*, ed. Jarvie and Agassi, 29–51, two books by Nicole Constable, and one by Allen Chun. Barbara E. Ward (1965) and C. Fred Blake (1981) wrote on inter-ethnic relations in Sai Kung.
19. Myron L. Cohen, *House United, House Divided* (New York: Columbia University Press, 1976).

Down to Work

In June 1969, Elizabeth began her first interviews of women. It soon became clear that it would not be possible to interview as many as she had hoped, although 14 indigenous women did agree to be interviewed, as did 11 tenants. She conducted interviews in the afternoon, when women, at least those who were not employed full time, were more likely to have some free time after doing housework and shopping. The fact that they had a little free time did not always mean that they were available for interviews, however, as they often were playing mah-jong, watching television, or talking among themselves, as well as watching small children.

Elizabeth can only hope that the excellent rapport she had with the great majority of the women compensates in part for the small sample size. Once women came to trust her, they spoke in detail about their lives, their ideas, and their opinions. Some of them were quite emotional as they talked about themselves and their experiences. One reason for this may be that, in general, in Chinese society it is impolite to talk about oneself, and perhaps because of fear of gossip, people usually reveal little about themselves. When the women realized that she and her assistants were genuinely interested in them, they responded by talking far more freely than they would in ordinary conversation. Moreover, they appeared to find the kinds of questions we asked to be important. From what Elizabeth observed during the interviews, and because of her experience of living in the village, she has considerable confidence in the validity of the information which she obtained.

Several months after starting the women's interviews she also began to interview men. Although her approach and procedures were the same as those with women, and our assistant was a model of tact, politeness, and persuasiveness, she found it much more difficult to gain the cooperation of men. She approached only native men because of the nature of the questions she was asking, especially those on household division, inheritance, and lineage matters. There were also those whom she could not approach for political reasons. Elizabeth finally succeeded in interviewing fifteen men and completing interviews with nine of them. With those nine, rapport was excellent and the answers meaningful, but in the remaining cases they refused to allow her to come back to complete the interview, although they cooperated for the first meeting. There are a number of possible explanations for this. One is the political situation in Hong Kong and the village, for there quite certainly was a lingering distrust of our motives and affiliations. Some, including one man who worked twelve hours a day, simply did not have enough free time to talk further. Another is that the questions asked were not on subjects that men would normally converse about with comparative strangers, and some were on rather sensitive subjects. They certainly found it hard to understand why Elizabeth should want that kind of specific and personal information from them. Still, it remains to be explained why some men cooperated fully with us. Even those men who refused to talk further were invariably polite, which is some consolation.

To gain a broader comparative perspective, she also interviewed leaders from six other Tsuen Wan villages. The interviews varied in length, but some were very fruitful and they all helped her learn about and compare the central Tsuen Wan villages and their lineages.

Graham's Survey

It was here that there was considerable overlap with Graham's work. He was concerned with the town as a whole. Village life was an excellent opportunity to experience in detail a part of the larger picture. His work, however, extended beyond the boundaries of the village. Much of the information about the immigrant population, its efforts to cope with new and often socially disruptive ways of living, could not be gleaned from walking the streets or even from government records, valuable though they were. He believed it necessary to interview a group of those whom he could identify as leaders, both indigenous and newcomers, and ask a series of identical (standard) questions in order to explore Tsuen

Wan's distinctive development, which involved two very different populations caught up in economic and social change. To our knowledge, only one other scholar had conducted research in Tsuen Wan,[20] and Graham was the first to interview on a wide scale.

His research questions took some time to formulate, as did his methods of approach: devising a questionnaire, testing it, then locating key individuals to interview. It took him nine months not merely to ascertain important questions but also to determine the strategy whereby he could ask for lengthy interviews of busy men, and one woman. He completed his questionnaire by early January 1969, tested it in Kowloon, and began interviewing in earnest after the Lunar New Year holidays. His survey ran until October 1969. By November he had coded the data, and with the help of the computing centre at the Chinese University of Hong Kong, he completed a preliminary analysis. A feverish writing schedule resulted in a rough draft of his doctoral dissertation by May 1970, when we left Hong Kong after a rewarding two years.

Our Social Life in Kwan Mun Hau

In addition to the people we interviewed, there were many others with whom we talked in the village, and from whom we learned much that was relevant to our work. Within a short period of time, we had formed relationships that have remained strong to this day. Shortly after moving in, we noticed that a ceremony was being held in an open area just in front of the village. A young man who spoke English well began a conversation with us and explained that a funeral was in progress. He was a member of the Yau lineage and was the first of our many contacts within it. He worked as a translator for a Canadian agency and continued to talk regularly with us, rapidly coming to understand the purpose of our work. He has remained a lifelong friend and a valuable source of information. He had a successful career in banking and has been the accountant for the Yau lineage for many years. We became close to all of his family members, several of whom have been very supportive of our work.[21]

Another young person from the Yau lineage soon approached Elizabeth. She was a student at the Tsuen Wan Government Secondary School—the best in Tsuen Wan. She spoke excellent English and hoped to improve it. She, and all her family, became some of our closest friends and supporters within the village. They had and have a reputation for being intelligent and hard-working, with some members being among the best-educated in the village.

In addition, we were exceptionally fortunate in our immediate neighbours, Mr Kwok Yung-hing, his wife, his mother, and four daughters. We shared a common staircase to our second-floor homes, with facing doors. Their door was almost always open and, after we had installed a gate so that our baby would not fall down the concrete stairs, so was ours. They were ideal neighbours: intelligent, thoughtful, well-informed, observant, and open-minded. They quickly came to understand the nature of our work and why we were living there. They were not part of one of the local lineages, but Mr Kwok's father, who was Hakka, had arrived in Tsuen Wan in about 1870 and opened a shop selling miscellaneous products. Since the family had resided in Tsuen Wan while it was still under Chinese rule, and had various kinship relations there, they were widely accepted by local people and encouraged to rent a flat in Kwan Mun Hau. His wife had immigrated as a child with her family from Shunde *xian* in the Pearl River delta.

The youngest of the four girls was three months older than our son. While we were living in Kwan Mun Hau, we learned about a kind of godparenthood relationship that children sometimes

---

20. Baruch Boxer, a geographer, conducted research in 1964 and 1966. For his insightful summary article, see Baruch Boxer, 'Space, Change, and Fung-Shui in Tsuen Wan's Urbanization', *Journal of Asian and African Studies* 3, no. 3–4 (July–October 1968): 226–40.

21. We are especially grateful to his mother, Yau Tsang Yung-hei.

were entered into. This could exist between the child and a deity, a natural feature such as a special tree, or a person from another family. A relationship[22] between a child and an adult or couple could be initiated by the child's parents because they believed the child to be in need of the protection and help offered by additional relationships, or it could be initiated by an adult because of affection for the child. When Kin-man, their youngest daughter, was about two years old we asked whether she might become our goddaughter (契女). Her grandmother, who acted as the final authority on important family matters, agreed, and after we had given Kin-man auspicious gifts, her grandmother carried out ceremonies to inform the gods and ancestors and create the relationship. Our families have remained relatives to this day, seeing each other frequently and exchanging help whenever it has been needed. They have been invaluable for our research, because not only are they knowledgeable about Tsuen Wan history, liked and respected by the local people, but they have been able to give us insight into situations that otherwise would have been unfathomable. They also helped us by explaining Elizabeth's work to residents of Kwan Mun Hau. Furthermore, both parents are models of decorum, and have been valuable teachers to us of appropriate and polite Chinese behaviour.

During a short return visit to North America to attend a conference in the late summer of 1969, Graham was offered a teaching position at the University of British Columbia in Vancouver, Canada. This meant that when we left Hong Kong in the spring of 1970 we were fortunate enough to know where we would be in the future. At that time, though, we had no idea it would ever be possible for us to return to Tsuen Wan. Canada seemed very far away and travel was not easy.

Postscript

Life sometimes has a way of returning what we think we have lost. In 1975–1976, Graham had a sabbatical leave and for a year became a visiting scholar at Hong Kong University, where he was able to carry out archival research on the emerging situation in China. Elizabeth did not yet have a permanent position, as she had been busy writing her doctoral thesis, somewhat delayed because of the birth of a second son, then 4 years old. Given our ties to Tsuen Wan, and Kwan Mun Hau, we would not consider living anywhere else, especially as this would give Elizabeth the opportunity to do further research there. We had the good fortune to be able to rent the ground floor of a house owned by and adjacent to that of Mr Yau Shui-cheung and his wife Yau Chan Shek-ying. It was their daughter whom we had come to know so well during our first stay there.

During the intervening few years, Kwan Mun Hau had acquired a much more settled look. When we were first there it was quite stark, with a predominance of the concrete paving and facings of hillsides that are so common in urban Hong Kong. By 1975 people had planted trees, including guavas and bananas, among others. Some were raising chickens where space permitted on the terraces in front of their houses, and pet birds, dogs, and even cats were common. An anthropologist friend who visited us commented that it seemed like a rural oasis on the edge of the city.

Graham followed events in China as best he could, under the then difficult political climate. From 1979, he began to focus on a set of rural communities in the Pearl River delta region, which were undergoing dramatic economic change and in which Hong Kong entrepreneurs had major (and familiar) roles to play. He returned to Hong Kong in 1981–1982 for a sabbatical leave, and again in 1995–1997 to teach at the City University of Hong Kong. Each time he lived in Kwan Mun Hau, and although his work focused on the transformation that was taking place in the Pearl River delta region,

22. This type of relationship has been called fictive kinship, but might better be called 'constructed kinship', given the strong lifelong bonds it creates. Stone, *Kinship and Gender*, 302.

he never lost interest in the changes that were taking place in Tsuen Wan. Elizabeth also returned regularly[23] and continued to do research there whenever possible.

What Is to Follow

As the 'new town' policy of social and economic planning was applied, Tsuen Wan continued to evolve, providing a model for the other new towns that were later created in the New Territories, but with its own distinctive characteristics, including its industrial base. The greatest challenges in its path to becoming a more liveable society emerged during the period James Hayes has called 'The Battling Seventies'.[24] As the nature of its development has changed over time, we have found much to learn about its changing social fabric. We will present our findings in the later chapters of this book, following those derived from our original research in the late 1960s.

Our understanding of Tsuen Wan has been greatly enriched in an unanticipated way. Our initial intent had been to study the social dynamics of the contemporary society. To our great surprise, as time passed we found that we would have opportunities to gain insight into its earlier history, knowledge that was very important for our overall understanding of the town and district. These opportunities initially came to us through the testimony of elders. Elizabeth began this work in 1975–1976. She chose to focus primarily on women's lives before and immediately after the Japanese occupation and, by interviewing older women, learned about their daily life and work histories, as well as their remarkable tradition of mountain songs and laments. After beginning her curatorial career, she returned to Tsuen Wan in late 1979 to collect tools, clothing, and domestic objects no longer needed in the urban context. Collecting and documenting these with the help of Mrs Yau Chan Shek-ying gave her important insights into their earlier way of life.

In the late 1960s we had only one historical document to study, the Yau lineage genealogy, which had been duplicated for distribution to all member households in 1966. As time passed, other important documents were made available to us, which have helped to carry our research back in time. Furthermore, in the intervening years, historians, specifically James Hayes and David Faure, have published their important research. All of these sources have provided an unexpected, and most welcome, foundation for our work, which we will present in the next two chapters, before moving into our study of Tsuen Wan in the late 1960s, and beyond.

---

23. Elizabeth found a career at the UBC Museum of Anthropology, which allowed her occasional research leave.
24. Hayes, *Tsuen Wan*, 108–24.

2

Some Historical Background

If people don't explain these things, no one will know them in the future. The young won't know. . . .
It is important to record them.
— Ho Wing-Kwong, 1996

Tsuen Wan before the Japanese Occupation[1]

In the early twentieth century, Tsuen Wan—originally written, Chin Wan (淺灣) 'Shallow Bay'—was a predominantly rural district (*xiang* 鄉)[2] populated by Hakka villagers as well as some shopkeepers, about half of whom were immigrants,[3] in its small market centre. Unlike other areas of the New Territories, there were no Cantonese-speaking villages. It owed its development to the early Qing policy of Hakka resettlement on the then coastal frontier, after the Ming loyalist Zheng Chengkong [Koxinga] was overcome. Most of the villages likely date their origins to the eighteenth century, after the lifting of the Qing expulsion order which forced the existing coastal population to withdraw inland,[4] although some arrived later.

The Economy

The area was not prosperous. It occupied a narrow coastal shelf backed by Tai Mo Shan, the highest mountain in Hong Kong, and its coastal foothills. There were three rivers running from the mountain, and another draining into Gin Drinkers Bay. These were likely the most important sources of the ample supply of irrigation water for Tsuen Wan's agricultural economy, while one also powered its incense mills.[5] The valley floors provided virtually the only flat land in the area, except for reclamation in central Tsuen Wan. Elsewhere, the hill slopes ran straight into the sea, leaving little flat land for

---

1. 1941–1945. See Chapter 4.
2. A *xiang* was a unit of social organization throughout the Pearl River delta of Guangdong, composed of a group of villages focused upon a small market centre, with local political and ritual coherence. A plaque dated 1897 in the central Tianhou temple identifies Tsuen Wan as a *xiang*.
3. David Faure, 'Notes on the History of Tsuen Wan', *Journal of the Hong Kong Branch Royal Asiatic Society* 24 (1984): 99–100.
4. See Sung Hok-p'ang, 'Tsin-Fuk (being an account of how part of the coast of South China was cleared of inhabitants from the 1st year of Hong Hei [Kangxi] until the 8th year of Hong Hei)', *Hong Kong Naturalist* 9, no. 1–2 (1938): 37–42. See also Anthony Siu Kwok-kin, 'The Hong Kong Region before and after the Coastal Evacuation in the Early Ch'ing Dynasty', in *From Village to City: Studies in the Traditional Roots of Hong Kong Society*, ed. David Faure, James Hayes, and Alan Birch (Hong Kong: Centre of Asian Studies, University of Hong Kong, 1984), 1–9.
5. As of 1907 there were 24 water-powered sandalwood mills. See David Faure, 'Notes on the History of Tsuen Wan', *Journal of the Hong Kong Branch Royal Asiatic Society* 24 (1984): 93. See also James Hayes, 'Sandalwood Mills at Tsuen Wan', *Journal of the Hong Kong Branch Royal Asiatic Society* 16 (1976): 282–83.

farming. At the time of the New Territories lease in 1898, the population was agricultural, growing rice, pineapples, sweet potatoes, and catch crops, as well as raising pigs. Fishing was an important subsidiary occupation for land-dwellers, and there was also a community of boat-dwelling fishing people.[6]

Tsuen Wan pineapples were famous for their sweetness, and one of the first acts of the British in the New Territories was to set up a pineapple cannery, although no later record exists.[7] The living was generally secure, but people were almost universally impoverished and did not hesitate to describe themselves as such. Before the occupation, fuel-cutting was an important source of income. Women and girls climbed up into the hills, cut bracken (草) and pine branches, and carried the heavy bundles back, either to their homes or to purchasers, often agents selling to fishing people for breaming their boats.

One indication of poverty was the extent of men's out-migration in the late nineteenth and early twentieth centuries. Two plaques in the central Tianhou temple acknowledge donations for renovations in 1897, one recording donations from men who were then abroad, the other from residents in the district. The first lists more names and the largest sums of money, with contributions from Hawaii, Southeast Asia, the United States, Mexico, Central America, Australia, the Caribbean, and South Africa. Some men prospered, sending back remittances and returning wealthy; others returned poor, or not at all. Many went as contract labourers, 'sold as a piglet' (賣豬仔), whose outgoing fare was paid but whose return fare was not.

Even before 1898, Tsuen Wan had become a daily coastal market centre of some importance.[8] Records suggest that it attained this status in the mid-nineteenth century, as trade in local produce with Hong Kong Island developed.[9] By the early twentieth century, two local boats made the relatively short trip daily.[10] Entrepreneurs sent pineapples to Hong Kong Island by boat and brought back piglets, as pig-raising was an important economic activity for women in the central Tsuen Wan villages. It was a significant means of raising funds to meet expenses such as weddings and to pay off debts.[11]

In the early 1920s, the district was on the eve of important changes, albeit less momentous than those after 1946. Castle Peak Road, the ring road around the New Territories, passed through in about 1917, linking it to the growing commercial centres of Kowloon. Modest changes in the economy of the area got underway. At the same time, there was an influx of public works and industrial enterprises offering wage labour opportunities. The building of the Shing Mun Reservoir provided employment for local men and women in the 1930s. A lead mine functioned until 1941. A major brewery operated in Sham Tseng from the 1920s until 1996.[12] During the 1930s a silk mill, an iron pipe company, and an iron works were established, together with an automobile assembly plant. In 1937, Texaco, an American oil company which was active throughout Guangdong, created a depot on the coast near Kwan Mun Hau (關門口). A dozen or so smaller enterprises produced wine, soy sauce, ginger, joss sticks, noodles, and vermillion. The factories employed perhaps a thousand people.[13] The population of Tsuen Wan, according to the 1931 census, was only 5,331. The impact of these new forms

---

6. See Barbara E. Ward, 'Varieties of the Conscious Model: The Boat People of South China', in *The Relevance of Models for Social Anthropology*, ed. M. Banton (London: Tavistock, 1965), 41–60.

7. 'Report on the New Territory at Hong Kong by J. H. Stewart Lockhart with the Governor's Covering Despatch', Sessional Papers 1901. For a list of the various reports and documents in the early period of British rule, see James Hayes, *The Great Difference: Hong Kong's New Territories and Its People 1898–2004* (Hong Kong: Hong Kong University Press, 2012), 278–79.

8. Hayes distinguished coastal market centres from standard market centres *xu* (墟) in *The Hong Kong Region 1850–1911 Institutions and Leadership in Town and Countryside* (Hamden, CT: Archon Press, 1977), 15, 37–38. The shops of the former opened daily, together with the market (街市).

9. Faure, 'Notes on the History of Tsuen Wan', 49–50.

10. Faure, 'Notes on the History of Tsuen Wan', 93 n13.

11. One woman credited her widowed mother-in-law with saving her indebted family from dissolution by raising eight pigs to sell.

12. Hayes, *Friends and Teachers*, 144.

13. Ho Chuen-yiu (何傳耀) Quanwan Fazhan Shilu (荃灣發展實錄) [An outline history of the development of Tsuen Wan], *Wah-kiu Yat-po* (華僑日報) (Hong Kong), 7–9 July 1969.

of enterprise was therefore substantial. Due to the worldwide depression and Chinese exclusion acts in various countries, out-migration declined during this period, but internal developments were also significant.

By 1933 there was a regular bus service to Kowloon, and in 1935 a ferry service was established to Hong Kong Island. The nucleus of urban Tsuen Wan was formed when fifty or so two-storied shophouses were built in 1938, in what is now its commercial centre. A new market was opened by a group of businessmen who arrived in the 1920s, although a few businesses remained on the former site between Kwan Mun Hau and Hoi Pa (海壩) villages.

The non-indigenous population grew in this period, partly as a result of Japanese incursions into China. These newcomers were Hakka and Cantonese tenant vegetable farmers and businessmen, as well as rice merchants from the Chaozhou region. Buddhist and Daoist religious organizations from China established monasteries and temples in the hills above the growing town. Immigrants braved a disease said to result from pineapple cultivation or a toxic plant called *mahchihn* (麻纏) affecting the stream water, which outsiders used, unlike villagers, who had wells. In addition, there was endemic malaria, from which the local people also suffered. Their sayings reflected these dangers: 'If you have not had malaria you are not a Tsuen Wan person', and 'If you want to prosper, go to Gold Mountain; if you want to die, go to Tsuen Wan'.

Tsuen Wan's improved economy was symbolized by the formation, in 1938, of the Chamber of Commerce, although this was not the first association. In 1926 the Agricultural Products Society was founded as an agency (辦館) for importing seeds into the area and then exporting its produce. In 1929, a group of young indigenous men who enjoyed football founded a successful sports club. They acquired land for a pitch and formed a number of teams. All three associations were still extant in 1968, and we shall have more to say about them, and others.

Governance

Tsuen Wan had a political structure long before it became a part of the New Territories. Freedman noted that the district was once called 'the sz yeuk of Tsuen Wan'. A '*yeuk*' (約) was an alliance, and '*sz*' (四) indicates that it had four components, although their referents were unknown to Freedman. He stated that the alliance included all the villages from Ting Kau to Kowloon City, attributing this information to Sung Hok-pang, a well-known historian and folklorist of the 1930s.[14]

There was another political structure which was active before British rule and lasted until the occupation. The elders of the area met together as a body called the Tsuen On Kuk (荃安局) to deal with the political affairs of the district.[15] They acted very like the local gentry in Imperial China.[16] After 1946, it was formalized, in an expanded form, as the Tsuen Wan Rural Committee. The islands of Tsing Yi (青衣) and Ma Wan (馬灣) were integrated politically with the mainland. All village affairs, cooperation with government officials, and other matters such as inter-villages disputes, were dealt with by the elders (*fulou* 父佬) of the area.

---

14. Maurice Freedman, 'A Report on Social Research in the New Territories' (mimeo, 1963), republished in the *Journal of the Hong Kong Branch Royal Asiatic Society* 16 (1976): 191–261. Faure, 'Notes on the History of Tsuen Wan', 51, states that the Tsuen Wan *yeuk* had 12 components which James Hayes *Tsuen Wan*: 14n69 indicates were the 12 *jia* (甲) that the Qing system of local government, the *baojia*, had instituted.

15. 謝李陶 Xie Li Tao, ed., *Jinri Quanwan* (今日荃灣) [Modern Tsuen Wan] (Kowloon: 新界文化服務出版社, Xinjie wenhua fuwu chubanshe, 1965), 14.

16. See also Hayes, *Tsuen Wan,* 14.

[E]ach village has its elders or headmen . . . who manage its affairs and assist the District Officer in settling disputes. A number of these elders have been specially appointed by the Governor of Hong Kong. They usually meet in temples.[17]

In the pre-1941 period, despite its daily market centre and its connections to Hong Kong and Kowloon, Tsuen Wan was an administrative backwater. The district officer, Southern District, being based in Tai Po or Kowloon, was not at all convenient. The police station was small and inconsequential, there was no fire service, nor was there a hospital. The maintenance of law and order rested largely on the shoulders of the Tsuen On Kuk.

This body was largely concerned with internal matters. The appointments to which de Rome refers were a group of local men[18] of high prestige, who spoke for the district in dealings with government officials. One was Yeung Kwok-shui (楊國瑞), who had received his imperial degree in Guangzhou shortly after 1898 and received a visit of congratulations from the district commissioner New Territories.[19] Another was the well-educated headmaster of a local school and a leading member of a wealthy lineage. Others had either received a good education in China or had prospered abroad, returning as wealthy and esteemed figures. The British district officer was a political figure and a magistrate like his imperial Chinese *xian* counterparts had been, utilizing local talent in administering his area. He had many duties, and through him the impact of British rule on the New Territories was substantial, if remote. The degree of his influence was nonetheless critically dependent on the Tsuen On Kuk.

Settlement History

From our informants, and relevant publications, we were able to reconstruct an approximate history of the settlement of central Tsuen Wan. Both Shek Wai Kok (石圍角) and Lo Wai (老圍) have been described as the oldest of the Tsuen Wan villages.[20] Lo Wai has five lineages, and a representative of one, the Cheung, said in 1969 that they had been in Tsuen Wan for approximately 300 years. This would place their settlement just after the expulsion order had been rescinded.

Another relatively early arrival was the Chan lineage of Sam Tung Uk (三棟屋). They initially settled in Lo Uk Cheung (老屋場). They then prepared a site which they had purchased for 30 ounces of silver from the Cheng of Shing Mun (城門) and built their walled village. Their founder was the nephew of the founder of Kwan Mun Hau and Ham Tin (咸田) villages.

A stone plinth erected in Kwan Mun Hau in December 2016,[21] explains its history as follows:

According to village historical records, over 300 years ago (1705) the Chan (陳) and the Yau (邱) surnames settled in Lo Uk Cheung (present-day Tai Wo Hau) in Tsuen Wan, then called Chin Wan. Later, people of the Fan (範) surname moved here and settled down. Everyone, equally and without exception, practiced farming as their main economic activity. Subsequently, because the population increased, housing and arable land were insufficient. Without fear of difficulty, the people of the Chan, Yau, and Fan lineages moved mountains and reclaimed the foreshore. A dyke was built across the bay, and behind it cultivable fields were created and housing was expanded. The villagers farmed the land and fished for a living. A long strip of cultivated land was created to the south of Shing Mun. There was

17. F. J. de Rome, N. Evans, and E. C. Thomas, *Notes on the New Territories of Hong Kong* (Hong Kong: Ye Olde Printerie, 1937), 22.
18. Hayes, *Tsuen Wan*, 14, suggests that there were four who were especially prominent representing different segments of the alliance. This may answer the uncertainty about the early Tsuen Wan *yeuk*.
19. He was also a graduate of the Senior Teachers Training College in Guangdong. Other leaders are named in Xie Li Tao, *Jinri Quanwan*, 14.
20. Hayes, *Tsuen Wan*, 14.
21. The plinth is headed 'The Origin of the Nine Heroes' [Kau Wai Kung] of Kwan Mun Hau Village, Tsuen Wan' 荃灣關門口村九位宮由來. It continues with the history of one of their two protective deities, which we give in Chapter 3.

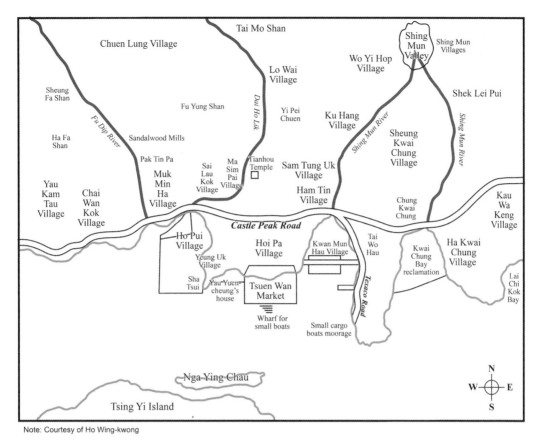

Note: Courtesy of Ho Wing-kwong

Map 2: Adaptation of sketch map of Tsuen Wan about 1920, drawn by Ho Wing-kwong. Areas of coastal reclamation are indicated by straight lines, with the original shorelines behind them.

an old gully through which sea water could flow in and out. A sluice gate was therefore built to control this flow of water. Thus, the people named the village, Kwan Mun Hau ['the village of the closing gate'].

The village's reclaimed lands were to the east of the area that became the market. A map provided by Ho Wing-kwong (何永光), a Tsuen Wan elder and dedicated local historian, clearly shows the reclaimed areas of Kwan Mun Hau and others in the central area with those of other villages to the west, together with the original shoreline.

The colonial land survey, conducted between 1900 and 1904, showed the existence of 160 lineage trusts of property in Tsuen Wan. James Hayes' initial research showed some 50 lineages in existence, almost all with at least one ancestral hall. These halls were and are typical of Hakka people, with a single tablet representing ancestors whose souls have been incorporated through the appropriate ritual,[22] and who remain seated in the hall in perpetuity. After studying these lineages and their genealogies, Hayes concluded:

> This is where the value of local genealogies is most clearly shown. They indicate beyond doubt that the lineages present in 1898, whose landholdings are shown in the British land registers and survey sheets at that time, had arrived in Tsuen Wan in the late seventeenth and early eighteenth centuries. It

---

22. The tablet in the Yau ancestral hall in Kwan Mun Hau village reads: 'The soul tablet of the ancestors, deceased fathers and mothers, of the Yau surname of this hall' (邱氏堂上始高曾祖妣神位).

is possible to state with a degree of authority attributable to no other source that the Tsuen Wan sub-district, as it was in 1898, was mainly repopulated by newcomers from south Fukien and north-east Kwangtung in the first half of the eighteenth century.[23]

Topography helped to determine the distribution of villages within the sub-district, which was relatively small: 9.25 square miles on the mainland, and the islands of Tsing Yi and Ma Wan. There was a cluster of villages around the bay, with its wharf and market, including, in all, about 1000 people in 1898. Other villages extended along the coast and up into the hills, including the Shing Mun villages.[24]

Villages and Lineages

Villages varied in composition from a single lineage, such as Sam Tung Uk, to Hoi Pa with more than 10 surnames. It is important to note that lineages were not necessarily contained within single villages. For example, members of the Yau lineage lived and live in both Kwan Mun Hau and Hoi Pa. Members of the Chan lineage live in Kwan Mun Hau and Ham Tin. Their ancestral hall was located in Ham Tin, but was resited to Kwan Mun Hau when the village moved. The Fan of Kwan Mun Hau are related to others in Hoi Pa and Ham Tin, and their hall had been located in Ham Tin. The Ho of Ho Pui (河背) and Muk Min Ha (木棉下) are one lineage, with their hall in Muk Min Ha. There are people of the Fu lineage in both Sham Tseng (深井) and Hoi Pa. The villages were geographically separate, each distinct from the others.

Many of these names indicate the villages' proximity to the sea before recent land reclamation for urban development began, with Kwan Mun Hau being an example. Hoi Pa means sea barrier or bund, while Ham Tin means salt fields, which likely was the nature of the land when reclaimed.

Wells and Shrines

Until a public water supply was installed, wells were especially important for the survival of villagers because of the toxic stream water. Tenants of villagers normally gained the right to use their water.

Likewise, each village had one or more earth god shrines.[25] Their role was to guard the village, to keep it safe and its households peaceful. The general term used for these guardian deities by Hakka people is Baak Gung (伯公).[26] Their shrines were and are dedicated to various gods, including Dahuangye (大皇爺), Hongshenggong (洪聖公), and the Kau Wai Kung (九位公). The last was only worshipped in Kwan Mun Hau, and in that village the last character on the shrine, and the one dedicated to Hongshenggong, was recently changed to the homonym meaning 'palace' (宮), to reflect the grandeur of their shrines.[27] This term was said to denote a higher rank than Tudigong (土地公) and Tudipo (土地婆), the terms for male and female earth gods used by Cantonese people, because their responsibility for protecting the village was so great. People who were not indigenous to the villages were welcome to worship at their shrines, and this was taken as a sign that the god was especially efficacious (令).

23. James Hayes, 'The Tsuen Wan Sub-District from Chinese Genealogies', *The Rural Communities of Hong Kong* (Hong Kong: Oxford University Press, 1983), 116–19.
24. Hayes, 'The Tsuen Wan Sub-District from Chinese Genealogies', 115.
25. Ho Wing-kwong stated that there was no higher-level earth god, but conflicting information exists. See Hayes, *Tsuen Wan*, 45.
26. Such earth gods, called by the same term, were common in the Hakka region of Taiwan studied by Myron Cohen, *House United, House Divided: The Chinese Family in Taiwan* (New York: Columbia University Press, 1976), 8–9.
27. The character (公) has multiple meanings. In its initial usage it signified a god's official status.

Internal Relations in Tsuen Wan

From all reports, Tsuen Wan was a peaceful place, with little history of conflict among or within its villages or lineages, the one major exception taking place in the mid-nineteenth century.[28] We heard no evidence of any village considering itself to be superior to any of the others, despite the fact, for example, that a member of the Yeung lineage had achieved an imperial degree. There was sufficient water for irrigation, so that was not a problem, and there were not substantial differences in wealth among the residents. Some who had gone overseas had come back with means, or at least had sent funds back to their families even if they had been unable to return. Others earned a comfortable living through businesses that they owned in the town and sometimes elsewhere, but elderly people in general said that Tsuen Wan was a place characterized by poverty.[29] This self-image is significant, and we shall examine it further in the next chapter.

In general, poverty was not extreme, and people did not die of starvation except during the Japanese occupation. Everyone could gain a living by farming their own fields, renting those of others, or cutting fuel. The better land produced two crops of rice per year, but people with poorer land or fewer fields often ate sweet potatoes. During the winter, people planted white radishes (蘿蔔) and other vegetables that could be salted and preserved, as well as peanuts, sweet potatoes, and taro. With a few exceptions, however, even those families with sufficient fields ate a monotonous diet with little protein except for lower grades of seafood, including small, strong-flavoured fish steamed with rice. It was only families with business interests who could sometimes eat meat. Although many families raised pigs, the one pig killed in the Tsuen Wan market on the first and fifteenth of the lunar month could barely be sold in its entirety, so few were the people who could afford to eat pork. Pork was a highly valued food, offered and exchanged at festivals, and eaten only very occasionally or given in minute quantities to children to supplement their diet.

Families could rent additional hill land from the government, paying a small yearly levy to grow pineapples, grass, and pine trees. It was designated by the name of the particular hill, so people would recognize who had the rights to it. To supplement subsistence farming, their coastal location was advantageous, and women gathered shellfish during the unusually low tides on the first and fifteenth of the lunar month. They were joined by women from Sha Tin (沙田), who walked over the mountain passes to gather sea snails. Some men also fished, either using stake nets or fishing from small boats similar to Hoklo boats, with raised and pointed bows and sterns.[30]

Regardless of their family's economic status, younger women universally worked at farming. Their ability to do heavy work was often used as a measure of their worth, especially by their mothers-in-law.[31] The older women of the household, if there were any, looked after the children as best they could while doing housework and caring for pigs.[32] Many younger women could manage an ox and plough, even with a baby on their back,[33] and as a result, a household could be self-sufficient even though there were no men present because they were overseas. In other cases, a man might be present but virtually useless, especially as opium addiction was fairly common during the early twentieth century,[34] disappearing only in the late 1960s, as the last addicts died. An addict might not only fail to contribute to

---

28. A minor exception was reported by a Fan lineage man, some of whose fields he said had been registered under the names of the more numerous Yau and Chan lineages, leaving them primarily hill lands suitable only for growing pineapples and grass for fuel. A Tsuen Wan leader told a variant of this story to James Hayes.
29. See also Hayes, *Rural Communities*, 123.
30. Families also engaged in salvage after typhoons. One exceptionally fortunate couple found bamboo poles filled with gold and opium, which they buried under their sweet potato plants and gradually sold.
31. This continued after they became engaged in wage labour.
32. The pigs raised must have been sold on Hong Kong Island and in Kowloon.
33. Those who could not sometimes exchanged their labour with those who could, cutting grass for them, for example.
34. Licensed opium divans were only made illegal in 1909–1910. Hayes, *Tsuen Wan*, 26.

the household economy, he might also steal his wife's wages. One man described how the addiction of his well-educated father had brought the family from relative wealth into penury, while the father of another had sold the family's fields. Other men were addicted to gambling, another way of losing the household's income, while some were lazy and just loitered around doing little for the household. Such problems led to Tsuen Wan being called by the shameful name *yeuhng gung* (養公), 'where husbands are supported', although this was by no means universal.

Security

Perhaps because of the relative economic equality that prevailed, families did not have to send members out at night to guard their ripe rice crops, although they had to watch ripe pineapples. In general, there were no problems with violent theft, with the exception of two businessmen who were murdered, one for his year-end cash and the other perhaps out of envy, according to their descendants. Elderly people told us that there had been no need to organize village guards until just before the occupation, when it was harder to maintain order during this transition period.[35] Bandits attacked a shop in the market, and, when the owners resisted with a gun, set fire to it. The fire spread to adjacent shops and houses, causing significant losses. Each village recruited several strong young men to patrol against thieves at night (治衛隊). Another period of disorder occurred during the seamen's strike in 1922, when the port was closed and some people resorted to stealing grain.

In general, however, older people described Tsuen Wan as a peaceful place in which villagers cooperated and people looked out for each other's welfare. They offered help with weddings and funerals, for which the young men carried the coffin.[36] Elders were asked to adjudicate any disputes that arose, after being invited to a meal.

The security of the area was substantiated by many women's testimony. They said that they felt safe and that their surroundings were peaceful (安定).[37] They emphasized that this was the case, despite the fact that they often worked alone in their fields, and fuel-cutting took them far up into the hills. They went in groups to some mountainous areas, but on their own hillsides they often worked alone. They also walked over mountain paths to visit their natal families at festivals and on special occasions.

Women reiterated their sense of security in various ways. One said that village men dared not even look at young women before they were married. Young men and women were expected to keep conversation to a minimum. Women emphasized that they had no fear of rape. They said that they knew everyone and could recognize any strangers. Furthermore, they were well able to defend themselves and did not hesitate to do so, both verbally and physically. If they were away from their villages and saw a man acting abnormally, they attacked him with their grass-cutting knives and heavy wooden grass-carrying poles, which had iron points. We were told of just one exception, a man from Sheung Kwai Chung who bothered women there, especially young widows of men in his lineage, who was not stopped because he was of a senior generation.

---

35. Hayes, *Tsuen Wan*, 35.
36. See also Patrick Hase, 'Observations at a Village Funeral', in *From Village to City*, ed. Faure, Hayes, and Birch, 129–63.
37. This contrasts with stories of confrontations and rape experienced by girls from the Punti lineage village of Ha Tsuen. Rubie Watson, 'Chinese Bridal Laments: The Claims of a Dutiful Daughter', in *Village Life in Hong Kong*, ed. James L. Watson and Rubie S. Watson (Hong Kong: Chinese University Press, 2004), 233.

Plate 8: 'Shing Mun Village with Its Sacred Grove', 1923. Stuart Schofield, the photographer, was a Canadian geologist who surveyed potential water resources in Hong Kong. Courtesy UBC Museum of Anthropology, Vancouver, Canada, Stuart Schofield fonds 039798.

Conflict

There was one conflict in the mid-nineteenth century which was said to have lasted three years. For an event that was both significant and unusual, the lack of contemporary clarity about its nature is puzzling, especially as it is commemorated with a shrine in the central Tianhou temple.

The conflict took place between the villages of central Tsuen Wan and those of Shing Mun, the latter possibly supported by Pat Heung, a name that is in itself confusing.[38] We were given an essay, attributed to the 'Information Office', perhaps an arm of the Rural Committee, which says that Tsuen Wan had a market and a public scale, the commission from which paid the administrative costs of the villages and the temple. One group of villages disagreed with the commission, among other issues. Shing Mun attacked, and the fighting lasted for three years. Tsuen Wan relied on local young men to fight for them, and 17 were killed. The conflict was finally settled by village elders. Rites are held every year to commemorate the 17 martyrs, and in 1933 the community leader Yeung Kwok-shui had a plaque created to inform succeeding generations, and to pay respect to the heroes' spirits in heaven.

While this suggests that the commission was a cause of the dispute, elders gave various alternatives, stating that the issues were geomantic sites, or fields. The clearest and most comprehensive account was given in 1969 by an elderly man of the Chan lineage, Mr Chan Siu-cheung, who lived in Kwan Mun Hau. He stated that his grandfather had taken part in the fighting when he was about 30 years old. Mr Chan said:

> The relationship between Tsuen Wan and Shing Mun was not very good, but we had a good relationship with Shek Lei Pui (石梨背), a small hill village to the east. Once, some people from Shing Mun planned to take property from Shek Lei Pui, and they sent a note saying when they would come and what they wanted. The people of Shek Lei Pui were terrified, and so some went to Tsuen Wan and told

---

38. The Shing Mun villages were known as the 'Pat Heung' (八鄉), as was the *xiang* on the other side of Tai Mo Shan.

them. Between 60 and 80 young men united and hid around Shek Lei Pui to wait for the robbers, ten of whom came. They caught them and took them to Tsuen Wan, but they didn't know what to do with them, as there was no law here then and they didn't want to kill them. They held them in a big boat and took them to Nantou (南頭), the seat of local government, but at Kap Shui Mun one prisoner broke loose and hurt a Tsuen Wan man. They took the rest to Nantou, but the escaped prisoner swam to shore, and told his fellow Shing Mun villagers that the others had all been killed. They were very angry and attacked the Shek Lei Pui people with no warning. They beat them with weapons and took all their property, but some escaped to Tsuen Wan and said that everyone had been killed. Then more than 200 Tsuen Wan natives united and marched to Shek Lei Pui and fought there without stealing anything. They couldn't enter the village, as a big fire was burning in front of it. About 20 Tsuen Wan men and more than 100 Shing Mun men were killed.

After this, Shing Mun people took pigs, cows, and chickens over the mountains as gifts to Pat Heung, and said that they wanted to enter into an alliance with their district. Then that group united and started to attack Tsuen Wan. Usually they fixed a day to fight. Wo Yi Hop (和宜合) was the battlefield, as was Chuen Lung (川龍), not Tsuen Wan town. Lots of people from both sides were killed, but no one could win because few people fought and they retreated after a few had been killed. This went on for three years.

The conflict was settled because a wealthy man from Chuen Lung was tired of having his village used as a battlefield. So, he didn't talk to either group, but one day he took money, livestock, and so on to Pat Heung and said that Tsuen Wan wanted to talk. Another day he did the same with Tsuen Wan. He deceived both sides. All thought that he was being a middleman. They had a peace talk in Chuen Lung, each thinking that the other side wanted peace. They negotiated what should be given to each side, and then there was peace. Only the man named Tsang lost property. Then the names of the people from Tsuen Wan who had been killed were written on a paper and placed behind a big tablet in the Tianhou temple, where they were worshipped every year. . . . [A]n educated man spent a lot of money to renovate the temple, building a small chamber for them, and inscribing their names in stone to be worshipped in the Heroes' Hall.

Plate 9: Mr Chan Siu-cheung in the Chan ancestral hall, Kwan Mun Hau village, New Year, 1969. His grandfather had participated in the fight between Tsuen Wan and the Shing Mun villages.

My grandfather used a big gun carried by two men, with sand and small pieces of iron for bullets. Tsuen Wan also had a cannon, which was their most important weapon.

Within 20 years the two sides had forgiven each other, and the bad relations had ended. When the Shing Mun villagers had to move because of reservoir construction they also installed a plaque commemorating their 17 dead in the new temple that they built near Kam Tin, where some now lived.[39] James Hayes was given two other versions of the story, one from the Shing Mun perspective and the other from the Au-Yeung lineage of Tsuen Wan.[40]

Relations with Others

According to oral testimony, in the early years of settlement in Tsuen Wan and Tsing Yi, local people paid rent to the large and powerful Punti Tang lineage.[41] Ho Wing-kwong said that this was because they had opened the land to cultivation before the arrival of the Hakka people. One of the major tombs of the Tang of Kam Tin, still worshipped by them, testifies to their interest in Tsuen Wan, but the Tang were said to have caused no problems to the Hakka settlers when they came to worship at it. Land rent was no longer paid to them after 1898, reflecting the colonial policy of granting rights to established tenants, and perhaps even earlier. Tsuen Wan was also protected from their control by the mountainous terrain and by distance. As Ho Wing-kwong said: 'You can control only as far as the length of your whip'.

Some wealthy members of large and powerful Cantonese lineages in the New Territories had owned slaves. They had been purchased and kept as status symbols, doing demeaning tasks for anyone of the lineage who made demands of them. Wives were found for them, and the family continued in that capacity. The practice stopped at the end of the Qing dynasty, but some remained living near the villages.[42] Tsuen Wan people had not kept slaves for a very long time, although Ho Wing-kwong said they had purchased children in the distant past. Some might treat them well if they were willing to work and adopt them instead as godsons: *kaaijai* (契仔) or *gonjai* (幹仔).

Tsuen Wan people with some means and who needed help sometimes hired short-term workers, or else they hired long-term workers, dependents called either *cheuhnggung* (長工) or *cheuhnggang* (長耕) depending on their role, a practice that ended with the occupation. The workers, who were men, came from poor areas of Guangdong and Fujian. Some were given small houses to live in. Many lived and ate with their employers and were treated almost as family members, occasionally even being left some property. At a minimum they were given housing, meals, and some money. They had their place in the community (有地位). *Cheuhnggung* were hired to help families who did business, while *cheuhnggang*, who had farming experience, helped with farming. Ho Wing-kwong's family had some:

At that time the living was very hard in China. If you gave him two meals a day and one or two dollars he would think you were the emperor. Then things were entirely different; people were different. If you gave them food and money and shelter they would work for you for life. Some people treated them well, and a better-off family might get a man a wife. Both would then work for you. The worker was a free body, not on contract; he wasn't bound to you.

Occasionally there was a family without sons who had a *cheuhnggang*. If he was deemed appropriate, they might invite him to marry one of their daughters in uxorilocal marriage, in the hope of having

39. The eight Shing Mun villages had to give up their land and move to completely new locations in 1928 to make way for the reservoir construction, a 'traumatic' experience. Hayes, *The Great Difference*, 87–88.
40. James Hayes, 'A Village War', *Journal of the Hong Kong Branch Royal Asiatic Society* 17 (1977): 185–98.
41. See also Hayes, *The Rural Communities of Hong Kong: Studies and Themes*, 119.
42. James L. Watson, 'Chattel Slavery in Chinese Peasant Society: A Comparative Analysis', in Watson and Watson, *Village Life in Hong Kong*, 125–44.

descendants.[43] The man would take responsibility for their care in this life and the next, and would inherit their property. His children would carry this on. This form of marriage was called *yahpjeui* (入 贅), the second character meaning to 'patch together', 'link', or 'connect'.

Another group of people who were separate from the Tsuen Wan indigenous land-dwellers were the boat-dwelling fishing people. Until about the 1960s, they had no opportunity to study and were extremely poor. They sold their fish through land-based intermediaries, which made them appear inferior, exacerbated, no doubt, by pre-existing prejudice against them.[44] Some people said that in earlier years they were not treated well when they were on land, and that bullies broke their water containers, which they carried on their heads. A local man said this was because the Tsuen Wan people had not yet 'become civilized'. The fishing people did, however, worship at the various local Tianhou temples.[45]

As the land dwellers began to learn Cantonese, mutual understanding became easier. Aside from their interaction at the temples, they sometimes entered into special relationships. The fishing people's living conditions were harsh, and their children even less likely to survive than those of the land dwellers. In desperation, some approached the land-dwelling families to ask them to be godparents. One man said that six or seven out of ten fishing families did this, in part, also, as a way to avoid bullying. The relationship enabled them to say they were someone's godson, and then the bully would stop. The boat families also could store their extra clothing and nets in the godparents' houses to keep them dry. A Kwan Mun Hau woman said that Hakka people had many such relationships:

> There was a boat family whose children had died. On the first and fifteenth of every month they would bream their boat on land. They had only one son surviving. The mother was afraid he would die and urged my father-in-law to become the godfather.[46] The family sent him some fish, shrimp, and crabs. Then at every Mid-Autumn Festival they sent gifts, including pork. My family would send back white radishes, *chahgwo* (茶粿), and salt vegetables because those people didn't have these things. At New Year my father-in-law sent sweet year cake (年糕), and they gave him dried scallops and other foods. The man came when he had time, when their boat was here, maybe once a month. We had no ceremony to establish the relationship. He had no language in common with my mother-in-law. We didn't have to inform him when she died, as he wasn't a true relative.

In addition to these godparenthood relationships, there was at least one marriage. It had taken place in the early twentieth century between a Kwan Mun Hau man who had gone abroad to work, without success. His first wife had died of heartbreak in his absence. He then married a woman from a fishing family.

This raises the question of how newcomers were treated who came for other reasons, such as marriage. We heard nothing suggesting that the woman mentioned above had not been accepted. One Cantonese woman who married into a Kwan Mun Hau family in the pre-war period had been referred to by some people as 'snake woman', a derogatory term, but once she had learned to speak Hakka and do the heavy work that was expected of the local women, she was accepted. The same applied to a Jamaican woman who had married a Kwan Mun Hau man who had gone there to work. He brought her back with their children and she adapted quickly to the conditions of life in Tsuen Wan. She learned to plough and harrow, and to gather shellfish. She also learned to speak Hakka and earned the local people's respect. Ultimately, she had to return to Jamaica because of economic duress, adopting out her twin boys to lineage families, but her name appears in the Yau lineage genealogy.

---

43. Cohen found this form of marriage in a Hakka community in Taiwan, see *House United, House Divided*, 34.
44. Hayes found, also, that they purchased food and vegetables from marine hawkers, rather than going ashore, see *The Hong Kong Region*, 37.
45. The bell in the central temple was donated in 1743 by a man surnamed Lai, a name common among boat people but not present in the land population. Faure, 'Notes on the History of Tsuen Wan', 49.
46. She said her father-in-law likely had been chosen as he had three sons, and daughters: a 'good fate'.

In the pre-war period, about half the shopkeepers were not local.[47] Among these were immigrant Hakka men, some of long-standing, some Cantonese men, and some Teochiu. The natives called themselves and immigrants of long-standing *Tsuen Wan buntouh* (荃灣本土); recent immigrants were called *Tsuen Wan loihlouh* (荃灣來老).

Tsuen Wan developed the reputation of being accepting of outsiders. According to Ho Wing-kwong:

> Out of all the New Territories, Tsuen Wan was the earliest place to be open to others (開放) and civilized (文明). You could say that it was the first place for outside people to do business from early times. There was no discrimination (排斥). Only a few were of this level: Yuen Long (元朗), Tai Po (大埔), Tsuen Wan. Of these, Tsuen Wan was the best for immigrants to do business peacefully, assimilating easily. Now it is true, then it was true. Why was it harder to do business in, for example, Yuen Long? People wouldn't shout at you or bully you. For example, if you went to Yuen Long and opened a business the local people wouldn't buy from you; they would only buy from locals. But Tsuen Wan [was different], perhaps because it is closer to Hong Kong and Kowloon, so it may have received more outside influences. So, it was more 'open' and 'civilized'. When people came to do business, no one would make distinctions among them. Even if the newcomers didn't have an association (同鄉會), it was easy for them to cooperate with people here. The fact that there are lots of surnames together here is a good thing about Tsuen Wan as a place. Others, like the Tang, are more conservative and have an old-fashioned way of thinking.

The Market and Marketing Relationships

In 1898, Tsuen Wan was a bustling market town, although smaller than Yuen Long, which had 74 shops.[48] Yuen Long, like Sheung Shui (上水), Tai Po, and others, was a periodic market., Tsuen Wan's shops and market opened daily. As Ho Wing-kwong explained, it was initially highly informal:

> You could say that the Tsuen Wan market belonged to Kwan Mun Hau people named Yau and Chan. They managed it. The area was next to Kwan Mun Hau. They had lots of land and were wealthier. They used part of it for a market. At that time, mainly because the land belonged to Kwan Mun Hau, people just set out their products. Later, more than 100 years ago, the Yau and Chan ancestors thought that since people gathered there to sell things, they should consider setting up a market structure, with shelter and fixed stalls. Then they divided the space into separate areas where meat, fish, and vegetables were sold. They rented the stalls out, but for very little. The Kwan Mun Hau Yau and Chan ancestral trusts oversaw this. The Yau and Chan also had some shops built. Around the market there were also shops belonging to Hoi Pa, Yeung Uk (楊屋), Ho Pui, and Muk Min Ha people who had property, so most shops were opened by local people. This market was not governed by rules but was simply organized by the vendors themselves.
>
> The establishment of shops was different. Within the past 100 years, people began to think of establishing shops. There were houses clustered near the sea. There was little room near the market for those people who wanted to set up businesses, but if one of the residents was willing, he could sell his house, and the purchaser could use the front of the house for a shop. This became the business area on Old Street. Later, in 1936–37, a new market, two new streets, and modern style housing were planned and built, causing a great increase in land values in the adjacent areas,[49] although about 60–70% of the old business area remained. Because of the fire, though, it was diminished, and not worth rebuilding.

---

47. Ho Wing-kwong provided a diagram and list of shops with their owners circa 1920, reproduced in Faure, 'Notes on the History of Tsuen Wan', 99–101.
48. James Hayes, 'The Pattern of Life in the New Territories in 1898', *Journal of the Hong Kong Branch Royal Asiatic Society* 2 (1962): 95.
49. See also Hayes, *The Great Difference*, 51.

That business area remained primarily in the hands of local people, whereas the proprietors in the new market were immigrants. From about 1960, the fishing people joined in the market activities.

Although there were shops in Tsuen Wan, local people also went elsewhere to buy things they needed, and to sell their produce. Until urban development began in earnest, pineapples were their most important product, and it was possible for a skilled person to make a good living as a pineapple merchant. A Kwan Mun Hau woman said:

> There was a wooden boat that went to Hong Kong side, rowed by two people, and with one to control the sail. My father-in-law was a pineapple agent. The boat left here at 4 a.m., after being loaded the previous night. After it arrived in Hong Kong he would employ some coolies whom he knew to carry the pineapples to the shops where they would be sold. . . . Farmers from Tsuen Wan, Tsing Yi, and Kwai Chung (葵涌) carried the pineapples to Tsuen Wan market to sell them. My father-in-law then bargained for them and sold them in Hong Kong. He also acted as an agent locating baby pigs for people, so if people asked me who I was I would say 'daughter-in-law of the pig-seller' (豬頭仔的新抱) and then they would know.

He delivered the pineapples to various locations on Hong Kong side according to their quality, taking the best to customers by rickshaw, and sometimes also selling sweet potatoes and firewood. He was a member of the Yau lineage resident in Kwan Mun Hau, and had an impressive reputation as a good wholesaler, a businessman who increased the family property.

If Tsuen Wan people needed more rice, they could buy it in Sham Shui Po (深水埗), together with seasonings such as soy sauce and fermented bean curd. There were Hakka people there with whom they had kinship relations. Women from Tsuen Wan sometimes walked there to sell fuel, and people with surplus fish sold it there.

Another market where local people sometimes bought special items was Yuen Long, which they reached by walking over mountain paths, until the bus route was developed. An elderly man said that when young he would walk there to buy sugar to make *chahgwo*. The sugar available there was superior, he said, because of locally grown sugar cane. In the early twentieth century, they also went to buy farm tools, livestock, and 'mountain products' such as basketry trays and containers. Thieves were a problem on those mountain paths back then, so they often went in groups for security. People also sometimes carried their rice to Yuen Long, where there was a milling machine, and this saved them the labour of milling it by hand.

Local Governance and the Central Tianhou Temple

Order was maintained in Tsuen Wan, as we have indicated, through the well-established system of local governance, based on a close relationship between their governing body and the central temple dedicated to Tianhou, called Ma Leuhng (媽良) by Hakka people.[50] According to their accounts, from the earliest times they farmed, but as they were also fishermen they needed to worship Tianhou so that they would have peace and prosperity.[51] A local legend says that the image of the goddess was caught in a fishing net by men of three surnames from Lo Wai. It became heavier and heavier until it could no longer be moved, and so it was left in that place, which became the site of the temple. Another story was that it had been dug up and could stand upright only on that site. During the Qing (Kangxi), the local people contributed funds and materials so that a temple could be built. However, they then faced the problem of maintaining it, carrying out repairs as needed, and hiring a caretaker (廟主).

50. There were four other temples dedicated to Tianhou in the district.
51. See James L. Watson, 'Standardizing the Gods: The Promotion of Tian Hou ("Empress of Heaven") along the South China Coast, 960–1960', in Watson and Watson, *Village Life in Hong Kong*, 269–310.

Plate 10: Central Tianhou temple as seen across vegetable fields in 1968. The large building beyond is likely a weaving shed, with a mansion nearby.

The solution they reached was to establish a public scale that was located by the temple until about 1960, giving it the authority of the deity and establishing public trust. Local men bid on an annual basis for the right to operate the scale. All significant goods sold in the area, such as pigs and large amounts of vegetables, were weighed there, and commissions charged. Thus, the temple had an annual income from the bids, which was used for its expenses, for the ceremony of giving thanks, and for social welfare in the district.

Later, wealthy businessmen, who had prospered because of the benevolence of the deity, bought and donated fields near the temple, which also yielded income. Another source of income for the temple, one that was very popular in the first half of the twentieth century, was an event called *jouh seh* (做社). All households that wished to participate, or had the means, contributed money. On the first day of the second lunar month, the event called *faan sehyuhk* (分社肉) took place, and pork that had been used to worship Tianhou and cooked in wine was divided and distributed to all participating households. Households bought shares, and 'won' pieces of pork accordingly. People agreed that it was especially sweet, as it had been used to worship the deity, and they believed that eating it would bring them peace and good fortune. It could be cooked with vegetables at home and thus served to all family members. As people were fortunate if they had pork even once a month, this was very special indeed, and described with great enthusiasm.[52]

---

52. Variants of this ceremony and feast were held in many New Territories villages and village clusters, although the feasts were often eaten communally at the shrine or temple. See Faure, 'Notes on the History of Tsuen Wan', 61–68. See also David Faure, *The Structure of Chinese Rural Society* (Hong Kong: Oxford University Press, 1986), 73–74, 96–97, 103, 141. Kwan Mun Hau people did so until the village moved. Men and women bought shares 'like an association' and worshipped at their shrine to Hongshenggong with a roast pig, and then divided the pork.

Tsuen Wan as a Community

At this point, we should consider the quality of social relations in Tsuen Wan as a community in comparison to other districts in the New Territories. With the exception of the relationship between land and boat people, Tsuen Wan was quite egalitarian.[53] No one village or lineage dominated the others, and all shared in a similar lifestyle that included cooperation among its people to maintain order. The various lineages coexisted amicably, and did not maintain boundaries either within or around the territory. Unlike many New Territories communities, Tsuen Wan people had no specific memories of ceremonies to protect and purify their territory (*dajiu* 打醮),[54] although some said they may have been held in the past. Many districts held these ceremonies at regular intervals, and they believed them to have a protective function against pestilence and unsettled spirits.[55] Some elders did remember occasions when Tianhou had been taken out in procession, carried by two unmarried men, when an epidemic occurred.[56] According to a Fan elder, they made a one-day circuit around the central Tsuen Wan villages, starting in Ho Pui, while other village groupings within the district had their own processions.

Why did they believe that these protective rituals were not needed? This may be related to the fact that these Hakka people do not believe it necessary to appease 'hungry ghosts' in the seventh month,[57] and maintain that their ancestors will protect them. They did not, it seems, perceive their social and spiritual world in an adversarial or fearful way.

They had no hereditary enemies, being protected by topography, and were vulnerable only to sporadic attackers, such as pirates, who might come by water. We found no evidence of the concept of hereditary enemies in their worldview, or of entrenched hostility or rivalry within Tsuen Wan itself. The elders, representing the people of Tsuen Wan, worked together to govern them through the Tsuen On Kuk, with the power of their temple behind them. Tsuen Wan, like many other small multi-lineage communities in the mountains and coastal valleys, was almost entirely self-governing through cooperation and an agreed-on system of local representation,[58] even during the first decades of British rule.

Once the British were established on Hong Kong Island, and then in Kowloon, their proximity, and Tsuen Wan people's exposure to them, may also have helped them to understand relationships that were different than those that governed other parts of Xin'an. We refer here to the areas dominated by the large and powerful Punti lineage villages, where a contrasting way of life had developed centuries before.

This fundamental comparison between two very different ways of building communities in the New Territories was first articulated in 1977 by James Hayes.[59] His analysis is based on his first-hand observations and discussions with elders in many of the small village groupings of the New Territories, especially those on the islands, and his careful reading of the literature on the large single-lineage communities. As he states, it was quite possible for members of multi-lineage communities to maintain a peaceful and orderly existence, even though some may have had to pay land rent to large and powerful lineages, capably managing their own affairs, creating a 'flourishing, self-regulating community life'.[60] This theme was further developed by others, such as Judith Strauch,[61] thus beginning to right the

---

53. With occasional exceptions, as stated.
54. For a discussion of the complex meanings of *dajiu*, see Faure, *The Structure of Chinese Rural Society*, 80–86.
55. See, for example, Hayes, *Rural Communities*, 156–64.
56. See also Faure, 'Notes on the History of Tsuen Wan', 50, citing couplets dated Guangxu Gengyin (1890).
57. An exception was the 1969 community-wide 'hungry ghost' festival to settle the war dead. See Chapter 6.
58. Hayes, *The Hong Kong Region 1850–1911: Institutions and Leadership in Town and Countryside* (Hamden, CT: Archon Books, The Shoestring Press, 1977), 194–201.
59. Hayes, *The Hong Kong Region*, 194–201.
60. Hayes, *The Hong Kong Region*, 200.
61. Judith Strauch, 'Community and Kinship in Southeastern China: The View from the Multilineage Communities of Hong Kong',

balance against the predominance in the anthropological literature of the major Cantonese lineages and their worldviews. The village that she studied was similar to Tsuen Wan in its protected location and its residents' loyalty to their lineages, while also maintaining a strong and united multi-lineage community whose members were economically relatively equal.

It is important to compare their way of life and worldview with those of the wealthy and powerful Cantonese-speaking single-lineage communities on the northern plains of the New Territories. These were long-settled, some having been present since the Song dynasty. They possessed the best rice land, with its flat and rich paddies.[62] Their settlements were organized on the basis of kinship, with large single-lineage villages or village groupings, and a substantial percentage of their land held in lineage trusts.[63] Their lineages were hierarchical, with some men having extreme wealth and even official status, while others lived in poverty.[64] The primary goal of these lineages was to maintain their wealth, power, and territory, as well as tight control over their nearby tenants, who were much later arrivals. They viewed similar lineages as rivals against whom they were engaged in perpetual power struggles, while forming alliances when it was politically expedient to do so.

The British did not recognize the concept of subsoil and surface land rights, and quickly ended this relationship.[65] Under colonialism, the large lineages lost some of their income and power because distant fields to which they had claimed subsoil rights were awarded through the land registration process to the tenants who were farming them, resulting in considerable bitterness.

Lineage rivalry continued into the twentieth century. The decennial *dajiu* mounted by the Tang lineage village of Ha Tsuen, for example, is aggressive in the extreme, involving a three-day march around the boundaries of their territory by about 1,000 young men, with particular bellicosity when it passes their rival lineage village of Ping Shan. Its purpose is to demarcate their territory and to settle the spirits of martyrs from the Tang lineage and satellite villages (which are pressed to contribute) killed in conflict with neighbouring lineages.[66] Such attitudes and conduct have been virtually unheard of in the small multi-lineage communities of the New Territories. In Tsuen Wan, this was true not only of their day-to-day life, with the exception of the mid-nineteenth century conflict with Shing Mun, but also of their ceremonies and festivals. When supernatural threats were mentioned, people almost always reiterated their confidence that their ancestors would protect them.

Relationships among Families and Lineages through Women

There was also a complex web of kinship relations that drew together not only lineages and their branches, but also those created by marriage. Some men rarely visited their wives' families, apparently being somewhat embarrassed to do so, although there were exceptions. They did, however,

---

Journal of Asian Studies 43 (1) (November 1983): 21–50. In her study near Tai Po, she found no oral history revealing 'fights, disputes, bullying, and all-round uneasiness' that Baker expected would be found in such communities. Hugh D. R. Baker, *Chinese Family and Kinship* (New York: Columbia University Press, 1979), 65.

62. The Man lineage was an exception, in that its fields were reclaimed and saline, but the red rice they produced had its own value, and they had other sources of income as well. James L. Watson, *Emigration and the Chinese Lineage: The Mans in Hong Kong and London* (Berkeley: University of California Press, 1975).

63. An example is the Tang lineage village of Hang Mei in which, in the early 1960s, 93% of the land was collectively owned, the majority by lineages and their branches. Jack M. Potter, *Capitalism and the Chinese Peasant: Social and Economic Change in a Chinese Village* (Berkeley: University of California Press, 1968), 96.

64. James L. Watson, 'From the Common Pot: Feasting with Equals in Chinese Society', in Watson and Watson, *Village Life in Hong Kong*, 117; Rubie S. Watson, 'Class Differences and Affinal Relations in South China', in Watson and Watson, *Village Life in Hong Kong*, 76–79.

65. Michael J. E. Palmer, 'The Surface-Subsoil Form of Divided Ownership in Later Imperial China: Some Examples from the New Territories of Hong Kong', *Modern Asian Studies* 21, no. 1 (1987): 1–119.

66. James L. Watson, 'Fighting with Operas: Processionals, Politics, and the Specter of Violence in Rural Hong Hong', in Watson and Watson, *Village Life in Hong Kong*, 314–23.

acknowledge the relationships created by the various types of marriage, and the resulting kinship ties, through terms of address and the appropriate behaviour that these implied. Mr Kwok Yung-hing, now in his eighties, said that his family addressed men of the Yau lineage as 'mother's brother' (*kaufuh* 舅父), because one of his lineage older brothers (堂阿哥) had married a woman of the Yau lineage. They were thus *jihgeiyahn* (自己人), 'our own people', a meaningful term used for relatives and others with whom people have a close relationship. Their wives were addressed as *kaumouh* (舅母). Women visited each other at festivals with gifts of pork and fruit, even when we were first there, and men and women used these terms into the 1990s. He said that they also addressed men of the Chan lineage as *kaufuh*. The reason for this was more complex. His mother was his father's second or 'replacement' wife, called *tihn fong* (填房), meaning 'filling the room', the first wife having died. She had come from the Chan lineage, and so the Kwok families acknowledged the relationship by addressing Chan lineage men as *kaufuh*. The Chan people allowed them to use their well water.[67]

Furthermore, the second marriage created a relationship between the *tihn fong* wife and the family of the deceased first wife. She was referred to as *bohk geuk* (駁腳), a woman who had been 'grafted' onto the natal family of the deceased first wife. Their various family members were then referred to as her '*bohk geuk*' (kinship term), and they interacted as though she was a married-out daughter, exchanging visits at festivals and attending each other's celebrations.

This same man's maternal grandmother had been born on Tsing Yi and married to a man in Longgang, Bao'an (寶安縣龍崗). Her daughter married Mr Kwok's father in Tsuen Wan, and her son came to live there, where he was much loved by his sister's family, to whom he was their *kaufuh*. He had no children, and since his death his soul has been worshipped by his maternal nephew, thus demonstrating another possible kind of relationship, rare, because of the usual emphasis on patrilineality, but not unheard of.[68] A sister of the woman born on Tsing Yi married a man of the Lau lineage of Wo Yi Hop village. Mr Kwok said that for this reason they addressed the Lau men as *louhbiu* (老表), with *biu* being used for cousins related through women. He said that they strictly adhered to the acknowledgement of these relationships and their appropriate terms of address, and that 'people at that time were concerned to build up relationships as much as possible'.

While many marriage relations were within Tsuen Wan, the relationships known to us were also more widespread. Many married to and from Sha Tin, Tai Po, and Pat Heung; there were fewer relations with Sham Shui Po and Bao'an. We never heard of any marriage relations with Sai Kung, Cheung Sha Wan, or any of the islands.

Festivals and Entertainment

The annual cycle of festivals brought people together in shared activities and worship at the ancestral halls and shrines, often with unicorn dancing (舞麒麟). These gave some relief from the hard work of their daily lives, and the opportunity to enjoy special festival foods, including the meat prepared for offerings. Women worked hard to make them and enjoyed them because they could not go to restaurants and teahouses. Sugar, a special treat, was featured in almost all of them. Those called *chahgwo* and *goubaahn* (糕粄) were especially important and were exchanged by families on special occasions. Both were round cakes several inches in diameter, made from glutinous rice flour, water, and brown sugar, leavened through a sourdough process, and steamed on banana leaves. 'Year cakes' were unleavened but of the same ingredients, steamed for hours because they were very large, and cut into pieces for distribution at New Year. *Chahgwo* had fillings of peanuts. The savoury variety, made for the Winter

---

67. In contrast, see Rubie S. Watson, 'Class Differences and Affinal Relations in Ha Tsuen', in Watson and Watson, *Village Life in Hong Kong*, 79–80. Such relationships were not acknowledged there, although they were in other parts of China.
68. Caring for the souls of matrilateral relatives without descendants was said to be not uncommon.

Plate 11: Mrs Yau Chan Shek-ying making *chahgwo* filled with popcorn, peanuts, and brown sugar, winter, 1979–1980. They would be steamed on banana leaves.

Solstice, were filled with radish, green onion, mushrooms, preserved meats, if available, and seasonings. *Goubaahn* were like *chahgwo*, but flatter, and without fillings. Various sweet specialties were made to eat and exchange at New Year, which was celebrated similarly by most families. All members should have new clothes, especially children.

According to a Fan man:

In the past at New Year, and also now, we had to clean the entire house. At 12:00 a.m., we burned firecrackers. Everyone had to have a bath with pomelo leaf infusion.[69] Then we would be a year older. We still do this. The women were very busy. On the first day of the New Year we stayed home, as family was important, and we ate vegetarian food, using new bowls and chopsticks, as the old ones had been used for meat.[70] Early in the morning of the second day we went to worship at the shrines with firecrackers, did unicorn dancing, and so on. That day opened the New Year. Everyone tried to be the first to go to the temple to worship, and then we worshipped the shrines together. We couldn't sweep the floor until the third day. My father says this even now, but it gets very dirty, so we do it. He says we can only sweep back, not away. On the third, we sweep, sweep, to send away the ghosts of poverty.

Children received red packets of lucky money, and everyone rested as much as possible. Younger women were entitled to return to their natal families (外家), carrying gifts of festival foods and pork, to have some days of rest and emotional support. On the fourteenth or fifteenth day, the lineages raised lanterns for new sons who had been born.

At Qingming, when families worshipped their recent ancestors at their graves and tombs, women made another variety of sweet *chahgwo* called *seungchahngbaahn* (雙層粄) or *jeuijaibaahn* (蕝仔粄), 'little boy's penis cakes'. They consisted of sets of three small rolls steamed on banana leaves.

---

69. Pomelo leaves are believed to be purifying.
70. Yau lineage members did eat meat on this day.

For the Dragon Boat Festival, women made *jung*, both savoury and sweet, from glutinous rice steamed in tightly wrapped bamboo leaves. The *chahgwo* for that festival were black and flavoured with a plant believed to prevent illness, as were the willow leaves they hung over their doors. In the earliest period, young men of the coastal villages raced their fishing boats. The races were organized by the Tsuen On Kuk.[71]

In the eighth lunar month, the Mid-Autumn Festival was important, especially for children, who had lanterns to play with while their families made offerings to the moon. In the ninth month, at Chongyang, lineages and their branches worshipped higher-order ancestors at their tombs, and enjoyed meals cooked at the tombs or afterwards at the halls. During the Winter Solstice, considered to be the most important festival, women made savoury *chahgwo*.

Their lives were also punctuated by the memorable ceremonies that acknowledged significant changes in their lives: the birth of sons, special achievements, marriages, and deaths. In subsequent chapters we shall explain what we learned about these events, and how their acknowledgement changed over time.

In the years before the occupation, Tsuen Wan people engaged in various forms of group entertainments and activities when time permitted. In the 1920s and 1930s, almost every village had a group of young men who met to build up their strength and practice unicorn dancing. Masters were hired to teach the young men, who could then defend their villages against thieves if necessary. Their unicorn dancing,[72] and playing of gongs and cymbals, added to the meaning and festivity of occasions such as New Year, the lantern-raising ceremony, and village or lineage temple worship. They also played to accompany weddings and funeral processions. All of these occasions have their own special rhythms. However, as the government strengthened the protection of the area, it was no longer necessary for young men to learn martial arts.

An especially meaningful form of entertainment was the singing of Hakka mountain songs while working outdoors. This was very popular in the generations before the occupation, and for approximately 15 years afterwards. They were sung between a man and a woman, addressing each other as 'older brother' and 'younger sister', or by groups of women.

The songs expressed various emotions: love, jealousy or suspicion, flirting, sexual innuendo and desire, humour, and competition or aggression. Many were described as *liuh* (撩) 'flirting', and they were not only competitive in nature but also could be suggestive or even risqué, as well as using coarse language and even vulgarity. These were generally improvised, and some people were extremely skilled at this. They gave unrelated men and women an otherwise forbidden opportunity to communicate, especially given their content.

Others were learned or remembered, often after being heard only once by those who were gifted. Some that were said to be very old, dating back two or three generations, expressed love or jealousy between a man and a woman who were engaged or married, and facing separation or infidelity due to emigration. Their tunes were beautiful when sung.

Mrs Yau Chan Shek-ying remembered a remarkable number of them, and sang them for us to record.[73] For example, she remembered that when she was 12 years old, in the 1930s, a boat that

---

71. The way the dragon boat races were held changed within memory. After the occupation, the Rural Committee, along with fishing people's representatives, organized the events.
72. Unicorn dancing was and is believed to bring the blessings of a good, peaceful, and gentle long life, according to Ho Wing-kwong.
73. Recordings of about 45 mountain songs, and wedding and funeral laments, have been deposited in the Audrey and Harry Hawthorn Library & Archives at the UBC Museum of Anthropology in Vancouver, and the Richard Charles Lee Canada-Hong Kong Library at the University of Toronto, where they are readily accessible to the public. They were sung in Hakka by Mrs Yau, in an old style that not even her son could fully understand. They include her discussion of their meanings in Cantonese, and written transcriptions.

had come from Kowloon could not return that night due to wind conditions. A local man sang to a woman on the boat, who had come to cut grass, flirting with her.

> You Kowloon woman can't return.
> Spend the night at my house
> I have beds and covers.[74]

Mrs Yau said that the Kowloon woman could sing well, and could respond because she was from Kowloon, whereas it would have been shameful for a local woman to do so. If she had not been able to sing back, she would have shouted at him instead. Those who could sing improvised rebuttals were admired and were considered to have won the competition. Some people were skilled at improvisation, but they also could learn from others. There was an older Kwan Mun Hau man who taught the young village women how to sing in the evenings after they had finished working at Texaco, but sometimes men also learned from women.

The following includes suggestive imagery:

Girl:
> High mountain-top water sounds hoh hoh
> The surface of the water spreads out for growing pineapples
> The best pineapples have no fruit
> The best younger brother has no wife

Boy:
> On the top of the tall mountain grows a pine tree
> Branching out to hang lantern(s)
> One pair of lanterns hanging together
> The best girl has no husband.[75]

Some songs that she remembered were not flirting songs, but instead convey love between a couple, something that again was not to be publicly expressed. One described a returned sailor's suspicion of fine new things worn by a woman to whom he is engaged, but she responded well to him:

Boy:
> You wear a white dress with blue trim, Ah Muih
> Who made your dress for you?
> Who gave you your golden hair ornaments?
> Who gave you the ring you wear on your hand?

Girl:
> I am wearing a white dress with blue trim, Ah Go
> It was cut and sewed by me.
> My hair ornament was given by my father.
> I bought the ring with money earned from selling hemp thread.[76]

Others, even older, express women's fear of separation from their emigrant husbands, and their husbands' possible infidelity.[77] In one, a woman's sister-in-law told her that her husband would return from abroad that evening. The woman did not believe her, as she had received no letter from him. Her mother-in-law had told the sister-in-law, but not her. The sister-in-law was malicious and bet her that if

---

74. An audio recording of the song can be downloaded at https://www.hkupress.hku.hk/+extras/1681audio/.
75. This could be word play between 'husband' and 'pants'. An audio recording of the song can be downloaded at https://www.hkupress.hku.hk/+extras/1681audio/.
76. An audio recording of the song can be downloaded at https://www.hkupress.hku.hk/+extras/1681audio/.
77. Elizabeth Lominska Johnson, 'Singing of Separation, Lamenting Loss: Hakka Women's Expressions of Separation and Reunion', in *Living with Separation in China: Anthropological Accounts*, ed. Charles Stafford (London and New York: RoutledgeCurzon, 2003), 27–52.

he did come back the woman would have to embroider ten lotus flowers for her. He did in fact appear, and he woke a number of times that night to call her to bed with him, but she still hadn't finished the embroidery. As a result, at dawn he was very angry and left the next day instead of staying for a week as he had planned. She then sang him this song:

> I hold a golden cup in two hands, asking when you will come back.
> I go along the upper road where there are many white flowers [other women], many, my husband.
> I go along the lower road where there are many stones.
> My husband, you are now leaving; when will you return?
> When on the road you should not pick up the wild flowers,
> Within the house there is already a plum blossom [herself]

Another song concerns a woman whose husband has gone overseas to work with a group of friends. The friends return, but he does not.

> Woman:
>> Put away the hemp weaving, put away the stool,
>> waiting for my husband to return.
>> He went with you but did not come back with you.
> Man:
>> Little sister, don't ask.
>> Talking about your husband will make you very angry.
>> Your husband has a relationship with a Vietnamese woman; it's very serious.
>> During the day they act as travel companions.
>> At night they act as a couple.
> Woman:
>> Worship heaven, worship earth, so that whenever that Vietnamese woman becomes pregnant the babies will die,
>> So my husband can earn money and return.[78]

These songs were part of an oral tradition of long standing, as the women who sang them were illiterate. When groups of women went out to work, cutting grass or doing wage labour, they worked and sang at the same time, which made them very happy together (很熱鬧). Even though some were very upset—if they had worked from dawn until dark and been berated by their mothers-in-law, and the family had gone ahead and eaten their dinner, treating them as though they were not human—they could overcome their bitterness by singing.

In addition to the songs sung by local people, itinerant Hakka singers sometimes arrived, either individuals or couples. They sang mountain songs or opera songs, and sometimes accompanied their singing with clappers, or carried props, such as a miniature dragon boat. While the local people were sitting outside working in the evenings, the singers would appear and sing for several hours if they were paid. After the occupation, they sometimes came from distant Hakka areas, such as Meixian. They would sleep in barns or cow sheds, and the local people, who would gather in large numbers, would also give them food. Some were good at improvisation, including references to the locality, for example.

There were also gambling games that people enjoyed, as was apparent in the delight of the man who described them. He was especially enthusiastic about the *jouh seh* festival, which included gambling. In one game, a ceramic pot was hung by a string, which was burned after people had bet on what the handle would weigh when the pot fell and broke. Another game (字花) involved betting on 36

78. An audio recording of the song can be downloaded at https://www.hkupress.hku.hk/+extras/1681audio/.

numbered cards representing historical figures. Finally, there were Hakka cards, a game on which men and women could also gamble, with the prize sometimes being a piece of pork.

Education

Almost no girls had the opportunity to go to school until after the occupation. There was one Christian school for girls, but the idea of educating them was not accepted by most families. Only those who were relatively wealthy gave their daughters any education in the immediate pre-war period. A wealthy man from Chuen Lung also established a free school that accepted girls. We knew of four literate women born or married into Kwan Mun Hau, one educated through form one. There was a school that offered evening classes for girls, but most could not be spared for this.

Virtually all boys had at least several years of education; those with less came from extremely poor families or were mentally handicapped. The history of the development of local schools is complex, and the precise dates of their existence are unclear. In central Tsuen Wan there were some lineage schools of the traditional type, including schools in Lo Wai, Sam Tung Uk, and that of the Yau lineage. They were initially for lineage boys, but also were open to others. For the Yau lineage school, fees were adjusted according to the family's means, the poorest paying only rice, firewood, and service to the teacher. The pupils learned how to read, including classical Chinese; to do calligraphy; to use the abacus; and how to carry out proper rites. Places were reserved first for the Yau, then the Chan, and finally others if there was room. This school existed until 1941. Those who went on to a somewhat higher level also learned some Chinese history, and old stories were told to them by the teacher. The teacher in the school in Lo Wai had an imperial degree (秀才). The fees were quite high, but it even attracted students from elsewhere in the New Territories. Before the occupation, there was also the Catholic Tak Shing School attached to the mission in Tsuen Wan, which had been established in the mid-nineteenth century. The language of instruction had been Hakka, but it was later changed to Cantonese. There were no local secondary schools until the 1950s, so boys from wealthier families commuted to Hong Kong Island for middle school. Others taught themselves beyond their basic education through reading, and some became surprisingly literate.

Villagers' Economic Status

Those men who were able to acquire higher levels of education could work at more comfortable and lucrative jobs than farming or might go into business. Those few families who were fortunate enough to have a member who had been financially successful overseas also benefitted.

Furthermore, women's ability to do heavy subsistence farm work gave Hakka people several advantages. First, it may well have helped them to open for cultivation land that others would have considered to be impossible to work because of the labour required to do reclamation or terracing. In addition, this enabled men to do non-agricultural work, depending on their training, thus diversifying their employment. Women's agricultural skills also allowed the men in their families to emigrate in search of economic betterment.

When wage labour became available, this improved the economic situation of Tsuen Wan people, virtually eliminating the need for men to go abroad to work. As was the case with doing business, those people living in the central villages had advantages. Employment for women consisted primarily of carrying loads, in addition to their routine work of carrying grass. Women from Muk Min Ha carried incense materials to the nearby water mills that would pound them into incense powder. Chai Wan Kok (柴灣角) specialized in the production of bean curd skim, a specialty which was also made possible by the abundance of fresh water.[79] Once construction on the Shing Mun Reservoir got underway, many local people were employed on the project, primarily those from Kwan Mun Hau, as well as some from Hoi Pa and Sam Tung Uk.[80] Women's roles were to rotate very large drills that went into the earth, work that they did even when they were pregnant, and to carry the extremely heavy sacks of cement from the pier a long way up the mountain to the construction site. Each sack was carried on a pole between two women and weighed about 100 *jin* (240 lbs.). Men operated steam hammers and excavated tunnels for water to go through the mountains. The local people initially feared the dam, as they had never seen such a structure, which was about ten storeys high.

The best opportunities for employment came when the Texaco Oil Depot opened, especially for people in Kwan Mun Hau, which was adjacent to the depot. Men worked there making steel containers and filling them with oil products. One spoke of working below decks on the ships, filling containers under stifling conditions. Women's work at the depot was also dangerous, as they often had to carry heavy cans of kerosene on carrying poles while walking on planks between ships and the land. Occasionally, one would lose her footing although none drowned. In all cases the women were doing extremely heavy carrying work, with loads greater than their own weight. Still, they were considered fortunate to have this employment. The work for Texaco was initially scheduled according to need, and paid on a piecework basis, but later was regularized.

All these kinds of wage labour became available by or during the 1930s. Some, such as the carrying of materials for making incense and bean curd skim, probably had a much longer history. Despite these changes, most Tsuen Wan people, with the exception of those in business, remained relatively poor, and although their economic situation began to improve, they still ate and dressed very simply.

---

79. Faure, 'Notes on the History of Tsuen Wan', 75.
80. Migrants from elsewhere were also hired.

3

The Early Years of the Yau, Chan, and Fan Lineages in Tsuen Wan

Trees have their roots; water has its source. How could people not know their ancestors and lineage?
—Yau lineage genealogy

For 300 times 3,000 [years], respectfully maintain the ceremonies, so as to continue the ancestral virtue.
—Chan lineage genealogy

Lineage Histories

Of the more than 50 lineages present in Tsuen Wan in 1983, more than half had written genealogies, varying in length and amount of detail included.[1] The great majority were in manuscript. Twelve more had them until the occupation, during the chaos of which they were lost or destroyed. It is impressive that, even within these small and relatively poor lineages, there were men with a sufficient level of literacy to create and maintain their genealogies,[2] and who believed that it was important to do so.

Men from both the Yau and Chan lineages gave us copies of their genealogies. Both had been updated and reproduced in book form shortly before we received them, and distributed to all member households. It is noteworthy that they put so much time, thought, and energy—not to mention resources—into revising and printing them at a time when Tsuen Wan was evolving around them at such an astonishing pace. Rather than turn their complete attention to contemporary matters in this rapidly changing environment, they demonstrated their loyalty to their ancestors and the values that they attributed to them.

According to the Chan genealogy, an early compilation was by two sixteenth generation scholars during the Daoguang years of the Qing dynasty (1821–1851). About 100 years later, eighteenth-generation member Chan Fuk-cheung of Kwan Mun Hau edited it, adding information specific to Tsuen Wan. He laboured over this task with great commitment, according to his son.

When my father was young he found it disappointing that we didn't have this information and he was eager to have a genealogy, so he went to villages of related branches to gather it. He found one in Luk Keng that had information from the Ming dynasty to the beginning of the Qing, so he borrowed that. He worked by kerosene lamp in the old village to copy all that pertained to our branch. This was our first genealogy, with information from all the families in the village, including his generation, connecting with the old genealogy. Four or five years before his death, many lineage brothers and elders thought that we should have a complete genealogy, and asked him to prepare it. He must have spent a

---

1. 'The Tsuen Wan Sub-district from Chinese Genealogies', in Hayes, *Rural Communities*, 117.
2. Hayes, 'The Tsuen Wan Sub-district from Chinese Genealogies', 124.

year doing it. He included the information from the past, which had to be rearranged, and then he had to add current information. He also asked neighbouring villages if they had information, and added the children. The old genealogies are different from the new ones. The old ones had sparse information, just the person's name, who his wife was, and where they were buried. For the new one he tried to add more personal information, such as dates and education. In the past they recorded nothing about daughters. . . . We were a male-centred society, including only wives as ancestors. He thought daughters should be included, so the generation after him includes sons and daughters. Then the next generation on the daughters' side will be able to understand their mothers' family history.

He added that his father also visited tombs to copy their inscriptions. They printed the new version in 1979.

This genealogy begins with a preface, including a mythical surname history. A concrete history follows, starting in the Ming with an apical ancestor and his wife, whose nine sons founded branches that spread over several provinces. After a eulogy and name poems, used for assigning formal given names by generation, there is a list of ancestors for the first 12 generations. The last is the founding ancestor of the Tsuen Wan branch, who arrived in Qianlong 15 (1727). Considerable detail is given on the life, death, and tomb of this ancestor, who lived to be 84. He had five sons, the first of whom was adopted. The last died as a child. Their ancestral hall (or trust) is called the 'Chan Sam Ying Tong' (陳三英堂), the 'Three Heroes Trust', named for the three sons who apparently established it. Alternatively, it is called the 'Chan Hau Tak Tong' (陳候德堂), honouring the name of the founder.

The ancestor's biography states that at the present location of Tai Wo Hau resettlement estate, he 'bought good fields, ploughed the land, evaporated salt, and engaged in trade; he founded the two villages of Kwan Mun Hau and Ham Tin, where the lineage lived together'. It then describes the creation of the 'satellite town' and construction of the Mass Transit Railway [MTR], when the two villages moved. 'The lineage prospered in descendants and wealth, living in peace and content with its lot. This was bestowed through the ancestor's blessed protection.' It then gives the present location of the ancestor's 'blessed shrine', or hall, and its couplets, which incorporate the 'three heroes'. It identifies the managers of the ancestral trust, the donor of the gold-lettered stone lintel, and describes in glowing terms the celebration of the completion of the hall, which included a banquet of 100 tables, many guests, and a visit by the governor of Hong Kong and other officials.

In the genealogical information that follows, much attention is paid to the geomancy of tombs, whose orientations were frequently adjusted. The eleventh-generation father (1660–1730) and mother of the Tsuen Wan founding ancestor were reinterred in Tsuen Wan in 1820. Although there are few individual details until the seventh generation, some are given. For example, an ancestor born in 1763 died tragically without heirs at the age of 30, when his boat capsized as he was travelling to the provincial capital to take the civil service examinations. The twentieth-century entries vary greatly, some being sparse and others having considerable biographical detail. One man, born in 1910, 'always liked to study' and obtained a teaching degree; his wife, surnamed 'Tang', was 'very intelligent and able', and raised successful children. Several men born post-war had studied in Canada and England, one marrying a woman with an English name. Deaths overseas, principally in Panama and San Francisco, are also recorded.

The Tsuen Wan Yau genealogy was first compiled by Yau Yuen-cheung (1865–1937), a noted local scholar,[3] and edited in 1944.[4] It was updated in 1966, with a handwritten version reproduced for all member households by mimeograph. The addition of remote ancestors was based on a genealogy borrowed from a related lineage in Lufeng, Guangdong, thus solving the 'two difficulties' of unrecorded remote generations and the dispersal of early lineage members. In 1984 a new edition was

---

3. 邱元章. He was a returned emigrant who had prospered in Jamaica. The substantial house he built in Hoi Pa has been preserved.
4. A surprising date, as it was during the occupation.

printed in book form so that it would be 'elegant, refined, and durable'. Its compilers emphasize the importance of maintaining and updating the genealogy to know 'the origin and flow of the ancestral line'. They acknowledge that 'revising a genealogy and copying it as a book is time-consuming; few have been copied and not all descendants have had access to them', resulting in members' ignorance of both their distant and close ancestors. 'For these reasons, we specifically got together and everyone expressed their agreement that we should produce more copies . . . so that members would be able to continue the genealogy themselves. Kin-cheung and Kin-king were enjoined by the lineage to try their best at this difficult endeavour, and took on this responsibility without daring to be careless.' Their preface states:

> When our ancestor Yi-sau moved from Dongguan to Tsuen Wan, he did not bring a genealogy. He only knew that our founding ancestor was Jilong, therefore later generations had no way to trace the earlier ancestors and could only continue the genealogy downwards.
>
> The seven generations from Yi-sau to the Kin generation name were all recorded in detail, clearly and correctly. . . . The fourth generation ancestor Yuen-cheung had been concerned that later generations would lose the thread and therefore compiled this genealogy. However, he recorded only the near relatives and their offspring, but did not know about the remote ancestors. Fortunately, we met our classificatory brothers Jintu and Weiching of the Shima branch [in Lufeng] who on the occasion of a visit to Hong Kong in the autumn of 1949 copied and presented to us a volume [of their genealogy]. This enabled our lineage to connect the upper and the lower [strands] and to compile a complete genealogy. These few words are to commemorate our brothers' gift and to express our gratitude.

An essay from one of these brothers follows, expressing his deep gratitude for the warm hospitality he received from the Tsuen Wan members, and confirming their shared descent.

The resulting volume is entitled 'Genealogy of the Henan Yau Lineage'. It explains the change in the Yau character to 邱 in 1732 to respect the taboo on using Confucius's name, lists the first author and seven revisers, describes their movement to Henan and then south, gives the names and locations of ancestral shrines (halls) in Fujian and Guangdong, and the couplets in the Tsuen Wan hall, among which is:

> South of the Yellow River the ancestral generations succeed each other
> North of the Wei River their reputation is transmitted.

These are followed by numerous pages of historical information, including prefaces written at various times and lists showing single lines of descent, with information on outstanding achievements and experiences of male and female ancestors.

The Tsuen Wan section begins with the 1944 preface and an introduction to the 1949 supplement and revision, followed by name poems and a long and eloquent preface emphasizing the importance of knowing and maintaining their lineage history, and introducing their founding ancestor, Yi-sau. It first gives his immediate descent relationships and movements in Guangdong from Shima, Lufeng to Guanlanxu, which was then in Dongguan. It continues:

> In his youth Yi-sau had high ambitions and with all his strength sought to lay foundations and build enterprises, always regarding it as his duty to glorify his ancestors and enrich his descendants. Afterwards, in the Qianlong years, he again moved, to Tsuen Wan. He first dwelt at Lo Uk Cheung. . . . The ancestor of the neighbouring Chan surname had already migrated there. Yi-sau maintained harmonious relations with his neighbours; he surpassed others in loyalty and honesty, and moreover was laudably industrious and frugal. He was esteemed by the Chan ancestor who subsequently gave him his daughter in marriage, thus forming a marriage alliance. Yi-sau produced two sons, the ancestors Kun-man and San-man. Later, on account of the population's growth, there was not enough land to live on and till. The elders of the Chan and Yau surnames did not shirk from painful exertions; they moved mountains and filled in the ocean to build a dyke connecting two seashores. The sea in front

of the dyke they used for fishing; the area behind the dyke they developed as arable fields. When food production increased, they built houses on the dyke and lived in them peacefully and content. Within a few years a village formed there, the old Kwan Mun Hau village, which has now been developed as an urban area. This fortunate policy was all due to our ancestor's spirit of determination which enabled him to establish these great achievements. When the village was firmly established, our ancestors chose a place within it so that the descendants could always remember and sacrifice to their ancestors [in an ancestral hall].

It then describes the government's need to develop the urban area, and how the hall had been dismantled and reconstructed at a superior 'Blue Dragon site', 'which certainly bodes well for the descendants' prosperity and the development of the lineage. In 1964 the whole village, the Chan and the Yau, together moved here'.

The genealogy includes a migration map and a number of charts organizing historical and genealogical information for ease of comprehension, including a clear chart showing the descent lines in Tsuen Wan, with details indicating sons who died young, wives' surnames, adoptions, many birth dates or sometimes life spans, and often the burial sites of descendants and their wives. It also gives some biographical details, such as those who achieved public office and those who went overseas, including those who died there. It includes, in addition, biographical material on three historical figures, appropriate wording for an announcement on the death of a parent, couplets used for mourning, the phrase used for dotting the ancestral tablet, the ritual for the wedding ceremony in the ancestral hall, and the prayer text to be used when announcing a marriage to the ancestors.

An important foundation document of the Yau lineage, copied and preserved by Yau Yuen-cheung, set out the terms of the property division in 1837 between one son of Yau Yi-sau and the widow of the other, who indicated her assent in her own surname (Wong). The document is called the *bafang fenjialu* (八房分家錄).[5] The 'eight branches' establishing the lineage structure are descended from Yau Yi-sau's eight grandsons. It is a proper legal document, 20 pages long, clearly written by a legal clerk of Lo Wai village and detailing a precise division of all the property.[6] It established the foundation and basic trust of the lineage, the 'Yau Luen Fong Tso' (邱聯房祖), the 'Yau Trust of the United Branches'.

Yau Po-sang (邱寶生), a mid-twentieth-century civic and lineage leader, wrote, or rewrote, another important document, a village handbook setting out the correct forms of interpersonal behaviour in speech and writing. Like the strict acknowledgement of kinship with people of bride-giving lineages, this handbook demonstrates the importance of correct interpersonal behaviour.[7]

The origin and arrival date of the Fan lineage is not clear, as they had no extant written records, but they were said to have arrived later. They had not maintained contact with a related lineage in Shek Kong. They had an ancestral hall in Ham Tin, but it had been sold after the occupation due to poverty. One member said that they regretted this loss but had no recourse. Their numbers in Tsuen Wan remained small, he said, as they always had more daughters than sons.

The Settlements

The three villages occupied by these lineages, Kwan Mun Hau, Hoi Pa, and Ham Tin, were located in central Tsuen Wan. Kwan Mun Hau, their principal village, had two earth god shrines. One was

---

5. Literally, 'A Record of Family Division among the Eight Branches of the Lineage'. See Appendix to this chapter for an abridged translation.

6. James Hayes argues for the importance of literacy and shared cultural understanding gained through local education in giving villagers the ability to manage their affairs effectively and independently. This document is an example. See 'Preface' to *The Hong Kong Region 1850–1911 with a New Introduction* (Hong Kong: Hong Kong University Press, 2012), xxi–xxiv.

7. Made available to us courtesy of James Hayes.

dedicated to Hongshenggong, a popular Hong Kong deity honoured by fishing people, and said to have been worshipped by Kwan Mun Hau people because of their many fishermen. The other was dedicated to the Kau Wai Kung, the 'Nine Heroes'. The text on the plinth erected in 2016 next to their shrine in the resited village continues as follows.[8]

> During this period, when the villagers created fields by reclaiming mountain land and the foreshore, resulting in a long strip of cultivated land, methods of cultivation changed and additional agricultural labour was needed to meet various problems. To resolve manpower shortages, the villagers hired nine long-term agricultural workers to help with farming.
>
> At that time pirates were ferocious and violent, and came to Kwan Mun Hau to rob and plunder, which severely affected the livelihood of the villagers. The nine labourers protected the lives and property of the villagers without regard for their personal safety, and bravely sacrificed their lives.
>
> Thereafter, the villagers conveyed to their descendants that they should never forget the indomitable spirit of eschewing self to serve the public good. At that time, a shrine was erected to the Nine Heroes in the centre of the village, at which incense and candles could be burned in homage and respect.
>
> Today this plinth is erected to inform future generations and provide information about the origins of the Nine Heroes, exhorting them never to forget this history and to pass it on, one to another.
>
> The Management Committee for the Kau Wai Kung
>
> Erected on a lucky day, 2016 (Bing Zhong year)

A Yau elder, who was born in 1919, talked with us on a number of occasions about their history. He said that the relationship among the people of the three surnames was close, and that they lived next to each other in old Kwan Mun Hau with the surnames intermingled, although the Yau were more compact. He added that initially the Yau lineage could not build an ancestral hall, so they used the ancestor's original house until the late nineteenth century, when they built a hall using funds from individuals and the founder's trust. We were shown their locations on the government survey map, together with the Yau lineage school (聯房書室).

As old Kwan Mun Hau was by the shore, the village and its fields were subject to flooding during typhoons. According to the survey map, the Yau fields were irregular in shape, and were dispersed from present-day Texaco Road, which extended out onto a peninsula, up to the present village site. The fields that were individually owned were as many as could be cultivated. Those people who opened more fields could use them to establish a trust in the name of an ancestor. They could be rented out to yield income to the lineage or lineage branch in whose name they were established. Significantly, the elder told us that after 1898, under British administration, people stopped creating trusts, as they had to be registered under their own names, and 'they began to realize the value of private property'. The Chan fields were larger and more regular, extending between Kwan Mun Hau and Ham Tin.[9] Fan fields were dispersed around the area, with a cluster near Ham Tin.

Before the occupation, trusts were used only to support the worship of ancestors, 'as they were the ancestors' property', and to pay the land tax. The land started to become valuable when immigrants came and paid high rents, almost certainly because of the development of the new market.[10] The property and income were managed by the lineage head (族長), or manager (司理), who also had responsibility for adjudicating disputes within the lineage. Those chosen were educated, honest, senior, and willing to do this unpaid work.

---

8. Continued from Chapter 2.
9. Some may have belonged to the Chan of Sam Tung Uk.
10. See Hayes, *The Great Difference*, 51.

When the government resumed the land between the present site of Kwan Mun Hau and Texaco Road, the Yau lineage was offered money for the trust lands but decided instead to exchange them for property and buildings in Tsuen Wan. According to a member of the Chan lineage,

> In the past the Chan had a lot of agricultural land and received substantial amounts of rice in rent. The Yau just had some house plots with broken-down houses. No one wanted them and they had to pay property tax. The Chan lineage sold most of its land in the past as it was good land. We sold it for money and it was used up, spent. The Yau fields in the past were salt fields, which no one wanted, as they couldn't grow anything. They made a great fortune, which was fate, not planned.

Another said:

> Compared with other Tsuen Wan lineages, the Chan and Yau are the most successful, because we have kept our property, we have a lot, and we manage it well. The Chan have less money, because we were richer than the Yau in the past and many of us worked elsewhere: abroad, in Kowloon, in Hong Kong, so we learned more than the Yau did. Our eyes were opened earlier. We learned new things and stopped such rituals as the lantern-raising sooner, before the occupation, because they were too much trouble.
>
> The Chan and Yau both sold some ancestral plots in the past but we mostly divided the money while the Yau tended to use it to buy more buildings. Dividing the money is useless because then there will be nothing left. One sub-branch sold all its property and divided the money, so it's all gone.

Lineages and Rites

The Yau elder quoted above said that before the occupation only a few men went to the *Chongyang* (重陽) worship of ancestors at their tombs. The expenses were covered by income from the ancestral trusts. Those of the founding ancestor and his wife are located on a mountainside near Nam Wai in Sai Kung, and he credited a related lineage there with helping them to find the site.[11] The wife's tomb was originally near the Tsuen Wan village of Shek Lei Pui, but was moved to make way for reservoir construction.

Some women accompanied the men to help carry necessities, such as woks and rice, as they cooked at the tombs. They left at 4:00 a.m. and walked over the mountains, arriving at midday. After clearing undergrowth from around the tombs, conducting the rites, and cooking, they walked back, arriving in the evening. Alternatively, they hired a boat that took them to Kowloon, where they bought fresh pork and wine before continuing on foot. At the tombs they conducted the rites, and cooked stewed pork with preserved bamboo shoots, salt fish, and bean vermicelli with dried shrimp. They eat vermicelli on good occasions as they are symbolic of long life, and the stewed pork represents the Hakka people. Later they added steamed pork belly meat (扣肉), layered with taro.

The Chan lineage also had the custom of cooking and eating these special Hakka foods at the tombs during the Chongyang rites. They worshipped with higher-order branches from Hong Kong and the mainland at the tomb of the founder's father, Man Tai Kung, in Sha Tin, as well as those of the founder and his sons.

Some men were especially skilled cooks, cooking for lineage banquets as well as for events such as weddings, assisted by women. On these occasions, temporary outdoor stoves were built to supplement their large indoor stoves. This custom continued at least through the 1980s.

Older boys and men also contributed to lineage events by playing gongs and cymbals with the special rhythms appropriate to the occasions, often with unicorn dancing, which some also learned.

---

11. He said that their founding ancestor and Yau Yi-sau were brothers, while they have a distant relationship with the Yau of Tseng Lan Shue in Sai Kung.

Plate 12: Yau lineage men serving a delicious Hakka dish of stewed pork, for a village banquet the evening before a young man's wedding in 1981.

They played during the New Year hall worship, and at the lantern-raising, when the rhythm played in the procession meant 'produce sons' (添丁). The solemn one played to accompany a funeral procession meant 'to be at peace going up the mountain', while they played festive rhythms at weddings. In the early 1900s, boys could learn these skills and martial arts under a Hakka master hired for this purpose.

Livelihood in the Early Twentieth Century: Men's Roles

From about 1880 until the 1920s, little local employment was available. The Yau elder said: 'People had to go away to work then. All they could do here was farm. There was very little business to do, and there weren't enough fields. They had to earn money.' His own father had gone to Panama to work on the canal, and then tried to establish a business there, which failed, so he returned to operate a stake net and market the fish.

The employment of men who remained in Tsuen Wan before the occupation depended on their abilities, their families' economic situations, and their families' needs, all of which helped to determine their level of education. We knew of only two older men who were actually illiterate, one because of a disability and the other because of his family's poverty. Another man born in about 1910 had studied for only one year because his father had died when he was 8 years old. He said that he often had to guess at characters, which was embarrassing. He also had little opportunity to learn Cantonese. He had a complex employment history, starting at age 12 carrying beef to a boat from an abattoir on Hong Kong Island, then selling fish, farming, and working at Texaco, first as a labourer and then at semi-skilled work. After the occupation he worked in gambling establishments and then in the Country Village Store.

Like him, poorly educated men in impoverished families lived by farming and doing miscellaneous kinds of manual work. A Fan man, born in about 1890, studied only a few years in a village school taught in Hakka, and then had to stop to care for his mother. His son also had to decline educational opportunities because the family needed his help. The father initially did fuel-cutting and watched cows, but he also farmed on land rented from others, growing rice and pineapples. He later did many other kinds of work, including cooking for the crew on the local ferry, marketing fish caught by fishing families, digging water tunnels for the Shing Mun Reservoir using a steam hammer, and carrying kerosene from the storage facility at Texaco.

One man of the Chan lineage had only three years of village education but still obtained employment as a salesman at the Sincere Company, where he increased his literacy and learned some English. Another found employment as a waiter on a passenger liner, and 'got fat from eating steaks every day'. After the occupation he worked as a customs inspector, and later for a cable car company.

At the higher end of the economic spectrum were those whose families could educate their sons well. One elderly woman said that her husband had a better education than most because his father had sent remittances from overseas. He worked for a shop as a purchasing agent, carrying messages to and from Hong Kong Island every day, and did not know how to farm. Two of the better educated men were teachers, although one later worked as a foreman for Texaco. A Chan man worked as an apprentice mechanic on a motor boat from age 15, sailing out from Hong Kong. During the occupation he returned to Tsuen Wan and opened a teahouse, which he ran until the 1960s. Two other men worked long-term for Texaco and were rewarded with gold watches for 25 years' service. One operated a forklift truck for much of his career and was justifiably proud of his award.

There were others who worked in businesses, some their own and others for which they worked as employees. A Chan family of three brothers ran a successful medicine shop business in Tsuen Wan and Kowloon, starting in the pre-war period. One had worked as a driver in his youth. His undivided and relatively well-to-do family had owned a transportation company. They grew sufficient rice for their needs and had nearly 30 people eating together, including several full-time labourers. Starting in 1934, from the age of 20, he worked as a lorry driver in the New Territories and was then recruited by the Chinese and the British governments to drive heavy lorries around south China. After the war he returned, and although their transportation company had been destroyed, he was hired to drive military cars at a good salary.

A well-educated Yau man worked in a European-run shop on Hong Kong Island, returning home on Sundays. As he was a friendly and talkative man, he would describe events there to Tsuen Wan people, earning him the nickname 'radio broadcaster'. When that business closed, he returned and became the overseer of the market. His son, who had studied English, worked on Hong Kong Island for British civil servants as a cook and an interpreter, returning after the occupation.

Those few families whose male members were fortunate enough to have the education and attributes that led to success lived in a reasonably comfortable way. Men could improve their families' standard of living through hard work and capable decisions,[12] or destroy it if they succumbed to addictions.

Most shared in Tsuen Wan's general poverty. Families like the one described above, whose members could eat rice all year around, were probably few; others often ate it cooked with sweet potatoes. Those who had more than two sets of clothes, or a second set to wear over the first to try to keep warm in the winter, were considered fortunate. They had no special clothing for cold weather or rain, with the exception of palm-leaf capes and pointed hats, which were not adequate. Many, if not most, houses had dirt floors and earthen walls, which were impossible to keep clean. There was little comfort of any kind.

---

12. Capable women could do this in their absence.

Women's Contributions to Their Families' Livelihood

No one denied the fact that all women had to work hard, regardless of their family's economic standing. This was emphasized by many people, who acknowledged that they always worked, and that they generally worked longer and harder than men, although men sometimes did heavier work. Carrying water was women's work, regardless of their health, as was grass-cutting, which girls learned when in their teens; men did these tasks only under duress.

In most families in the early twentieth century, women had primary responsibility for growing rice. Older women dried it while attending to housework and child care, while younger women grew and processed it, husking and milling rice on days when it was raining too heavily to do outdoor work, or in the evenings. If a family had enough women and fields, they could grow sufficient rice for their needs. Between wage labour and farming, a woman could support her mother-in-law and her children. As wage labour became available, younger women combined this with their other work. Rice agriculture must have diminished correspondingly, as families became increasingly involved in a cash economy and could buy at least some of their rice.

A woman born in about 1905 described her daily schedule, which was typical:

> Every day I got up at 4:00 to carry water. Then I applied water and pig manure to the fields, and returned home to eat rice with salted vegetables at 8:00 with the family. I was 30 years old before Texaco offered carrying work. I carried kerosene, paraffin, and sheets of steel, 280 *jin* (斤) [336 lbs.] between two women. My mother-in-law cared for the children, and during the harvest brought rice for us to eat in the fields. She also took care of the pigs and watched the rice as it dried. The senior wife raked the fields, washed the clothes, cut grass, and sometimes worked carrying kerosene. She didn't have to carry steel, and was more comfortable than I was. When there was no carrying work, I had to cut grass and firewood; there was no time to stop. When I worked building the reservoir, another woman and I carried six or seven bags of cement in a day, one bag at a time. It was a very long way uphill. Then I carried water. After 7:00 we ate again, and then I milled rice and cut up pig vegetables until 10:00 or later.

Wage labour for some women began in the 1920s, or perhaps earlier, in the small-scale enterprises that existed then. The Shing Mun Reservoir project employed many Kwan Mun Hau women during the 1930s, and the oil depot, which was conveniently located, offered increasing employment opportunities.

Another important economic activity for women was pig-raising. This, too, was hard work, and unrelenting, as the pigs had to be fed regularly on plants that were cut up and cooked. The water hyacinth that was their primary food was grown in water, and harvesting it was heavy and unpleasant work. Raising pigs involved families in a cash economy, as did selling grass and wage labour.

Women's work was heavy and unceasing, making virtually no allowance for their state of health or for childbearing. As one woman said, 'We had time to die, but no time to be ill'. They worked long hours, generally carrying loads heavier than their own weight on carrying poles. This made their shoulders sore and thickly calloused, as were their feet, as they often worked barefoot. Their mothers-in-law were their taskmasters, as they must have seen their sons' wives as women who would help to release them from their own burdens, and it was their responsibility to manage their households. In the immediate post-war period, the younger women were rarely home in time to eat dinner with the family. One, a mother of eight children, said that the best situation was when, after a day of cultivating and harvesting vegetables, cutting grass, and working at Texaco, she returned at 5:00 to apply pig manure to the vegetables and feed the pigs. She then carried water for the family and returned home at 6:30 for dinner. More commonly she could not return until 10:00 when she ate leftover rice and scraps of salt fish, as the best food had already been eaten by others. They were treated, she said, 'as though we were not human'.

These work routines continued during pregnancy, the exception being that pregnant women did not carry steel, as that was considered to be too dangerous. The woman quoted above told of how, when she was heavily pregnant with her second son and had a carrying pole loaded with grass, she fell about 20 feet onto a field of green onions. She was pinned there until someone finally came and shouted at her for flattening his onions. She asked him for help lifting the pole. When she got home her mother-in-law also scolded her. Fortunately, her baby survived and was born one week later. Her first son had been born only about two hours after she had finished carrying water for the family. A few days after she had given birth to another baby she had to go into water up to her waist to harvest food for their baby pigs. Other women said that they had to carry water within a few days or a week after childbirth, as there was no one else who could or would do it. One woman actually gave birth while she was on a mountainside cutting grass. Fortunately she was with other women, who cut the cord with a grass-cutting knife, wrapped the baby in an apron, and supported her on the way down.

Their daily schedules and activities varied somewhat, depending on the woman's age, and the size and composition of the family. Some mothers-in-law were reasonably supportive, whereas others were harsh and critical. Furthermore, there were women with no mothers-in-law, but who had to work regardless. Without an older woman in the family, there was likely no one to care for the children while their mother was out working, and they were neglected. Small children were left at home alone, often tied to a table leg, dirty, crying, falling asleep on the floor. One elderly man attributed his leg problems to such a childhood. He said that he ate cold rice, or occasionally congee if an older woman relative gave him some. Young girls learned how to do basic cooking, and sometimes were left with responsibility for small siblings, who were strapped to their backs. Life was cheap, women said, and the babies might live or die.

Women's Relationships

Outdoor work gave older girls and women many opportunities to be together, to talk, and to sing mountain songs. Unlike Cantonese women, they had no maiden houses where unmarried girls might stay together to be taught womanly knowledge by an older woman,[13] and there were no bachelor houses for young men. Women's work required that they be outdoors, and they enjoyed camaraderie in this context.

Women stayed together in age groups to cut grass and do wage labour:

> Women used to go in groups of 20 or more to cut grass, all from Kwan Mun Hau: Yau, Chan, and Fan together. We would call to each other to leave, and then wait for each other to return. We each would gather and bind together four bunches of grass, weighing in all more than 100 catties. We went out even in the rain, as otherwise we would have no fuel. We also went in groups to gather shellfish. Old women would go along for that. If young women in their teens wanted to go out in the evening to get measured for clothes we would get several together and ask an older woman to go along. Otherwise the tailors might feel us here and there while they were measuring us, and people would say that we had no shame.
>
> In the past there were a lot of songs. Now I don't remember all of them. We felt very happy then, with nothing to worry about. Whenever we went to cut grass we would sing. Sometimes we sang when we were carrying kerosene, but mostly when we were cutting grass. You could just follow the group and learn how to sing.

---

13. Judith Strauch, 'Community and Kinship in Southeastern China: The View from the Multilineage Communities of Hong Kong', *Journal of Asian Studies* 43, no. 1 (November 1983): 38; Rubie S. Watson, 'Chinese Bridal Laments: The Claims of a Dutiful Daughter', in Watson and Watson, *Village Life in Hong Kong*, 221–50.

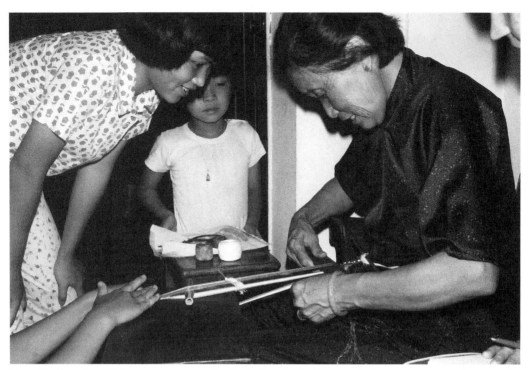

Plate 13: Members of the younger generation, including Kwok Kin-wa, enjoying a rare opportunity to see the weaving of *fadaai*, 'patterned bands', by Mrs Yau Tsang Yung-hei, 1976.

They even imitated laments[14] that they had heard. Some were wedding laments, those sung by a weeping bride to her parents and her 'sisters' (姊妹), the group of young women, including lineage sisters, with whom she had worked. If a member of their group was getting married, the others might pool some money from their savings to buy her a gift: an alarm clock, a pair of vases, a length of cloth for a set of clothes, or, most extravagant, a silver ring, perhaps also giving her some money from what was left. Although there were no maiden houses, they might spend two weeks beforehand together with an older woman, learning wedding laments and giving support to the bride, who was young and afraid. A bride who could learn well might lament for as long as four evenings before her marriage. A woman born in Sha Tin said she had done this, with the villagers gathered outside listening. She was unusual among pre-war brides in that she was literate, as remittances from her emigrant father had allowed her to study, so she learned some laments from a book.[15]

After marriage, 'sisters' also supported each other if they were mistreated at home: if the family had saved no breakfast for them, for example.

> Someone had fed it to the pigs. So when I went to work that morning people asked me what I had had to eat and I said 'nothing', and so they all gave me a little piece of whatever they had. Sometimes husbands gave money to their wives. When we worked together we would talk about it: how much did he give you? People would admire the women who could get more money from their husbands. This was to be kept secret. No one should tell their mothers-in-law. If they did, the mother-in-law would be angry, asking why he gave money to her. If a woman told the mother-in-law, that woman would be blamed and not allowed to enter the group of women anymore.

---

14. C. Fred Blake, 'Death and Abuse in Marriage Laments: The Curse of Chinese Brides', *Asian Folklore Studies* 37, no. 1 (1978): 13–33. His work derives from notebooks of Sai Kung Hakka bridal laments, recorded by literate girls.

15. Some villages, including Wo Yi Hop, had books of funeral laments written by men, although most women could not read them.

Plate 14: Mrs Yau Chan Shek-ying showing how a traditional Hakka head cloth (頭搭) was worn, with a patterned band that was made in 1930 in Sheung Kwai Chung, her natal village, 1980.

Women's marital status was indicated by the only ornament that they wore on their otherwise plain dark clothes. These were beautiful, colourful 'patterned bands' *fadaai* (花帶) ending in tassels made of silk or cotton thread. They wove them on the rare occasions when they had a little time, in the evenings or on days of heavy rain. Women who had not learned to weave got them from others.

The tassels, colour combinations, and patterns varied between districts, and were minutely named. Unmarried girls and older women wore those in darker colours, whereas young married women's bands featured red or pink with yellow. This showed men how to address them, as different terms were used for young married women. They wore them to fasten their head cloths, with the tassels on one side; to fasten their aprons; and on their 'cool hats' (涼帽), flat hats with a round opening at the top and a fringe of black cloth about five inches long to shield them from dust and the sun. The tassels hung at the sides, and one of the mountain songs describes how attractive this made the wearer to a man:[16]

> The hat is new, the person looks so smart.
> It is not your hat I like;
> I like the two *fadaai*.

Brides were expected to spend the days before their weddings weaving large numbers of them to give to women relatives and to wear themselves. They also served as ritual objects in their weddings, and decorated the lanterns celebrating the birth of sons.

---

16. Elizabeth L. Johnson, '"Patterned Bands" in the New Territories of Hong Kong', *Journal of the Hong Kong Branch Royal Asiatic Society* 16 (1976): 81–91. The character for 'patterned' also means 'flowers', with their implied fertility symbolism, or 'colourful'. See Emily M. Ahern, 'Affines and the Rituals of Kinship', in *Religion and Ritual in Chinese Society*, ed. Arthur P. Wolf (Stanford: Stanford University Press, 1974), 286–88.

Marriage Forms and Arrangements

Women were supposed to contribute substantially to the families into which they married. They were seen as labour force, and were treated as such. This was reflected in one woman's description of the procedures leading up to her marriage when she was 12 years old, in the 1930s.

> My own marriage was introduced by people who were not my relatives. My husband's family had already looked at two girls and rejected them before considering me.
>
> They sent two men to a pineapple hill to look at me, an uncle and another old man. My mother sent me to gather pine cones to cook fish, carrying my younger brother. The two men approached me on the road, asking if we had any small pigs for sale, or any pineapples. I answered them: 'Who would have pineapples at this time of year?'
>
> They watched me, seeing how I walked. I said: 'So rude, watching how people walk!' They were the only ones who saw me, not my husband. He was only 14 years old. They liked how I looked, that I looked strong and sturdy enough. They didn't care whether I was pretty or not.

Primary marriages in the pre-war period were blind, and arranged either by professional match-makers or through relatives. Sons' marriages were arranged by their fathers, if present, whereas those of daughters could be arranged by their mothers. What the matchmaker said had to be taken on faith, and families might be deceived about the man's family's property, the number of brothers who would share it, or the personalities of the man and his family.

It was customary for women married before the occupation to say that they had been sold into marriage: 'When I was sold here. . . .' In 1984, Elizabeth heard the son of one such woman responding with incredulity and some derision when his mother said this, asking her: 'How much were you sold for?' This was a specifically Hakka way of describing marriage, and could also be used by mothers-in-law as a way of expressing power over them.

The wedding negotiations included reaching agreement on the amount of bride price and the gifts to be given to the woman's family. It was impressive to hear how precisely women could remember these, as though they were, in fact, a calculation of their value. The woman quoted above said:

> His family said that they wanted a matchmaker, so they got a red paper with my name and horoscope and brought it to their house. They waited for three days, and if during that time nothing bad happened, nothing was broken, no cats died, and so on, I was considered acceptable. Then they sent the bride price (帶禮), which was different then. The gifts included:
> one hen and one rooster
> one big pot of rice and more than 30 catties of glutinous rice
> one big pot of wine
> nine salt fish
> nine duck eggs
> nine squid
> mung beans
> vermicelli
> one measure of pork
> My family accepted everything, and poured 2 measures of water from washing rice into the wine pot, leaving one catty of rice in the rice pot to return, and returning the rooster.

In her case, the bride price was 99 dollars. The matchmaker was paid about 40 dollars, as well as a pig's hind leg.[17] For her dowry, her mother gave her a chest, three sets of clothes, a wash stand, a small

---

17. See also Hayes, 'The Transmission of Custom Through Written Guides', *The Rural Communities of Hong Kong* 193. This is called 掛薪水, 'to hang the wages' [for the matchmaker]. In addition, the bride was expected to make a formal visit to her on the first New Year after her wedding, with gifts of pork, wine, and *chahgwo*.

bucket, a ring, and a foot-washing basin, which did not use all of the bride price. The foot-washing basin was a fertility symbol, as women gave birth into them at that time. Her future husband's family also gave her some sets of clothes, which meant that the bride price could be less.

On the day of her marriage, she was carried in a sedan chair, as cars were not used until the 1950s, with gongs and cymbals, unicorn and lion dancers, and a piper: 'really festive'. On the second day she poured tea for her new husband's relatives, receiving lucky money, and the couple was presented to the ancestors in the hall. On that day her husband's family held a banquet, cooked by village men on temporary outdoor stoves at which she had to worship. On the third day women and children from her natal family came with gifts of wine and special foods, an occasion called *sung chah* (送茶). The groom's family normally provided a banquet for them, and they stayed overnight. The next day they would be given sweet congee and a midday meal,[18] and then escorted on their way.

A very old woman, born in about 1890, said she had been engaged at the age of two, when the boy's family gave the bride price of money, sugar, two catties of pork, fish, and vermicelli. She was not married until she was 19. Just before her marriage, unmarried girls came to stay at her house, some for as long as a month, to accompany her and lament for several days, learning from the older married women. She lamented because she did not want to leave her parents, and to thank them for raising her.

On the night before her wedding, the bride was seated in her family's main room for the ceremony of *seuhng tauh* (上頭), in which a woman with a 'good fate', as she had both sons and daughters, combed her hair into a bun with ornaments while saying auspicious phrases, and the bride lamented her pending separation from her 'sisters'.[19]

> I am very close to my sisters
> I hold a sugar cane and divide it. I want to break it.
> I am very close to my sisters.
> I hold a piece of malt candy. I will divide it equally
> At night I slept in the same bed with my sisters, but
> I will become a bride.
> You will return to sleep with your parents
> Each evening we could use each other's shoes.
> We could exchange our clothes.
> Tonight I am going to see the God of Hell (閻王).
> Tonight you will see your father and mother.

She also cursed herself:

> Since I was small I never wore a set of new clothes.
> Today I am wearing a full set of new clothes.
> I am like grass being dried in the sun to die.[20]

She also could curse the matchmaker in a lament, but she had to follow this with a lament to release her. She lamented her coming separation from her mother, who wept or lamented in return, and also from her father. If he had died, she lamented in front of his tablet, and wore a white belt.

She was taken to her ancestral hall to make offerings, the only time in her life she worshipped there: 'The white flower worships 1,000 times; the red flower worships once.'[21]

---

18. In one of the Sai Kung marriage laments, the bride urges her female relatives to come to 'eat all their flesh and all their bones, too'. Blake, 'Death and Abuse in Marriage Laments', 30.

19. The format and tunes are like those of funeral laments, with the exception of one that may be a mountain song, expressing sorrow at this parting.

20. This derogatory imagery is like that in the laments analysed by Blake, 'Death and Abuse in Marriage Laments', 13–33.

21. Girls are called 'red flowers' in mountain songs and laments.

> Along both sides of the hall are many people,
> Brothers and their wives fill a table.
> Worshipping at the hall, the lane full of people of high repute,
> It is my turn to worship a single time.
> Many guests attend my wedding.[22]

When the sedan chair came to get her, the bride cursed for the last time before her transformation into a wife began:

> My younger brother scoops some sand in front of the door
> To allow those people from hell (陰間) to place their flags.
> He sets down a bucket of water to send them on their way.[23]

The elderly woman said that on the day of her wedding, she had worn a 'phoenix crown' and bells. Her uncles and parents, wearing formal robes, accompanied the sedan chair, with gongs, cymbals, and a dancing unicorn, halfway along the road, until they were met by her husband's people. They might then have held a banquet for relatives and friends in their village, financed by the bride price. Three days after the wedding, her parents sent gifts of rice wine and dried seafood.

The grooms' families made their own preparations for weddings. Details changed over time, but there normally was a gathering of village people, primarily women, to make red dumplings, *tongyuhn* (湯圓). The groom worshipped in the temple, and then worshipped the ancestors in the hall for the ceremonies of *seuhng tauh* and the initial audience with the ancestors *yit jou* (謁祖). For these ceremonies, his hair was combed by lineage elders. He wore a hat in which gold ornaments were inserted, and sat on an inverted rice measure placed on a flat basket to receive congratulatory words (祝文) from the master of ceremonies, a senior man skilled at reading these texts. On the morning of the wedding he worshipped at the temple, and then he, or his representatives, went to meet the bride at her home, accompanied by lineage brothers: unicorn dancers, and others playing gongs and cymbals. After the bride's ceremonial arrival, she descended from her conveyance, now sheltered under a red umbrella. That day or the next, the couple worshipped the Baak Gung, and then the ancestors in the hall for the rite of *gaau jou* (告祖) or *gaau jih* (教子) that is the principal marriage ceremony.[24]

When the bride arrived, if there was a baby under one-month-old in the village she had to walk from the sedan chair on flat baskets, because her *saat hei* (殺氣)[25] was extremely powerful and could harm the baby. Likewise, small children were kept facing away from her, as were other people, including the women carrying her dowry.[26] Her pathway to his house was marked with water in which red rice had been soaked. The groom's family then held at least one banquet for their relatives, the number and scale depending on their means.

Brides were made to feel their place in their new families on the second day. They were wearing new clothes, and the family might confront them with a wok filled with hot greasy water. In it were nine 10-cent coins, nine bowls, and nine pairs of chopsticks. They poured water onto the ground, and the bride was made to kneel in it and retrieve the objects with a spatula, placing them in her apron, then putting them into a kerosene container and pulling it into the house. New clothes were rare and special, and this was very hard. Some with stubborn temperaments refused, which probably did not

---

22. These lines of a wedding lament were sung by Mrs Yau Tsang Yung-hei in 1996.
23. An audio recording of the lament can be downloaded at https://www.hkupress.hku.hk/+extras/1681audio/.
24. This detailed information was provided by Paul Siu-kwong Yau. We lack specific information for the Chan lineage.
25. This might be translated as 'killing breaths', extremely powerful negative forces emanating from unburied corpses and from brides. These may result from brides' liminality: while in transition they are neither members of their natal families nor of those of their husbands-to-be. See James L. Watson, 'Funeral Specialists in Cantonese Society: Pollution, Performance, and Social Hierarchy', in *Death Ritual in Late Imperial and Modern China*, ed. James L. Watson and Evelyn S. Rawski (Berkeley: University of California Press, 1988), 109–34. See also Ahern, 'Affines and the Rituals of Kinship', 284–86.
26. Should a child face her, he had to be bathed in water in which her trouser cord had been soaked, so that he would recover.

earn them favour in their new homes, while others cried. Another way of teasing the bride was to hold up a chicken head or a piece of orange and tell the couple to eat it, or to have her light his cigarette. This proximity would have been extremely embarrassing.

Several elderly women spoke of how marginal they had felt when newly married. They did not presume to eat with the family or, if they did, dared not look up, and just reached for the food. One did not know for some months what her husband looked like. Another said that when her mother-in-law boiled pork soup she was not given any. One said that this poor rapport had a negative impact on the number of children they bore, as there was no relationship between husband and wife. The young women were shy, and dared not talk to their husbands. Women also were expected not to draw attention to their sexual characteristics. They bound their breasts, and dried the breast-binding cloths out of sight under the bed after washing them. If they breast-fed their babies on their doorsteps, older men would hit them.

A number of people emphasized the fact that marriages then were not based on love, and may never have evolved into love, although some did. There was no reason why the couple should be compatible, and if they could even cooperate this was fortunate. One very old woman said that her husband certainly did not help her, and that if he did not shout at her this was good. Another talked about the preparations she had made for her death, saying that she had moved to the ground floor so that her body would not have to be carried downstairs 'but if I have to be with that man in the underworld, then I would prefer to live longer'.

After the occupation, marriage customs changed and the couple had some chance to get to know each other or, at a minimum, to see each other. One form that disappeared quite abruptly post-war was 'small daughter-in-law' *sanpouhjai* (新抱仔) marriage, in which a girl was brought in as a child, and actually married when the couple were mature.[27] Many families had chosen to marry their sons this way before the occupation because it cost less and brought a worker into the family. The wedding ceremony could be simpler and less expensive. Some girls were brought into their future husbands' families when they were only a few months old and were fed their mother-in-laws' milk together with their future husbands. One had been only 40 days old, from a poor family. Her husband's family gave nothing for her, as her family was considered fortunate that they did not have to raise her. She was actually married when she was 19 years old, and she could then visit her natal family. Others were small children, or a little older. One had been carried in under a red umbrella when she was about 6 years old, wearing a necklace of red cloth. When she was about 16 and was married, they sent gifts to her natal family. The girls were expected to work hard for the families, and people reported that their condition in general was poor, as they were dirty and dressed in ragged clothes. They were taught to address the boy's parents as he did, and to address him as older brother. When they reached maturity, their marriage was completed with the basic ceremony of combing her hair, pouring tea for the family members, and worshipping in the ancestral hall. The mother-in-law bought them a bed, and said: 'You are now adults, husband and wife. Be good to each other; don't quarrel like you did when you were children.'

A mountain song relates to this form of marriage:

Older brother is poor; younger sister is poor.
We work together.
Older brother does not have good trousers to wear.
Younger sister does not have a good head cloth.
Younger sister, suffer every day.

27. See also James Hayes, 'San Po Tsai (Little Daughters-in-Law) and Child Betrothals in the New Territories of Hong Kong from the 1890s to the 1960s', in *Women and Chinese Patriarchy Submission, Servitude, and Escape*, ed. Maria Jaschok and Suzanne Miers (Hong Kong: Hong Kong University Press, 1994), 45–76.

Suffer one or two more years
When you have a son life will be good.
When you have a daughter-in-law, it will be splendid![28]

The mother-in-law was expected to give the bride some gifts, including lucky money after the bride had poured tea, and, if she was wealthy and willing, a pair of gold bracelets or, at a minimum, a ring. Her natal family might also send gifts to her. If the family had the means, they might hold a banquet. Three days after the wedding, her female relatives would come for *sung chah*, with gifts of *chahgwo* and special foods. They were offered meals in exchange, as with any other wedding. After one month the bride could visit them, giving them *chahgwo* and pork, and staying overnight. The woman whose wedding procedures were described earlier was technically a small daughter-in-law, as she was only 12 years old, but her husband's family decided to have a full wedding ceremony when she was brought in, thus compressing the rituals with a ceremony that was more lavish than was usual for such marriages. She then slept with her mother-in-law for three years. When she was 16 years old, her mother-in-law told them that they were adults, got them a bed and their own room, and they began sleeping together.

After the occupation, however, there was a full-scale rebellion by young men against this form of marriage. The young women did not have this power. The men did not want to marry girls with whom they had been raised, and the girls had been teased because they were addressing their future husbands as brothers, and his parents as though they were their own, perhaps without fully understanding what was to come. The boys also were teased, and would tell the girls not to address them this way. The mother might then tell the girl to avoid addressing him, or to call him 'small husband' (老公仔). Furthermore, as the girls were often maltreated and made to work hard, they likely did not appear attractive to their future husbands, and their long-term proximity undermined attraction. To have sexual relations with them was felt to be incestuous, and believed to be shameful.[29] Men then refused to marry the girls their parents had raised. Their ability to resist probably came in part because by that time they could be independently employed, rather than being dependent on their families, and the young women began to have alternatives. Furthermore, by then couples were beginning to have a degree of free choice in marriage.

The girl could be treated like a daughter or *kaaineuih* and married to someone else, returned to her natal family if her parents were still alive, be introduced to someone else and married out from a relative's house or, most likely, she could run away. Elizabeth was told of five women who had run away from Chan families and three from Yau families, all within a relatively short period of time. As long as they were still virgins they could marry another man. Virginity was important, and those who were not virgins could remarry only in a very simple way, just wearing red clogs.

The situation of widows was rather like that of rejected small daughters-in-law in the solutions available to them. Much depended on whether or not they had children. As one woman said: 'Some did remarry, because if they had no children and were neglected by their husbands' families and had become strangers in their parents' homes, they should remarry. If they didn't, they were like fish in a dried pond'. These decisions depended in part on the structure of the family. If they had sons who were the family's only descendants, the sons might be considered essential to its continuity and their mother more likely to stay. One woman gave an analysis of the various situations of widows and their children, saying that if the widow had no mother-in-law she could take her children with her when she remarried, but if the children were mistreated by their new family, they might think of returning.

---

28. An audio recording of the song can be downloaded at https://www.hkupress.hku.hk/+extras/1681audio/.

29. For a detailed analysis of this form of marriage, and related attitudes and social practices, see Arthur P. Wolf and Chieh-shan Hwang, *Marriage and Adoption in China, 1845–1945* (Stanford: Stanford University Press, 1980), esp. 82–93. The age of the girl when brought in may have been an important variable in the outcome of the marriage.

Their uncles might not want them back, however, as sons might claim shares of the family property. The most fascinating aspect of what she said was that if the children stayed with their mother they would keep the surname of their deceased father, but if their stepfather was good to them, getting wives for the boys and marrying the girls into good families, then they might also use his surname: 'Their bones might be surnamed Yau and their skin surnamed Ho.' This was analogous to the traditional system of land tenure, in which the surface rights were referred to as the 'skin' (地皮), and the subsoil rights as the 'bones' (地骨).

If a small daughter-in-law or widow decided to leave, she was expected to do so in secret. She might take a basket of clothes, pretending that she was going to wash them, and, if a widow, perhaps some small dowry items. She then would disappear under cover of darkness without telling the family, and by late afternoon they would know that she had left. She generally would never be seen in the village again, as she had no place there, although we knew of several exceptions.[30] For men married to small daughters-in-law, one solution, if they were dissatisfied, was for them to take a second wife if family finances permitted this. In the pre-war period polygyny was practiced openly, and the two wives were expected to live together. In one Chan family there were three successive generations of polygynous marriages. The senior wives in the first two generations had been small daughters-in-law, although in the third generation the wife who appeared to be senior had been married in as an adult with full ceremony. In fact, she was not senior to the other, but equal, as this marriage was another form, called *pihngchaaih* (平儕), in which a man married two equal wives at once. His family had raised a small daughter-in-law for him, but he did not like her, and wanted them to find him someone else. The arrangement they made, which they kept secret from the incoming bride and her family, was that he would marry both at once and that they would be of equal status. The son agreed because he thought this would add a worker to the family. Both women wore bridal regalia and worshipped in the hall together. When they were teased, they had to cooperate in lighting a cigarette for him. The small daughter-in-law remained a virgin, however, as he did not enter her bedroom. The occupation soon followed and she left to marry another man.

Another kind of polygyny could occur if an engaged woman died before marriage. In one case, her incense pot was brought into the groom's village at the same time as his new bride, so that her soul could be worshipped as his first wife.[31] His second wife, the one brought in as a living woman, died before bearing any children, so he then married a woman who was, in effect, his third wife, who bore his children. In a similar case, a woman to whom a Kwan Mun Hau man had been engaged was killed in an accident before they were married. When arrangements had been made for him to marry another woman, her family insisted that a sedan chair be sent to their home to receive her soul tablet. His family sent another chair to pick up the living bride, but the one represented by the tablet was considered to be the senior wife. Her family probably wanted this arrangement so that her soul would have a final resting place (歸宿) and would not be untended in the next life. This belief may also have been a reason for families giving their daughters as small daughters-in-law, because if they died young their souls would still be cared for.

Adultery was taken extremely seriously, although we heard of no cases in which women were complicit. Men caught in adultery were actually put into pig cages for their fates to be determined, and then likely sent away. Even if adultery was not the woman's fault, she could be blamed. There were several such cases in Kwan Mun Hau. In one, a man in Sheung Kwai Chung went out and told his wife to leave the door open for his return later that evening. His uncle heard him and went in and raped the woman. She was immediately married out to a man from a poor family in Kwan Mun Hau, who could

---

30. An elderly woman was warmly welcomed at the 1969 Yau *Chongyang* banquet; she had remarried during the occupation taking her son, who thereby lost lineage property rights.

31. This happened in Tai Lam Chung. One of the children was a woman who married a Kwan Mun Hau man.

not afford to be concerned about her lack of virginity. She was given a pair of covered baskets to take with her and wore red clogs; there was no other ceremony. One reason why they were willing to give her up was that she had been a small daughter-in-law, and therefore not expensive.

Childbirth and Children's Survival

In addition to working for the family, women were expected to bear children. Both were necessary, but their working conditions were such that they made childbearing, and the survival of their children, difficult and precarious. Women sometimes suffered miscarriages from carrying heavy loads. Before the occupation and for a decade or so thereafter, babies were delivered at home either by older women, such as neighbours or relatives, or sometimes even by the mother herself, alone. Women who helped others as midwives were said to be skilled, but they could not manage if there were complications, and some women died. The lack of medical care, such as suturing, after birth, and the fact that most women had to resume carrying work within a few days meant that some suffered a prolapsed uterus, which could not be cured with the medical care then available. A few fortunate women had older family members who were aware of this risk and encouraged them to rest after childbirth. A woman who had given birth tried to do somewhat lighter work for a while, but if there was no one to help she got little respite.

Especially in the earlier years of the century, women stayed in the birth room as much as possible. Their husbands would not enter, as the room was believed to have the odour of birth pollution. The new mother could carry the baby out so that he might see it. She would not enter others' houses because she carried pollution. When their work took them outdoors, women had to wear hats, as the discharge made them appear like a spot of blood, offensive to the heavenly gods. If they did not, they risked having a spot of blood appear on their foreheads. During the first month, the mother was expected to sit only on a designated stool, and to be given food rather than helping herself. After the first month, the room, the furniture, the bedding, and the woman herself were cleansed by washing them with pomelo leaf water.

During the first month, people, especially strangers, were warned not to enter the house by certain protective objects such as rice husks placed in a ceramic container outside the front door, and objects hung on the bedroom door. Among them might be an old mirror, a grass-cutting knife, a brush, fishing nets, a rain cape, an almanac, or old shoes. People believed that these objects were *pixie* (辟邪), supernatural barriers to prevent malevolent influences from entering the house. This practice stopped in the early 1950s, when they began to gain more confidence in Western medicine and thought of it as an old custom that was no longer needed.

In the early twentieth century, when the new mother was in the room with her baby she might see ghosts coming with chains to take it, and she would hold it tightly. Other people couldn't see them. She would try to keep it from crying, perhaps because that would attract ghosts. At that time some babies were believed to be locked to life for a certain number of days, after which they would die. Under the conditions of life then, their lives were indeed precarious, and on average women lost half the babies they bore. The experiences of some were especially tragic. One woman gave birth to 12, one each year, and lost 11. The last, a son, was fed by a wet nurse, as she herself had no milk, and he survived. Another gave birth to seven, three of whom were sons, but lost six. Only a daughter survived. The first was killed at birth by her mother-in-law, who was said by others to be a truly black-hearted woman. Measles and smallpox were especially common. The only medical knowledge available was that of old women, who gave sick children 'tea' made by pouring boiling water over cockroaches, centipedes, or spiders found in the toilets, following the principles of sympathetic medicine: that poison destroys poison. Alternatively, they touched them with burning grass.[32]

The fact that women generally had to leave their children while they went out to work put them at considerable risk. A grandmother might feed a baby *wuhjai* (糊仔), sweet rice flour paste, but they sometimes used their fingers, which was not hygienic. Babies often got diarrhoea, especially once they could crawl and were teething, which was a risky time when many died. Women fed them breast milk, but if they had been out for some hours the baby might vomit it, and they also feared that if they drank unboiled water while out this might make their milk unsafe. Tinned condensed milk became available in the 1920s, and those who could afford this fed it to their babies, using a bottle fitted with a nipple.

New mothers were believed to be at risk from supernatural powers. One of these was called *fung* (風), or *saang jaifung* (生子風). If a woman opened a window or did not wear clothes that fully covered her, she was at risk of being blown on by these 'winds', making her fall unconscious and die suddenly. Women were still taking precautions against this in the 1960s. In contrast to some parts of China, however, a woman who died in or shortly after childbirth could receive a normal but simple burial, and her soul could be installed in the ancestral hall when she would have reached the age of 60 and there were no family members senior to her still alive.

On the twelfth day after the birth, women from the mother's natal family came to visit, bringing rice wine, pigs' feet, *chahgwo*, chickens, and eggs for her. It was customary for her mother to bring gifts for the baby: a baby carrier, a hat, and some clothing. The chickens and wine were to be used for worship at the family's earth god shrine and at the Baak Gung, as well as in the ancestral hall. They were restoratives for the mother, together with ginger cooked in sweet vinegar, and salt duck eggs, if her mother-in-law treated her well.

If the baby was a son and they had the means, the family might hold a full month (滿月) banquet. His grandmother could take him to the ancestral hall to worship, offering a chicken that his mother's natal family had brought. If the baby was a girl, they might worship without her. After the month was over, the mother could return to visit her natal family, taking as a reciprocal gift some of the chicken cooked in wine.

Families resorted to various means, natural and supernatural, to try to protect the lives of their precious children.[33] Some were based on a belief called 'spirit sadism': that evil spirits took children who were especially valued. To protect them, people avoided praising a child, and if someone mistakenly did this, a family member would respond with a special phrase to counteract it. They might also call a child by a derogatory name such as 'little dog', or address a boy as if he were a girl. Children might also be taught to address their parents as though they had been adopted, calling their father 'younger uncle' (阿叔), for example.

Childlessness and Adoption

To be without children was tragic, as a couple had to have at least one son to help them in this life and to care for their souls in the next. Women who remained childless, or who only bore daughters, risked being criticized and, furthermore, their husbands might take second wives. If the second wife did bear children, the first could become marginal in the family. One such woman, brought in as a small daughter-in-law, was pathetic in her old age. She said that she was useless, as she could not bear children. She had wanted to adopt a daughter, but her mother-in-law refused to care for the baby while

---

32. People described a number of other treatments.
33. The euphemism for illness in children was that they were 'disobedient' (唔聽話).

she worked. Another childless woman did this, a widowed second wife. She decided not to remarry, and adopted a baby girl, with the agreement of her two mothers-in-law. She got her from a family in Sha Tin, and said that the procedures were very simple, just like getting a puppy or a piglet. She walked over to get her, gave her a piece of sugar cane, and carried her back. Later her family gave twenty dollars 'lucky money' (利是) to the baby's family, although they had not asked for anything. Her mother-in-law cared for the child while she worked, and the child slept with her at night. She and her daughter remained close throughout their lives.

The belief existed that if a childless couple adopted a daughter she might 'lead in' younger brothers and sisters. Furthermore, a knowledgeable middle-aged woman[34] said that her mother-in-law's generation believed that without a daughter to lament, the funeral rites would not be efficacious in settling the soul, and that it would remain in hell (陰曹). She remembered being taken at age 14 to a funeral in which a young woman had been adopted after the death of her 'mother'. Her lament began:

> When she was alive I did not lament her.
> Mother did not see me lament as a daughter.
> Now my mother has died.
> I was carrying grass down the mountain.
> At the side of the road my brother asked me to be her daughter and lament.
> So I came to lament.

The 'daughter' was well-compensated with a cow and three *mu* (畝) of fields, as her assent had meant that she had to be in the presence of a corpse. From then on, she was considered to be affiliated to two lines of descent, her own and that of her 'mother', and to be given spiritual protection by the woman she had lamented. This belief continued at least into the 1980s, although by then young women no longer learned to lament and simply served as daughters in the rites. At that time, an elderly woman who was blind hoped that a daughter could be adopted to lament her, because her eyes would thus be opened in the underworld.

In addition to this important role, there was further evidence that daughters had value, and that families wanted to have both daughters and sons. A mother of four sons and five daughters in a poor family said: 'Someone in the village suggested that we should send one or two of my daughters away, but my mother-in-law berated that person, because my husband had been adopted and the family wanted to have as many children as possible. She said we wouldn't send them away 'even if we were dying of hunger'. A man from another family also refused requests from two families who wanted to adopt one of his daughters.

Decisions about adopting sons in or out were complex and challenging, given sons' value and importance for continuing the family line. A man from a relatively wealthy Chan family said that his family was unusual because they had adopted no sons for several generations, unlike his related neighbours. The Yau genealogy and statements made by people of both surnames testify to the precariousness of maintaining family lines. In some cases, this resulted in lineage branches with very few members, a source of potential conflict with regard to property matters, as profits from lineage property are divided equally among the branches.

In adopting a son, the fundamental decision was whether he would come from within or outside the lineage. Sons brought in from outside had to be bought. One man explained his purchase by his parents because their two sons had died, the second by drowning during a flood. His adoption was called 'replacement exchange' (帶親), because he replaced the son who had died. He compared this to *tihn fong*, or 'replacement' marriage. The term he used for such adoptions by purchase was *hohbaaujai*

---

34. Yau Chan Shek-ying.

(荷包仔), 'lotus-wrapped son', and the woman who had adopted the baby girl from Sha Tin referred to her as a *hohbaauneuih* (荷包女).[35]

We wrote earlier of a woman who had lost six of the seven children she bore, a truly hard fate, made worse by the fact that her husband then took a second wife, whom he favoured. Ultimately, she adopted a son. He was six years old when she adopted him, and as his birth family was very poor, her family gave them several hundred dollars and some rice. He was a good son, and remained with her, unlike some others, she said.

Adoption between descent lines within the lineage is called *gwo gaai* (過繼) and was quite common in the pre-war period. The Yau genealogy shows that among the 80 men in the first six generations in Tsuen Wan, there were 19 sons recorded as dying young, ten childless men who adopted sons from within the lineage, and two from unrecorded sources. Six men remained childless, four at the time when emigration was common. There were various possibilities for adoption within a lineage (過房).[36] One was between brothers. An older brother had the right to adopt the first son of a younger brother, whereas a younger brother could adopt a younger son of the older, if he had one.

A Chan man said that they preferred to adopt from a brother, as he is their own flesh and bones, but that there were potential complexities. For example, the oldest son of a younger brother might be nearly grown, unwilling to live with his uncle, and his father reluctant to give him up. He might, therefore, continue to live with his birth father, but as the son of the adopting father. If he was his birth father's only son, he might continue both lines.

Not everyone agreed that adoption within the lineage was a preferable form of adoption, however, because the relationship was so close and might lead to disputes over property, so some people preferred to buy sons from outside. Such boys were called *lo jai* (羅仔),[37] and families tried to get them while still young.

There was the risk of conflict around all cases of adoption, and some people gossiped about adopted sons behind their backs, referring to them as 'wild son' (野仔), or 'bought son' (買仔). It was common knowledge which men had been adopted. Even if their adopting parents didn't tell them about their status, some people looked down on them. When children fought with them, they might call them derogatory names. Another risk was that they might leave when grown, after spending the property they had inherited from their adopting fathers, without meeting their obligations to maintain the family line and care for their parents' souls.

Another kind of adoption was significant and may remain so: the adoption of a brother's son to a man who had died childless. The older brother of a man whom we knew had died while in his teens, probably in about 1930, and still unmarried. When the man's wife consulted a spirit medium she was told by the deceased brother, very clearly, that he wanted to have a son and grandsons. She told him that their second son had been adopted to him; they had already decided this.[38] He was incredulous, so they wrote it on a paper and burned it to inform him. This made him very happy, and he said he would ensure that the young man prospered. He had been an outstanding scholar, as is the son adopted to him.

35. An alternative translation is 'wallet boy' (or girl), as the characters also mean 'wallet' or 'purse', and imply that the child had been bought. Acknowledgements to Kwok Yung-hing.
36. James L. Watson has analysed the complexities of adoption in a large lineage: 'Agnates and Outsiders: Adoption in a Chinese Lineage', in Watson and Watson, *Village Life in Hong Kong*, 53–71.
37. Meaning 'to net a son', or perhaps 攞仔 'to take or choose a son'.
38. We also heard that he had designated this heir before his death.

Dong Ga (當家): The Management of Household Finances

In most families there was one person who was responsible for managing the household finances. This system probably came into effect once Tsuen Wan people became involved in a cash economy.[39] It seems that this role was often, but not always, filled by women. Some people said that women were more trustworthy, and less likely to smoke, drink, or gamble. In a family in which there were two women of the same generation and appropriate age, then the decision might have been based on capability.

Women's lack of formal education did not prevent them from capably carrying out this responsibility. All employed members of the household, married and unmarried, were expected to turn over their earnings so that she could manage the household budget, make financial decisions, and distribute money to members for their day-to-day needs. If there was some special occasion in a younger woman's natal family, or she needed new clothes, she had to request these funds. Employed women kept back only a small amount of their earnings for themselves, if they kept any at all.[40] Those who kept some back apparently did so only if they believed that the financial manager was not meeting their needs: not saving enough food for them, for example, or not buying them new clothes at New Year. They also might keep back a little at times when they were engaged in high-paying work, such as carrying steel.

The manager maintained her position until she became too old to do so, and a member of the next generation was old enough to take it over. The process of selection seemed to be a natural one, with the woman who was the obvious successor, normally the most senior, then taking charge. This gave her considerable responsibility. She had to make crucial decisions affecting the entire household, such as when and how pigs should be sold. The purchaser would come to the house and bargain with her. She might also participate in a rotating loan association if the family needed to borrow money. In a household with more than one couple, men liked their own wives to be the managers, as this gave them more power in the household and influenced how much they could keep back from their earnings for personal expenses, such as cigarettes and hospitality. A man's own wife would likely allow him more money in order to maintain his good will and loyalty to her. As younger wives had less chance of attaining this position, their power in the household tended to remain less.

The financial manager, if a woman, did not control property matters, however, as these were men's affairs. The only exception was if there was no man present, due to emigration or death. In that case she would have to manage the property, despite the fact that it was in the man's name, and could buy or sell fields or houses, or arrange a son's wedding. There was the very occasional financial manager, however, who secretly kept money back and accumulated it over time, little by little. She could do this if her husband was working elsewhere but sending back money, and by eating very frugally. Eventually she might have enough to buy some property, such as a house. Her husband might not find out, and the property would not be included when the family divided, as it belonged to her alone. Ultimately, however, it would be passed on to her son.

Women did have personal property that was theirs alone. This included their dowry items, gifts from their group of 'sisters' when they were married, gifts of money they received, and any gifts given to them by their natal families. Money that they had been able to set aside was theirs, and it was called by the Hakka term *se-koi* (私額), private money, a term that men would not use.[41]

---

39. For possible nuances in the management of household finances, see Myron L. Cohen, *House United, House Divided*, 91–97.
40. Unmarried girls might be an exception, if the family could afford to let them keep their earnings.
41. Cohen, *House United, House Divided*, 178–91, 198, 210–11. During a medical emergency in one family, a woman asked her young daughter-in-law for her bracelets, and she agreed that they could be sold for this purpose.

Married Women's Relations with Their Natal Families

Married women referred to their natal households as their *ngoihga* (外家): their 'outside' house-holds.[42] This term reflects the fact that once a woman had been married out, she could never again be a member of her natal household, and explains why young women learned bridal laments or, even more impressive, learned to improvise them so they could cry from their hearts. When a bride lamented, her mother almost certainly would lament in response, or at least weep. Before the occupation, brides were young and frightened, as they had no idea where they were going, with whom they would live, and what their futures would be. Almost certainly they knew all too well that the status of young married women was low, and that they would have no power to make their lives easier unless they were fortunate enough to have exceptionally kind mothers-in-law or sympathetic sisters-in-law.

Another fact was absolute, however, and this was that they had the right to maintain ties with their natal families. Even the strictest mother-in-law could not prevent them from visiting on special occasions and staying overnight. During the brief time they were gone, their mothers-in-law had somehow to manage what they could of their workload. Mothers-in-law rarely visited their natal families, as their parents would have died, and members of the next generation should visit them instead. As one woman said:

> Once your parents are dead it is not meaningful to go back. When they are alive they will ask about you, your husband, and your children. This is true. In the past, mothers were very devoted to their daughters. If your mother-in-law treated you badly you could go and tell your mother. She wouldn't have known the mother-in-law was so bad. The mother would pity the daughter. How would a sister-in-law pity her? A sister-in-law would expect her to leave after one night. Her mother would want her to stay an additional night.

There were only a few factors that could keep daughters from making these visits. One was distance, and a woman who married from Bao'an or another distant place was unlikely to be able to return, especially as most were illiterate at that time. If her natal home was as close as Sha Tin, for example, she might leave early in the morning and return the same day. Those from nearby might make brief, frequent visits, as was the case with the woman born in about 1890 in Chuen Lung. She could stop in to see her mother and have something to eat when she was out cutting grass. Once a woman had children, she might not have been able to return if her *ngoihga* was so far away that she would have to stay overnight.

Another impediment was if the bride had somehow lost contact with her natal family. This happened to the small daughter-in-law whose marriage at the age of 12 we described above. Her father had died, as had her younger brother and sister. Her mother arranged her marriage, and she was able to return at New Year for a visit (called *san daam* 新擔) when she was first married, with gifts of pork and *chahgwo*. Then her mother remarried two years later, leaving the girl with no way of contacting her, while her brothers went to live with relatives. She had three paternal aunts, one of whom lived in Kwai Chung and had been asking people about her. By chance they met when the girl was carrying kerosene at the Texaco Oil Depot. They both wept, and she learned where her aunt lived. From then on she knew how and where to contact these members of her *ngoihga*, which gave her new-found power in her husband's family. She had the acknowledged right to visit them at festivals and special occasions, carrying gifts of festival foods, wine, and pork, and staying overnight. Women generally stayed one or two nights, but at New Year they might stay longer, from the fourth until the tenth of the year. The principal constraint was that they had to return on the specified day, or their mothers-in-law would scold them.

---

42. Called *niangjia* (娘家) in *putonghua*.

Mothers-in-law who forbade these visits were seen to be violating their daughters-in-law's rights. One with an especially harsh mother-in-law asked to return to her *ngoihga* at New Year, and the mother-in-law refused and locked her in the house. Others told her that she had the right to go, but that she herself should buy pork to take. It is noteworthy that pork was among the gifts taken by women to their natal families, given its cultural significance and the fact that it was a luxury food. When they left, their natal families sent reciprocal gifts with them for their husbands' families.

Women from her *ngoihga* also visited her during celebrations and festivals, when it was expected that they be given a generous meal. These visits were more likely to happen if they were relatively young, and the distance was not too great. One woman said that her father's sister who lived in Sha Tin made the journey over the mountain passes only if she had problems, such as sick children. That aunt would bring them rice and sweet potatoes, because by then they had stopped growing them.

When the younger woman made a return visit, the gifts of food she brought could be used as offerings to worship her natal ancestors, although this was done on a table at her aunt's home, not in the ancestral hall. The ancestors' spirits were invited from the hall to receive the offerings. The niece could not participate, because once she was married she could not worship her own ancestors. There was one important exception: if there was no one to worship them in her natal family, then she could make offerings to them at her husband's home, but only outside the door, as his ancestral spirits and earth god would not let them enter.

Women's Funerals, and Their Laments

When a woman died, members of her *ngoihga* were notified by her husband's relatives, unless she had specified otherwise. They took special notices written on white paper to her relatives, who burned them after receiving and reading them, and gave lucky money to the messenger. Both men and women came to her funeral. When they arrived, the woman's sons and grandsons knelt outside the door to receive them, and her *ngoihga* relatives had to raise them up. Then those women would begin to lament, followed by women in her husband's family.[43]

Funeral laments were heart-breaking, reminding those who heard them of their own losses. Other women would weep and might lament in turn, while men often were moved to tears at the sound of the women's unrestrained voices, half singing, half wailing, often improvising as they expressed their feelings, mourning their loss and calling to the person who had died at the end of each line. The laments are called *haam* (喊) *oi* or *gew oi*. *Gew* and *oi* are Hakka words, *haam* and *gew* meaning 'to weep for' and *oi* meaning 'mother'.[44] Women lamented the dead at particular points in the rites, but also when they were moved to do so by their own feelings.

Laments were also called *haam naahnmehng* (喊難命), weeping for bad fortune, and women often used them to express their misery at their hard fates, and even to air their grievances against others.[45] Whether they were heard was less important than the opportunity this gave to release their pent-up feelings. For example, a woman married into a poor household, and whose mother had died, might lament her:

43. Men who heard them might sob; women would comfort the lamenting woman or, if they were criticized in the lament and able to lament extemporaneously, rebut her in kind. See Elizabeth L. Johnson, 'Grieving for the Dead, Grieving for the Living: Funeral Laments of Hakka Women', in *Death Ritual in Late Imperial and Modern China*, ed. Watson and Rawski, 135–63. Elizabeth Lominska Johnson, 'Singing of Separation, Lamenting Loss', in *Living with Separation in China: Anthropological Accounts*, ed. Charles Stafford, 27–52.
44. 'Oi' can also mean 'mother-in-law', as women addressed their mothers-in-law in the same way as their mothers,
45. Chan Shek-ying was among them, using her laments to criticize family members, such as relatives who put her aunt (father's sister) in hospital at the end of her life, rather than caring for her at home.

Having a bad fate, I was married into a poor household.
Today I come; I have lost my mother.
I came and I saw my mother's tablet.
I have lost my mother and I am miserable.
My mother listened to others
and married out this struggling girl with a cursed fate.
I am so poor that I carry loads until my shoulders look like rough granite.
If I had been married better, I would not be so wretched now.
My feet are full of holes like a rice-drying basket.
When I came for special occasions and festivals my mother came to
greet and caress me.
Today I have lost my mother, who came to greet and caress
this person with an accursed fate.[46]

If women wept and then told her that her sisters-in-law would take her mother's place, she might answer:

My sister-in-law acting as my mother is not like my real mother
Whenever I had any problem, my mother would ask about me.

When she was 14, many years previous, Chan Shek-ying heard a relative's lament for her father's sister's husband (*daaihgujeuhng* 大姑丈), expressing her bitterness over the deaths of her children and her husband's neglect of her in favour of his second wife:[47]

My *daaihgujeuhng* you are at peace.
You have a son and everything is fine, *daaihgujeuhng*.
Daaihgujeuhng could never eat all his food, could never spend all his money.
I met *daaihgujeuhng* at the end of the street, and asked if his wife was well.
How could I be well? I have only forty dollars a month.
If I were like other people, I would have a good fate.
I should have children pulling at my shirt,
children clinging to my legs.
If my children were still alive,
I should have three pulling at my clothes on the right,
three pulling at my clothes on the left.
My *daaihgujeuhng* also had a second wife.
He as a husband treated them both equally.
Towards the second he showed no special favour.

At one funeral we witnessed, the first wife of the deceased, whose husband had left her for another woman, lamented at his coffin, although she was not in mourning. She was said to have been accusing him of lechery.

The theme of encountering the reality of death and loss was important in women's laments for their mothers and other senior relatives. For example, a woman might begin her lament for her father's older sister (*daaihgu* 大姑):

I come today to lament my *daaihgu*.
When I came for festivals my *daaihgu* laughed 'ha ha'.
Tonight, a white paper says my *daaihgu* has passed away.
I came to my aunt's door and she was not here.

---

46. An audio recording of the lament can be downloaded at https://www.hkupress.hku.hk/+extras/1681audio/.
47. This was the woman described earlier.

A daughter-in-law might include in her lament:

Every morning when I open the door my son could not call his grandmother.
Your grandson and baby now have no grandmother and could not call her.
In the morning I take out one less pair of chopsticks.

In another lament, a daughter blamed the young daughter-in-law for her father's untimely death, and the daughter-in-law was skilled enough to rebut (*bok* 駁) her in kind. Antiphonal, competitive lamenting critical of others was characteristic of funerals, and was reminiscent of mountain songs in the improvisational skills it required.[48]

Women were expected to lament for their senior relatives, and those who could not, or did so inadequately, were looked down on. By the 1960s, however, the ability to do so was being lost, as the context for learning this skill had disappeared.[49]

Economic Relations between Women and Their Natal Families

We knew of two cases in which women, with their husbands, had given support to their natal families in the pre-war period, although generally they kept their affairs separate. A Fan lineage man had married a woman from a poor family in Sam Tung Uk. Her mother sometimes came to eat with them and lived with them in her later years to help care for the children after his mother had died.

In another case, a woman from Kwai Chung who married a Kwan Mun Hau man in about 1905 had lost her mother when she was a child of seven. She had no brothers or surviving sisters. Her father was poor, and worked at cutting firewood. She helped him as she grew older. After she had married into a relatively well-to-do family, her father was too old to work. He had his own house, and she supported him by giving him some of the money that she earned by cutting fuel. Her husband and mother-in-law knew that she did this, and her husband also occasionally gave him money, which he came to collect every week.

In cases in which an old couple had no male descendants and no means of support, they might live with a married daughter and then leave to her whatever property they had. The woman described above, who had supported her father in his old age, inherited his property, as there were no men left in his lineage branch. This gave her the responsibility for being the chief mourner at his funeral and ensuring that his soul was worshipped. When she grew too old to do this, the responsibility devolved onto her son, together with the inheritance. His responsibility for the soul of his mother's father was considered to be unusual, but it was a logical outcome of the situation. There was a somewhat similar case in the late 1960s, when an elderly couple had two daughters but no surviving sons, their adopted son having died. Their closest descendant was their deceased nephew's widow (任新抱), who cared for them in their old age. They died within two weeks of each other. She was then responsible for being the chief mourner at their funerals, carrying their tablets and performing the rites, and inheriting their house in return.

---

48. It was said not to be appropriate to criticize the relative who had died (although we heard of examples), but was possible to use the opportunity to air grievances against others.
49. Chan Shek-ying, from whom I learned about them, said that when her time came there would be no one to lament her.

Appendix: *Bafang Fenjialu* of the Tsuen Wan Yau Lineage

The Yau Luen Fong Ancestral Trust was established this way in 1837:

[The legendary history of the family and its growth]

It is true that the branches of a tree are reproduced naturally, just as other life grows naturally. Likewise, the members of a family increase in numbers. As a result, it becomes difficult to have sufficient resources to support them.

The head of a family must therefore think prudently. I considered the fact that my elder brother and I both came from Lufeng and Guanlan, and then settled together in Tsuen Wan. As we worked hard, we earned enough to support our households. Later on, my brother Kwun passed away. I worked with my sister-in-law and our descendants to carry on our business, and we earned a lot of money. My brother Kwun had three sons and I had five sons. All of them have married, and thus our worries have been lessened. As we are now almost eighty years old, I sought my sister-in-law's consent to divide the majority of our property into eight equal shares, for the benefit of our future descendants. Once this has been confirmed, no one should be excluded, and our prosperity should be maintained. We should make a general copy of this document, and eight additional copies for the eight branches to hold in safe custody.

Dated Daoguang sixteenth year [1837] second month sixth day good hour.

Set up by Sun Man and Madam Wong.

Witnessed by paternal cousins Yee Pong and Tak Chiu and maternal cousin Cheung Wing-wah

Deed written by Cheung Ting-yiu

This article was copied from the original by Yau Yuen Cheung in 1925.

Rules and Obligations

1. The main chamber of the Ancestral Hall, the space inside the door, and the area extending in front are the property of all held in common.

2. Regarding the shops: there is an old shop on the main street, which extends from east to west. There are seven stalls in a row from the front to the back, and on the front from west to east there is a row of five large and small stalls. On the southern side of the main street there is a shop with four stalls from east to west, and a place to store grass. The properties are divided into eight shares and cannot be divided.

3. The study hall is to be used to enable all descendants to advance their careers. The rooms in the study hall are for the education of the younger generation and cannot be encroached upon for business or living purposes.

4. Descendants who achieve prominence [through examination success] will be rewarded with 10 taels of silver.

5. Descendants who are successful in obtaining a first degree from the local academy [*xiucai*] will be awarded 2,000 catties of grain.

6. The descendants' school fees will be supported by the ancestral [trust], but the daily expenses of the teacher will be shared by the parents of the students.

7. The expenses of any descendant who sits for the post-secondary examinations will be partially supported by the ancestral [trust].

8. The expenses needed for the annual sweeping of the tombs, the New Year decorations, and the celebration of the birthdays of the deities will be covered by the yields of the following fields, worked each year by two families in rotation. These properties include an area of 60,000 square feet in Lower Kwai Chung, the Hoi Pa Main Road, and an earthen house.

9. Once the oxen and cattle have been divided among the eight branches, there should be no objections or complaints.

10. All the title deeds pertaining to the fields and houses have been distributed to every family, whereas the remainder are being kept in the main chest for safe custody.

11. These rules and obligations have been selected by Siu Kwong in 1997.

4

The Japanese Occupation, Recovery, and Transformation
1941–1970

The Japanese Occupation

The Japanese occupation of Hong Kong lasted from December 1941 until August 1945.[1] Virtually all normal life stopped during this time, including the sources of employment that had been developing. Some people fled out of fear to Chuen Lung and Tsing Yi when the Japanese first arrived, and about 30% left Tsuen Wan for various reasons, including long-term labourers who no longer could be employed. Those who were especially patriotic left to join the fight against the Japanese occupiers. Others could not accept the severity of foreign domination, and so they left to escape it. Still others could not survive in Tsuen Wan, so they left to try to find a living. These included well-educated people without knowledge of farming, many of whom escaped to the mainland or went abroad, some never to return. Others had special skills that were valued elsewhere. Some men worried that their wives would leave them to escape the hardship.

Japanese domination was brutal. At a minimum, people had to bow when they encountered Japanese soldiers, or else they were beaten. They also witnessed horrifying behaviour on a regular basis. According to a man of the Fan lineage, who was in his twenties at that time:

> It was terrible living under the Japanese. I saw horrible things. A man was starving and stole two pieces of ginger candy and they shot him. I saw a lot of people tortured and shot. If people were caught stealing food they were blindfolded and shot by three men. I saw this done to a man, whom they wounded. He fell into the water and tried to crawl out. No one dared to help him, and they returned and killed him. People were tortured if they could not work because they were too hungry. I saw a woman stripped of her clothes. People were terribly hungry, so thin that their legs were just bone and their faces hollow. People from Kwan Mun Hau starved to death. People who had food wouldn't share it as they didn't know how long the Japanese would be here.
>
> The place where you are living was the worst during the Japanese occupation. They brought five or six people there every night and beheaded them. How many would that be in more than three years? People did not dare walk there at night, but now it has been exorcised by monks. Once you were caught by the Japanese you didn't have a chance, as they were just soldiers and there was no law. People caught by them were put in a little cell that was too low for the prisoner to stand up, given nothing to eat, and just kept there in their own filth.

People were left with terrible memories, such as hearing a prisoner screaming all night. Prisoners captured by the Japanese and taken to the present site of Kwan Mun Hau were not only executed there,

---

1. The most thorough general account is Philip Snow, *The Fall of Hong Kong: Britain, China and the Japanese Occupation* (New Haven and London: Yale University Press, 2003).

but also buried on that hillside. Their bones had to be removed before the village moved,[2] and families did their own purification rituals in addition to the exorcism that had been performed.

The occupation was especially terrifying for young women, as the soldiers would chase them, and rape them if they had the chance. They would ask the older women where the young women were, and they lied to them, so the soldiers sometimes hit them. One young woman was seized by the Japanese, who abused her for several days. Some disguised themselves as boys as a way of escaping them.

> The Japanese used to chase the girls; two chased me. They were very ugly, with short legs and big eyes. The soldiers asked my mother-in-law for me, and she told them a wrong way, so I escaped to my uncle's house, which had iron doors. They continued to chase girls, and my uncle suggested that they provide them with some prostitutes, as those women would be doing that work anyway.

An elderly woman said that larger villages did set up brothels for the soldiers, so that they would leave their women alone.

People lived on what they could produce from their fields, which was often inadequate. Some had to eat bark and wild plants. Those who grew rice did not dare dry it for fear it would be stolen, so they simply cooked it in a wok. They stopped raising pigs for the same reason, and also because they had nothing to feed them, given that even people did not have enough to eat. As one woman said: 'The matchmaker for my marriage died: her whole family, sons, daughters, all died. If you have nothing to eat, you die.' One very old woman reiterated something that many people said, which was that if the Japanese had stayed one week more than the three years and eight months of the occupation, they would have died of hunger, as by then they had nothing to eat. Those families without agricultural skills often sold their fields. One family survived better than others because they were well-managed and had land and three adults. The mother and daughter-in-law farmed, growing rice and vegetables. Others with no land helped them in return for food. The son had a bicycle, which he used to take fish to Kowloon each day, keeping one to eat.[3] People also cut firewood to sell in Kowloon, as people there had none. For the first three years, some families grew plants that yielded oil for the Japanese occupiers.

> We fled from them for one year, and then came back and worked for them growing oil plants, earning two dollars and four ounces of rice per day. Many people starved to death—I saw them die. They ate a kind of fertilizer made of dried vegetable stems. Then they drank water and it swelled and killed them. People also ate sweet potato vines. My husband smuggled, and thus ran the risk of being killed. He smuggled gasoline so that we could buy rice. We boiled it into congee.

Some men and women worked for the Japanese building Route Twisk over Tai Mo Shan, for which they were paid in rice, one level measure per day. If they did not satisfy their overseers, they were beaten with rods. They had to live on the site most of the time because of the distance.

All education and normal employment ceased, as did ceremonies such as worship at ancestors' tombs, unless it was done in secret, resulting in a major hiatus in people's lives. When the occupation was over and boys were able to study again, they were often very old to be in primary school. Some lineages said that they lost their genealogies during this time because of the disorder. A few men were employed by the Japanese as their plainclothes police, resulting in rifts in the community that were not soon forgotten. The mutual responsibility system that was imposed was also destructive, as it was very different from their familiar form of social organization.[4] Even their physical environment was

---

2. District Office files include villagers' expressions of concern about the treatment of human remains during site formation. Villagers then provided mortuary urns for those uncovered.
3. He also took food to his widowed sister's baby boy. She had remarried because life was so hard, leaving him with his grandmother.
4. Hayes, *Tsuen Wan*, 37. Chapter III is very informative. For example: 'In Hong Kong, whilst there are indications that the *pao-chia* system had been applied under Chinese rule, it had probably only been loosely and occasionally imposed. Moreover, the British administration had generally emphasized the individual's responsibility under English law. The reimposition of mutual responsibility in Occupied Hong Kong under severe and much more stringent police controls was assuredly one of the most feared and

dramatically changed, because Castle Peak Road had previously been lined with large trees, which were cut down by the occupiers for their wood.

The occupiers converted the automobile factory into one that produced tanks. Some Tsuen Wan men benefited from this:

> Soon the Japanese used the engineering works to make tanks. It expanded and they needed a lot of skilled workers. They asked for apprentices and hired me. I studied for six terms, and my fellow apprentices were all Tsuen Wan natives. At first, I did not work. I studied Japanese for three months, and then observed in the factory for several months. I learned mathematics, draughtsmanship, physics, everything. After three months we worked for a long time in each department to see what we were suited for and liked to do. Then we became workers, being paid 50 cents occupation money per day and one-half catty of rice, but at the end of the occupation the factory was sometimes bombed by the allies, so the Japanese started to retreat. They removed the machinery and asked us to go to Hung Hom or Japan, but we didn't want to leave the village during the war. About half went, but many of them were killed by bombs. I didn't go, but worked instead on road construction at the top of Tai Mo Shan, getting four ounces of rice and four of wheat flour each day. Everyone got very thin.
>
> At end of the occupation I sold the family's last plot. Then I worked [at short-term engineering jobs]. Some years ago, I started my own business. I gave my knowledge, and others gave capital. This was in old Kwan Mun Hau. I didn't work there, I hired people. When the village was resited, I found the small scale inadequate so I bought more machinery by hire-purchase. Now I have three flats in a resettlement factory. . . . I have more than ten employees. I am very satisfied with my career, from nothing to establishing a factory, from agriculture to a skilled factory worker. I have to thank the Japanese, as without them I would not have had this career.

In contrast, the woman who later became his wife did underground work for two years on behalf of the communist East River guerrillas who were combating the Japanese on the mainland. She observed the activities of the Japanese, and then carried messages over mountain paths from Tsuen Wan to the Yuen Long area—a five-hour walk. This was very dangerous work indeed.

There were few children born, and many deaths. If children got sick and needed medical care, people sometimes had to sell fields to pay for it, as they did to pay for the interment of elderly relatives who died. Even worse, they sometimes were unable to give relatives a proper burial. Some people also had to give or sell their children to others, if they could not support them. Families sold sons as well as daughters. One Kwan Kun Hau couple paid an agent (水客) to try to find their son after the occupation, and wept for days when he did not succeed. To add to the misery, malaria was also pervasive, perhaps because of the general disorder.[5] Those who were ill could not work. Many households divided during the occupation. We have puzzled over the reason for this, but perhaps they believed that members of smaller family units would struggle harder to survive.

Recovery

The occupation was severe in its impact on Hong Kong in general. A government report stated:

> At the end of August 1945, the economic life of Hong Kong was dead. The population was greatly reduced in numbers, utilities were barely functioning, there was no food, no shipping, no industry, no commerce.[6]

---

detested aspects of Japanese wartime rule'.

5. This also may have reflected the termination of the stringent anti-malarial measures undertaken by the government to protect the health of the Shing Mun Reservoir labour force. Hayes, *Tsuen Wan*, 23.

6. *Hong Kong Government Annual Report 1946* (Hong Kong: Ye Olde Printerie, Ltd. 1947), 1. For details, see Snow, *The Fall of Hong Kong*, 206–18.

And yet, like a phoenix, Hong Kong in general, and Tsuen Wan in particular, were reborn into new roles in the period after 1945.

The post-occupation society was to be very different from its pre-1941 form. The modest beginnings of industrial development in Tsuen Wan continued at an accelerated pace. This formerly rural district, with the beginnings of industry and other occupations that offered wage labour, was to become in the space of 20 years the most intensively developed industrial area in Hong Kong. Its population was to grow from perhaps 8,000 in 1946 to over 250,000 by 1968, when we arrived.[7]

Civil war in China and the resulting establishment of the People's Republic of China in 1949 were important events in the demographic and economic history of Hong Kong. From 1946 until 1962, especially in the early period, large numbers of people moved from China to Hong Kong. Hong Kong had experienced panic migration in 1937 with the Japanese invasion of China, which led to squatting and street sleeping on a scale previously unknown in Hong Kong. The movement of people from 1948 to 1952 was immense and without precedent. A government report of the time noted:

> At the time of the fall of Shanghai in May, and later in October, when the communist capture of Canton was imminent, the number of Chinese flocking into the Colony reached at times over 10,000 in one week.[8]

The capital, skills, and people that flowed into Hong Kong contributed enormously to its economic success and transformation in the 1950s and 1960s. As early as 1947, land had become a scarce resource. Potential factory owners saw in Tsuen Wan not merely cheap land but also certain advantages as a site for industrial use. For textile entrepreneurs, the abundance of water from the hills behind Tsuen Wan was important, as was the direct road to Kowloon, and its proximity to Victoria harbour, along with its own potential harbour facilities.

From 1948 onwards, such entrepreneurs, often from the Shanghai area, were a critical part of the migration from China to Hong Kong. Even before the establishment of the new government in China, government sources noted:

> [T]he tendency of Shanghai industrialists to move to Hong Kong continued and it must be confessed that they have brought into the Colony modern methods and machinery which have proved a welcome and effective spur to established industries.[9]

The Shanghai entrepreneurs brought not merely their capital and their own entrepreneurial talents, but very often their skilled workers as well. By early 1950, more than 30 factories were established in Tsuen Wan, and the population had grown to an estimated 20,000.[10] By then, the indigenous Hakka people no longer constituted a majority of the population.

The movement of Shanghai capital to Hong Kong was the first indication of the changes that were to be characteristic of its economic development. Shanghai textile entrepreneurs had returned to their war-ravaged city in 1946 with the general expectation of re-establishing their industries. They ordered the most modern textile machinery from Britain, which had a dominant role in the supply of Shanghai's textile industry before 1937. An economic crisis and a terrible winter delayed shipments until 1948, by which time the political situation in China was changing. The entrepreneurs diverted their orders for delivery to Hong Kong, and in late 1948 and early 1949, as communist forces moved to take north China and to threaten Shanghai as well as the Yangzi delta, it was a relatively simple task to move their capital investments and experienced workers to safety in Hong Kong. Thus, from an early date, modern air-conditioned mills, in the hands of skilled labour, and with an abundant additional

---

7. The figures are unpublished estimates from the Tsuen Wan District Office.
8. *Hong Kong Government Annual Report 1949* (Hong Kong: Government Publications, 1950), 2.
9. *Hong Kong Government Annual Report 1949*, 22.
10. Population estimate was given in a speech by the chairman of the Tsuen Wan Federation of Societies.

supply of cheap local labour, were operating in Tsuen Wan.[11] By 1950, the textile industry was one of the more significant in Hong Kong. In 1951 it was estimated that there were 7,500 industrial workers in Tsuen Wan, which was about 8% of the total Hong Kong labour force.[12]

Hong Kong's economy shifted after 1950, from one dominated by the China trade to another which was much more diverse and in which industrial production was of growing importance. It was increasingly affected by global political forces, which began to change the nature of the international economy and Hong Kong's role within it. War in the Korean Peninsula, in which Chinese forces confronted American troops and their allies, resulted in an American blockade of China. This brought Hong Kong's China trade to an abrupt end, and dramatically shifted the post-war economic trajectory in East Asia. Hong Kong 'lost its hinterland'[13] and somehow had to adapt to new circumstances and reinvent itself.

Industrial growth in the early 1950s occurred within a policy vacuum of a government committed to a laissez-faire approach to social affairs. Rehousing of its enormous number of squatters did not get underway until 1954, when it was clear that the immigrant population was unlikely to return to China. It was also soon obvious that the newcomers were hardworking and central to Hong Kong's economic future.

Tsuen Wan as a growing industrial presence was challenged by a lack of development of new housing. In the central area, only 50 or so shophouses, which were built shortly before the occupation, were residential alternatives to village housing, outbuildings, and land, all of which were rented out to immigrant tenants.

By 1955, the population had grown to over 51,000, with a substantial preponderance of men aged 15 to 50, suggesting the presence of immigrant workers.[14] An official report on the situation in Tsuen Wan stated:

> [T]he development of industrial sites has far outrun what should be the parallel development of housing sites and for lack of proper accommodation the increasing population has had to find room for itself in squatter units. The problem is being attacked but it will be some time before a material improvement can be effected.[15]

Some of the factories provided dormitories for their workers and some 5,831—more than a tenth of the population—lived in them. A further 8,337 workers, some with families, were living as tenants in the villages and their surrounds.[16] The villages in the centre of Tsuen Wan became disorderly, congested, and unsanitary collections of traditional village houses interspersed with a motley array of temporary structures. The 1955 census of the New Territories indicated that 6,134 pigs were being raised in Tsuen Wan—more than in any other sub-district—suggesting an additional reason for unsanitary conditions. It is also somewhat surprising that so much livestock was being raised in the midst of dramatic industrial growth. That said, raising pigs was an important subsidiary occupation for both immigrant and local women.

Squatter structures were not only used for residential purposes. One feature of the Hong Kong industrial economy in the 1950s was that it was not confined to large up-to-date and well-capitalized factories such as those established by Shanghai entrepreneurs in west Tsuen Wan. Rather, a notable

---

11. Other former rural areas in North Kowloon also urbanized, but under much less favourable conditions. See Hayes, *The Great Difference*, 26–27, 111–13.
12. *Commissioner of Labour Annual Report 1950–51*, 8.
13. Ezra F. Vogel, *One Step Ahead in China: Guangdong Under Reform* (Cambridge, MA: Harvard University Press, 1989).
14. From an (unpublished) partial census of the New Territories conducted by the District Commissioner New Territories with the Department of Agriculture and Fisheries. Courtesy of James Hayes.
15. *New Territories Administration Annual Report 1956–7*, 7.
16. *New Territories Administration Annual Report 1956–7*, 7.

characteristic, especially in Tsuen Wan and northern Kowloon, was the 'small industrial unit'.[17] There were large numbers of tiny establishments, characterized by founder-management, a shortage of capital, weak bargaining power for both raw materials and the prices of finished products, and often poorly housed in flimsy structures. A factory survey conducted in May 1955 found 61 factories in Tsuen Wan, 29 of which employed less than 50 workers and only 12 of which employed more than 200. The larger factories fell into a narrow range of industry, namely cotton textiles, silk weaving, and enamelware, the enterprises begun by Shanghai émigrés beginning in the late 1940s. The smaller concerns covered a wider range, although dominated by silk weaving, but also including small metal workshops, carpentry, food processing, and the manufacture of ritual goods, including incense powder and joss sticks.[18] The six villages in the centre of Tsuen Wan had among them a total of 51 factories employing 1,208 workers. Population densities in the old central villages were very high, reaching 322 per acre in Kwan Mun Hau, 302 in Ho Pui, and 270 in Muk Min Ha.[19] Life was not easy in the overcrowded villages of central Tsuen Wan, compounded by the fact that Castle Peak Road was now several feet higher than it had formerly been because of a large water pipe from the new reservoir of Tai Lam Chung, some miles away to the west. The difference in elevation brought terrible flooding in the rainy months from May until September.

By the mid-1950s, Tsuen Wan was facing a crisis, as its increasingly urban space was developed with little or no planning, and its burgeoning industry grew with little direction or oversight, creating

Plate 15: Continuing a long history: making incense sticks in a squatter workshop in northern Tsuen Wan, c. 1968.

---

17. D. J. Dwyer and Lai Chuen-yan, *The Small Industrial Unit in Hong Kong: Patterns and Policies* (Hull: University of Hull Press, 1967).
18. Unpublished records held in the Crown Lands and Survey Office, Public Works Department, Hong Kong Government.
19. Unpublished figures from the Tsuen Wan District Office. The density in Kwan Mun Hau was therefore 206,000 per square mile, in traditional village housing, outbuildings, or squatter structures.

major problems for villagers and immigrants alike. There were three possible ways to ease the increasingly desperate situation. Land could be reclaimed from the foreshore and hillsides could be torn down, creating space for development and providing fill for reclamation; and, most dramatically, native villages could be resited to new locations, to make way for more efficient land use in dealing with the issues that were daily becoming more pressing.

Policy decisions in 1954 marked a watershed in the social history of Hong Kong and shifted the colonial government to an interventionist strategy of a kind that it had never before pursued. After the disastrous fire in the Shek Kip Mei squatter area on Christmas Day 1953, the government embarked on a housing programme that, by 1968, made it landlord to a third of Hong Kong's population, and marked the end of government non-involvement in social policy. For Tsuen Wan, this resulted in much greater intervention by the government in the affairs of the district. This involvement had two aspects. One was the formation, in 1957, of a new administrative district in the New Territories, corresponding to the historical dimensions of Tsuen Wan *xiang*, with its district office in the town. The other was the selection of the area as the subject of a Feasibility Report by engineering consultants in 1958. As a direct consequence of this report, a Town Planning Board was established, which began to create a development plan for the district. In 1961, Tsuen Wan thus became Hong Kong's first 'satellite town' (衛星城市)[20] modelled, more or less, after the British 'new towns' of the post-war period in which the intention was 'to seek to create a balanced community—a new town instead of an existing urban area'.[21] The direct effect was to increase population movement to Tsuen Wan and to extend the industrial base.

The 1950s were a time of great confusion in Tsuen Wan and there were a number of conflicting social currents at work. Industrial activity expanded throughout the decade and there were over 300 factories by 1960—a tenfold increase over the decade. In part, this was a consequence of more land becoming available for factory expansion, with significant reclamation of the foreshore in front of the old coastal villages in central Tsuen Wan. The growth of industrial establishments continued into the 1960s.[22] With it came population growth, fuelled in part by the increased demand for factory labour. These immigrants exacerbated the housing problems. There was some addition to the housing stock on the new reclamation, but it was insufficient to meet growing needs, and much of the new population continued to crowd into the villages or squatted on the hillsides above the town. A significant element consisted of non-Cantonese speakers from poorer rural regions of eastern Guangdong.

Social relations in general were orderly, despite the inadequate housing, extreme overcrowding, lack of amenities, and cultural diversity of the population, for reasons that we shall attempt to explain in the later chapters.[23] There were labour problems, however, and 'Shanghai' workers were in the vanguard of disputes with their 'Shanghai' employers who, with few exceptions, were not resident in Tsuen Wan. Workers' organizations had been formed from an early date but were split ideologically, with competing allegiances either to the People's Republic of China or the Nationalist government on Taiwan. We will deal with questions concerning worker and manufacturer associations in a later chapter. The tensions came to a head in 1956 with a series of disturbances having both political and economic underpinnings, which left eight people dead and caused over HK$250,000 in damages.

---

20. It was created not long after the launch of the 'Sputnik' satellite by the Soviet Union, which had an enormous popular impact. The idea of Tsuen Wan being a 'satellite city' was, and remains, a powerful image among the local population.

21. The background and later developments are detailed in Roger Bristow, *Hong Kong's New Towns: A Selective Review* (Hong Kong; New York: Oxford University Press, 1989).

22. The official reports of the New Territories Administration indicate that the number of factories grew from 337 in 1961 to 555 in 1964. The 1968 figure is 405, but does not include the many small establishments in the 'flatted factory' buildings.

23. James W. Hayes, 'The Old Popular Culture of China and Its Contribution to Stability in Tsuen Wan', *Journal of the Hong Kong Branch Royal Asiatic Society* 30 (1990): 1–25.

In order to bring some rationality into the uncontrolled influx of industry and population, policy makers were faced with complex and often competing interests. The creation of new building land was relatively straightforward. The government had undisputed rights to the foreshore and there were few challenges as to how it dealt with hill slopes. On the other hand, there were major issues when it came to tackling the problems of the congested native villages. Tsuen Wan lay within the leased New Territories and the descendants of the pre-Convention inhabitants had traditional rights to land, which were not easily brushed aside. Most of the land in the central area, where the problems were the greatest, was held by the descendants of the original inhabitants, and they could point to detailed records in the Land Registry to bolster their claims. At the extreme, the government could resort to resumption, which is the forcible, if necessary, seizure of land, but this was unpopular and politically unwise.

The situation was not easy and it illustrates much that is fundamental to an understanding of industrializing and modernizing Tsuen Wan. Its tremendous growth after 1947 had occurred on a base population of indigenous villagers, who retained their political influence despite their rapidly diminishing portion of the total population. It existed due to the distinctive legal status of New Territories' people. This was a critical aspect of 'the great difference' which Lockhart had noted, and Hayes had expanded upon. Despite this, village removals were absolutely essential for the development of central Tsuen Wan.[24]

Village removals, or, to be precise, resitings, were not unknown. Many were to make way for the building of reservoirs. As early as 1900, a village had been removed on Hong Kong Island.[25] In 1928, the Shing Mun villages had been resited. In the 1950s, Tai Uk Wai (大屋圍) was built on reclaimed land to the south of the original Tsuen Wan foreshore to rehouse the population of two villages displaced by the Tai Lam Chung reservoir. In 1960, most Shek Pik (石碧) villagers chose to relocate to Tsuen Wan from Lantau Island, when the reservoir was built.[26]

The details of all these removals were rather special. The people had no alternative but to move and were compensated accordingly, although this resulted in profound changes in their livelihoods. The Tsuen Wan villages were not being threatened by reservoir construction, but instead by rapid urban growth. In some fashion they had to be encouraged to move to new locations that would allow their ancestral land to be used for development purposes. Fair compensation had to be negotiated for the surrender of their land and adequate locations for new villages had to be found.

In 1964, three of the villages did move to a site just outside the central area, overlooking the new Tai Wo Hau resettlement estate—the culmination of a six-year period of negotiation. The land slump, which began in 1964 and continued into 1969, and the complicated nature of land tenure in one of the remaining central villages, prevented further agreement on village removals until the 1970s, when the dynamism of Hong Kong's economy brought renewed vigour to Tsuen Wan.

The early 1960s marked the beginning—although not the end—of the development of modern Tsuen Wan. Reclamation had extended available building land far beyond its 1946 limit, creating further sites for housing development or industrial use. By the end of 1962, Tai Wo Hau resettlement estate had a population of over 20,000 in 12 domestic blocks (and one factory block) including two blocks entirely populated by resettled boat squatters. Their presence in the boat anchorage had long impaired the final reclamation of the harbour, and theirs was the first systematic clearance of boat squatters in Hong Kong. By 1968, when we arrived, there were three resettlement estates and one low cost housing estate. Three large resettlement estates and a number of smaller ones were under

---

24. Boat-dwelling fishing people, and those who had moved onto land, were once again disadvantaged, as they did not meet the criteria for rehousing. Hayes, *Tsuen Wan*, 151.
25. See James Hayes, 'A Chinese Village on Hong Kong Island Fifty Years Ago – Tai Tam Tuk: Village Under the Water', in *Hong Kong: A Society in Transition*, ed. Ian Jarvie and Joseph Agassi, 29–52.
26. Representatives of each of the removed villages sat on the Tsuen Wan Rural Committee.

construction. In total, 60% of the population of 250,000 was living in various forms of government housing—a far larger proportion than anywhere else in Hong Kong, except Kwun Tong. The squatter population was still substantial, about 35,000, exceeding those in private sector flats (about 28,000) and village housing (about 20,000).[27]

The commercial sector extended far beyond the bounds of the 50 shophouses from the 1930s. A small, but increasing, number of buildings of 16 or more storeys housed commercial establishments, banks, schools, private flats, and even churches and temples, although there were not yet any modern hotels. At this time, there was little middle class development, and Tsuen Wan remained a working class town. In terms of its contribution to Hong Kong's economy as a whole, Tsuen Wan accounted for 55% of the cotton spinning output, 80% of silk weaving, 70% of enamelware, 44% of chemicals, primarily the large oil storage and transfer facilities in the long-established Texaco Oil Depot. It was without question the most intensively industrialized area in Hong Kong.[28]

Plate 16: Factories in western Tsuen Wan, c. 1969, with the Fou Wah Weaving Mill on the right.

Plate 17: Factories seen over the roofs of one of the west Tsuen Wan villages, c. 1969.

---

27. Unpublished records, Tsuen Wan District Office.
28. Lai Chun-yan, 'Some Geographical Aspects of the Industrial Development in Hong Kong' (unpublished MA thesis, University of Hong Kong, 1963).

Plate 18: Factory producing enamelware, with the brick kiln on the right. The basins, spittoons, trays, and chamber pots were sold locally, but also exported to Africa.

Plate 19: Workers in an enamelware factory, one of Tsuen Wan's important industries in the late 1960s. Conditions were hot, back-breaking, and polluted.

The scale of operation of cotton textiles, enamelware, glassware, and the chemical industries was substantial, but an important part of the local economy remained village-based, of small scale, and little changed in its essential respects from its situation in the 1950s. Much was still carried on in the villages that remained *in situ* in central Tsuen Wan, although part had shifted into the three new villages that had moved to the edge of the town in 1964.

In the older villages, conditions were as chaotic as they had been a decade or so earlier. Hoi Pa, which was still in place, had precisely doubled its population between 1957 and 1967, with 8,000 people crammed into an area of about 20 acres.[29] Much of the silk weaving industry was carried on in small workshops erected on some of the former rice fields of Sam Tung Uk, although there was one

---

29. Tsuen Wan District Office files.

Plate 20: A landscape of small industry, looking west from Kwan Mun Hau, 1968. Dyed cloths hang on racks, sheds shelter looms weaving silk brocades, and conical baskets protect preserved fruit. Fuk Loi Tsuen is in the distance.

flatted factory block in a government-developed factory area devoted to silk weaving, with especially high ceilings for the looms. Muk Min Ha, closest to the factory area in west Tsuen Wan, below the level of Castle Peak Road, had many small machinery shops, as it met some of the repair needs of the larger cotton textile mills. The Kwai Chung area was preparing for an enhanced industrial capacity, undergoing site preparation for new factory areas and resettlement estates, while the Gin Drinker's Bay reclamation continued.

The scale of immigration and the singular nature of economic enterprise in Tsuen Wan made for a population composition that differed in some important respects from other areas of Hong Kong (see Table 4.1). Hong Kong–born people were less than 5% of the population in 1968 and there were larger numbers of Chinese people born outside Guangdong/Guangxi than anywhere else in Hong Kong. There were also large numbers of Teochiu people, born in the Chaozhou region of eastern Guangdong. Hong Kong's only other major concentration of Teochiu people was in Kwun Tong, Kowloon's 'new town', which was similar to Tsuen Wan in many respects, although wholly built on reclaimed land and without a core indigenous population.[30]

The early growth of Shanghai-operated factories accounted for the 'northern' population. This part of the population was comprised to a large extent of immigrants from Jiangsu and Zhejiang, so-called 'Shanghainese' or, from a Cantonese perspective, 'northerners'. The Teochiu population was among the last to arrive in Hong Kong, after the influx of Cantonese speakers from the Pearl River delta region. For these later migrants, Tsuen Wan, with its economic opportunities, was a viable

---

30. Kwun Tong became a focus for the Social Research Centre at the Chinese University of Hong Kong. See Ambrose Y. C. King and Rance P. L. Lee, *Social Life and Development in Hong Kong* (Hong Kong: Chinese University Press, 1984).

Table 4.1 Hong Kong population: origins, 1966

Origin	Tsuen Wan	New Territories	Hong Kong Island	Kowloon	New Kowloon	Total
Hong Kong*	4.9	23.4	3.3	2.3	2.4	6.7
Delta[†]	47.4	44.4	52.2	50.2	46.1	48.0
Siyi[‡]	17.1	11.2	19.1	21.1	22.5	19.3
Chaozhou[§]	12.7	9.0	8.0	6.7	16.7	10.9
Guangdong/Guangxi**	4.7	4.3	5.0	7.6	7.2	6.0
Other China	12.6	6.3	10.2	10.3	5.7	7.7
Other	0.5	1.0	2.2	1.7	0.4	1.3
Unknown	0.1	0.1	0.1	0.2	0.1	0.1

Notes:
* Hong Kong, Kowloon, New Territories, and Colony waters.
[†] Guangzhou, Macao, and adjacent places.
[‡] The then counties of Taishan, Kaiping, Xinhui, and Enping.
[§] Eastern Guangdong, but excluding Hakka speakers.
** Elsewhere Guangdong and Guangxi.
Source: K. M. A. Barnett, *Report of the By-census, 1966* (Hong Kong: Government Publications 1968), 34–35.

settlement alternative to Kowloon, where land was often fully occupied. In the late 1960s there were still large numbers of Teochiu squatters in Tsuen Wan, and one resettlement estate already had a large Teochiu-speaking population. In addition to the Cantonese-speaking immigrants, who were in a clear majority, there were a significant number of Hakka-speaking immigrants from southern Dongguan and Huizhou. They were part of a long-established migration which dated from pre-British times.

Tsuen Wan was thus a community of considerable cultural diversity. With each speech group there was some occupational specialization. 'Shanghainese' were almost wholly involved in industrial enterprises either as managers or foremen, or as owners of small textile or engineering establishments. Many silk weavers left the employ of one large silk weaving factory in the early 1950s to set up their own businesses. Cantonese-speaking Pearl River delta migrants formed the bulk of the textile workers. Teochiu people were especially strong in the retail rice trade—an old established link with Chinese migrants from the Chaozhou region in Thailand and Vietnam—but were also involved in petty business such as food hawking and food retailing. They also worked as coolies, and groups of men, sun-tanned and often stripped to the waist, sat by the roadside with carrying poles and grappling hooks, waiting for casual hire. With some exceptions, the Teochiu were the poorest of the land-based population. There was a small, but solidary, population of migrants from Fuzhou, whose male members were typically seamen. The retail meat trade was wholly in the hands of Hakka migrants from Huizhou and Dongguan. Dongguan migrants also predominated in pig and poultry raising, vegetable production, and fruit hawking.

This was Tsuen Wan when we initially saw it, and began our first-hand observations. We focused on the coping strategies of both the indigenous and immigrant populations in this situation of profound change, hoping to learn how they created and maintained support networks in a society that, initially, offered little security. The relationships between the two groups were also of fundamental interest to us, and we were fortunate in being able to follow these questions on to the present millennium—a continuing period of change.

5

Settling In: Kwan Mun Hau, 1968–1970

When we moved into Kwan Mun Hau in late 1968 it consisted of ten neat rows of two-storey gable-roofed houses, on a terraced hillside above Castle Peak Road. A formal gate marked the principal entrance, with Kwan Mun Hau Village in bold calligraphic characters on the cross-beam, the Chinese name of the district officer, and the date: 1965. On the reverse was an aphorism: 'From benevolence comes righteousness' (遵仁由義). Behind the gate was a wide staircase, with houses on both sides. One side was darker, as it was flat, and more cluttered with workshop materials and products on the terraces. A road passed above this area to a car park, dividing Kwan Mun Hau from the adjacent new villages of Yeung Uk and Ho Pui. The two Baak Gung now served their protective role from a terrace near the car park,[1] and the Yau and Chan ancestral halls, similar in size, construction, and materials, could be clearly seen.[2]

Our new home was the upper floor of a house owned by the principal trust of the Yau lineage. Its location directly above the Country Village Store ensured that we were surrounded by activity, including the clatter of mah-jong games downstairs, and people coming and going on another staircase leading from the village.

Missing from the new village was any evidence of agricultural activity, a dramatic change. Eventually some people created tiny vegetable plots and raised chickens at the edges of their terraces, but otherwise they had no use for their agricultural skills. The sources of their new livelihood were apparent: the tenants of diverse origins who lived among them, many on the ground floors so they could operate small workshops; the factories that were very much in evidence in the town itself; and, less visible but also important, buildings in the town from which some families, and the lineages, received rents.

The Decision to Move

The world changes; we must follow and also change.
　　—Kwan Mun Hau native, 1969

How did it happen that the residents of an entire village came to an agreement to move, after previously fruitless discussions with the District Office? The official records are revealing on this subject.

---

1. The land the Kau Wai Kung had occupied had been exchanged for a two-storey house in the new village, which yielded income. One floor served as a village hall, a place where all surnames could meet together rather than separately in their ancestral halls; income from the other maintained the shrines, and subsidized village activities. Not all villages moved their Baak Gung with them; some became 'modernized', held ceremonies of thanks, and sent them back to heaven. Villages that moved in segments were less likely to move theirs.
2. Most lineages that moved in later years had halls similar to these. Muk Min Ha and Sam Tung Uk were exceptions.

Plate 21: View of Kwan Mun Hau from Tai Wo Hau estate, 1968. The village gate is on the lower right, and the Yau and Chan ancestral halls are on the third and fifth terraces. The playground has since been replaced by the Tai Wo Hau MTR station.

Plate 22: An industrial playground: children in Kwan Mun Hau, with our goddaughter Kwok Kin-man, her sister Kin-ping, and our son among them, playing on machinery components from a village workshop, 1969.

The problems are set out in a memo from the district officer south to the district commissioner New Territories, 11 October 1957.[3]

> The layout for the Tsuen Wan area took no notice of the existence of villages occupied by the descendants of pre-Convention inhabitants of the area. In most instances the villages are now at wrong levels and the implementation of the first stages of layout refinements have endangered the lives and property of the villagers. Since the introduction of industry to the area the villages have become swollen, offering as they did for many years the only permanent housing in the area. It is these unsanitary and comparatively heavily populated pockets bristling with traditional rights guaranteed them by the Peking Convention that are preventing the normal and natural development of what will one day be the City of Tsuen Wan. . . .
>
> We have tolerated these villages thinking perhaps that the villagers would, with some encouragement, build modern houses in conformity with the layout and all would be well. I submit that this laissez-faire attitude is impracticable because the land-holdings of the villagers cannot be made to conform to the layout. . . . At the moment the acceptance of a 'plan' for the area is causing hardship to the original inhabitants and this hardship is causing the people to become vociferous against this administration and the Government in general. They say, quite rightly, that a man has every right to build on his own building land and that the District Officer has no right to prevent him as he is now doing—in Kwan Mun Hau and Ham Tin they are becoming a little tired of having their lives and property endangered by flooding and say that the Government is more than partially responsible in allowing [various development projects].
>
> We are criticized from time to time by the Secretariat, P.W.O. and general public for our tardiness. I submit that it is now time to state our problem and to urge extraordinary measures to solve it. I submit a solution which I consider might possibly solve it, provided we handle the matter with sufficient political tact. . . .
>
> . . . our problem [for all of central Tsuen Wan] is the demolition of 297,302 square feet of housing (not including pigsties or temporary structures) in which at least 18,549 people and 54 factories are housed and then persuading 561 landowners or groups of landowners to build modern housing in accordance with a layout imposed upon them without consultation and with little thought for their future welfare. I repeat that left to themselves very little will happen—the villages will hamper essential development and the areas daily become more slum like.
>
> The introduction of this proposed scheme to any one village should be made dependent on the acceptance of all the landowners in the village. The scheme itself may appear over-generous. I myself do not think it is and consider that it will take a great amount of talking and propaganda before we shall be able to obtain the villagers' consent to leaving their pigs, their old houses, and what remains of their traditional way of life.

The District Office files include repeated exchanges regarding the situation, with one from Kwan Mun Hau representatives and 'all the villagers' concluding:

> Furthermore, we most earnestly declare that Government shall be held wholly responsible for whatever loss of life and property which resulted from the development plan by the Government. We write you this letter with the request that you would adhere to the fine tradition of loving your people as your sons and assist us with this matter so we can live a happy life.[4]

Government memos give many details of possible terms and complications, but one states the occurrence of a sudden, and apparently unexpected, change:

---

3. DOTW 33A/388/57.
4. DOTW 33A/388/57.

Now that the opposition to the construction, through one corner of the village, of the No.1 culvert has turned into a spontaneous demand for the removal and reprovisioning of the village to preserve its entirety, an opportunity has arisen and should in my submission be grasped.[5]

The people of Kwan Mun Hau agreed to the revised scheme in early 1963, thus expressing their commitment to preserving the integrity of their village. This is set out in the following news report:

Wah Kiu Yat Po (25/3/63), translated (by the District Office Tsuen Wan [DOTW]) as follows:

The Tsuen Wan Kwan Mun Hau Tsuen has reached agreement with DOTW to remove their village to give way to Tsuen Wan Development. The new village site is on a terraced hill beside the Tsuen Wan Police Station, overlooking Castle Peak Road. 98 house site ballots were drawn yesterday and removal compensation is expected to be paid before April.[6] Terms have been agreed upon are as follows:

A) Government to purchase old house lots at $300/square foot
B) Government to sell to the villagers new house sites at $6/square foot. Villagers will get back a 675 ft site for each old site of 0.01 acre (436 sq ft) surrendered.

Other conditions are:

1) Government undertakes to connect water mains to the new village, opening drainage system and erecting railings.
2) *Tun-fu*[7] fees for removing ancestral halls should not be exceeding $4000.
3) Government agrees to pay transportation for removal.
4) Government agrees to consider . . . transfer of deposits on metres of electricity and water from old village to the new.
5) Erection of pigsties in the New Village will be discussed after removal.

The move that followed apparently went smoothly for everyone except those families whose houses impeded other construction. According to a woman from one, they had to leave their old house earlier than did the others, and live for three years in Tai Wo Hau resettlement estate. She found the experience to be traumatic and the surroundings dirty, and was so distracted that she was hit by a bicycle and injured.

A geomancer confirmed the appropriateness of the new site, although the government had to cover the costs of exorcism because of its history during the occupation. It is conveniently located, as it is close to Castle Peak Road and not far from central Tsuen Wan. Three tenants, former and present proprietors of shops, also moved with the village; the others were moved to Tai Wo Hau.

Before the houses could be built, the two ancestral halls had to be completed and their fittings installed, as senior generations should have priority. The ceremony of moving in is called *yahp fo* (入 夥). Moving the incense burner was very serious, as it represents all the lineage members. Each incense burner and tablet was moved on an auspicious day by men of a senior generation. Assistants ensured that the tablet remained upright, and unicorn dancers accompanied them. The lineages held celebratory banquets when they moved.

The new village was ready for occupancy in late 1964. The ceremony to celebrate its completion was held in the nearby park, with a banquet for nearly 1,000 people. The district officer and assistant district officers attended the ceremony, and the governor cut the ribbon. All households received photographs of the old village, and could also order photographs of those assembled for the celebration.

When we arrived, four years later, we found that the people seemed to be comfortably settled and that they had found new tenants. Those homes we saw were clean and bright, some well-decorated and furnished, but others, belonging to poorer families, relatively bare. We never heard how the discussions

5. DOTW 33A/388/57. DOTW copied from (163) in TW 89/155/88.
6. Villagers had responsibility for arranging for construction in these early resitings, while the government did so in later removals. Hayes, *Tsuen Wan*, 67. He describes the complex discussions leading to the resiting of Ho Pui on pp. 68–74.
7. 尵符. A Daoist charm to counter malevolent spirits and invoke good fortune.

on pig-raising were conducted, but there were no pigs. The villagers later realized that their agreement was inferior to those achieved by other villages, in that their houses had only two storeys, rather than three, and that no provision had been made for the right to build houses (丁屋) for adult sons. Men acknowledged that they did not know to ask for better terms, probably because they were the first to move.

The enormity of the decision the villagers had taken, and the profound changes taking place in their livelihood, as well as in the city and broader community around them, raised many questions as to what their lives would be like after 1964. Tsuen Wan was an extraordinary place at that time, urbanizing and industrializing at a remarkable pace and in a manner that was barely controlled. Kwan Mun Hau and the other removed villages seemed like oases of order in this near-chaos, but their members were inevitably involved in the rapid urban development around them.

What effects did this new environment have on their kinship groups: their households and lineages? What decisions did they make to try to maximize the benefits of their changing situation, and which were imposed on them? How did their distinctive situation as Tsuen Wan natives differentiate them from the immigrants around them, such as their tenants? Certainly, the way they had approached the move, asserting their desire to remain together rather than moving piecemeal to new locations, made a clear statement that they considered the village to be a meaningful unit, with ties among them that should be retained. The emphasis that the lineages placed on building and consecrating new halls affirmed their commitment to their ancestors, and to each other. Many questions remained, however, as to what might happen to these bonds over time.

Standard of Living after the Move

In 1969, a thoughtful Yau man gave his perspective on the different phases the villagers had experienced:

> In the new village we are not much better off than we were in the past. Our income is not stable and we have to think of how to manage. In the past, if we worked hard we would have a good harvest. We produced almost everything we used: rice, vegetables, and fuel. We could catch seafood for free. We raised pigs and chickens. We used money only occasionally to buy clothes; we native people rarely used money. We could eat preserved radish and other such foods. Now everything requires money. We have to buy rice, pay our electricity and water bills, school fees, and transportation. Even the children's breakfast requires 20 to 30 cents. Now if you don't work you can't manage.
>
> There have been three stages. The first was before government raised the level of the area, long before the occupation; it was easy to get useful things. We got our fuel from the hillsides. Our harvest wasn't large, but we still would have some free time. Then we mostly grew rice, bananas, pineapples, and pine trees for oil and firewood. We were closest to the sea, in the delta of the stream, so our fields were fertile and our harvests the largest in Tsuen Wan. We had a small pool by the shore to store sea water and catch the water after rain, so there was no flooding. We had fish from there.
>
> The second stage was after government developed the area and raised it, which led to floods all the time. It was very bad for our houses, and there was lots of stagnant water, which bred mosquitoes. There was flooding with every rain, so we had to move up here, the third stage. The first stage was the best, the second the worst and this stage is in between. The first was one generation above me, the second was after the occupation, and the third is the present.

An elderly Fan man agreed with him, saying that life was better in the past. 'It was hard working in the fields, but we could start and stop when we wanted to. We had to buy very few things, only cloth, and we got our food from the sea and fields. Everything was cheap. We could get fish or crabs just outside our doors. Now we can't even buy them. The water is polluted from the factories and the air is very dirty.'

One has to ask whether women would agree with these statements, however, given that their lives in the past had consisted of unrelenting hard work. One woman, who was about 40 years old, said that she had once envied the young women who worked in factories, as they remained clean and wore nice clothes. She found farming to be dirty and smelly work. However, once she had moved from farming to factory work she decided that she preferred the previous lifestyle, as factory work required standing for long hours, with no time out to eat. She was about to return to work six weeks after giving birth.

Families' standard of living after the move depended primarily on the amount of property they had owned. If they had only a portion of a house in poor condition, and had sold their fields, then they might have received no more than one floor of a house in the new village or, worse yet, they might have had to take a ten-year low-interest loan to pay for it. In addition, they had to partition, decorate, and furnish the new house, and install a kitchen, perhaps borrowing even more. Those who had substantial property, in contrast, might have received several village houses and possibly even the exchange rights for a building, or a portion thereof, in the town. Thus, some families had to repay a loan and had no rental income, so that they were forced to work, while others could live comfortably from rents as well as whatever employment they might have. If they did not like their working conditions, they could leave. Each floor of a village house rented for about $200 per month, which was equal to at least half the income that men earned at the kinds of jobs that they reported they had. These differences in living standards were readily apparent inside people's homes.

Education and Employment

A major change that had taken place since the occupation was the widespread availability of public education. By 1968 all children, boys and girls, attended primary school, and illiteracy was rapidly disappearing. A new primary school, the 'Three Village School', had been built directly behind the village. The change to universal literacy among young women happened quickly, and some girls entered or completed middle school, which gave them access to new types of employment. They no longer had to depend upon manual labour but instead could find factory work or clerical employment. Not long after, some went on to university, including one who then became a teacher. The same was true of boys, some of whom had completed middle school while several were attending university by the 1970s. The cost of secondary education remained a problem for some families, but committed young people worked, and went to school part-time. One result of universal education was that all the younger people were fluent in Cantonese, the language of instruction and Hong Kong's lingua franca.

Another change was that those native women who were not from very poor families could simply be housewives, with occasional putting-out work. Doing housework was still hard, as they did laundry by hand and often had many children to care for, but it was easier than their earlier work, and they were well aware of this difference. Some still had traditional stoves, but they now went to construction sites or markets to collect scrap lumber for fuel. Some of this was very heavy, so that their carrying poles bent under the weight. The wood had to be cut and split before it could be used. Such shared activity reinforced the bonds among native women.

Women who were not working or caring for many children sometimes had spare time, making possible leisure activities such as mah-jong or television. One said that the old women had trouble understanding this change in lifestyle: that women no longer were forced to spend all their time carrying heavy loads. They did not even have to carry water, as it was piped into their houses.

Those families whose children had achieved higher education benefitted, as they could obtain better-paying jobs. It was customary that employed children, both sons and daughters, should give most of their earnings to their parents and grandparents. The amount they gave was a common topic of conversation. For example, one woman said that her oldest daughter earned $135 every two weeks

Plate 23: A village woman adjusting the weight of her awkward load of firewood as she carries it up the stairs to the village shortly before the birth of her sixth child, 1968.

and gave $100 to her, $15 to her grandfather, and kept $20 for herself. Her second daughter earned less, but still gave her $70 every two weeks, and their four children had told them that when they were old and unable to work they would help them. Like so many people, this woman was preoccupied with all the bills that had to be paid, now that their economy was completely cash-based.

Men worked according to their qualifications and initiative. Some were drivers, and employers preferred to entrust their valuable vehicles to native men who were not going to damage them and then leave. Others bought cars themselves and worked as unlicensed taxis. Those who previously had family businesses generally continued in them, unless they had retired. The Fan man who had been trained by the Japanese as a machinist continued to run his factory with a partner from the Yau lineage, and since he knew how to alter his machinery to diversify the products, it was flourishing. Several young village men worked in clerical positions, in such contexts as banking, and one was a teacher.

Some men simply depended on rents, and were criticized behind their backs for setting their sons a bad example. Others had trouble finding any consistent and satisfactory employment, making their families' financial situations precarious if they had no rental income. Factory jobs were readily available, but they offered relatively low pay and demanded long and inflexible hours. According to one factory worker, who like many others his age had relatively little education:

> In the factory I work 12 hours per day with six days a year off. . . . If I have any family trouble, I have to take special leave. So whenever I am free I have a lot to do. Friends and relatives wouldn't choose my holidays for weddings, meetings, funerals, or village rituals, so I have lost almost all opportunities to participate in these things. Sometimes I don't even know about them. This makes a person dull and stupid, with no time to do anything. I'm not human anymore; I always work like a machine. The work isn't hard, but the hours are very long: I have to be in Kowloon from 7:30 [a.m.] until 6:30 [p.m.].

He said that employers prefer native people, as they don't change jobs so much: 'If you tell us to fly away we can't, because our property is here.' His family was one that clearly was having trouble making ends meet. He, his wife, his mother, and five children lived on one floor of a poorly furnished house. His wife sewed dolls' clothes as putting-out work.

There were others, like him, who worked outside Tsuen Wan, including one who did skilled work at reservoirs in Castle Peak and Lantau under much better working conditions. He had Sundays and statutory holidays off, as well as ten days' annual holidays. Furthermore, he said that he had income from rents. Many Kwan Mun Hau people continued to work at the Texaco depot, as it was conveniently located and offered secure employment.

In contrast to the situation elsewhere in the New Territories, where emigration was so common, we found only one man who, with his wife, worked in a restaurant in England, although we have since learned of another. His family was poor, and neither of his brothers worked, as one was ill and the other unemployed. They somehow lived on money that the émigré sent back to support his children, who lived with the family, and his brother's wife's factory wages. Her husband readily admitted their poverty, saying that they were 'a very poor and simple family'. He, too, had gone to England to work, but had soon returned because he could not stand the cold, thus incurring major expense in airfares that the family could ill afford. This situation caused great stress to their elderly mother who, in addition, was caring day and night for her blind and terribly feeble husband.

Social Changes

Television had become available to Tsuen Wan in 1967, and quickly became popular. Some people saw it as positive, and an elderly man who was barely literate said that it introduced him to ideas and places that he never would have dreamed of in the past. People used it as an important source of news. It opened new worlds to them, and served to destroy some deep-seated ideas, such as legends about the moon once they had seen moon landings take place. It is hard to imagine how people interpreted some of what they saw. For us it seemed most incongruous to see elderly women in their traditional Hakka clothing watching programmes about Superman, for example, or violent westerns. Its offerings of Cantonese opera, however, had special appeal. Television's social effects were profound. Its increasing prevalence meant that there was less conversation and fewer groups gathering outdoors for discussion. It also undermined younger people's knowledge of Hakka.

In addition to television, Tsuen Wan now offered other diversions for people with a little time and money. There were several cinemas, and one elderly woman was known for going daily. They acknowledged that their new situation gave them many more such opportunities. According to one elderly man:

> People are also fond of spending money in teahouses, and usually go to the best. Even old women will spend three dollars in a teahouse, whereas in the past they spent ten cents for congee with fried bread. Now we all have become wealthy, not from our efforts but instead from our ancestors. We became wealthy from the village moving and our property increasing in value. Previously people had a lot of money but they didn't spend it; now they spend it. Now they have many enjoyments: television, educating their children, going to the teahouse, and having good food.

People also gambled, playing mah-jong and other games, some for high stakes. The older women liked to play Hakka cards and also gambled with them for small sums.

Another change was in people's personal appearance. During the previous decade, most middle-aged and younger women had their long hair cut, rather than wearing it in a bun, following changing fashions, and some later had it permed. They still wore Chinese pant-suits (衫褲), but younger women often had them made from patterned cloth instead of dark colours, and they sometimes were fitted, with short sleeves. Older women continued to wear loose-fitting black pant-suits, with distinctive Hakka head cloths, long rectangles that covered their hair, or dark scarves. In great contrast, teenage girls and young women wore Western-style clothes, with fitted pants often in the bell-bottom style of the time, and colourful blouses.

Men said that they had worn Chinese-style clothes, which they praised as being comfortable and durable, when young, but only the most conservative still wore them. Children usually wore Western clothes, with the exception of some girls' school uniforms. Traditional baby carriers, made of red or pink cloth with auspicious symbols, were still in common use.

Medical Care and Its Effects

An especially significant change was the ready availability of modern medical care, both Western and Chinese. Parents usually took their children to Western doctors because of their treatment's effectiveness, whereas elderly people generally preferred the preventive properties of Chinese medicine. Everyone seemed to be aware of the vast difference that had been made by modern medical care. By this time, a general clinic and at least one maternity clinic existed, in addition to the privately run Seventh-Day Adventist hospital. From these clinics, patients could be referred to larger government or private hospitals in Kowloon or on Hong Kong Island if necessary.

The availability of effective medical care, as well as the benefits of an improved diet and sanitation, made a deep impression on everyone old enough to remember the previous conditions, when the only remedies were based on folk knowledge, which could do more harm than good, especially when the victims so often were young children. Many people expressed beliefs like those of this woman:

> Now one birth means one alive, for which we must thank the scientific Western doctors. Even in the past we didn't trust the Chinese doctors, but we had no choice. There was no permanent Western doctor in Tsuen Wan before the Japanese. Afterwards there was only one for a long time.

Furthermore, many babies were being born. In one year there were four lanterns hung in the Yau ancestral hall, and another year there were six. The Chan lineage of Sam Tung Uk had discontinued their lantern-raising ceremony, but when eight sons were born in one year they held it again.

These increases in the numbers of children surviving were good, but also created pressure on families' resources. In the late 1960s the realization that every child born almost certainly would survive was momentous. Many families felt the financial pressure of supporting the large numbers of children whom they suddenly had, especially given that all, boys and girls, would attend school, with its fees and many incidental expenses. Simply managing and caring for six or more children was also challenging, made easier only if a mother-in-law was available, and willing and able to help. Even childbirth now involved expense, as people realized the benefits of giving birth in a modern medical setting. The cost varied according to the kind of care received. Some women had been mistreated by clinic staff, who were unsympathetic, treating them like ignorant peasants who were bearing too many children, but this situation was improving.

At that time, a major concern was how to effectively space and limit the number of children born, moving away from the past situation in which women 'bore children until they could bear no more' (生到冇得生). Fortunately, birth control was a benefit of the available medical care, and women frequently discussed the effectiveness and possible risks of the methods offered. Everyone, even the oldest women and men, knew about the availability of birth control. There was no perceptible objection to it, although it was considered to be women's responsibility. They learned about it through the clinics and hospitals where they now gave birth. Family planning workers met with them, and explained the various methods so that they could choose which was best for them. A few were sterilized, despite the fact that it involved surgery, if they were certain that they did not want any more children and their husbands were willing to sign consent forms.

In the late 1960s families were still large, ranging from four to eight and even ten children, but it was certain that they would decline in size in the near future. People frequently discussed the number of children they wanted and their fears that they might become delinquents (*feijai* 飛仔), especially as opium addiction was being replaced by heroin addiction. Furthermore, couples saw the value of having girls as well as boys. Many said that a girl was as good as a boy, or better, although almost certainly there were none who would say that a family should have no sons, as a male heir was still needed. Girls were valued for their income, their filiality, and their household help. Most commonly, people said that they would like an equal number of each, two boys and two girls, as two would leave (at marriage) and two daughters-in-law would come in. There certainly were examples of people who had no daughters and hoped to have at least one and others who hoped for a more equal balance.[8]

A middle-aged man summarized the situation:

> In the past more children were born, but now there are more alive. In the past, if a child got seriously sick he had a 70% chance of dying. Now not so many are born, as we have birth control. In the past, people wanted to have as many as possible. Because we Fan have only a few people, we always wanted more, especially my father. If our numbers could increase, then we could speak with a loud voice. The best number to have is four, two sons and two daughters. To have two is useless, with no investment or increase. Some say that three is best, but for our Fan family four is best.

Care at the End of Life

The one situation in which families rarely used modern medicine was in caring for the very elderly. If death took place in a hospital, they did not allow the body to be brought back into the village,[9] although the funeral could take place on the immediate periphery, whereas if it took place at home the rites could take place in and near the person's home. In the past the Chan lineage customarily permitted a dying person to be carried to the ancestral hall, where the funeral could be held, but this was no longer done. When we were there we knew only one older man who died in hospital, but several others who were cared for at home regardless of their families' means, as people believed they could offer them better care. Doing all that was needed for a bedridden elderly person was exhausting, especially if they were old men whose equally elderly wives took primary responsibility for their care. One Yau family with some means engaged a Chan couple who, like other villagers, were called 'our own people', to stay with the 90-year-old grandmother of the family at the end of her life. The woman cared for her during the day, and the man sat with her at night. More of this responsibility would doubtless have been taken by her daughter-in-law if she had been there, but she was away in hospital following serious surgery.

One reason why death should take place at home was that it helped to ensure that family members would be there with the dying person. It also guaranteed that older women were present who had detailed knowledge of the rites that should be carried out before, during, and after death.[10] When an old person was about to die, the women of that surname were called, regardless of the hour, if they were not there already. They were not afraid to be in the presence of death, as they knew how it should be managed for the benefit of the dying person and subsequent generations, and without harm to

8. See Janet W. Salaff, *Working Daughters of Hong Kong: Filial Piety or Power in the Family?* (New York: Cambridge University Press, 1981).
9. We later heard of one exception; an elderly woman whose funeral was held outside the door of the Chan hall, although she had died in hospital.
10. See Patrick Hase, 'Observations at a Village Funeral', in Faure, Hayes, and Birch, *From Village to City*, 132–33. James L. Watson, 'Funeral Specialists in Cantonese Society', in *Death Ritual in Late Imperial and Modern China*, ed. Watson and Rawski, 116–17.

themselves.[11] When death had occurred, they dressed the body before it stiffened, helping men if the deceased was a man, or dressing him themselves if no men were available. One such woman said that she often helped with marriage, funeral, and lineage rites, as she had learned what should be done from watching older people, she had many sons and daughters ('a good fate'), and was willing and poor, so she appreciated the lucky money she received. Everything had to be done properly, with no mistakes or inappropriate things said.

Great attention was paid to how and when the person died, as this was considered to affect not only their wellbeing but also that of their descendants. A young Yau woman told me about her grandmother's death:

> She died peacefully. She was smiling. The time when she died was good: the tide was high then, and it was an auspicious day. . . . She understood everything that we said until the end, and knew that my sister had given birth to a son. She said that she felt comfortable. A few days previously her daughters had bathed her in pomelo leaf water. After that she couldn't move her legs. They said that meant that she had a clean life and would have a clean death.

Initially, she was laid out on a mat on the floor of their house, dressed in 'long-life clothes': a black robe with a rank badge and a skirt, and a gold paper headdress with pompoms. Her face was covered with a special paper.[12] In her right hand was a willow branch, and in the left a chopstick with five cakes speared on it, because on the third day she would reach a river, where she would wash her hands. After noticing that they smelled bad she would realize that she had died. She would find a bridge to cross the river to enter the underworld, and the cakes were for her to give to dogs there so they would not chase her.[13] A brick was against her feet, with another perpendicular to it holding an oil lamp. On each side was a bowl of rice, one holding one chopstick and the other holding two. Beyond them was a big clay pot holding incense and candles.

The women had arranged these symbolic objects, and also directed her immediate family members, who were sitting silently on both sides. Outside it was noisier, and village people were present,[14] as well as her coffin, with its lid propped open. The funeral offerings included pigs' heads, one given by each daughter.[15] Hakka funeral priests conducted the rites, directing the mourners, chanting Daoist texts while beating percussion instruments. Their roles are to guide the soul and ensure that it is settled in the underworld and does not wander lost.[16] Villagers came in and offered incense, receiving 'lucky money' in return.

The silence indoors was suddenly broken when a closely related elderly woman came in and after a long pause started to lament, each line ending in sobs. It was unrestrained, unselfconscious, and deeply distressing. From time to time she lifted the paper covering the deceased woman's face and appeared to call her.

---

11. A Cantonese neighbour said that these Hakka women came to give help without being asked, in contrast to Cantonese women.
12. Once in her coffin, special covers given by sisters and daughters were placed over her, large numbers of them being said to make a great impression in the afterlife. In addition, women relatives gave pieces of cloth with the donor's name applied, which were displayed in the house and the procession, and afterwards kept or used. In the past, her clothes would have been washed and then used to make clothing for the family's children, as would the white mourning robes. The mat on which she had been laid out could be used for the children to play on. All were believed to have great protective power. See, in contrast, James L. Watson, 'Of Flesh and Bones', in Watson and Watson, *Village Life in Hong Kong*, 368–70.
13. A lament advises her to testify to the officials that she died of illness, not suicide, and had sons and daughters, so she will be allowed to cross.
14. At funerals we observed, men who were not family members in mourning gathered outdoors, chatting, laughing, eating, and drinking. In all we observed portions of about five village funerals, of which this and one other were the most elaborate.
15. In the past these had to be eaten, but now they do not.
16. For comparison, see J. L. Watson, 'Funeral Specialists in Cantonese Society', in *Death Ritual in Late Imperial and Modern China*, ed. Watson and Rawski, 109–34, in which corpse handlers and pipers are described as being essential. The priest as 'choreographer' was similar, but without the atmosphere of fear described by Watson.

By evening the grandmother had been placed in her coffin and her descendants were wearing mourning clothes, differentiated according to their relationship to her. A younger man of the lineage had gone to inform relatives. During the night the priests continued their rites, but broke the mood with a play that they performed in the middle of the night. They wore costumes and used mime and paper objects to create an entertaining story about a magistrate, said to amuse the 'ghosts' so they would be kind to the deceased. By the next afternoon the coffin had been moved to an open area, where offerings were set out and men of both lineages worshipped. People were invited to take a last look at her face before the coffin was closed. It was late afternoon before they moved it into the van that would carry it, as they had to wait until the Agriculture and Fisheries Department staff went off duty before proceeding with the burial.

An impressive procession formed, and made a complete circuit around central Tsuen Wan. Before it set off, three women holding lighted sticks of incense in lanterns circled the coffin, speaking several phrases, and then were taken to the grave site in a ceremony called 'sending fire' (送火).[17] They circled the open grave, called the 'eye', three times to 'brighten the place', being careful not to meet the coffin as they returned. In the procession, one son carrying her tablet walked first, followed by nine lorries with wreaths (花圈) presented by related people and organizations, three bands, the van with the coffin, Yau lineage men playing gongs and cymbals, 20 cars, people walking, and a police car. Paper representing low-grade money was scattered in front of the coffin to appease any wandering spirits that might be present. We stopped at an open space where everyone bowed, and then a group of us, including one granddaughter, ran back to their house, where we had to step over a purifying fire before returning home. Her granddaughter turned on the lights 'so her soul could find her way back'.

The priests had left instructions as to what should be done on each of the five 'sevens' (weeks) that the family had decided would be the length of the mourning period. Women could lament on those days but not afterwards. Her soul tablet remained in the house during this time, together with paper offerings: a large house, nicely detailed; two servants; a set of clothes; and mounds of gold and silver foil, representing mountains of gold and silver for her use in the underworld. Her daughters had also bought fields for her, represented by green scrolls, 'because we are farming people'.[18]

A few weeks after her death, her two daughters and three women married into Yau families went to a temple to consult a spirit medium (問米婆). It is women, as *yin* (陰) beings, who act as mediums, and who consult them as needed by families. These women enquired about the grandmother's wellbeing, and that of other deceased family members. The spirit mediums are women said to have 'fairy bones' (仙骨), born with the ability to go into trances and communicate with the spirits of family members in the next life, speaking with their words.[19] The women first asked the Kitchen God, who gave details of the deceased person, so they knew it was the real Kitchen God. Then they communicated with the grandmother, her husband, their son who had died at age 15, and wives in two generations who had predeceased their husbands. They were particularly concerned to ask the grandmother her opinion of the ceremony, and whether she had met any family members yet. They also asked her what she would like for the ceremony at the end of mourning, and asked the others whether they were peaceful and happy, and what offerings they wanted.

---

17. They repeated this procedure on the two subsequent days, 'taking fire' to the deceased and saying that now he or she must start to cook and eat there, but also 'brightening the road' for the soul to return home. The family also should save a place at the table for the soul during the initial mourning period, serving him or her food, and on each of the 'sevens' that followed. Had the deceased been a man, the rite would have been performed by two women, also village residents of any of the three surnames and considered to have 'good fates'.

18. Such offerings are burned at the end of mourning to send them to the soul in the underworld for whom they are destined.

19. See also Jack M. Potter, 'Cantonese Shamanism', in *Religion and Ritual in Chinese Society*, ed. Arthur P. Wolf (Stanford: Stanford University Press, 1974), 207–31.

The oldest daughter of the family had given birth to a son on the day that the grandmother had died. Normally her mother would give her clothes and a carrying strap for the baby, and special foods for herself, but her mother was still hospitalized and unaware of the death. The older women were adamant that birth and death should not be mixed, and so these things could not be done. The baby's mother had to stay away, the family could not visit her, nor could they have the small feast they had planned to celebrate the baby's first month. They worshipped at home ten days later instead.

In the night at the end of the fifth week, the final ceremony was held, presided over by the priests and the women. More offerings appeared, including 18 paper chests of paper money and clothing given by her married daughters. The family bathed in purifying pomelo leaf water, having already purified the bowls and chopsticks. Women made red *tongyuhn* in sugar syrup, to signify happiness. The priests chanted, but then everything fell silent. Soul tablets representing the grandmother's deceased son and her oldest son's first wife were dotted by a relative, the dotting being to prevent the spirits from unintentionally harming the young men who would carry them.

At daybreak there was frenzied activity. The offerings were burned, red threads were pinned on people and objects, and the family threw their mourning clothes onto the fire. Some ran through the house carrying burning paper. The ceremony (上臺) to install the grandmother's soul into the ancestral hall then began.

The family had agreed, after consulting with spirits of other deceased family members, that they should be installed with her at this time. A system of seniority prevails, in which no one can be installed in the hall until he or she has reached at least 60 years of age (in total, before and after death), with no surviving relatives who are older. A woman's husband must have predeceased her. When an older relative dies, those junior to him or her could be included in the ceremony and 'be seated in the ancestral hall' (坐祠堂). In this case, the grandmother's middle son and her first daughter-in-law, both of whom had died childless, had said through the spirit medium that they wished to go at that time. Her son would not yet have reached the age of 60, but this did not seem to pose problems. Likewise, the daughter-in-law's husband was still alive, but her wishes were honoured. She may have requested this because her husband and his second wife had been neglecting her, leaving her soul tablet behind when they moved house, so she did not know where to find them. She had taken revenge on his wife by pulling her off her motor scooter, injuring her. She wept through the spirit medium, as she had died young and childless, and they had not even taught their children to care for her soul.

Six tablets were included in the ceremony, as it was also offered for others to enjoy, including a tablet for all the gods ordinarily worshipped, one for all their ancestors for three generations above them, and a tablet for the grandmother's husband and his deceased first wife. The grandmother's youngest son, sheltered under an umbrella held by his brother, carried a pair of baskets on a carrying pole to the ancestral hall, one holding her tablet and the other her incense burner. Her deceased son's tablet was carried in his incense pot by this brother's second son, who had been given to him in adoption. The childless daughter-in-law's tablet was carried in her incense burner by a son born to the oldest son's second wife. The young men carrying the tablets were protected by wearing red sashes and being sheltered under umbrellas.

A red cloth representing a road was stretched between the altar table and the altar itself, and the priest, who directed them in Hakka,[20] took ashes and incense from each of the incense burners of those to be installed, and placed them in the main incense pot. From then on, the three souls were considered to be at peace, seated with their ancestors.[21]

---

20. The older women were also important in determining complex details of the ceremony.
21. It was clear from these ceremonies and the way people viewed them that women were considered to be ancestors in their own right, as were men. A knowledgeable Yau lineage elder affirmed this when asked. Rubie S. Watson states that in the Punti village of Ha Tsuen women might become temporary domestic ancestors, but never lineage ancestors. 'Class Differences and Affinal Relations in South China', in Watson and Watson, *Village Life in Hong Kong*, 97–98.

On the third night after a death, families expected that the soul would return home to see his or her family, and they looked for signs that this had happened. This seemed to be that aspect of the soul that was associated with the grave, not that which was making its journey through the underworld. Families were pleased if a soul returned, as this meant that she had loved her home. Signs of return included the consumption of offerings, sand from the grave that appeared on the floor, and sounds and movements typical of the person. Furthermore, after the grandmother's daughter-in-law's hospitalizations, she heard footsteps on the stairs. She then felt her mosquito net being pulled aside, heard sounds of the tea that was by her bed being drunk, and saw a black shadow. This pleased her, as she believed it showed that her mother-in-law cared about her, and the family. People's only concern was that the soul not touch the living, especially children, who were especially vulnerable and could be made ill by this.[22]

Children's illnesses that could not be cured by normal means were thought to be possible signs that a deceased family member needed something, and in response a woman might consult a spirit medium. For example, an illness of our neighbours' baby daughter was unresponsive to conventional treatment, so her mother then consulted a spirit medium, and learned from her own father's spirit that he was concerned that his sons were now grown and should not get involved with bad women. He told her that there were other spirits with him who needed money, so she burned some ritual paper money for them.

The next life is much like this one, a social world in which family members can be together, make friendships, and remain in contact with those in this life, the world of light (陽), the next being the world of shadow (陰). Entering the shadow world takes three days, and involves crossing a river and testifying before the god of the underworld. Family members meet the newly deceased person and give him or her an introduction to life there, such as taking him to where he can receive offerings.

Sometimes people who died violent deaths, such as by murder or suicide, remained unsettled, and disturbed the household by moving furniture and making strange noises. This could be very upsetting indeed. One woman's husband had been murdered in the 1930s, and he did this. She had to consult a spirit medium to ask him to stop, as the children were still young and were being frightened.

The soul, then, had (and has) three locations where offerings could be made and communication could take place. One was at its grave and then, once the bones had been lifted out and arranged in a mortuary urn, ideally in a tomb. The soul should be informed when this transfer is to take place, so that it would not be separated from its bones and unable to find them. The second aspect of the soul is in the underworld, and the third in its soul tablet. Not many souls had individual domestic tablets; some of those who had died young had them, for example, and others did not.[23] This likely depended on whether there were younger members of the family to worship them. If a tablet's location was changed, it was important that it be led to the new location with burning incense, otherwise the soul could wander lost. They could then be incorporated into the hall tablet when they reach appropriate seniority.[24]

Qingming remains an important festival during which families make offerings to recently deceased family members in their graves, and to those more distant ancestors in whose memory trusts of property have been dedicated. More distant lineage ancestors are worshipped only in the autumn, at Chongyang.

It is important to note that most of what we have discussed above applies specifically to natives. Immigrants could worship their ancestors and communicate with them through spirit mediums, but

---

22. In comparison, see James L. Watson, 'Of Flesh and Bones', in Watson and Watson, *Village Life in Hong Kong*, 355–89.
23. Senior family members often have large formal portraits hung facing the front of the house. There sometimes were individual paper tablets on the west wall of the Chan hall, presumably to receive offerings until they could be installed in the main tablet.
24. Even those who had died as children could be installed in the hall tablet when the time came if brought by a senior family member, an example being a boy who had died at the age of seven.

they were not living in their own territory and could not hold a funeral in their houses or bury a deceased family member on a mountainside. They had to hold funerals in public spaces or funeral parlours, and bury their dead in public cemeteries or use cremation, placing the ashes in monasteries.

Marriage and Its Rites

During our first time in Tsuen Wan, a number of weddings took place, but they were all marriages of daughters. The reasons for the lack of men's marriages may have been the paucity of births during the occupation, and the fact that men tended to be older at marriage than were women. Negotiations were underway for the marriage of one man, an oldest son who was 32 years old. He was to marry a woman from another Tsuen Wan village. His family was looking for housing for them, and also was meeting with her family to determine the nature of the exchanges that would take place. By that time villagers were marrying non-Hakka people. One of the weddings we witnessed was between a native woman and a Cantonese man.[25] In these situations, accommodation had to be made to each other's ceremonial gifts and procedures. For example, Hakka people did not shelter the bride under a red umbrella as she left her natal family, believing this to be unlucky, and they would not compromise on this custom. Once the bride approached her husband's home, however, her family's customs no longer applied.

Other aspects of marriage had been changing since the occupation. Couples tended to be older when they married, and although some were introduced, they still were able to meet and make their own decisions. Marriage laments were gone, as there was no context in which to learn them. Women had chosen their future husbands, and knew they would be able to see their natal families frequently. Perhaps most startling was the fact that some women were pregnant when they married. This was laughingly called a 'modern dowry' (摩登嫁妝), a not altogether negative term. The bride could still be presented to the ancestors in the hall, as long as the pregnancy did not show.

Marriage rites still consisted of several stages, starting with meetings between the families to negotiate the various exchanges. We saw the departures of several village brides, from the distribution of cakes by their parents, to the *seuhng tauh* ceremony after her purifying bath in pomelo leaf water, the gathering of village women to make red *tongyuhn*, to the groom's arrival the next day to meet his bride, heavily made-up, in her red dress. After pouring tea for her parents and senior relatives, the couple departed, preceded by her dowry carried by women with 'good fates', and with the bride's ritual actions directed by older women.

We were not able to witness the wedding of a man until our return visit in 1975, but we saw many of the proceedings because he was from a family whom we knew well. Marriage formalities at that time consisted of the same procedures as they had previously, with the important difference that the groom himself, accompanied by his men, some with gongs and cymbals, went to the bride's home at the agreed-on auspicious time to meet her.[26] His entrance was barred by the young women accompanying her, with whom he had to bargain for access. Once inside, the bride was brought to him at an auspicious time, and they bowed three times to any ancestral tablets or portraits that were there, after which they respectfully poured tea for her seated parents and other senior relatives, who gave her jewellery and gave the couple lucky money. As the couple left, her parents wept. They went to Kwan Mun Hau by car and entered the village through the gate with a blast of firecrackers, gongs, and cymbals.

In the main room of his parents' home, the couple poured tea for his parents and other senior relatives in descending order after pouring a little on the floor for the family earth god. His relatives gave the bride jewellery and lucky money, and the older women instructed her on how to address

---

25. We were told that some immigrants were reluctant to marry local Hakka women because of their ability to do heavy work, as it would be 'like marrying a water buffalo'.
26. He first went to worship at the hall and temple, accompanied by senior men and women.

Plate 24: Village women carrying a bride's dowry out of the village, 1968. The foot-washing basin, now made of plastic instead of wood, is a symbol of fertility.

Plate 25: Women carrying a bride's dowry chest past rosewood planks from a furniture workshop in the village, 1976.

each of them. Hung on the wall were blankets or lengths of cloth identified with the names of the husbands of the married-out female relatives who had presented them. The bride then waited in their bedroom where a pair of dragon and phoenix candles burned, and the bed had been covered with sweets, symbols of a happy union, by women with good fates.

They then went to the ancestral hall with his father for the *gaau jih* ceremony, conducted by a senior man of the lineage who was fluent in Hakka and could read the text, and organized by the senior women. The ceremony was very formal and serious, except when an older woman intervened to correct the leader, and everyone laughed. The groom and his father worshipped first, and then his father stepped back and the bride was brought to stand by her husband to continue the ceremonies of hand-washing, offering incense, and kowtowing as prayers were read. An assistant burned paper offerings for the first three generations of ancestors. The couple left the hall facing the tablet, walking backwards so as not to turn their backs on the ancestor.[27] A restaurant banquet followed.

Family Membership in the New Context

Elizabeth: 'How many people are in your household?'

Yau elder (annoyed for the first time in our experience with him): 'Even members themselves cannot always say how many people there are in their households. Some members may live in Kowloon. Parents may live separately but eat with their children. Who can say how many people are in a household?'[28]

His answer was astute in that households may be defined in various ways, including those based on commonly held property, and those defined by people living and/or eating together. The former may include more than one of the latter, as households defined by property held in common sometimes include more than one domestic unit. In Chinese these can be identified by the terms used when they divide: 'dividing the property' (分家), 'dividing to live' (分開住), and 'dividing to eat' (分開食〔吃〕). Anthropologists call them joint families if they include two or more married couples in any one generation living together (Chinese: 'large household' 大家庭), stem families if they include a married couple in one generation and one, or the survivor of one, in the generation above living together; and nuclear families if they include only a couple and their child or children.

There was the possibility that members might live elsewhere, but this was rare, given the availability of local employment, although a few were studying abroad. Of 19 households,[29] the only family defined as a 'large household' by a member was actually made so only by including a couple living overseas. Those presently living together included the elderly parents, a son with his wife and children, an unmarried son, and the children of the overseas couple, so they were defined as joint only by common property (their house) and economy. Of the remainder ten were stem families and eight nuclear families,[30] leading us to conclude that present circumstances did not foster the maintenance of very complex families, although stem families were possible and apparently valued.

Several government policies had affected household size and structure. In the years leading up to the village resiting, it may have been hard for households to divide to live, because policy did not allow

27. The leader said it had been simplified, and should have included a pig, or at least a boiled pig's head, among the offerings. They also should have worshipped once between the two altar tables.
28. Myron Cohen: '[T]here may be more to domestic units than meets the demographer's eye'. 'Developmental Process in the Chinese Domestic Group', in *Family and Kinship in Chinese Society*, ed. Maurice Freedman (Stanford: Stanford University Press, 1970), 27.
29. In the interview sample.
30. A complication was that three households had people living with them who were not part of the patriline. Two included married daughters, and another had two of the wife's sister's children co-resident but not members. A further complication was that six men known to us had or were said to have second wives, all living separately from the first, but this was too sensitive to discuss. They were taken without ceremony, and their children may or may not have been recognized in the father's lineage.

the expansion of houses or the building of new ones. At the time of the move, the District Office had urged families to settle any outstanding property matters, however, so as to minimize complications.[31] Finally, houses in the new village were uniform in size and configuration and could not be expanded,[32] restricting the number of people who could live together. Some of the poorer households were very crowded, with up to 12 people in a floor space of 675 square feet, but it was virtually impossible for large joint families who still held their property in common to eat together, although brothers with sufficient property might live in adjacent houses, as each floor of a village house has its own kitchen space and toilet. To actually live and eat as a single unit would, as one man said, make their houses crowded 'like a chicken coop or a pigeon cage'.

Elizabeth's interviews included questions comparing household size and structure in about 1940 with those in 1969–1970. The average size of 15 of the 19 households, as defined by people living and eating together and ignoring those defined by common property for the moment, had increased substantially, from an average of 4.4 to 7.8. This growth can be explained by the great increase in the number of surviving children. Seventy percent of household members in 1969–1970 were unmarried people under the age of 30. The four households that were smaller than they had been were ones that formerly had been joint, but had since divided to live and eat. Two had also divided their property. Several of these had been very large, and if their changes in size since 1940 are included in the comparison, the amount of relative growth in the size of households was actually less, from 7.3 in 1940 to 8.2[33] in 1970.

Ascertaining household structure in about 1940 with confidence was difficult, as this was also dependent on memory, sometimes that of married-in women. It appears that five households had been joint,[34] four stem, and ten nuclear. In comparison, there was a significant increase in stem households, to ten, by 1970. This may reflect a decline in mortality among the elderly.

People's opinions about married sons living with their parents, and couples in the same generation living together, were mixed. Whether this was even possible depended on the space available, of course, although people's tolerance of crowding and lack of privacy impressed us. A few said unequivocally that sons should live with their parents, and two men, one middle-aged and one older, said that it is amusing for old people to be with younger people and children, one adding that the older members can help in the household while the younger ones work. He said: 'Although our furniture is always broken by children jumping on it, I prefer that to having a sofa for 10 or 20 years with no one sitting on it.'

The majority said that the generations' ways of thinking were likely to be different. With regard to forming joint families, some said that sons' wives were unlikely to get along, sharing one kitchen, as they now were educated and were marrying in from diverse places. Likewise, some said that in the past all men had the same kind of education and worked in agriculture, so there were not differences among family members as there are now. Several people said that if a son was able to move out, this would show that he had initiative. In sum, almost everyone expressed a degree of ambivalence about this matter.

Regardless of whether elderly parents lived with their sons, several people acknowledged that they might need their financial help, as there were no public pensions. Those people without descendants faced serious challenges. An elderly couple we described earlier depended for their care on their nephew's widow, who was poor and still responsible for most of her nine children. We also heard of two women without descendants who had entered old people's homes, when resorting to institutions of any kind was rare.

---

31. Unpublished records, Tsuen Wan District Office.
32. With one exception, that of a man with special connections.
33. Excluding co-resident affines.
34. Of these, one man had lived in Kowloon with his second wife, the first remaining in Tsuen Wan with his brother's family.

Men said that sons would normally divide the family property after their parents' death. The oldest son should get first choice, or somewhat more, because he would have primary responsibility for the care of their souls. Two men discussed contemporary inheritance law, some aspects of which went against their traditions as New Territories natives, they believed. One man said that a division of property would be a new experience for them, because they had never had property to divide. At the other end of the scale was one of the wealthiest households in the village, with businesses and property held in common, although they did not live together. According to a middle-aged member:

> My father's generation divided to live at the end of the occupation. They didn't want to but were forced by circumstances. It was hard to manage so many people. Many households divided to live at that time. . . . We three brothers divided to live when we moved here, as these houses are too small.

Another man said that his household had wanted to divide to live at the end of the occupation, but was prevented by government restrictions on the expansion of housing space. They had divided when the village moved.

The Lineages after the Move

Various features of industrial cities would be expected to work against the survival of lineages as co-resident groups, holding common property, and maintaining their traditional organization. This was not the case for the Yau and Chan in Tsuen Wan, however, although there were some differences between them by the late 1960s. The lineages, especially the Yau, were virtually unaffected by such factors as the dispersal of members through migration, the demands of industrial employment, the transformation of property relations, and the encroachment of new values. Their location in central Tsuen Wan benefitted corporate kin groups because of the increase in the value of their trust property. The situation of the Fan was rather different, as they held no property in common, and were fewer in number.

At that time, the Chan lineage included 55 households, and the Yau 31. Of these, 33 Chan households lived in Kwan Mun Hau, while the rest were in Hoi Pa and Ham Tin, with a few elsewhere in Hong Kong and one in Southeast Asia. The Yau were all resident in Kwan Mun Hau except for six households in Hoi Pa and one in China, while the Fan had three households in Kwan Mun Hau and two in Hoi Pa.

Lineage members, and their branches, tended to live in clusters in the new village, but the clusters of each surname were intermingled with the others. The Yau and Chan frequently referred to the original marriage between them, and were careful to avoid any expression of competition. Their rites were not competitive, and they invited guests from the other lineage to the banquets that followed.

Both lineages held trust properties focussed on their founders, and others focussed on various ancestors below the founders and their sons and grandsons. The government policy of Letters of Exchange had allowed the trusts to exchange their holdings for building land, with shares in the resulting building being divided between them and the contractor if necessary. They thus had regular rental income.

According to a Yau elder:

> The founder's property has increased in value very rapidly during the past 10 or 20 years, because we exchanged the land for houses and buildings, so we have a lot of money every year to buy more buildings in Tsuen Wan. I am very proud that the founder's property has increased, not decreased.

They managed their property well, having regular office holders: an informal head, two managers, an accountant, and a treasurer,[35] with quarterly meetings of representatives of the eight branches at which accounts were presented. At three out of four meetings, shares of profits were distributed, divided on a branch basis, the traditional way of managing lineage finances. This principle was sometimes challenged, as the branches varied greatly in numbers. The lineage appeared to be trying to counteract this by giving lucky money on a per capita basis at New Year and Chongyang. The cash payments at Chongyang 'in lieu of pork'[36] started in 1964, when they also began holding a banquet afterwards. These reflect the increasing prosperity of the lineage after the move, according to a member.

The profits for the fourth quarter were used to finance the Chongyang rites at the tombs of the founder and his wife, his two sons and their wives, whose tombs had to be moved to Sheung Shui from Tsuen Wan in 1973; and his wife's parents, with a person identified as a long-term labourer, in a tomb below Chuen Lung.[37] After the occupation, more people participated, riding in vehicles so that children could be included. In 1969 this was an impressive affair, with five busloads of people going to the various destinations, banners flying that said 'The Yau Ancestral Trust Sweeps its Tombs', and a banquet in and around the ancestral hall afterwards.[38]

Plate 26: Yau lineage men, having presented their offerings that include a very large roast pig, and accompanied by a geomancer of the same surname, kowtow three times, concluding the Chongyang worship at the tomb of their founding ancestor, 1969.

Plate 27: The tomb of the Yau founding ancestor after the 1969 Chongyang rites were completed. Mrs Yau Tsang Yung-hei had assisted by carrying baskets of offerings.

---

35. All of whom received nominal stipends.

36. Pork had been distributed to families at Chongyang in the pre-occupation period.

37. The tomb identifies them as the mother-in-law and father-in-law of the Yau lineage founding ancestor. Lineage members refer to her as *jepoh* (姐婆), the Hakka term for maternal grandmother, but the identity of its occupants has elicited much discussion. The tomb has a trust of property, and they owe its occupants an obligation. We found other examples of care being given to the souls of unrelated individuals and those in the matriline, sometimes sharing a tomb with patrilineal ancestors. James Hayes cites several such examples, two of which were expressions of gratitude for help given in the distant past. The obligations were expressed either through maintaining the benefactors' tombs or, in the case of Muk Min Ha, by honouring his soul in an ancestral hall attached to theirs. 'The Old Popular Culture of China and its Contribution to Stability in Tsuen Wan', *Journal of the Hong Kong Branch Royal Asiatic Society* 30 (1990): 20–21.

38. They later began to worship at the tomb of the founder's father in Guanlan in Bao'an on the other side of the border.

Likewise, Chan lineage men joined men from related New Territories lineages in rites at the tomb of their founder's grandfather, Man Tai Kung; his father; and their founder, Hau Tak Kung, who is worshipped by descendants of his sons who settled in Tsuen Wan and elsewhere in the New Territories and across the border. They still cooked and ate by at least one of these tombs. The largest rites were those at the tomb of their founder in Sha Tin. In 1969, three busloads of men, women, and children participated, followed by a restaurant banquet for men. They said they should worship the most senior first, but the worship at the founder's grandfather's tomb was always on the eighth of the ninth lunar month to facilitate planning. Men of both lineages also worshipped at the tombs of those branch ancestors that had trusts of property, and had not been closed for reasons of bad geomancy.

The Chan lineage did not hold regular meetings, although accounts were posted at the hall at New Year. The officers included three managers and a treasurer, all long-term positions; and an accountant, who held his position for two years. They had sold some of their property, apparently at the insistence of some of the poorer members, but still retained enough to divide profits on a branch basis. This happened when $40,000 had been accumulated, according to some, at which time one-half could be divided.

The Chan had two permanent lanterns in the hall, and families who wished to celebrate sons' births could worship individually and hold banquets.The Yau continued the tradition of a lantern-raising ceremony for sons born into the lineage the previous year. They celebrated new sons on the 14th night of the New Year with a procession organized by young lineage men, who set off firecrackers and played the rhythm meaning 'increase sons' on gongs and cymbals. They went to the homes of families with new sons in both Hoi Pa and Kwan Mun Hau. The fathers came out carrying elaborate 'flower lanterns' with auspicious components representing such values as good fortune and cleverness, accompanied by women relatives carrying the babies and the offerings.

Plate 28: The Yau lineage lantern-raising festival, 1969. The father of a new son joins the procession carrying his lantern, as lineage men play gongs and cymbals.

Plate 29: The mother of a baby boy carries offerings in the procession, first to the ancestral hall, then to the Baak Gung, then back to the ancestral hall, where the lanterns are raised.

Plate 30: The lanterns, with their auspicious symbols, are suspended from the roof beams and raised. Portraits of two ancestral couples in Qing robes hang on the walls.

Plate 31: Men who still know how to do unicorn dancing celebrate outside the hall after the ceremony, 1970.

These were taken first to the hall to worship, then to the Baak Gung, and then back to the hall, where the lanterns were raised. The beams from which they were suspended reflected the babies' generation order. Following the ceremony, a banquet was held in and around the hall, cooked by lineage men assisted by women, and paid for by the families and the founder's trust.

Aside from these opportunities for the collective worship of ancestors, families could do so on the first and fifteenth of the month, when the halls were opened, and at major holidays. It was almost always women who worshipped on these occasions, taking offerings to the halls,[39] the Baak Gung, and sometimes to the Tianhou temple.

An advantage of belonging to a lineage was the welfare benefits that it might provide. At that time, the Yau lineage gave loans to the needy from the founder's trust, the amounts being inversely proportionate to the size of recipients' branch. The lineage also contributed to the costs of the lantern raising and of funerals, if needed, as well as offering help with school fees. The Chan lineage contributed to funerals, the branches gave loans, and the small trusts helped students. Both lineages also mediated internal disputes as needed, an important intangible benefit.

Leaders provided some comparative information on other Tsuen Wan lineages. Some small lineages had sold their property when under duress, especially during the occupation, or because poorer members wished to do this. The situation in Lo Wai, with its five lineages, was distinctive. The Tsang lineage was the largest, although they, like all except the Cheung, had sold their hall during the occupation. Those lineages without halls did not have property to finance the worship of distant ancestors, although they did so when constituent households pooled resources. The Cheung continued their Chongyang worship, with a banquet afterwards, as well as the lantern-raising festival,[40] although two-thirds of their households were Christian. They had no profits to divide.

In the mid-nineteenth century, the Lo Wai lineages decided to pool their property and slaughter pigs at the end of the year to give the elders a banquet and an opportunity to meet. They formed a property-holding organization named the Tung Wo Seh (同和社), which eventually had enough property, some donated by individuals, to establish an excellent school and provide welfare benefits to residents. As Tsuen Wan industrialized, the Tung Wo Seh received substantial sums from rental income. It therefore created a welfare association and a registered company that owned a profitable minibus service (see Chapter 6).

The Chan of Sam Tung Uk apparently had been wealthy, and they renovated their hall when we were first in Tsuen Wan, but they recently had sold much of the property in their founder's trust, as had all except one of the four lineage branches. The first decision apparently was made because members of three small branches would receive significant amounts of money from the sale. The fourth, larger, branch had only one vote of the four, and so had to concede. The principal trust still paid half the fees of all primary and middle school students, a significant commitment. The Ho of Muk Min Ha and Ho Pui had sold some property and their hall, once splendid, was partially ruined, although accounts and couplets were posted.[41] The Tang of Hoi Pa had also sold some property. Some of the Ho and a majority of the Yeung of Yeung Uk were Christian, but the Yeung still had trust properties yielding income for worship at Chongyang, and profits to divide. The Chan of Sheung Kwai Chung, with members also in Sam Tung Uk, Kowloon, and Kuala Lumpur, still had a hall and maintained their rituals. Although

---

39. Men had worshipped ancestors before the occupation, as they had more time then. Women's frequent worship of lineage ancestors in the halls contrasts with available information on Cantonese lineages. Rubie S. Watson states that women worshipped lineage ancestors only as brides, worshipping domestic ancestors after marriage. 'Class Differences and Affinal Relations in South China', in Watson and Watson, *Village Life in Hong Kong*, 98, 102. Maurice Freedman says: 'Only when she was dead was a woman admissible in the shape of an ancestral tablet, into the ancestral hall.' *Lineage Organization in Southeastern China* (London: Athlone Press, 1958), 32.

40. There was one permanent lantern in their hall, so none was actually raised.

41. The hall had been abandoned when its geomancy had been compromised by the building of a hospital above it, exposing red earth and said to have resulted in many deaths.

they had sold some property, as requested by poorer members, their common property paid for rituals. The Lo and Tsang lineages of that village were very small, but also had well-maintained halls. From what we could ascertain, none of the Tsuen Wan lineages had property that was as profitable as that of the Yau and Chan, who were reputed to be the wealthiest, and the most conservative in maintaining their ceremonies.

To conclude, the Yau and Chan lineages of Kwan Mun Hau were unified and prosperous, which might be explained in various ways. The property of the lineages and their constituent trusts included urban buildings, houses, and factory plots, which gave them significant incomes. The Yau, in particular, had benefitted because they had sold little or no property. Any differences between them might be explained by several factors. First, the Chan property in the past was said to have been of higher quality, and hence more easily sold. Second, the Yau had no Christian households whereas the Chan had several, although the head of one was the man who had researched and written their genealogy. Third, there were greater wealth differences within the Chan lineage, and men from wealthy families were more likely to be well-educated and to have business interests outside the village. The Chan also had more members living outside Kwan Mun Hau, either in other villages or elsewhere. They also appeared to be more divided along ideological lines than the Yau. They had a fairly large right-wing faction, some of whose members went to Taiwan every year, and others who were markedly left-wing. One Chan man had actually sold his house to an outsider and 'fled to Taiwan', we were told. This was one of several houses owned by immigrants or members of other lineages at that time, bought from village families. The Yau had been poorer in the past, and fewer members had come back wealthy from abroad. Most shared the same political ideology, and were more unified in their loyalty to their lineage.

The Yau and Chan lineages were doing well in their new urban context. There were a number of reasons for this. First, they had not needed to emigrate to find employment, unlike men in most of the New Territories at that time. Income came to them in the form of rents from property, for those families that had it, and urban employment, although the latter could be profoundly disruptive of lineage and village participation. Members also benefitted from their shares of profits from lineage property, and their welfare benefits. Furthermore, the lineages remained protected by Hong Kong government policies pertaining to New Territories natives, and their own commitment to staying together. Had Kwan Mun Hau not moved as a whole, with its ancestral halls and shrines, their property almost certainly would have been sold piecemeal, the lineages disbanded, and the families dispersed. There had been no land reform like that which had taken place on the mainland and on Taiwan,[42] and the property of lineages and families remained secure in accordance with their traditions. Finally, their commitment may also have derived from their awareness that the government at that time offered virtually nothing by way of a social safety net, a vacuum that was filled in part by their lineages.

Tenants and Their Relationships with Villagers

If there were no immigrants, then we natives would have no one to rent houses to. The relationship is like fish to water.
—Yau lineage man

When the village moved, the villagers apparently had little trouble finding new tenants, given the scarcity of housing in Tsuen Wan. Some rented out whole floors, while others rented out rooms partitioned off within their own housing, sharing the kitchen and toilet. The standard partitions were generally raised off the floor and ended below the ceiling to allow for ventilation, so the rooms were

---

42. With the exception of the British colonial government's granting of rights to the tenants of absentee subsoil owners after 1898.

not at all soundproof. Some tenant families or groups lived on complete floors, while others used them as small factories or workshops, sometimes living on the premises. This was revealed through Elizabeth's census.

The census, done near the end of our stay, sampled one out of every three houses. This was facilitated by the regular layout of the new village and the consecutive numbering of the houses, of which there were 110, and two that were not numbered. One served as the Village Hall. Our assistants gave much-needed help with this work, essential because of the numerous variants of spoken Chinese we encountered. The questionnaires were relatively short, asking about household size and composition at various times, when they had divided to live separately and had divided their property (if they had any), how much space they occupied, the education and occupations of members, and their religious practices. In the case of the many small factories and workshops, we asked about their products, other questions about their operation, the number of employees, the calculation of their remuneration, whether any lived on the premises, and why they chose to be located in Kwan Mun Hau. We did not ask about lineage members and tenants elsewhere, in urban buildings or in other villages.

In our sample we found 21 native households, including one of the unrelated but long-established families. The average size was 7.6, and they included thirteen nuclear families, six stem, and two joint. Several had matrilateral relatives sharing their homes: married daughters and daughters' children. One family did not own their flat, but rented it from the Yau ancestral trust.

Our sample found 61 tenant households, indicating that they occupied much less space per household than did the natives. Furthermore, not all tenant households were composed of families, as seven people lived alone and 22 in groups of friends or workmates, the largest including six cheerful male textile factory workers with a big piano. In addition, there were 27 nuclear families and five stem families, a total of 173 people in all. In general, they occupied relatively small spaces, many only single rooms, and one young woman lived alone in a cockloft. The largest family included a recently widowed man and his eight children.

The three shop proprietors, tenants who had moved with the village,[43] lived at the back of their shops. They included one couple and two older men. Two shops sold food items and the other sold Chinese and Western medicines. There also was a barber shop, but the partners did not live there. Some employees of workshops stayed overnight if they worked late or traffic conditions were bad, and a few actually lived on the premises.

There were nine workshops in the sample, three making or finishing fine furniture, one making machinery parts, one making leather parts for textile factory machinery, two repairing such machinery, one manufacturing blocks of camphor, and one making metal office furniture. One machinery factory partner lived in the same house as their factory with his nuclear family of four, and three partners. Two workers in a furniture workshop lived on the premises, and in another the owner and his nuclear family of six lived on site. Another manager of a furniture workshop lived upstairs with his nuclear family of six, doing the varnishing there. Two people did putting-out work at home. Finally, an elderly *putonghua*-speaking labourer used his flat as a temple for a Buddhist religion of his own creation.

The shopkeepers said that business was poor, as there were not many customers. They were located in the lower part of the village, where only one native family lived, and faced competition from the Country Village Store, run and patronized by villagers. The owners of the furniture-making workshops also said that it was hard to do business, although this was not the result of the location and space available; on the contrary, these were beneficial. Their challenge was the recruitment of new workers, as they had to do at least a three-year apprenticeship, when young men could find better-paying work in factories.

---

43. According to James Hayes, this was not government policy in the 1970s, and probably was not earlier. There may have been an agreement between the tenants and their landlords, perhaps because at least two were Hakka.

A few of the tenants in the sample were Hakka, but only three of these were New Territories natives. Tenants' origins were extremely diverse, even though we spoke with only one representative of each household or workshop. Many came from various counties in Guangdong, including some who were Hakka. Others were Teochiu. Others came from much further afield, including Honan, Hubei, Shandong, Wuhan, Shanghai, Ningbo, Burma, and Singapore. The owners of some factories were said to be Shanghainese, and they tended not to live on-site. They also did not offer their workers the bi-monthly worship of a patron god and special meal (做禡),[44] although a Cantonese furniture workshop manager did. Four of the tenant families were Christian, in contrast to the villagers.

When asked why they were renting space there, the representatives of workshops and factories gave a number of reasons: the rents were low, transportation was convenient, there was space to store their materials and products, and the air was fresh. Tenants often spoke positively of the villagers, and said that they were good people. None said anything critical, which corroborated the positive interactions we observed during our time there.[45] There were tenants who mentioned the differences in their situations, however, and said that they themselves had no property, or that 'natives rarely have to work, and so mainly play mah-jong'.

The fact that most tenants had come from the mainland meant that they likely were separated from their wider families, and that some may have had no family members at all in Hong Kong.[46] Their lives had been disrupted by their flight from China and loss of any property they may have had, while their situation in Hong Kong was generally characterized by insecurity and hard work with long hours. The indigenous people, in contrast, were surrounded by people to whom they were related through both men and women, and enjoyed a level of security that was rare in Hong Kong at that time.

We asked native men in the interview sample, as well as other native men, how they compared their situation with that of immigrants at that time. They knew that they enjoyed many benefits, especially in their privileged relationship to the government as landowners in the New Territories. They received compensation and exchange rights for any land that was resumed. They often believed that the compensation was inadequate, but immigrants had nothing comparable. They also received tangible benefits from their lineages, including the security of being members of organized descent groups so that they did not need to belong to associations, which they believed in general to be inferior. Their lineages and villages were festive (熱鬧) on special occasions. Their lifelong unity was reflected in the nicknames by which they referred to each other, which often derived from idiosyncrasies of behaviour or appearance that were funny but generally not flattering.[47]

A number of thoughtful men, however, perceived some disadvantages in their status. Most important was the fact that they were not free to leave, even in war, as they were tied to their property. They believed that outsiders learned a lot and gained experience by having to make their own way in life, thus making them more capable. They had to work harder than natives, and hence could earn money faster. As they were not part of localized groups, they were less prone to internal conflicts. Still, overall the natives recognized and appreciated their special position in Hong Kong at that time.

The situation is greatly improved in new Kwan Mun Hau since the village moved. It has been good for living conditions, good for prosperity, and good for kinship, as people remain living together. Before

---

44. Celebration of this was very much in evidence at small shops throughout Tsuen Wan, the fronts of which were roped off, with the employees and shop owner eating inside, and incense, candles, and offerings at their shrines.

45. In contrast, James Watson reported distance between Man lineage members in the large Cantonese lineage village of San Tin and their outsider tenant farmers, and the Mans' negative comments about them. James L. Watson, *Emigration and the Chinese Lineage: The Mans in Hong Kong and London* (Berkeley: University of California Press, 1975), 47–48.

46. A native man spoke of how, as a child, he was saddened by passing a shop with a Shanghainese proprietor who always played Beijing opera recordings expressing loneliness.

47. Married-in women, with a few exceptions, were referred to by their surnames followed by a kinship term, or their husbands' names; village-born women often had their own nicknames.

the move, the Yau Luen Fong Tso had no profits to divide; now we do. We were the first village in the New Territories to move, except for those moved for reservoirs, whose conditions were quite different. Kwan Mun Hau is also very well located.

It is also good because for some decades before we had no educated people; now we have a lot with university degrees. Relationships are cooperative, and it is peaceful and orderly here. We have lost a lot of land to development, but also have done well. We have retained many of our customs, and also have retained the landscape, with people living together in a village, the same people.

6

Coping with Change

The Roles of Associations, 1968–1970

The contrast between the situation of original inhabitants and immigrants was typical, not only of Kwan Mun Hau, but also of Tsuen Wan as a whole. Graham decided to examine the coping strategies of these newcomers, studying the associations they had formed in order to learn what benefits they offered their members. He approached this by interviewing office holders from the list of associations that was available in District Office files.

In the 1960s, studies of associations and their leaders in Chinese urban settings were few and focused almost entirely on overseas Chinese communities.[1] Crissman produced a concise summary of the characteristics of the structure of urban overseas Chinese community organizations, as they had developed through the 1960s.[2]

There were also clues from China's urban past. China had been a traditional agrarian society, in which most of the population were cultivators and lived in rural villages. It nonetheless had a high degree of urbanization, and throughout its history had urban settlements of prodigious size, when compared to Europe at a similar stage of development. In the imperial past, rural migrants had lived and worked in urban settlements, and had adapted to urban environments through the creation of associations based upon criteria such as assumed kinship (same surname), locality of origin, or occupation, variously called guilds or *huiguan* (會館). These had been noted by observers, especially Burgess and Morse, and neatly summarized by Ho in a rich volume.[3]

In Tsuen Wan District in 1969, there were 91 registered voluntary associations; in 1947 there had been but three (Table 6.1). This proliferation of associations followed the growth and diversification of its population. Most Tsuen Wan associations were found among the immigrant population. Despite variation in the types of associations, their wealth, size, and success, they were all a response to the enormity of change that occurred in Tsuen Wan during its transition to becoming an industrial town populated largely by immigrants. They also arose in the context of a 'minimalist-state'[4] in which the Hong Kong government was not interventionist in the provision of social infrastructure, with the

---

1. Maurice Freedman, 'Immigrants and Associations: Chinese in Nineteenth Century Singapore', *Comparative Studies in Society and History* 3, no. 1 (1960): 25–48; Marjorie Topley, 'The Emergence and Social Function of Chinese Religious Associations in Singapore', *Comparative Studies in Society and History* 3, no. 3 (1961): 289–314; G. William Skinner, *Leadership and Power in the Chinese Community of Thailand* (Ithaca, NY: Cornell University Press, 1958); Donald E. Willmott, *The Chinese of Semarang: A Changing Minority Community in Indonesia* (Ithaca, NY: Cornell University Press, 1960); William E. Willmott, 'Congregations and Associations: The Political Structure of the Chinese Community in Phnom-Penh, Cambodia', *Comparative Studies in Society and History* 11, no. 3 (1969): 282–301.
2. L. W. Crissman, 'The Segmentary Structure of Urban Overseas Chinese Communities', *Man* 2 *(NS)*, no. 2 (June 1967): 185–204.
3. J. S. Burgess, *The Guilds of Peking* (New York: Columbia University Press, 1928); Hosea B. Morse, *The Gilds of China: With an Account of the Gild Merchant or Co-Hong of Canton* (New York: Longmans Greene, 1909); Ho Ping-ti 何炳棣, *Zhongguo Huiguan Shilun* 中國會館史論 [Historical materials on Chinese *Landsmannschaften*] (Taipei: Taiwan *Xuesheng Shuju* 台灣學生書局, 1966).
4. Ian Scott, *Political Change and the Crisis of Legitimacy in Hong Kong* (Honolulu: University of Hawai'i Press, 1989).

notable exception of housing. It was primarily left to private sector interests to paper over cracks that appeared in the social fabric. Personal crises were challenging for the majority of immigrants, who had arrived in Hong Kong with few financial resources and often with only small family networks. Sickness, unemployment, birth, marriage, and death could all have major impacts, which associations remedied in various ways. Associations were created to meet obvious, and sometimes dire, social needs—a response derived from a long tradition in Chinese culture.

Table 6.1 Tsuen Wan: association types, 1969

Economic	29
Fellow-Countrymen's Associations	12
Neighbourhood	9
Welfare	5
Leisure	10
Political	4
Religious	27

Economic Associations

Given the rapidity of economic change in Tsuen Wan, it was not surprising that associations with a predominantly economic orientation were most numerous. The economic sector was a wide-ranging one, and within it there were a number of different kinds of associations: nine cooperative/mutual aid societies, six associations oriented towards commercial activities, 12 trade unions, a union of manufacturers, and an association of both workers and owners from small industrial units. Members of some included both natives and immigrants, as both needed organizations to help them cope with Tsuen Wan's rapid economic growth.

Cooperatives

The cooperatives were, with one exception, oriented towards primary production and were to be found in the still-rural sections of the district or among people who made their living from primary production, which in the late 1960s was still important. Four were fishermen's cooperatives, which combined the functions of marketing, money loan association, and mutual aid. The number of fishermen's associations was a consequence of the requirements of different types of fishing, and also of specific ritual ties. The capital costs of deep-sea fishing were high. Two cooperatives focused on deep-sea fishing, which had become totally mechanized in the 1950s. Two recruited members from those who fished, and lived, in the waters off Tsuen Wan and Ma Wan respectively and had their ritual focus on separate Tianhou temples.

The other fishermen's cooperative recruited from both the land-based and water-based population. It functioned as an intermediary between the government and its members. Its office was the centre of organized activity for the Tsuen Wan fishing people and became the association headquarters for the fishing cooperatives. The fishing associations had one important element in common—they all participated in the annual festivals honouring Tianhou through their related religious associations, which we shall detail later in the chapter. The fishing cooperatives demonstrate the diversity of associational behaviour. They were ostensibly economic in their orientation, but also had religious, leisure, welfare, neighbourhood, and in one case through formal incorporation into the Rural Committee, political functions.

The oldest society in Tsuen Wan was the Agricultural Products Society (荃灣農產合作社), which was either established by indigenous people or long-term residents. Its precise founders were no longer known. It was a farmers' cooperative long before such organizations were officially sponsored and dated from the 1920s. A government-sponsored cooperative took over its economic functions towards the end of the 1950s.[5] By then it constituted a declining membership of elderly farmers who kept up the society for death benefits, help in times of sickness, and the mediation of disputes. In the late 1960s, it still ran an agricultural school for members' children and grandchildren. It became, however, a casualty of the process of economic change in Tsuen Wan as agriculture diminished.

Commercial Associations

Commercial associations were diverse, but of two broad types. There were those with a community-wide referent such as the Chamber of Commerce. More numerous were those with a sectoral referent, such as a particular trade. Such associations dealt with the specifics of trade, but also focused on welfare, mutual aid, and leisure. This type of association most closely resembled the traditional guilds of urban areas in Imperial and Republican China. They were all of recent origin. None dated from before 1965, and one was formally inaugurated only in late 1968.

The Chamber of Commerce

The Chamber of Commerce (荃灣商會) was another of Tsuen Wan's oldest associations, founded in 1938 by a combination of indigenous and immigrant business interests. Its constitution stated that 'all shops and factories established in Tsuen Wan by Chinese shall be eligible for membership'. In the mid-1950s, it included virtually every business in Tsuen Wan, including the large Shanghai-invested factories. Its importance was reflected by its inclusion in the Tsuen Wan Rural Committee, where it had two seats. As late as 1964, the chamber ran a free evening school for 1,300 pupils, and its clinic saw 30,000 patients a year. It was also at the forefront of relief and community welfare projects. The formation of the Manufacturers' Association—a union of the owners of the largest factories in the area—in 1958, signalled a decline in its influence. Other business activities that it formerly encompassed evolved into specialized associations of their own, such as the butchers' association. Its previous paramount position in the provision of welfare benefits was likewise taken over by other sectoral associations. Until 1960, the Chamber of Commerce was the most prestigious association in Tsuen Wan, combining political, economic, welfare, and leisure functions. As the 1960s progressed, Tsuen Wan and its problems grew too large for one association to handle. By the late 1960s, membership consisted of small businessmen with permanent shop space, who used the chamber as a vehicle of communication with the government over such questions as licensing. The formerly successful school was closed and even the clinic became less important, in part because of increased government-funded facilities. The decline in influence of the chamber in local politics was underscored by the emergence of a federation of immigrant interests, which could represent their views in a much more effective way than the chamber, with its formal incorporation into a political structure that was increasingly irksome to immigrants.

There were two additional community-wide commercial organizations which included both indigenous and immigrant members. The New Territories Chamber of Commerce attempted to do what the Chamber of Commerce had done for Tsuen Wan in terms of united action on common commercial interests. It was founded in 1959, when Tsuen Wan had reached a momentous stage in its

---

5. Many of the needs of immigrant vegetable farmers were met by formal government organizations.

development. Another Chamber of Commerce was founded in 1968 in the small industrial town of Sham Tseng, which was dominated by three large industrial undertakings—a textile mill, a bakery, and a large brewery. Its formation was a reflection of the growing economic differentiation and population growth in the community.

Butchers

The butchers' association (荃灣肉行商會) recruited its members from the licensed butcher shops of Tsuen Wan. Membership was group-based and one representative from each business, usually the owner, participated in the activities of the association. The leaders of the association stated that its members joined together to create a platform to air their collective views on common business interests. The chairman's speech at the formal inauguration of the association was clear. He said:

> Our members have had a long history in the operation of the meat business in Tsuen Wan, but there has been little liaison with one another. Today, with the ever-increasing prosperity in Tsuen Wan, along with the sharp increases in the population, the demand for meat has risen with every passing day. The question of whether the meat sold is up to the health standard is a matter of paramount importance to the people's health. It is our goal to secure an adequate supply of meat up to the health standard that has prompted us to start this organization.

The aims of the association were not wholly altruistic. Since its inception, the association had regularly petitioned the government for adequate meat-slaughtering facilities in Tsuen Wan. In the late 1960s, the nearest slaughtering facilities were in North Kowloon, five miles away. A slaughterhouse in Tsuen Wan would clearly save on costs. Not all meat, however, was slaughtered outside Tsuen Wan. Many pigs sold in Tsuen Wan were illegally slaughtered locally. This clearly posed a health hazard, which the association raised. Moreover, locally slaughtered pigs were often hawked by unlicensed butchers whose profits were high and whose business detracted from that of association members. As with the guilds in traditional Chinese cities, there was an element of restricted competition. Also analogous to traditional Chinese guilds, a locality tie underpinned the solidarity deriving from a common occupation. The butchers were invariably Hakka from Huizhou, Dongguan, and Bao'an *xian*[6] in the eastern Pearl River delta region. Hakka was the language of communication within the butchers' association office. The butchers' association represented a significant informal pattern in Tsuen Wan. Hakka-speaking migrants, some of whom were owners of small business, had a privileged position among the immigrant population. They spoke the same variety of Hakka as did the Tsuen Wan natives. Part of the success of the butchers' association derived from this informal solidarity with the local Hakka population. It was not the only reason. Butchers were, on the whole, prosperous businessmen. Their association office was one of the more elegant in Tsuen Wan, and their leader was one of the most respected figures in the area, having lived there for over 50 years. Business interests were not the sole concern of the association. It ran a successful football team and was also important for the general welfare of the members, especially through death benefits. On the death of a member, the association granted $500 towards funeral expenses, which was a significant sum.

Hawkers

There was a general hawkers' association in Tsuen Wan. It called itself a business association (荃灣 得牌小販同業會) and one of its objectives was 'to exchange knowledge so as to promote members'

---

6. 惠州, 東莞, and 寶安 were *xian* (縣) located in the eastern Pearl River delta. Migration to Tsuen Wan from these areas was common even before British rule.

business'. This objective did not take precedence. Rather the main goal was 'to enhance feelings of mutual obligation and unity among members' (聯合會員恩情) and to provide welfare benefits.

The provision of welfare benefits was a characteristic of most Tsuen Wan associations during the 1950s and 1960s, as with much of the Hong Kong population in the 1950s and 1960s, living was precarious. Within a short space of time after its founding, a 'ginger and vinegar' fund was established and 'compensation' for childbirth established. The main thrust, however, was directed toward meeting the costs associated with death. Each member paid an entrance fee to the 'funeral fund' of twenty dollars and an annual subscription of two dollars. On the death of a member each had to contribute one dollar towards the cost of a wreath. The constitution stated:

> In case any member shall unfortunately pass away, his or her beneficiary shall report to the association one day before burial. Upon verification of the fact [of death], the beneficiary shall be paid $1,000. The association shall furnish a floral plate [for the hearse], moveable decorations, a funeral band, and members to attend the funeral service. Each member shall receive one dollar travelling expenses. Benefits are to be denied if a member fails three times to contribute to the funeral 'floral wreath fee', if his membership is cancelled in the society, or he has committed suicide. If a member dies without kinsmen, this association will take over all the funeral arrangements and the name and photograph of the deceased shall be hung in the premises of the association for the everlasting admiration of others.

The hawkers' association was the largest in Tsuen Wan, with a paying membership of over 4,000. The members of the butchers' and hawkers' associations were both involved in retail trade. The butchers' association derived its strength from the similarity of its members' business orientation, and also from a locality tie. The hawkers' association was not merely diverse in the business interests of its members that included the retailing of a multitude of goods, but there also was little in the way of a locality tie. Most were from Guangdong province, but that meant little. Natives of various localities in Guangdong tended to be involved in specific branches of hawking. Thus, Teochiu were typically hawkers of cooked food, Hakka sold vegetables, and fruit was sold by natives of Dongguan, who were generally Cantonese-speakers. The leadership (office holders) reflected this diversity: it was composed of people from 18 Guangdong *xian* and one from Shanghai. Its members did, however, share one characteristic. They were often in conflict with certain government authorities—especially the police and/or the Hawker Control Force. Their difficulties over the question of hawking pitches could be resolved, in part, they believed, through the vehicle of associational strength. An important aspect of their work was mediation between members and the police, and this was a crucial aspect of the economics of hawking.[7]

Industrial Associations

Trade Unions

From almost the beginnings of modern factories in Tsuen Wan, workers' associations were established. With one exception, all the trade unions were founded before 1955. In the major industrial sectors in Tsuen Wan: cotton spinning, weaving and dyeing, silk weaving, enamelware, and rubber production, there was some degree of unionization. In each major industrial sector there were competing unions looking either to China ('left-wing') or to Taiwan ('right-wing') for ideological leadership, with much inter-union rivalry, which had been ongoing since their formation. As early as 1952, right-wing unions

---

7. The other issue was official corruption, which was widespread and unchecked until the government intervened in the 1970s. Unlicensed hawkers (and others, such as unlicensed taxis), were obliged to give payoffs to police or the Hawker Control Units, which then allowed them to continue in their business activities. The payments were onerous but, from the hawkers' perspectives, an inevitable cost of business.

made attacks on left-wing union premises. The smouldering conflicts burst into the open in 1956 when, as an extension of a riot in Kowloon, the right-wing unions attempted to win a dominant position in the labour world through a series of actions against left-wing unions and factory management in Tsuen Wan. The Tsuen Wan events began with an incident in a factory dormitory over hanging a Nationalist flag to celebrate the National Day of the Republic of China.[8] The incident quickly expanded and right-wing union members broke into a factory and set it afire. Then they began to systematically attack left-wing union establishments, welfare centres, clinics, cooperatives, and union headquarters, setting fire to them as they were taken. The official report on the riots describes the Tsuen Wan events as follows:

> The principal characteristics of the riots in Tsuen Wan were: firstly, a degree of organization among the mobs, which were led by men with large Nationalist flags, responded to whistle blasts, used a system of white wristbands as a mark of recognition, and were amenable to withdrawing from a factory, the management of which had hoisted the flag, paid the requisite protection money, or met other demands; secondly the concerted and destructive attacks on buildings housing communist sympathizers, whether union premises, houses, or shops, together with brutal and humiliating treatment of the occupants, especially if they tried to defend their premises; thirdly, the cases of extortion under the threat of arson or wholesale destruction of a factory and through the widespread forced sale of Nationalist paper flags; fourthly, the tendency to use the occasion to pay off old scores, either against the political opponent or against the former employer; and fifthly, the attempt to establish right-wing unions in a position of monopoly by securing undertakings in writing from factory managements that left-wing workers would be dismissed and replaced by people acceptable to those unions.[9]

Eight people died in Tsuen Wan during the riots, two of whom were leading right-wing trade unionists, who subsequently became martyrs in the cause of right-wing unionism. The scars left between the two factions as a result of the 1956 riots were still visible in the late 1960s, and relations between the two sides were poisonous. The conflicts between the two factions were by then rarely violent. It was suggested by one trade union leader that 'the river water doesn't violate the well water' (河水不犯井水), that is, the competing unions maintained their positions, and their distance.

There were two major aspects to the work of trade unions. One was the provision of welfare benefits such as funeral, marriage, and childbirth payments.[10] They often sponsored clinics with both Chinese and Western-style medicine, and conducted classes in literacy, sewing, cooking, and the like. The provision of leisure activities such as football, basketball, table tennis, or Chinese operatic performances were common, as were annual gatherings such as banquets, film shows, picnics, and songfests. Unions helped members find jobs if they became unemployed, and their activities extended to conflict resolution, such as the mediation of family disputes. Their welfare work was very important, but the aspect of union work that distinguished it from a welfare society was that it supported members in industrial disputes, some of which ended in either strikes or lockouts.

The right/left ideological split was clearly an important element in understanding trade union behaviour in industrializing Tsuen Wan, but class interests were of equal significance. A 1949 government report noted that 'the great degree of [industrial] unrest characterized the spinning industry which is largely in the hands of employers from Shanghai . . . who have a fierce distrust of all forms of workers' unions'.[11] Such distrust was still evident after 20 years of operation in Tsuen Wan. There was at least one case where a trade union maintained secret cells in a large factory whose management did

---

8. The People's Republic of China celebrates its national day on October 1, the Republic of China on Taiwan celebrates its national day on October 10 ('Double Ten').

9. *Hong Kong Government Report of the Riots in Kowloon and Tsuen Wan October 10th to October 12th 1956* (Hong Kong: Government Publications, 1956), 42–43. The Chinese version is 九龍及荃灣暴動報告書 and the summary is on page 28.

10. The funeral benefit for most trade unions was about $300; $20 was given for the birth of a child and double that for twins. Marriage benefits were usually $30.

11. Commissioner of Labour Annual Report 1948/49 (Hong Kong Government Publications, 1949), 44.

Plate 32: 'Grasp revolution, promote production!'. Sign celebrating October 1 outside the China Products Store, typifying the heated political situation in the late 1960s.

Plate 33: 'Long live the Republic of China!'. Sign celebrating October 10, put up by the Silk Workers Free Trade Union. Signs on the adjacent cinema advertise current attractions, 1968.

not allow union membership. Ironically, the largest membership unit in the union was the one with secret cells.

The overall rate of unionization was not high; one reason was political. After the events of the summer of 1967, when political conflict was rife, individuals were reluctant to make open commitments. In only one workplace was there an exception to this general trend. The workforce in the Texaco Oil Depot was almost wholly unionized. The depot was distinctive in that almost half of the workers, and virtually all department heads, were Tsuen Wan natives. The union won a number of significant benefits from the company, including virtually free medical care and subsidized eating facilities. The unusual solidarity of almost complete union membership, plus the locality tie, was of great importance.[12]

In common with workers' movements in the early stages of new economic growth, most trade unions in Hong Kong exhibited fragility. As economic pressure groups in the emerging industrial economy, the ideological split in the creation and effectiveness of trade unions into rival factions was one element in that fragility. It was not the only element, however, nor was it necessarily the most significant, although it received the most attention, especially in official comments on the trade union movement in Hong Kong. The colonial economy, and especially the emphasis on governmental laissez-faire, gave the decisive power to employers. It was clear that under the colonial system, prosperous middle-class, avowedly a-political organizations, with a leadership that could maintain or create channels of influence, would inevitably be more successful, whether these organizations were composed of butchers, manufacturers, or indigenous villagers. The question of leadership could not be divorced from the nature of associations. This is an issue that we shall leave for consideration in the following chapter.

The Owner-Worker Association

Ideology was an important element in the life of associations and most took an ideological stance. Workers' associations were unusual in that there were large numbers of workers' unions with competing ideological positions. It was our impression that in the late 1960s, in Hong Kong in general, and certainly in Tsuen Wan, most associations overtly or covertly took a Nationalist position. Only a minority held a position of support for the People's Republic of China. Part of the reason for this was the nature of the migration to Hong Kong at about the time of the establishment of the People's Republic of China. Many people were political refugees, broadly defined. For some, such as former capitalists or landlords, Nationalist officials, and the like, it was a matter of necessity for them to leave China in 1949, or shortly thereafter. Others were simply fearful of the potential for radical change and how their class positions might put them at a serious political or economic disadvantage. It was a period of great uncertainty. Association leadership was largely middle class and these were the very people who had the least to gain from the new socialist government in 1949. Ideological sympathy may thus have been one factor in the formation of associations.

In the summer of 1967, widespread social disturbances occurred throughout Hong Kong. The disturbances began with a labour dispute in Kowloon. The succeeding events are by no means clear, but with reference to the Cultural Revolution on the mainland, they quickly took on the nature of a political confrontation between the Hong Kong left and the colonial government. Unlike the events of the 1950s, which were predominantly right-wing inspired or supported, or the 1965 Kowloon riots about ferry fare increases which seem to have been largely apolitical, the events of 1967 were left-wing

---

12. Women could join the union, but only under their husbands' names.

supported, and for the first time since 1949, crossed the harbour to Hong Kong Island and extended into the New Territories. Over 50 years later, the factors that created the conflicts are still unclear.[13]

There was a growth of associations during 1967 and 1968. Many of these newer associations had ideological positions to maintain. The owner-worker association began as a response to the events of 1967. It recruited its members from among the owners and workers of the silk weaving and metal working trades, two sectors that were overwhelmingly small scale and largely non-Cantonese. The original sponsors consisted of three from Shanghai, five from Zhejiang, and one from Jiangsu. The chairman of the association prefaced the application for incorporation with the following statement:

> Since the premeditated disturbances and sabotage stepped up by the left-wing elements, the business of small factories has been hardest hit. Hence, as peace-loving citizens who seek social stability, to maintain law and order, to preserve peace and prosperity, and to promote justice, in the quest of self-help, self-defence, and self-salvation, with a view to showing my stand, I have met the requests of my fellow businessmen to start the preparation [of this association]. If both the employers and employees of the [two] trades are joined together in the formation of a social organization then it would suffice to check the left-wing organizations and social stability would be easily achieved.

The owners (and workers) felt a need to create solidarity, not merely as a bulwark against ideological challenge, but also because of the essential marginality of many of their operations. With the gradual passing of the ideological threat, as political changes in China saw the easing of left-wing government tensions, economic issues came to the fore. The organization grew to 200 members and established an office. The association had two major concerns. One was to help business enterprises find orders and thus dispense with the need for a middleman and his commission. The other was to find employment for its unemployed members. They attempted to pool business information, and loans were sometimes given at low rates of interest. Many of the members were drawn from small enterprises in government flatted factories. Given the small scale of these concerns, there was a lack of eating facilities for workers. The association successfully petitioned the government for a modest canteen in the area of the flatted factories. The ideological emphasis of the owner-worker association gave way to one that concerned the economics of small-scale production. Its office had no evidence of an ideological position, except for a picture of the queen, although it did take an active part in the planning of the 'Double Ten' celebrations in 1969.

The Manufacturers' Association

The Manufacturers' Association (荃灣工廠聯合會) was founded in 1958. It was dominated by 'Shanghainese' industrialists who were the first industrial entrepreneurs to arrive in Tsuen Wan in the late 1940s. Its impact in its first ten years of existence was but slight. The failure to achieve its objectives, which were at best broadly defined, contrasted with the experience of workers' associations. The Shanghainese managers and owners, who formed the core of the membership of the association, with only a few notable exceptions, were oriented away from Tsuen Wan. They were enormously successful men. Only very few had been self-made and many had a university education either in Shanghai or abroad. Many knew English and had friends among the numerous 'old China hands' who removed their business base to Hong Kong after it had become impossible to continue in post-1949 China.

---

13. See Committee of Hong Kong Kowloon China Compatriots of All Circles for the Struggle against Persecution by the British Authorities in Hong Kong, *The May Uprising* (Hong Kong: n.p., 1967) and its related pictorial account, *We Shall Win! British Imperialism Will Be Defeated* (Hong Kong: n.p., 1967) for left-wing views. There was no official report which dealt with the upheaval. One account, which is generally sympathetic to the Hong Kong government, is J. Cooper, *Colony in Conflict: The Hong Kong Disturbances May 1967–January 1968* (Hong Kong: Swindon Book Company, 1970). See also Gary Ka-wai Cheung, *Hong Kong's Watershed: The 1967 Riots* (Hong Kong: Hong Kong University Press, 2009), esp. 'The Impact of the 1967 Riots', 131–42.

Shanghai industrialists were welcome in Hong Kong, once it became clear to the colonial authorities that the revolution of 1949 had forever changed the political and economic climate of China and obliged Hong Kong to shift away from a reliance on the entrepôt trade. The Chinese system of power and influence, understood and accepted by the colonial authorities, was preserved and strengthened in post-occupation Hong Kong. The new industrialists were one of the groups to enter the system in the immediate post-war period. They accepted, with remarkable ease, many of the assumptions of the system of prestige. We shall later outline some aspects of this process. Suffice it to say at this point that the problems of management and ownership were solved by the owners of industrial establishments that they initially founded in Tsuen Wan—and which brought about Tsuen Wan's dramatic transformation—in Hong Kong–wide associations. The Manufacturers' Association had only a modest role to play in the future of Tsuen Wan.

Fellow-Countrymen's Associations

Fellow-countrymen's associations[14] have a long history in China and are to be found throughout overseas Chinese communities. The immigrant character of Tsuen Wan was reflected in its fellow-countrymen's associations. There were two that recruited their members on the basis of a 'north' China tie, one that was composed of natives from Fujian (specifically the city of Fuzhou), while the rest, including two surname associations, were from Guangdong (Table 6.2), although only one was Cantonese-speaking.

Table 6.2 Tsuen Wan: fellow-countrymen's associations, 1969

Association	Area of Recruitment	Speech Group	Membership
Northern Chinese Welfare Association	All China except Guangdong	Putonghua	1,050
Subei	Northern Jiangsu	Shanghainese	1,000
Fuzhou	Fuzhou, Fujian	Hok-chiu (Fuzhou)	160
Dongguan	Dongguan, Guangdong	Hakka/Cantonese	500
Zengcheng	Zengcheng, Guangdong	Cantonese	520
Boluo	Boluo, Guangdong	Hakka	120
Huizhou	Huizhou, Guangdong	Hakka	800
Teochiu	Chaozhou, Guangdong	Teochiu	450
Tsing Yi Overseas Chinese Fraternal Association	All China except Hong Kong	Cantonese, Min'nan (Southern Fujian)	500
Ho Clansmen	Lufeng, Guangdong	Teochiu	300
Tsang Clansmen	Chaozhou/Huizhou Guangdong	Teochiu	300

Most of the fellow-countrymen's associations were founded after 1958, although a few had parent organizations in urban Hong Kong that pre-dated them. The largest was the Northern Chinese Welfare Association (NCWA). It had been founded in the early 1950s as the 'Tsuen Wan Shanghai People's Welfare Association', which more accurately reflected the nature of its membership. Its constitution specified 'all persons who are native of any province in China, except Guangdong, . . . are eligible for membership'. Most members were from Jiangsu and Zhejiang. The definition of fellow-countryman

---

14. There is no adequate translation of the Chinese term *tongxianghui* (同鄉會), except for the cumbersome 'fellow-countrymen's association'.

was thus wider than for other similar associations which typically specified county of origin, and in one case, a specific city. The unifying principle for the NCWA was linguistic, and this was key for others, underpinned in all cases by a locality tie. The first migrants from Zhejiang and Jiangsu had been surrounded by people speaking mutually unintelligible varieties of Chinese (Hakka and Cantonese), and they sought familiarity in an organization that spoke their version of Chinese. Later arrivals were also deeply aware of the speech-group issues. Only in the 1970s did speech-group identity dissipate, when the children of the first generation of immigrants to Hong Kong came to maturity in the context of a thriving Cantonese-speaking mass culture in which a Hong Kong identity began to emerge.

Despite variation in the criteria for recruitment, fellow-countrymen's associations had similar purposes, although the ability to achieve their objectives depended upon their wealth and the characteristics of their memberships. The 'northern' associations and the Teochiu associations were the more successful because of their large potential memberships. The two clansmen's associations and the small Fuzhou association could not hope to achieve such numbers, although their memberships were very closely integrated. The range of socio-economic status was in general much narrower in the smaller associations, which had implications for their general ability to achieve stated goals. A shared class position gave an added element of solidarity to locality or speech-group characteristics. Class composition was therefore an important key to understanding the operation of Chinese associations in the 1960s in Hong Kong in general and Tsuen Wan in particular. Smaller associations without a middle-class leadership component did not have access to the channels of influence then typical of colonial Hong Kong.

These points can be illustrated with reference to the characteristics of the membership of various associations and their leaders. One example is the NCWA. The bulk of its members were workers in textiles, enamelware, and metal work. About 20% consisted of businessmen and professionals such as teachers, doctors, dentists, and accountants. The seventh-term office holders (1967 to 1969) consisted of one banker, nine managers of local factories, two school headmasters, four clerical workers, and only one worker. There was no significant difference in the pattern of leadership over time. Patterns for other associations in this category were similar. The membership of the Teochiu welfare association, for example, was overwhelmingly working-class, and members were typically squatters, or living in resettlement estates or tenements. Its leadership was composed of businessmen and educators.

The small Fuzhou association and the two clansmen's associations differed. There were less than 200 families from Fuzhou living in Tsuen Wan, and the majority belonged to the association. Hokchiu, the language of Fuzhou, is very different from Cantonese and indeed from any other variant of spoken Chinese then common in Tsuen Wan. Most members of the association had arrived in Tsuen Wan after 1962, fleeing food shortages in China caused by Great Leap Forward policies. Moreover, most of the family heads were seamen, who left their poorly educated wives and young children in the linguistically unfamiliar Cantonese-speaking environment of Tsuen Wan for long periods. Leadership of the association was in the hands of those Fuzhou men who remained in Tsuen Wan, largely as workers in the shoe industry. They were newcomers, poorly educated and with modest Cantonese language skills attempting to hold together families that were fragmented by the primary earners' employment as seamen.

The two clansmen's associations were also largely working-class and based on same surname ties. The members of one were natives of a large market town area in Haifeng in eastern Guangdong. Most were recent migrants who came to Hong Kong after 1961, but a sizeable number came after 1966. A few members were small businessmen, but most were factory workers. The other clansmen's association was similar and newly established. Its members spoke Teochiu. It owed its origin to the events of the summer of 1967 during which a much larger same-surname association split into right-wing and left-wing factions. The right-wing faction grouped in Tsuen Wan and those with left-wing sympathies were rigidly excluded from membership. There were coolies, construction workers, and small businessmen among its members, but the largest number were workers in garment factories making shirts. All had arrived after 1962.

The objectives of the fellow-countrymen's associations typically included welfare and relief work, both for members and non-members; the provision of clinics; assistance to members in finding employment; mediation of disputes; funeral benefits; help with costs of birth and marriage; the provision of leisure activities; and the promotion of unity and friendly relations (感情) among members. The larger associations were all actively involved in educational activities, the largest and grandest being the government-aided Teochiu school. Generalized welfare benefits ranked as a high priority for all, which for the richest associations extended to non-members. The NCWA, for example, dispensed rice, quilts, and cash in significant amounts, especially in the 1961–1965 period. In 1968 and 1969 over 4,000 people used the association clinic.[15] Most other associations had similar concerns, although only the largest provided welfare for non-members. Death benefits were extremely important in the work of fellow-countrymen's associations. They varied from $300 for a small association to $700 for a larger one.

The aims of the smaller associations were more modest. It was impossible for the clansmen's associations to run schools, although they offered basic activities such as sewing and cooking classes. Rather, they tended to emphasize welfare functions, which were of direct concern to members and their dependents. The Fuzhou association helped its members find work on ships, but it also helped with the remittance of funds from seamen to their dependents in Hong Kong. This aspect of the work was aided through the parent organization in urban Hong Kong. For the smaller associations, death, marriage, and birth benefits loomed very large in their work, and they often gave members loans to cover certain expenses, particularly medical bills. Without clinic facilities, this was an important service.

For small associations, the provision of leisure activities, even if merely a table and a mah-jong set, was of great significance. One of the clansmen's associations practiced Chinese boxing on the roof of the association premises. It was an activity that was very important in the homeland and the members practiced without the aid of a tutor, merely guidance from older members. One of the larger (Hakka) fellow-countrymen's associations had two formally constituted 'boxing academies', with tutors, and a membership of over 200 students. These kinds of associations will be discussed later in the chapter. Only one of the associations had a patron deity, namely the Subei association, which honoured Confucius on his feast day. One leader suggested that his association was in decline, as were fellow-countrymen's associations in general, because potential members were more interested in religion and sports, neither of which were significant for such associations.

Most fellow-countrymen's associations had clauses in their constitutions which specified that potential members should be 'showing good behaviour' (品行良好), which was a euphemism for non-left-wing sympathies. Some associations were more overt in their sympathies than others, but with only two exceptions, and these were smaller associations, support for the Guomindang was apparent at 'Double Ten'. In many association offices, the image of the patron deity was replaced by a set of portraits—those of Sun Yat-sen, Chiang Kai-shek, and Queen Elizabeth, along with the British and Nationalist flags. Some of the leaders of the fellow-countrymen's associations belonged to, and held office in, other ideological organizations in Hong Kong, and were invited to Taiwan to take part in the celebrations on October 10, as representatives from left-leaning unions were invited to China on October 1. Most of the associations extensively decorated their premises, erected billboards with a highly political content, replete with messages exhorting the Chinese (Nationalists) to retake the mainland, and held banquets, film shows, and the like. October 10 was a highlight of the year for many of these associations and they actively participated in planning for it with fellow sympathizers.

15. Tsuen Wan did not have a public hospital until 1973. A government polyclinic was established in 1967.

Ideology and its celebration was a highlight but should not detract from the important work of a non-ideological nature, which they also undertook. Ideology gave the associations an added element of solidarity, which during Chinese history had been focused upon the ritual connected with a patron deity.

The names that many fellow-countrymen's associations adopted were often the district name prefaced by 'temporarily in Hong Kong' (僑港 or 旅港), which suggests that the founders imagined their sojourn away from the point of migration was of only short duration. Even in 1969, there was a tendency for older people—first generation migrants—to belong to these associations and for their children to belong to newer, specialized ones, more in keeping with an emerging identity as Cantonese-speaking Hong Kong people. For the NCWA, 80% of its membership was 40 years old and above, and less than 5% younger than 20 years old. The pattern was little different in other fellow-countrymen's associations. Locality ties were important in industrializing Tsuen Wan. Fellow-countrymen's associations appeared to be significant in the initial stages of migration. In the longer run, these particularistic ties were destined to weaken, as they have throughout the overseas Chinese world.

Neighbourhood (*Kaifong*) Associations

In the late 1960s, there were a number of land-based settlement types: native villages, shophouses and tenements, low cost housing flats, Housing Society flats, resettlement estates, and squatter areas. Generally absent were middle-class housing complexes. In each of the settlement types there were examples of associations which recruited their members from within the settlement type (the *kaifong* [街坊] or neighbourhood). Specifically, there were three resettlement estate *kaifong* associations, an association in a Housing Society estate, a management association in a tenement complex, two associations in squatter settlements, and most unusual of all, an association based in a multi-lineage native village, as noted in Chapter 5. There was variation in terms of membership and the ability to achieve stated goals, but with the exception of one association in Lo Wai village, there was similarity of purpose. In general, their objectives were two—welfare and politics.

The neighbourhood associations differed from the fellow-countrymen's associations in that they saw local political work as an addition to general welfare tasks. In government and semi-government housing projects, the feelings of political isolation were acute. In 1966, over one-half of Tsuen Wan's population lived in such housing and the proportion grew dramatically during our two years in the town. There were no formal mechanisms of access to government, with one small exception. This contrasted strongly with the native village political structure of village representatives and Rural Committees. Village representatives had day-to-day contact with their constituents, and regular formal meetings with government representatives, usually the local district officer, as well as innumerable informal contacts with his staff.

Tenements were difficult to organize. The tenement population was a shifting one, and ecology constrained social interaction. Thus, only one middle-class apartment building had formed a management association. Squatter areas offered a contrast. Of the dozen or so squatter areas, five were either incorporated into the local political structure through formal membership on the Tsuen Wan Rural Committee or had an association which spoke on behalf of the neighbourhood.

The welfare work of the *kaifong* associations was substantial. They had clinics, kindergartens, and held classes in cooking, sewing, and at times literacy. They mediated disputes; one resettlement estate *kaifong* association dealt with three or four neighbours' conflicts a month and had dealt with 70 cases of husband-wife conflict in a year. They helped find employment and provided modest recreation facilities for the neighbourhood.

Neighbourhood associations had been prominent since the beginnings of Tsuen Wan's development. Tai Wo Hau, the oldest resettlement estate in Tsuen Wan, began as a controlled squatter area ('cottage resite') after a disastrous fire burned down a Tsuen Wan squatter area in 1954. As early as 1956, there were moves to start a *kaifong* welfare association based on the estate. The proposal ran into opposition from the authorities, who disapproved of the attempt to set up a school and a clinic. The District Commissioner New Territories deemed it inappropriate for a *kaifong* association to be set up in the New Territories. He argued that *kaifong* associations were more a feature of urban life, although even by 1956, Tsuen Wan was hardly the rural area of a decade previously. Despite a demand on the part of the government authorities to disband, it lingered for two years and finally disbanded through a peculiar compromise. In 1958 the chairman of the proposed association was co-opted onto the Tsuen Wan Rural Committee, where in 1969 he still sat representing 10,000 people. No other resettlement estate was thus represented, and in 1966 a fully fledged *kaifong* association was re-formed without objection.

A slightly different pattern was found among squatters. One such area was founded in 1950, adjacent to the native village of Kau Wa Keng on the Kowloon edge of the district. It was an unusual squatter area in that most of the residents enjoyed high social status, which they had been able to maintain in the transition to Hong Kong. The area was one of secure tenancy and pleasant villas and came to be called Kau Wa New Village. Its wealth contrasted strongly with other squatter areas. Like them, it was mono-class, but the residents were successful members of the middle class and the bourgeois atmosphere was very different from the proletarian atmosphere of most Hong Kong squatter areas. From the beginning, an association was formed which dealt with the provision of electric light, a village watch, sanitation, a market, a clinic, and a school. The sophisticated leadership was also able to secure, from a very early date, the support of the district officer, who was then based in Kowloon and easily accessed from the new village. In 1955 the two chief officers of the welfare association became village representatives with seats on the Tsuen Wan Rural Committee.

A much poorer squatter area tried a similar move to gain political recognition in 1958, which was resisted. Squatters on land adjacent to Muk Min Ha village, which was in sight of the newly established Tsuen Wan District Office, attempted to establish autonomy for their area and claim a seat on the Rural Committee. The village representatives of Muk Min Ha objected, and the movement failed. Only in 1967, as a consequence of the events of that summer, was a revived attempt at a neighbourhood association successful, although for the two years before then, a group of three residents, who were later to become officers in the neighbourhood association, acted as points of contact between the government and the residents of the area. The association gained approval by taking a political stand against the left.

An ideological element was implicit in all the neighbourhood associations except the one formed in Lo Wai village, although ideology was not as pronounced as in the fellow-countrymen's associations. The most ideological neighbourhood association was the one with the most homogeneous population, namely the middle-class *kaifong* association in Kau Wa New Village, which recruited almost 100% of the neighbourhood as members.

Most neighbourhood associations were of recent origin. Two were wracked by internal dissension, which made it impossible for them to function effectively. In the summer of 1969 a new element emerged. In a resettlement estate dominated by Teochiu residents, the *kaifong* association became the sponsor of a 'hungry ghost' festival, an activity that we shall discuss in detail later in the chapter. In another resettlement estate in which dissension had effectively hampered the work of the neighbourhood association, three hungry ghost festivals were held. Sponsorship of these festivals was distinctly along speech group lines, and it was on these lines that conflict occurred.[16]

---

16. For details, slightly later, see D. W. Sparks, 'Interethnic Interaction—A Matter of Definition: Ethnicity in a Housing Estate in

The development of associations can be seen as a response to problems implicit in Tsuen Wan's development primarily affecting immigrants. The native village association was different. The village of Lo Wai had a high degree of inter-lineage cooperation that was expressed in the mid-nineteenth century, when its five lineages pooled property and created the Tung Wo Seh. In the early 1960s, they rationalized their property management through a formally registered company. It called itself the Lo Wai Village Welfare Association.

The new association did not stop at property management. Like many of the immigrant associations it conducted relief work, mediated family disputes, helped members in their dealings with government officials, and pressured the government for water, sanitation, and village paths. It gave funeral benefits to resident immigrants, although only natives could become members. The leaders we interviewed said they did not look down upon the newcomers. Occasionally, the association helped young people find work, and it ran an excellent local school and an adult evening school. It also established a profitable minibus line between central Tsuen Wan and the village, which is close to local beauty spots in the hills above Tsuen Wan, and to several Buddhist and Daoist religious establishments. The buses transported villagers and local tourists from the market. Tsuen Wan villages and their lineages had coped successfully with the consequences of the industrial transformation of their agricultural heritage. None had adapted so radically to the change around them as Tsuen Wan's oldest village, which was never subject to a negotiated removal and has remained intact, if not unchanged, for almost four centuries.

Welfare Associations

These were the smallest and most homogeneous class of associations, apart from the political associations. With one exception, they resembled 'traditional' Hong Kong welfare associations, although there was a certain veneer of modernity about some of them. We have noted that welfare was a common element in most of the associations that we have discussed so far. In Hong Kong, and elsewhere in the broad Chinese diaspora, there were, and are, operative two concepts of 'welfare'. One refers to a concern by an association for the welfare of its own members and can be more nearly called mutual benefit. This was an important aspect of the work of all neighbourhood associations, the fellow-countrymen's associations, and all trade unions. We noted that the wealthier fellow-countrymen's associations broadened their welfare aims to include non-members, as did the Tung Wo Seh in Lo Wai.

Long-established Hong Kong welfare associations had, and still have, an almost exclusive concern for the welfare of non-members. Such associations are composed of groups of wealthy individuals who work to help those less fortunate than themselves. Thus, in urban Hong Kong there existed, and still exist, associations such as the Po Leung Kuk and the Tung Wah Hospital Board, in the New Territories the Pok Oi Hospital Board, and, perhaps most glamorous of all, the Royal Hong Kong Jockey Club,[17] which provide not merely a channel of welfare funds, but also a channel of status-honour.

The apex of prestige in terms of association membership in Hong Kong in the 1960s was a hospital board. There was a hospital board in Tsuen Wan which included every man (and two women) of note and wealth who had a connection with Tsuen Wan. The board was set up for the sole purpose of building and eventually running a modern public hospital in Tsuen Wan. The need was critical for a population that was approaching 300,000 and growing rapidly. Although the board had been established in 1960, modelled after the Tung Wah hospital board, building had not begun by May 1970 when we left Hong Kong, despite fundraising and a grant of land by the government.[18] Doubtless,

Hong Kong', *Journal of the Hong Kong Branch Royal Asiatic Society* 16 (1976): 57–80.
17. 'Royal' was dropped in 1997.
18. It was opened, as the Yan Chai Hospital, along with a nursing school, in 1973.

there were political problems. The directors of the board were all wealthy and busy men and women. Furthermore, the years after 1960 had not been easy. They included the death of one of its most dynamic members, a building slump, and the events of the summer of 1967. There were also other hospital boards, or similar organizations, in Hong Kong which detracted from the importance and the utility of the Tsuen Wan hospital board.

Other high-status welfare organizations included two fashioned after Western models, namely branches of Rotary and The Lions. These were small elitist associations whose major functions were to channel money for charitable purposes. Both The Lions and Rotary had direct concern with the problems of youth. The aid extended as far as medical treatment for schoolchildren, as well as books and school fees. Since many members were factory owners or managers, they encouraged many of their grantees with apprenticeship schemes. Both associations also acted as elitist social clubs for a small group of businessmen. They were dominated by well-educated 'Shanghainese'. Their memberships were, oddly, mutually exclusive. There was a further association, dominated by newcomers from the Pearl River Delta region, who were active supporters of the YMCA and its principles (荃灣聯青社).

There was an elite women's association called The New Territories Women and Juvenile Welfare Association. It was not specific to Tsuen Wan although it did maintain its office there. The wives of men with high prestige were represented on its executive committee. It had the usual admixture of public works and prestige that was, and is, so typical of Hong Kong's large welfare associations. Its objects were to solicit funds to be used for the particular needs of women. It ran nurseries, kindergartens, training classes, family planning clinics, and at times gave direct relief. It even loaned its facilities for weddings if the need arose. Its work was conducted in Cheung Chau, Ma Wan, and Yuen Long, in addition to Tsuen Wan.

Leisure/Educational Associations

In a non-industrial setting, leisure is not a problem. For the vast majority of the population in an agrarian society, living at subsistence level gives little time for a concern with leisure activities. The breaks from the agricultural routine, or other economic activities, are quite rigidly institutionalized around some ritual activity or an event like a periodic fair. Modern machine technology and its consequence, the factory organization of labour, determines a new pattern of living in which a worker's day is no longer geared to the hours of sunlight or the seasons. Factory organization typically leaves some time for the worker between work and rest, although there was very little in Hong Kong at the time. There arise, therefore, organizations that are predominantly recreational. The forms such organizations take depend on a number of factors including gender, age, migration status, and social class. To some degree, associations, particularly the fellow-countrymen's associations, provided facilities for adult recreation. For many Hong Kong adults, the opportunities for leisure time activities were limited. In a context created by a laissez-faire attitude to economic development, the typical work week was seven days and the average work day was ten-and-a-half hours. There were few public holidays, which were not always recognized by employers. This left little opportunity for recreation, except perhaps a visit to the cinema, which was popular, cheap, and air-conditioned.[19] Many of the larger factories instituted 'welfare sections' in which the workers could participate in sports and other leisure activities.

Another set of issues, which is related, is the lack of integration of the family into industrial society when compared to the situation in agrarian society. Thus, one feature of an industrial society is the existence of a 'youth problem' and attempts to provide organizations to cope with it.

In Tsuen Wan, there were a number of associations dealing with the potentially explosive situation of youth and recreation. There were four sports associations, a fifth which coordinated their

---

19. Television, although present, was not generally accessible until the early 1970s.

activities, a youth club, and several associations that dealt specifically with young people. These promoted cultural interests, such as dancing, music, calligraphy, and art appreciation.

In Tsuen Wan in the late 1960s, there were large numbers of children and young people. In the whole district there were only five sizeable gardens and sports grounds. Most of the population lived in public housing and given the density of population in these areas—especially the resettlement estates—recreational facilities were insufficient for the need. Parents' fears that their children might become delinquent were realistic under the circumstances. The Boy Scouts and the cultural associations, along with a number of church-sponsored centres, attempted to meet the deficiencies in public facilities. The leadership of these organizations was highly professional and composed largely of schoolteachers and successful businessmen.

Politics and education can be closely linked. Sports associations were not entirely free from political factors. In Chapter 2 we drew attention to the formation, in 1929, of a sports club which was founded by a group of educated young men of the district. Those men, by the late 1960s, were middle aged, and remained as leading figures in the association. It actively supported football and was represented on the government-sponsored sports federation. The club was dominated by Tsuen Wan natives and was headed by a popular local left-wing politician. After 1967, the venerable sports association was split ideologically, which severely hampered its operation.

Political Associations

In 1947, the system of village representatives and Rural Committees had been established throughout the New Territories. The system was formally highly democratic. Each village was allowed up to three representatives, depending upon its size. Each representative was elected on a franchise which included property ownership and indigenous status, or at least long-term residence in the constituency, usually a village. The election procedure was often a formality, although the process of selecting candidates could be long and arduous, and any person with a police record was disbarred from standing. In 1967, a new element entered into the equation of local political leadership when the government made a loose ideological sympathy with the British colonial administration a qualification for village representative status, as they were obliged to swear allegiance to Queen Elizabeth. In late 1967, a number of village representatives, including the chairman and vice-chairman of the Rural Committee, were dismissed after the chairman made a speech in the Heung Yee Kuk which was an attack, however mild, on the government's handling of the anti-British protests in the summer of 1967. The dismissals created consternation in the villages. It took several years, and new circumstances, to resolve the issues.

Overall, 65 representatives were elected to represent 25 native villages, former fishing people, and a number of other areas. From this group, 19 men[20] and two reserve members were elected to sit on the executive committee of the Rural Committee. Although the Rural Committee met as a body twice a year, the real power was with the executive committee and its committees.

The chairman and the two vice-chairmen of the Rural Committee, plus one other member, usually a former chairman, sat on the Heung Yee Kuk. On the smaller islands of Tsing Yi and Ma Wan a similar, though smaller, structure prevailed. These Rural Committees also had representatives on the Heung Yee Kuk.

The Rural Committee worked well for its constituency, but over a period of 20 years it became less and less representative of the growing Tsuen Wan population. With only few exceptions, the newcomers were excluded from formal political access to government. The non-native population, despite its overwhelming numbers, did not have the cohesive force, or political legitimacy, of the indigenous villagers. The Rural Committees in the district acted as native pressure groups when the need arose,

---

20. There were no women elected as village representative until the 1990s, when a woman was elected in Lo Wai.

which was frequent, and they fought strongly for the rights of the indigenous population, even if those rights impinged on those of the outsiders. They had a formal political relationship with the government, and the government was very conscious of the distinctiveness of the indigenous population, since it was derived from treaty rights.

The Tsuen Wan Rural Committee received a small subvention from government for its day-to-day expenses, and it was also trustee for the Tianhou temple, which received rental income from temple properties. Apart from its political functions, the committee was important for the mediation of disputes and conflicts, especially those concerned with property and inheritance. The committee was important in district-wide leisure activities such as the organization of the lunar New Year fair. It also consulted on the formulation of development plans for the district, especially in the town, since it was the representative of such a crucial segment of the population with enshrined land rights.

The smaller Rural Committees on Tsing Yi and Ma Wan were somewhat different, and the work that they did reflected the distinctiveness of their small island localities. The Ma Wan Rural Committee acted as government, police, postman, and fire brigade, and was a dominant influence on the lives of the villagers of the island. Tsing Yi was less isolated than Ma Wan, but on the island, the Rural Committee was both police and fire brigade. The Tsing Yi Rural Committee also organized annual celebrations in honour of Tianhou.

A new political association formed by immigrants emerged in Tsuen Wan in the latter part of the 1960s. It was called the Federation of Societies (荃灣區社團聯合會) and saw itself as a political counterbalance to the Rural Committee. The need for political articulation within this growing population became increasingly pressing. The division between indigenous people and immigrants was deep and there was a certain mutual suspicion between the two sides. The formation of the federation was recognition of the near-monopoly by the indigenous population of the effective channels of political communication. It was not, however, the only element that impelled its formation.

The federation was first mooted in late June 1967 when political conflict was approaching one peak. Ideologically, the sponsors and members of the federation were not neutral. The preparatory meetings had brought together associations, including some prominent in right-wing circles. Formal approval was given in September 1967, and shortly thereafter, all the right-wing trade unions attempted to join the federation. The government pressured them to withdraw their applications, for the implication of their being allowed to join was explosive. After the events of the summer, the colonial government did not wish to rekindle political sparks. Even before formal approval to the federation had been given, a Public Security Section (later called a Public Security Advancement Association—PSAA) had been set up 'to assist the government in maintaining law and order and promoting the economic prosperity of the Tsuen Wan District'. The PSAA functioned mainly as an intelligence-gathering service for the police. The section was headed by two prominent Hakka immigrants who were office bearers in a fellow-countrymen's association that was particularly overt in its right-wing sympathies and which had especially close relations with right-wing trade unions. For this aspect of its work, the federation received a small grant from the government.

It was one of the major aims of the federation to build solidarity among immigrants in Tsuen Wan, although it was a solidarity that derived as much from a feeling of outsiderness as from a threat from the left. If the Tsuen Wan Rural Committee was to maintain its dominance of formal political channels as the population grew and the issues of administering an urban and industrial settlement became increasingly complex, there was concern in the government about potential conflict on a greater level than had existed.

Rethinking the issues of local administration was already underway, even as the government was caught up in the unexpected left-wing challenges in the summer of 1967.[21] The policy rethinking was

---

21. *Hong Kong Government Report of the Working Party on Local Administration* (Hong Kong: Government Publications, 1967).

the result of a number of issues: local, regional, and global. The experience of coping with the complexities of Tsuen Wan's development in the decade after opening a district office in the town—and its implications for the New Territories as a whole—was important. Dramatic changes had occurred in the 1960s and were to continue in the 1970s as these issues had unimagined consequences.

Religious Associations

Religious associations of which we had knowledge included two temple associations, 13 boxing academies (健身學院), and five *fapaau* associations (花炮會). Religious behaviour was both highly visible and salient for a large proportion of the immigrant population of Tsuen Wan. Religious associations were the second largest category after those which we described as economic and which dealt with Tsuen Wan's central condition, that of economic transformation. Religious associations involved more people than any other category, indicating the strength of these essentially pre-industrial forms in a highly industrial setting. As with many associations they looked two ways, backwards to a pre-industrial society and forward to the present one. Like other associations, these reflected the subcultural characteristics of the Tsuen Wan population. Religious associations were, in general, the preserve of the newcomers. The indigenous population had its lineages, temples, and shrines which were the focus for its ritual activities. The process of migration had been divisive of organized kinship units for recent arrivals. This disruption must be seen as one important element in the formation of religious associations.

Temple Associations

The two temple associations were similar, although they differed in some details. The oldest and grandest, Yuen Yuen Hok Yuen (圓玄學園), represented a pattern that was common among the Chinese business community in Hong Kong at that time. A group of wealthy and highly respected, largely Cantonese-speaking, businessmen contributed considerable time, money, and effort, but mostly money, to erect and run a temple in the hills above Tsuen Wan, the only place in Hong Kong with a full-scale replica of the Temple of Heaven in Beijing. The need for such a temple complex was revealed by a Daoist sage, Lu Dongbin (呂洞賓), during a spirit-medium session.[22] The temple had shrines to a number of deities, and halls where members of the temple could place ancestral soul tablets for worship. For people with fragmented kin groups, this was of great importance.

It is not easy to classify the temple. The replica of the Temple of Heaven is a 'hall-of-the-three-teachings' (三教堂) devoted to the founders of Buddhism, Daoism, and Confucianism. The temple represented a sectarian movement which in Imperial China would have been highly unorthodox. Its general objectives were described by one leader 'to serve its purpose for religion, public morality and the tourist industry'. The temple association ran an old people's home within the temple and each resident was guaranteed a bed, food, and a funeral. It also served vegetarian food, some of which was grown within the complex, and was extremely popular with tourists, since it was both tasty and cheap.

The temple association was a registered company and its articles of association presented its objectives as follows: '3(a) to promote and protect the faith of the Buddhist and Daoist religions and to promote or oppose legislation and other measures affecting such religions and to study Buddhism and Daoism in all or any of their branches; 3(b) to erect Buddhist or Daoist shrines or altars for worship in the forms devised by the two faiths and to modify the same when desirable to suit local conditions'. Membership was open to any 'lay Buddhist or Daoist of Hong Kong and any merchant', and the association drew on a population which was scattered all over Hong Kong.

---

22. A process whereby individuals with special powers are believed able to communicate with, in this case, a god, and convey messages from the deity.

Plate 34: Yuk Ha Kok temple in the midst of a squatter area in northern Tsuen Wan, 1968.

There was no formal priesthood and the leading members of the board of management typically officiated in religious ceremonies of a formal nature. The association was involved in general relief work and at times the leadership invoked the blessings of various gods for the relief of catastrophes. In 1963, for example, at the time of great drought and water shortages in Hong Kong, there were invocations for rain. For a seven-day period in September 1968, there were religious services for 'the elimination of disasters and calamities'. The leading members remained in the temple during the period, maintained a vegetarian diet, and conducted religious services on a specially built platform.

The other temple association, Yuk Ha Kok (玉霞閣), was specific to Tsuen Wan and to the Teochiu population. Teochiu people were characterized by others as being highly religious. They were devout in their participation in temple festivals. The temple was founded in the middle 1950s, when in-migration to Hong Kong from the Chaozhou region had grown substantially. In the late 1960s it was located in a squatter area to the north of the town, where we had encountered it on our initial walks. The temple was likely the most spectacular squatter structure in Hong Kong.

Its organization was not unlike Yuen Yuen Hok Yuen, although it was not a registered company, nor did it draw its membership from as wide an area. The temple had three major aspects to its work. It was a Teochiu-language temple and place for the worship of a number of deities, some of whom advised those in need at regular spirit-medium sessions, typically carried out by the highly charismatic temple head. Another Daoist sage, Li Tieguai (李鐵拐) was a crucial deity as were 'The Great Sage Equal to Heaven' (齊天大聖) ['Monkey'], Matreya Buddha (如來佛) ['The Buddha to Come'], and Guanyin (觀音), the Goddess of Mercy. It was, secondly, a welfare organization for the local Teochiu community. Lastly, but by no means least, it provided a team of ritual specialists that was one of five serving the Teochiu communities in Hong Kong during the seventh lunar month, for their sponsorship of hungry ghost festivals.

Plate 35: Various structures of Yuk Ha Kok temple, including a mountain with monkeys and a red bottle gourd, all made of ferroconcrete.

During that month, but especially on the 14th day, many families, both Cantonese and Teochiu, burned paper ritual money and paper clothes, and presented other offerings to hungry ghosts—souls that are not regularly worshipped either through neglect, or because they had died violent deaths. Worship in the seventh month was, and is, an appeasement of these wandering spirits. For Teochiu people in Hong Kong in the 1960s, this worship occurred on a wide scale and also extended to ancestor worship, which distinguished Teochiu ritual from its Cantonese form. The temple sponsored its own hungry ghost festival at the beginning of the eighth lunar month, after all the others. The temple represented a sectarian movement, highly unorthodox, but of central importance in the lives of many Tsuen Wan Teochiu people, rich and poor alike.

It was focused on the medium cult, and one leader said that they believed in the power of the willow planchette or divining rod (扶乩) more than anything. It was the planchette that had the power to call down the true gods (神).[23] He stated that there were no problems with leadership, voting, future plans, or even the recruitment of members, for the planchette provided the answers, and at times even the names of potential members. There was a management committee drawn from the members of the temple and which ran for terms of undefined length. This committee was chosen through divination. The leading members of the committee with specific responsibilities for finance or general administration were all local businessmen. There was some overlap with the management committee of Yuen Yuen Hok Yuen, although it was not extensive.

---

23. A spirit medium held one branch of the planchette in one hand and an assistant held the other. Prayers were offered to the god and a request was made for the god, or an assistant of the god, to descend and speak through the medium. The planchette moved and traced out characters which the medium called out and which were entered into a book by a scribe. After the medium session was over the message from the god was interpreted.

Plate 36: A worshipper is possessed by a god and goes into a trance, biting a teacup and drawing blood, 1968.

Sometimes the god spoke through a medium other than the temple head. On one occasion that we witnessed, the name of a participant was traced out. Outside the area of the shrine, and out of sight and earshot of the divination ceremony, an elderly man in the crowd of worshippers, who had communicated with gods when still in his native place, immediately went into a trance.[24] He crushed a porcelain wine cup with his teeth and cut his tongue with the pieces. Blood from the cuts was stamped onto charm papers. He was brought from his trance by the master of the temple, who spat water infused with pomelo leaves, which had started the divination ceremonies, into the man's face.

On another occasion, the master of the temple was chosen to act on the god's behalf. He cut his tongue with a long and extremely sharp knife and proceeded to write charm papers with his bloody tongue for at least an hour. Some were very large and poster-sized, with characters three or more inches high. The charms were later sold at $25 each and in a very short space of time the temple collected many thousands of dollars. The medium also spat blood over other objects such as small yellow flags, plates, and other objects which were also sold. Possession of a charm with a medium's blood on it was believed to guarantee good fortune and peace throughout the year. They were stuck on doors or hung at the entrance of a house or a flat.

At the large hungry ghost festival, believers collectively worshipped before temporary soul tablets, presented offerings, and burned paper articles for the use of deceased relatives in the underworld. They also burned paper articles and made offerings for those who were not properly worshipped through some misfortune. This both aided the spirits of the dead and protected the living from the malevolent potential of wandering spirits—the hungry ghosts.

---

24. Graham was standing on a bench above the divination session. He could clearly see the god's message as it was recorded and was also able to see the crowded forecourt of the shrine. The elderly man, who was referred to by the Hokkien term *tan-ki* (童乩) ['spirit medium'], was surrounded by worshippers and indistinguishable from them, simply dressed in traditional Chinese clothing.

Plate 37: The temple head, in a trance and holding the planchette, cuts his tongue with a knife so that he can spit blood over the flags and charm papers, giving them supernatural power.

During larger festivals, groups of lay priests, who were attached to the temple but including some with permanent occupations, chanted Buddhist sutras. During the three days of the hungry ghost festival, a specific number of sutras had to be chanted. After each sutra had been completed, a copy of it was put into a gold paper container, placed on a white paper crane or red horse, and burned. Seated on the crane or horse was a paper messenger who carried a message from the faithful to the god to whom it was destined, indicating that the sutra had been chanted. A similar burning occurred after a set of colourful and hypnotic 'dances', which were a feature of all Teochiu hungry ghost festivals, representing the journey of a soul through the underworld.[25] Towards the end of the festival, large quantities of paper ritual objects, including an enormous brightly painted image of the 'God-Who-Looks-into-Hell' (大士爺), were also ceremoniously burned by the small stream that ran through the squatter area where the temple was located.

A Teochiu-language opera was held throughout the festival and was incorporated into the event by actors conducting an on-stage ritual involving two dolls, and then placing the dolls on the main altar. Sutras were chanted by family members for named ancestors who were represented by temporary soul tablets placed in a mat-shed behind very large soul tablets for deceased members of the temple and the unknown dead. As the festival ended, the poor gathered to receive gifts of rice and other vegetarian foodstuffs.

The colour of the large ceremonies was absent in the day-to-day divination sessions which were held in the temple and which constituted the bulk of the temple's work. The procedure was simple. A person seeking advice from the god went to a small table outside the shrine to Li Tieguai, and his or her questions were noted on a large sheet of pink paper. If there were a number of cases, the collected papers were taken into the shrine and a divination session got under way. The medium and his assistant

25. See Margaret Chan, *Ritual Is Theatre, Theatre Is Ritual: Tang-ki Chinese Spirit Medium Worship* (Singapore: Singapore Management University Wee Kim Wee Centre, 2006).

donned white robes, tied up their trousers with yellow ribbons, took off their shoes and petitioned the god or an assistant to come and give advice. The person who brought the problems knelt throughout the divination and was brushed lightly with the fly whisk, a symbol of Li Tieguai, before seeking advice from the god. The supplicant also drank a pomelo leaf infusion, which preceded all communication with the deity. The planchette was passed over the sheet containing the questions, and the god then gave advice, which was transmitted through the planchette and recorded by the scribe. The god also suggested the use of charms, which were kept on the altar. A supplicant could take the advice which the god communicated to a specialist to be interpreted after the divination, since the advice was often given in classical rhyming couplets, which are not easy to understand. Health, advice on business matters, family fortunes, and children's schooling were common problems that were addressed. The god at times advised the use of specific medicines, which could be readily obtained at a pharmacy related to the temple. After the divination was completed, the supplicant worshipped at the shrine and made a contribution to the temple. At the divination ceremonies, the officiants were all men, as were most of the supplicants, while at gatherings, especially at important festivals, there were large numbers of women worshippers. Many, from their dress, appeared to be domestic servants.[26]

The temple was enormously popular with the local Teochiu population.[27] It was significant that many were poor and of rural origin. The Teochiu version of spoken Chinese is very different from Cantonese, and the Teochiu population had some problems in adapting to the local milieu, alien as it was to them. A salvationist sect, offering considerable certainty in the ritual, figured largely in the life of the Teochiu people. The temple gave not merely spiritual support, although this was critical; it also ran an old people's home offering the destitute aged food and shelter, a funeral, and worship after death. In a situation in which migration had disrupted organized kinship units, an organization that provided many kinship-like services, such as spiritual care after death, was of great importance. The temple also provided certain leisure activities.

The temple was not short of money to carry on its work. Members, especially businessmen, donated large sums, and at the annual hungry ghost festival articles of no great intrinsic worth were auctioned off for huge sums. In 1969, contributions at the hungry ghost festival alone totalled $55,220

An Extraordinary Religious Event

In the late summer of 1969 we witnessed a significant, and almost certainly unique, example of cooperation between the original inhabitants and immigrants. It was unique in that we have no evidence that it was ever held again, and that it was not a kind of ceremony normally held by the local Hakka people.

A very large hungry ghost ceremony was held on a vacant site near the centre of Tsuen Wan. It was sponsored both by the Tsuen Wan Rural Committee and by immigrant leaders. The opening proceedings saw as extensive an array of local prestige as there had been during our two years in Tsuen Wan, more impressive even than a luncheon that was held in Tsuen Wan for the governor of Hong Kong.

---

26. In the 1950s and 1960s domestic servants were invariably Chinese. It was only later, in the 1990s and after, that Filipina maids and others from Southeast Asia became preponderant.

27. Information on Teochiu religion and ritual is sparse. It was thus not easy to compare the behaviour of Teochiu people in Hong Kong or Tsuen Wan during the 1960s with that of Teochiu people in the homeland or even overseas. There is a paucity of published information on the Chaozhou region in Western languages, although scholarly activities at Shantou University since the 1990s are increasing knowledge of this complex and important region. Chen Ta, *Emigrant Communities in South China: A Study of Overseas Migration and Its Influence on Standards of Living and Social Change*, English Version Edited by Bruno Lasker (New York: Secretariat, Institute of Pacific Relations, 1940), has a wealth of information on villages in the Chaozhou region, whose many emigrants were resident in Malaya. See D. W. Sparks, 'The Teochiu Ethnicity in Urban Hong Kong', *Journal of the Hong Kong Branch Royal Asiatic Society* 16 (1976): 25–56, which is an effort to define Teochiu ethnicity from interviews in a resettlement estate in Kwai Chung. It is clear that Teochiu ethnicity, like Cantonese ethnicity, is not homogeneous.

Plate 38: A couple, beautifully dressed for New Year, worship at the image of Maitreya Buddha in Yuk Ha Kok.

The organizing committee brought together political figures from both sides of the native-immigrant divide. The board of contributors was a roster of local prestige. Actively involved was a new association designed to promote the Tsuen Wan tourist industry, which included many of the local religious organizations.

The rituals lasted for four days, and during that time increasing numbers of soul tablets appeared. These were very expensive, in local terms. When we recently asked our reliable local Hakka informant about the festival, and why it might have been held in this way, he responded without hesitation: 'because of the war', adding that large numbers of people died or were executed in Tsuen Wan under the Japanese occupiers. He called the ceremony *taaipihngjiu* (太平醮), in other words, rites to achieve peace by settling restless spirits. It only needed to be done once, he said, and he and his wife went on to explain that Hakka people do not feel the need to appease hungry ghosts and do not have this custom. What they do, instead, is to worship their ancestors, in the belief that they will protect them. There was not a procession around the boundaries of Tsuen Wan, as in other *dajiu* ceremonies. This would have been logistically extremely difficult, given the size and complexity of Tsuen Wan at that time, with its factories and outlying squatter areas. What was important to us was the cooperation that it showed between the two categories of people, and that the local Hakka people felt the need to participate in this type of ceremony, following from the highly traumatic period of the Japanese occupation.

At the opening ceremony, the chairman of the Tsuen Wan Rural Committee, one important member of the organizing committee, spoke of the object of the festival as a concern with the relief of suffering of hungry ghosts in Tsuen Wan, especially the war dead. Once they had been settled, this would give a peaceful life to the populace. The chairman of the Heung Yee Kuk released a number of caged birds, a particular Buddhist act of merit. Each specific religious organization (including the two temple associations) had shrines where they conducted their own set of rituals. One hall was designated as a repository for tablets. It contained photographs of a particularly esteemed deceased former chairman of the Rural Committee, Ho Chuen-yiu, who was Christian, and the pre-war gentry figure Yeung Kwok-shui.

There were also general tablets for the deceased of all the Hakka households (presumably in Tsuen Wan), one for hungry ghosts in general, one for ancestors in general, and one for the war dead. Individuals were able to buy tablet spaces for named souls and they were worshipped for the duration of the festival. The soul tablet spaces were not cheap, ranging from $20 to $500 depending on their location. Before the end of the commemoration, every space was filled and they overflowed into a supplementary space. In all there were upwards of 2,000 temporary soul tablets installed during the four days of the festival. There was no opera and no auction. The activities were centred solely on the religious elements of a hungry ghost ceremony.

Boxing Academies and *Fapaau*[28] Associations

Boxing Academies

'Boxing academies' were established and headed by a tutor or master (師傅) who taught students Chinese martial arts. An academy had between 60 and 100 students. Some students studied for many years to gain competency in martial arts, and often aspects of Chinese medicine, to become teachers in their own right. They were typically between 17 and 25 years old, factory workers or middle-school students in the higher forms. Tutors saw their academies as places for the maintenance of social order by providing a place for young workers and students other than a gambling hall or street corner.

The boxing academies belonged to various sects (派) and branches (門) and they shared the same ideological roots as secret societies. Like many sects, there were generation names, 'genealogies', and a close religious brotherhood (結拜兄弟). With the existence of so many sects, and not unlike the fissions that occur in true kinship units, there was the potential for conflict. One of the more significant elements in the Tsuen Wan associational inventory was a fraternal association for the Tsuen Wan boxing academies. Reduction of tension was an important and necessary objective, although it did have other tasks to perform as well.

The major public appearances of boxing academies were at religious festivals. Students joined academies to keep fit and to learn martial arts, and also learned lion and dragon dancing. A student would invariably learn the rudiments of Chinese traditional medicine, certainly herbal medicine, and likely 'bone-setting', the manipulation of joints and tendons (鐵打). All tutors, without exception, were Chinese medical practitioners in their own right.

There was an immense variety in the types of armed combat and the kinds of martial arts that were taught. The reasons for this diversity are historical and closely related to ideology.[29] In identifying the emergence of the different varieties of skills, the history of boxing academies merges with that of Chinese secret societies.

Unlike monasteries and other religious sects, there was usually no set of formalized ranks. The brotherhood was reinforced not merely by worship before the tablet of the tutor's tutor ('ancestor'), but also by worship at graves in the spring and autumn, and on the ancestor's birthday. All the boxing academies had alumni associations, some of which were formally registered. Like many associations, such alumni bodies had welfare functions, aimed to develop good relations between members, and

---

28. The characters are 'flower' (*fa* 花) and 'bang' (*paau* 炮), and as a compound the term has little intrinsic meaning in either standard Chinese or English but denotes a 'portable altar' presented to a deity.

29. The history of the development of boxing sects is based upon interviews with a number of tutors. Most of them agreed on general principles, although there was some disagreement over detail. It differs little from some of the published accounts which concern the ideological background to secret societies. See J .P. Morgan, *Triad Societies in Hong Kong* (Hong Kong: Government Press, 1960); G. Schlegel, *Thian Ti Hwui: The Hung League or Heaven and Earth League* (Batavia: Lange & Co., 1866); J. S. M. Ward and H. G. Stirling, *The Hung Society or the Society of Heaven and Earth* (London: Baskerville Press, 1925); Li Chen-hua 李振華, *Jindai Bimi Shehui Shihluo* 近代秘密社會實錄 [True narrative of contemporary secret societies] (Taipei: Wenhai chubanshe, 1965).

helped members to find employment. All the boxing academies in Tsuen Wan were flourishing associations. Boxing masters said that membership was growing, and at virtually any time of the day or evening it was possible to hear the evidence of the vitality of the boxing academies with their constant practices for festivals, weddings, and shop openings.

In one respect there was a change. This was seen in the formation of the Federation of Boxing Academies, which signalled a break with the past in which conflict between sects and branches had been endemic. There was a general saying, repeated by a number of tutors, that 'a person never says he is first, a boxer never says he is second' (一名無第一武無第二). It was a reputation that still lingered for many and stemmed from the high conflict potential that existed with the schisms that have characterized Chinese boxing. This was uppermost in the consciousness of the leaders of the boxing federation.

Much of this reputation stemmed from a very close identification of boxing academies with secret societies in the past. It was said that especially in Guangzhou, Foshan, and Hong Kong, boxing tutors had more power than the police in the days before the Japanese occupation. Post-war Hong Kong was very different from pre-war Guangzhou or Foshan. The secret society leaders, who came to Hong Kong in the out-migration from China after the formation of the People's Republic, were either very closely watched by the police or encouraged to move on to Taiwan.

Boxing tutors in post-war Hong Kong either had to work or to concentrate their energies as practitioners of traditional medicine to earn a living. They were very severe in their control of their students, instructing them never to cause fights outside the academy, and never to fight with students from another boxing club. They were well aware that the line between a tolerated sect and the illegal triads was a fine one. Yet, given the factions, there was the potential for disastrous conflict. The federation was an attempt to develop unity among the different sects in order to forestall fighting between students of the various academies. The federation set up a committee to research aspects of the teaching of martial arts, and attempted at a modest synthesis, in published form, of the various kinds. In addition, as with so many organizations, there was hope of welfare provisions. Its critical goal, however, was the mediation of disputes and the integration of a group of societies and ideas that had previously been explosively disintegrative.

Fapaau Associations

Boxing academies and *fapaau* associations were intimately related. In Tsuen Wan District the feast days (誕) of three deities, Tianhou, Zhen Jun (真君), and the Dragon Mother (龍母), were celebrated in an impressive fashion. A *fapaau* association was composed of a group of people who came together in an organized fashion for the purpose of collective worship on the feast day of a deity. The men of the association carried a large paper altar (a *fapaau*), festooned with paper flowers, lanterns, and small figures, which was a blaze of colour. They also presented a whole roast pig, cakes, and other offerings to the deity.

Most typically *fapaau* associations had a basis in an occupational group such as hawkers, butchers or other small traders, or certain fellow-countrymen's associations. Most of the land-based *fapaau* associations had been formed within the ten years before 1968. They were wholly the preserve of immigrants, with the exception of those run by local fishing people. The land-based population of original inhabitants seemed hardly aware of their existence.

The association invited a boxing academy to help in the ritual and, most importantly, to provide the services of a lion dance team or, occasionally, a dragon. The biggest and most splendid celebration was for Tianhou's feast day. It was centred on the island of Tsing Yi and was held about a week after similar celebrations in other parts of Hong Kong.[30] The festival itself was organized by the Tsing Yi Rural Committee.[31] Groups from all over Hong Kong, including a number from Tsuen Wan, converged on the island in large, extensively decorated junks. A temporary shrine was erected for mass worship and there were other attractions such as opera, and activities which were of a questionable legal nature, including gambling and the cooking and selling of dog meat.[32]

On the morning of the Tianhou festival, one *fapaau* association paraded along Castle Peak Road and worshiped at a temporary shrine on Tsuen Wan's Market Street, erected around an earth god. The offerings and the *fapaau* were presented to the earth god and paper clothes were burned. The lion dancers paid their respects to the god before the group moved off through the town to the junk which took them across the narrow strait to Tsing Yi. During the procession through the town, the lion dance team stopped and paid their respects to those shopkeepers who had a close relationship with, or were members of, the association. Each shopkeeper hung lettuce and 'lucky money' outside his shop, which the lion proceeded to 'eat', while dancing. After disembarking from its junk, the association presented the *fapaau* and offerings before the image of the goddess, first in the small Tianhou temple, and then before the temporary mat-shed[33] shrine.

Plate 39: The Tianhou Festival in 1969: an earth god shrine in central Tsuen Wan has been specially decorated with a temporary shrine by a *fapaau* association.

---

30. Tianhou's feast day is the twenty-third day of the third lunar month; the Tsing Yi celebration was held the first weekend after the first day of the fourth lunar month.

31. The festival was also a source of income for the temple. The central Tsuen Wan Tianhou festival did not include *fapaau*, as it had its established sources of income.

32. The indigenous population was well aware of these attractions.

33. Mat-sheds (戲棚) are intricately constructed structures of bamboo poles lashed together to create temporary buildings for events such as opera performances, and covered with mats or, now, sheets of metal. Some are large enough to seat 1,000 or more people.

Plate 40: A *fapaau*, with another behind, being carried away by a boxing academy after presentation at the Tianhou temple on Tsing Yi Island.

In 1969, 74 associations from throughout Hong Kong, including seven from Tsuen Wan, participated in the festival on Tsing Yi. The many worshippers, each carrying three large and expensive sticks of incense and a set of paper clothes for the goddess, braved the heat and the crowds as a sign of their hope that Tianhou would bless them with her protection during the year. It previously had been the custom to fire a ritual rocket in the air when all the groups had presented their *fapaau* to the goddess. The group to catch the rocket, as it fell back to earth, would return with the major 'prize', an elaborate paper altar, the *tauhpaau* (頭炮), provided by the Rural Committee. This caused considerable rivalry, not all of it friendly. Drawing of lots replaced the ritual rocket firing, which was less dramatic but non-violent.[34] Each association had to bring a *fapaau* and after its presentation to the goddess was given a number. At the draw, held in the office of the Rural Committee, *fapaau* were matched at random with associations; thus, only rarely would an association return with the *fapaau* that it had brought. The first one in the draw took back two *fapaau*, one of which was the *tauhpaau*. After the rituals were completed, the association returned with its new *fapaau* and its own lion dance team, and celebrated the festival with a banquet where the ritual pork was divided.

At the banquet, the *fapaau* was broken up and the pieces were auctioned off. In this way, the association recouped much of the money for the expenses connected with the ritual and celebration, which could be as much as $10,000 for a large association. The winner of the *tauhpaau*, with its two *fapaau*, had a greater income at its disposal in the following year. The central element in the *tauhpaau* was a picture of the goddess. This had to be returned to the festival organizers the following year. It was either held by a member of the association, who could bid for the honour of keeping it for a year or was

34. J. L. Watson describes the traditional form before the advent of 'a rather tame and boring lottery' as 'sanctioned violence' among the large Cantonese-speaking lineages of the northwest portion of the New Territories. See his 'Fighting with Operas: Processionals, Politics, and the Specter of Violence in Rural Hong Kong', in Watson and Watson, *Village Life in Hong Kong*, 319–21.

held by the boxing academy which had helped in the ritual. Worship had to be conducted before the image on the first and fifteenth of each lunar month. Possession of the image was guaranteed to bring good luck and prosperity.

The worship of Zhen Jun[35] was smaller and was held a few days after the celebrations for Tianhou but also on Tsing Yi. The Dragon Mother festival was held at her temple in Tsuen Wan on the eighth of the fifth lunar month. In this case, lorries replaced junks in bringing the *fapaau*, the association members, and the boxing academies to the temple. The narrow dirt roads leading to the temple in the hills above Tsuen Wan were monumentally cluttered with worshippers and vehicles on the occasion.

Many boxing academies ran *fapaau* associations, and two of the biggest in Tsuen Wan were boxer-sponsored. If an association invited a boxing academy to help them the 'fee' was expressed in a number of tables at the banquet. It was usually two or three. A table consisted of 12 people and could cost up to $400 depending on the number and quality of the dishes served.

The form seemed unchanged in the transition from China to Hong Kong except that with the relative prosperity in Hong Kong the *fapaau* were more elaborate and the banquet food more expensive. The founding members of a *fapaau* association drew up a small committee to run the affairs of the association. It generally functioned informally, with none of the trappings of a constitution and formally democratic elections, which characterized most of the associations that we have discussed. No *fapaau* association was formally registered. Each had a chairman but the critical task of maintaining

Plate 41: A *huapai* erected on a restaurant by a boxing academy to show that their banquet celebrating the Tianhou festival will be held there.

---

35. Hayes, *Tsuen Wan*, 152, and *Friends and Teachers*, 168–69 offers some details on Zhen Jun (Chun Kwan) whom he calls 'The Righteous Soldier'. He suggests his worship on Tsing Yi was popularized by immigrant workers from the 'East River region of Guangdong in the early twentieth century', and that the mother temple was in 'Longjiang', possibly the Hakka-speaking area to the east of Shenzhen. There was substantial migration from this region to Tsuen Wan from the mid-nineteenth century, and it is close to the East River region, which is Hakka, although not within it.

the association between festivals fell to the treasurer, who collected the monthly subscription of between two or three dollars and held the balance of the money from the previous year's auction. One member of the committee was charged with recruitment, which was done by personal introductions. 'We do not recruit strangers', we were told. The size of an association was always limited by the size of the restaurant and the biggest had about 70 tables seating 850 people. The work of the organizing committee was concentrated in the period immediately before the festival. It was necessary to hire a boat (or lorries), build a *fapaau*, buy all the materials for worship, including the pork; provide token monetary gifts of one or two dollars for all the members; and arrange for the banquet. All of this could take considerable organization. A general meeting of all the active members some weeks before the festival selected those with specific duties. It was necessary, for example, to gain police permission to hold the procession through the town. Members who were former policemen or had good relations with the police were deputed to arrange this.

The *fapaau* associations were, in general, the preserve of Cantonese or Hakka immigrants, in contrast to the hungry ghost festivals, which were Teochiu-sponsored and run. Businessmen participated in *fapaau* associations and were the ones who typically bought the parts of the *fapaau* at auction. There was a strongly held belief that benefits flowed from these acts. Business organizations in China traditionally worshipped deities for much the same reason, although there is little ethnographic evidence which mentions the carrying of paper altars to a shrine on the occasion of a deity's feast day.[36] The participation in a *fapaau* association gave added solidarity to other particularistic elements such as speech group, territory, or occupation. That such pre-industrial forms continued, or were revived, in a town that had been subject to such considerable structural changes and social and cultural disruption was highly significant.

Some Conclusions

In this chapter we have presented a picture of associations in Tsuen Wan as we saw them in the late 1960s. We have tried to show that population growth, economic growth and change, in-migration, and the lack of government-provided social services, were important in creating the conditions for their development. New relations of production and a rapidly growing population of immigrants of diverse origins created new social relations and, in the absence of formal mechanisms to solve the problems and conflicts of the new order, they created voluntary associations. There were significant needs that are common to both industrial and pre-industrial society and which were met within the context of these associations. Hence, Tsuen Wan associations were not neatly specific, but their functions overlapped to a considerable extent. It was a feature of most associations that they were sources of aid for personal crises that in a pre-industrial setting would have been met by wider kin groups, and that were not adequately met by a government that was not interventionist. Kin groups were badly fragmented by the migration process that took place under the adverse circumstances of civil war and revolution, and new types of social networks were badly needed. One of the features of voluntary associations in a Chinese setting, and elsewhere, is that attachment to one's own group was commonly used as a basis for recruitment. At the same time, the aims of many, if not most, of these organizations were to gain some accommodation with the demands of a society whose major characteristics were universalistic. In a period of rapid social and economic change, particularism offers important mechanisms to meet the challenges contained within it.

---

36. C. K. Yang, himself Cantonese, mentions 'Rocket Societies', possibly *fapaau* associations, in a Guangzhou suburb, in his seminal book *Religion in Chinese Society* (Berkeley: University of California Press, 1959). See also Allen Chun, *Unstructuring Chinese Society*, esp. 164–70 where he discusses *fapaau* associations in the Shataukok region.

7

Leaders and Leadership

Questions of Approach

The importance of leadership in Tsuen Wan was impressed upon us, shortly after we arrived in the town, by a two-block-long display of large and colourful *huapai* (花牌)[1] along Castle Peak Road congratulating the newly elected members of the 14th term of the Tsuen Wan Rural Committee. *Huapai* also appeared periodically at the headquarters of various associations to celebrate new terms for their officers. Leaders of the many kinds of associations were essential in helping to meet the needs of the large and diverse population and to achieve social stability.[2]

Little had been written about leadership in the New Territories during the 1950s and 1960s. The most notable exception was Freedman, who had done exploratory work in the New Territories in 1963.[3] Village studies dealt with the topic only in passing.[4] Information on the historical dimension of leadership was emerging.[5] It seemed to Graham that a survey of the officers of voluntary associations in Tsuen Wan would tell him not only about the associations, but also about leadership itself. He hoped to discover the kinds of people who had emerged to take responsibility for the diverse groupings that were helping Tsuen Wan's people cope with the complex challenges they encountered.

He interviewed 91 leaders, defined as individuals who held some office in an association. The universe of association leaders in Tsuen Wan in 1969 was over 350. He was able to gain a partial list of office bearers from the District Office, as all registered associations had to file lists of chair officers. Additional names, and considerable information, were gleaned from occasional publications of various associations and from a regular reading of one Chinese newspaper which carried a daily 'New Territories Page'. It was not possible to interview some leaders, although Graham was able to gain limited data on their associations from District Office records. For some associations, he interviewed more than one office bearer. In a number of cases, one person was an office bearer in more than one association, and he therefore attempted to obtain information on those associations from this person.

1. *Huapai* are very large, painted floral plaques which draw public attention to events such as marriages, shop openings, special birthday banquets, village celebrations, and new terms for leaders of prominent associations.
2. James Hayes, 'The Old Popular Culture of China and Its Contribution to Stability in Tsuen Wan', 1–25. Hayes also draws attention to the various informal leaders who met needs for governance in squatter areas, for example.
3. M. Freedman, 'Shifts of Power in the Hong Kong New Territories', *Journal of Asian and African Studies* 1, no. 1 (1966): 3–12.
4. Baker, *A Chinese Lineage Village*, 132–53; Jack M. Potter, 'The Structure of Rural Chinese Society in the New Territories', in *Hong Kong: A Society in Transition*, ed. Jarvie and Agassi, esp. 14–18; J. L. Watson, *Emigration and the Chinese Lineage*, 92–95. See also Graham E. Johnson, 'Leaders and Leadership in an Expanding New Territories Town', *The China Quarterly* (March 1977): 109–25, and C. Fred Blake, 'Leaders, Factions, and Ethnicity in Sai Kung: Village Autonomy in a Traditional Setting', in *Leadership on the China Coast*, ed. Goran Aimer (London: Curzon Press, 1984), 54–89.
5. Hayes, 'Postscript: The Nature of the Political Situation in 1898, and Its Relevance for Local Leadership Patterns' in *The Hong Kong Region*, esp. 194–201. Also H. D. R. Baker, 'The Five Great Clans of the New Territories', *Journal of the Hong Kong Branch Royal Asiatic Society* 6 (1966): 25–48.

The Interviews

Between January and August 1969, Graham approached leaders whom he had identified by sending each a letter (in Chinese). About 20% sent a letter inviting him to visit them. Another 20% telephoned, agreeing to be interviewed. The rest were either telephoned for an appointment, or Graham and his assistant went directly to their association offices, or occasionally to their homes, to make an appointment. It was a frustrating and sometimes an uncomfortable business. Throughout most of the interviews, and many of the telephone conversations, Graham had the help of our research assistant, who was fluent in Cantonese and *putonghua*, and could understand Hakka. The language used in the interview was left up to the informant. Two interviews were conducted almost entirely in English, three in Shanghainese, (using a Shanghainese-speaking assistant), nine in *putonghua*, and the rest in Cantonese. A standard questionnaire in Chinese was used throughout the interviews. There were four broad sections: one consisted of questions focusing upon the leader's association and some general views of leaders and leadership, a second dealt with his career, a third dealt with family matters broadly defined, and the fourth with some general issues such as conception of social class and class relations. Almost without exception, the men that were interviewed (and the one woman) were busy people. Most interviews lasted over an hour and sometimes there was not enough time to complete the last section on general issues. In only a few cases was it possible to bother the informant more than once. The interviews were held in a number of locations, usually in the association office or at the office of the Rural Committee, but at times in our own village house, in the leader's residence, the leader's business address, and in a few instances, in a restaurant.

The conditions for interviewing were not always ideal, especially in the offices of an association or the Rural Committee, where privacy was often not possible. There were 39 leaders whom Graham had identified who would not consent to an interview. Refusals fell into a number of categories. Some village representatives refused out of suspicion regarding the aims of the research. They may be said to have been 'left-wing'. Others refused on the grounds that one village representative from their village,

Plate 42: *Huapai* on Castle Peak Road congratulating the newly-elected members of the Tsuen Wan Rural Committee, autumn 1968.

or one office bearer from their association, had already been interviewed. Village representatives from some of the outlying parts of district were not interviewed because of the difficulties of making contact. We interviewed representatives from all the central Tsuen Wan villages, except for two.

Failures to interview association leaders were related to a number of factors, not least of which was political strife within an association. It was difficult to interview leaders from the hawkers' association, since it was in the midst of a scandal in which the former chairman had absconded to Taiwan with HK$49,000 from the daily money loan association. The leaders were being pressed for repayment by the members and were understandably reluctant to talk about some aspects of the affairs of the association. Nonetheless, we had opportunities to talk with some of the leading members. Others refused to talk for no apparent reason, except for possible suspicion of the motives of a sociologist, who just might be something else.

There were thus many problems, not all of which were adequately solved. A certain resistance was understandable. The informants had no previous exposure to sociologists and their questionnaires, and it is thought impolite in Chinese culture to ask questions of a personal nature. The fact that he was received so courteously by so many is, perhaps, remarkable.

The group of leaders that were interviewed was not a representative sample in any strict sense, but it did include all but one of the most influential, or at least most prominent, figures in Tsuen Wan at the time. The data are inadequate in many respects and the findings have to be understood and interpreted against the background of the difficulties that we faced in executing research during a conflict-ridden time. We noted, above, that questions of ideology were important elements in the structure and functioning of Tsuen Wan associations, and that for the first time since 1949 village representatives were required to declare their allegiance to the colonial government. It was impossible to interview 'left-wing' village representatives, left-wing trade union leaders, or prominent residents of Tsuen Wan who had made an open commitment to the left in 1967. We did, however, have cordial relations with people whom we knew to have been associated with the left, but who refused to be interviewed.

Some Social Characteristics of Tsuen Wan Leaders

Most village representatives were, not surprisingly, indigenous to Tsuen Wan. The leaders of voluntary associations came from a range of places and reflected its general immigrant character. This was reflected in the fact that only two Tsuen Wan natives were office bearers in associations other than the Rural Committee. The overwhelming majority of leaders were born in their ancestral places of origin, their *heunghah* (鄉下). Only 14, three village representatives and 11 association leaders, had been born outside their native places. This characteristic of leaders was reflected in their speech groups. The village representatives were largely Hakka speakers, as were a significant proportion of association leaders, although the majority were native speakers of Cantonese. All Hakka- and Teochiu-speaking immigrant leaders were fluent in Cantonese, although in some cases their local accents were pronounced. The same cannot be said for Shanghainese immigrants, who usually spoke Shanghainese or *putonghua*, depending on the location of their native places or their educational background. Only two, a schoolmaster and a factory manager, who had to interact with Cantonese-speakers on a daily basis, were fluent in Cantonese with only slight northern accents. For the rest, their reference groups were entirely fellow-countrymen. We have discussed this feature of the Shanghai business owners in the previous chapter with respect to the Manufacturers' Association. Surprisingly, the same can be said of Shanghainese workers, who dominated the positions of skill in textile plants and who constituted the bulk of foremen. They invariably interacted with other Shanghainese-speakers, their fellow workers, and after 20 years' residence in Tsuen Wan had only a minimal grasp of Cantonese. This was not the case for their children, however, the significance of which will be highlighted later.

Tsuen Wan leaders were typically village-born. More association leaders were born in non-village settings than their village representative counterparts, but still over half were village-born. Over one-fifth of them were born in large commercial centres such as Shanghai or Guangzhou. Most village representatives still lived in their native villages and all remained resident in Tsuen Wan. Most of the immigrant association leaders were also Tsuen Wan residents, although only a few lived in villages. Of the 11 leaders who were not residents of Tsuen Wan, all were Shanghainese.

The modal age of leaders was 45, with immigrant leaders being somewhat younger than their indigenous counterparts. Most, therefore, grew to adulthood during the period of Nationalist rule in China and suffered the trauma of the Japanese occupation of China or Hong Kong. Many association leaders had suffered the additional trauma of the formation of the People's Republic of China. All but a small proportion would have been aware of the enormity of events in China in the late 1940s. Of the 51 leaders who were not Hong Kong–born, most had migrated to Hong Kong during the years 1946–1949, when in their late twenties.

Of the 91 leaders, only five (four village representatives and one association leader) worked in agriculture. Seven were not employed. The rest were predominantly in middle-class occupations. Over 50% were businessmen, although immigrants owned larger businesses than did their village representative counterparts. In terms of specific economic sectors, village representatives were typically found in commercial pursuits, and few were professionals or in manufacturing sectors. This suggests that Tsuen Wan's industrial development was almost entirely in the hands of newcomers and that indigenous leaders were oriented toward traditional occupations.

Those who were businessmen were typically running businesses that they themselves had begun; 33 ran their own businesses, eight ran 'family' businesses (i.e., a business begun by a relative), and six ran businesses in partnership with others. Only a few employed kinsmen in their businesses. Almost one-half employed no kinsmen at all and only five employed as many as three; these were all self-owned businesses. The scale of business was, however, quite small. Most of the businesses (34) had been established in Tsuen Wan at various times over the previous 20 years. Even those businesses not founded in Tsuen Wan had originated in Hong Kong. Only two had first been established outside Hong Kong.

There is no sense in which the Tsuen Wan leadership group, unlike the Chinese leaders in Bangkok in the mid-1950s and many other overseas Chinese settings, was backed by an extensive network of corporate wealth and business, expressed through 'an elaborate system of interlocking directorates and through kinship ties'.[6] Leadership was middle-class and a leader was typically a businessman. The businessmen, however, were not long-established in their businesses nor were they drawn from the ranks of the large businessmen, who were most responsible for the dramatic economic changes in Tsuen Wan after 1947. This again reinforces the point that the owners of large businesses, the natives of Jiangsu and Zhejiang (the 'Shanghainese'), were oriented away from Tsuen Wan. Only a few Shanghainese were connected with Tsuen Wan associations in anything beyond an honorary and non-participatory sense. One of the most important local figures, however, was Shanghainese, but he was a banker and property developer whose business interests, and his home, were in Tsuen Wan. Leadership was thus largely the preserve of the middle ranks of economic power. Part of the reason for this may be related to the recent nature of the extensive economic changes in Tsuen Wan, but it may also reflect the distinctive conditions for upward mobility that existed in Hong Kong in the late 1960s.

There were significant differences between the educational attainments of Tsuen Wan native and immigrant leaders. Most village representatives had been educated in a traditional setting, such as a

---

6. Skinner, *Leadership and Power in the Chinese Community of Thailand*, 177.

lineage school (variously rendered *sishu* 私塾) or more colloquially, *bokbokjai* (卜卜齋). Their association leader counterparts had studied at least in middle school, the modal category being university or technical school. While 62% of village representatives had only primary or traditional schooling, 68% of association leaders had completed middle school or had some post-secondary education. To some degree, education was not converted into extensive economic power. Part of the explanation here is age. Age was associated with educational achievement, and village representatives tended to be older, less well-educated, and less involved in large business. Shanghainese businessmen, on the other hand, owned large businesses and were almost universally well educated. These men had already made their marks. Some of the younger immigrant leaders were well-educated and had their careers before them.

Perhaps the four richest, and most influential, men in Tsuen Wan, all of whom were deeply involved in local affairs, unlike the rich Shanghainese, were unusual in terms of their educational background. Only one, a native, was educated through middle school; one was a native of humble origins and with only a very modest traditional education; the other two were both immigrants, one Teochiu, the other Shanghainese. Neither were particularly well educated. Both represented something of a 'rags to riches' story. One, the Teochiu, started in the rice trade in Tsuen Wan before the occupation; the other joined the migration from Shanghai to Hong Kong in the late 1940s and made a fortune in various kinds of amusements, banking, and land development.

Chinese versions of the Horatio Alger stories are part of the culture, and in Hong Kong in the 1950s and 1960s, with its extensive economic growth, the potential for upward mobility was substantial. Some leaders in Tsuen Wan came from humble origins, but they were the exception rather than the rule. The information on educational achievement pointed to the availability of resources in family backgrounds, and even for village representatives, the incidence of prestigious fathers or uncles (typically fathers or uncles who had accumulated wealth abroad) was high. For leaders, there was occupational mobility over time, some of the larger shifts relating to the changing character of Tsuen Wan (for the indigenous population) and to the nature of the migration (for newcomers). Thus, there was a pronounced movement from agricultural to non-agricultural occupations and also a shift out of both manual and white-collar worker categories. The biggest sectoral shift was away from agriculture and into commerce.

Despite the predominantly rural origin (birthplaces) of immigrant leaders, only seven had held occupations in the agricultural sector before their migration to Hong Kong. Apart from government employees, the largest group had occupations in the industrial sector. In terms of occupational status, the distribution was toward jobs that afforded modest prestige, although there was a lack of large businessmen. This once again indicates that the Shanghai entrepreneurs did not exercise an influence which their economic power might suggest they were capable of. With a modest start in occupational life, the social environment of industrializing Tsuen Wan allowed leaders to advance from the middle ranges of economic power.

Some Aspects of Leadership

By our definition, a leader was someone who held office in a Tsuen Wan association or was an elected village representative who may or may not have held office in the standing committee of a rural committee. As an objective measure of leadership, office holding is a rough and ready indicator and encompasses what can be called formal leadership. What such leaders do through their associations has been outlined in Chapter 6. The group of individuals we classified as leaders were asked how they would characterize a leader, why they thought people contributed time, money, and effort to serve in unpaid positions, and who they thought local leaders were. Their responses to these questions were illuminating. We were struck by the frankness of their responses.

A total of 33 men, 13 indigenous and 20 newcomers, were cited as leaders. We had interviewed all but eight. Of those eight, two were deceased (but still had enough influence to be ranked as leaders), one had emigrated to the United States shortly before we arrived in Tsuen Wan, one was a past (left-wing) chairman of the Rural Committee who would not consent to an interview during our initial stay in Tsuen Wan, and one a past vice-chairman of the Rural Committee whom we could not interview. The remaining three were Shanghainese businessmen, one of whom was ill for all the time that we were interviewing; the other two were rarely in Hong Kong since they were involved in business abroad.

Of those mentioned as leaders, almost half were local Hakka, and a third of the remainder were Shanghainese-speakers. Teochiu-speakers, Cantonese-speakers, and non-indigenous Hakka formed the balance in about equal numbers. One indigenous leader and one Shanghainese leader, both of whom were unofficial Justices of the Peace,[7] gained 62 and 60 mentions respectively, and were at the apex of the structure of prestige. No other leader came remotely close. Ranking third was a Tsuen Wan native, who held but one formal office, and who was not a member of the Rural Committee. He was a wealthy man but one who had very humble origins. The then-current chairman of the Rural Committee ranked fourth, closely followed by a young native leader, the son of a pre-war gentry leader. At the time of our interviews he was a member of the Heung Yee Kuk and was to become chairman of the 15th term of the Tsuen Wan Rural Committee. There was a tendency for members of speech groups to suggest leaders from their own speech groups and for leaders of newer, and less well-established, associations to be reluctant to name specific leaders.

Cynicism was the most common reaction to the question as to why people became leaders. The general response was that people shoulder the burden of leadership, burdensome in the sense that leadership of an organization or a village consumed time, money, and privacy, for some long-term, personal advantages, whether they were prestige or money. One leader said:

> Most become leaders out of self-interest and for the convenience of their business interests. They think only of rank. If I ask them to donate their time they demand photographs and want to make speeches. If they are not allowed to sit in the middle of the stage, they refuse. I cannot build a stage big enough for all to have the limelight.

These comments were not exceptional. Some did give a view that was positive and stressed the altruism of a leader. One argued:

> People become leaders because of their interests in charity (慈善). Many people recognize that they have made profits from Tsuen Wan and must return some of them to the poor and in this way gain higher status. An elderly man, if he is rich, will be pleased to do works of charity.

Despite the cynicism[8] there were some very clear notions as to what characteristics were necessary to maintain both association leadership and local prominence. People may well have become involved in public positions to benefit themselves in the long run, but initially the leader had to have the resources to become involved in the process of acquiring office and local prestige. This involved spending both time and money, but especially money. None of the leaders who ranked high were poor people, and some were very wealthy indeed. Two of the highest-ranking leaders held office only in the local hospital board. They were recognized as leaders not because of the influence they wielded through some powerful association office but because they were active in charitable affairs.

---

7. Unofficial Justices of the Peace (JPs) were honorary appointments of great prestige, dating from early in the colonial period. They were honours granted to prominent residents for public service and were important marks of social status. They contrasted with official JPs, who were ranking colonial civil servants. The appointment had a traditional ring in its Chinese translation (太平紳士). Both official and unofficial JPs continued to be appointed after 1997.
8. The catchiest response was a play on words that does not translate well into English: 'Leaders don't spend much money, don't make an effort, all they do is make a lot of noise!' (不出錢，不出力，出聲！)

This general context determined the cynicism with which leaders were regarded and also determined the views on the characteristics of the men who aspired to and become leaders. 'A leader is rich, that is all; if they are prominent they are rich' or: 'Prominence is proportional to wealth' were representative views. 'Charitable attitudes' or 'the ability to spend time on leadership matters' were also common responses, as was 'being a businessman'. The general Hong Kong pattern before the 1970s was that Chinese people achieved high status through public largesse.[9] Neither 'well educated', 'native', nor 'immigrant status' was significant.

The Need for Political Change

Through a policy of favouring indigenous villagers and their representative association, the Rural Committee, there emerged a gulf between natives and newcomers. In Tsuen Wan, voluntary associations were, in general, either exclusively immigrant or dominated by immigrants. There was no single structure in Tsuen Wan that served to bring the various interests together in the way that a chamber of commerce or a benevolent society was able to do in an overseas Chinese community. There were two political organizations, one, the Federation of Societies, which served to unite all immigrants, the other, the Rural Committee, which was the focus for the political activities of the indigenous population. There was little love lost between the two organizations. The tensions that existed were very apparent in our interviews.

In 1966, a government committee reported on certain proposals to institute local government reform in Hong Kong as a whole. In examining Tsuen Wan, the committee recommended that a local administration modelled after a British urban district council, with elected members responsible for certain elementary provisions, such as sanitation and leisure activities, should be instituted.[10] Its effect would be to replace the existing system of district officer administration which, with the advice of the Tsuen Wan Rural Committee, had been in charge of local affairs since 1957, when Tsuen Wan was already in the midst of massive economic change.

The proposal was a significant departure from tradition. The working party argued that for an industrial town of almost 300,000, which was expected to grow to one million, to have effective advisory powers in the hands of representatives of less than 5% of the population was anomalous. The establishment of a District Office in 1957 was recognition of substantial economic change underway and the need to establish a government presence in the growing town. When the report came down, Tsuen Wan had experienced even greater change than in the decade after 1947. Yet little came of the report's recommendation in the short term, largely because of the crisis brought on by the tumultuous events of the summer of 1967, and their aftermath. It was only during the governorship of Sir Murray MacLehose, beginning in 1971, that fundamental changes to the administrative structures of Hong Kong as a whole, and other equally dramatic policy changes, began to take effect. We will focus on these developments in the following chapter.

Deciding on the kind of political structure best suited for Tsuen Wan did unearth considerable bitterness, especially on the part of immigrant leaders. Equally, indigenous leaders were very frank about their desire to hold onto power and privilege, such as it was. 'The indigenous people should manage the affairs of the locality' (地方人做地方事) was a common argument used by them. There were few feelings on the part of indigenous leaders that their near-monopolization of formal channels of influence was in any way inequitable. A not uncommon characterization of the indigenous

9. H. J. Lethbridge, 'Hong Kong under Japanese Occupation: Changes in Social Structure', in *Hong Kong: A Society in Transition*, ed. Jarvie and Agassi, 77–127; M. Topley, 'The Role of Savings and Wealth among Hong Kong Chinese', in *Hong Kong: A Society in Transition*, ed. Jarvie and Agassi, 167–227.
10. *Hong Kong Government Report of the Working Party on Local Administration* (Hong Kong: Government Publications, 1967).

leadership by immigrant leaders was that it consisted of a set of country bumpkins (土佬) who were monopolizing effective channels of political communication. A generalized comment was that the indigenous leadership was acting selfishly and short-sightedly. In the words of one immigrant leader:

> It is selfish of the indigenous leaders to hang onto power. They cannot solve the problems of resettlement, of factories, and immigrants, and they especially cannot solve the problems of youth. They have influence only in the indigenous society and that influence stems only from the fact that they are large landowners. They want to hang onto status and rank. They are afraid of the loss of their authority and of their chance to make money. The indigenous leaders have the floor, but it must change.

This statement, which was not an isolated comment, indicated two central aspects of leadership in Tsuen Wan. It pointed to the areas in which immigrant leadership was effective, and it drew attention to the resource from which indigenous leadership gained its most important strength. It indicated the basic elements in the social structure of Hong Kong in the late 1960s, namely colonialism and its policies. The disproportionate amount of influence that the indigenous leadership possessed was directly related to the fact that it represented the new rentier class of the native population that emerged in Tsuen Wan in the wake of industrialization. Indigenous land owners had a strategic role to play in development efforts by providing land and housing, as we indicated in Chapter 4.

Freedman argued that 'power . . . comes to the village representative from the position he occupies in relation to the outside world'.[11] It was never easy to generalize about the New Territories, which was surprisingly diverse given its relatively small area.[12] The Tsuen Wan village representative in the 1960s was not typical of the kind of village representative that Freedman had analysed, for Tsuen Wan by the 1960s, and before, was like nowhere else in the New Territories.

The contrasts between large Punti lineage settlements which dominated the rich rice-growing areas, the linguistic diversity of the Sai Kung peninsula, and the varied characteristics of the population of the islands, were substantial. Yet the area was administered as an assumed homogeneous whole. The establishment of a District Office in Tsuen Wan in 1957 was recognition that Tsuen Wan had become distinctive and was no longer, if it ever had been, 'typical' of the New Territories. It was also during that same year that the Heung Yee Kuk was transformed and a clear conflict between the so-called 'Yuen Long' and 'Tsuen Wan' factions was resolved in favour of the 'Tsuen Wan' faction.[13] The issues in the conflict were, not surprisingly, about land values. They were also about 'development', and what the Tsuen Wan faction was able to do was to question the historical dominance of the larger lineage groups in the politics of the New Territories, and to make room for alternative views of the role of the New Territories in Hong Kong affairs. It was to lead to major policy shifts only in the 1970s, when the significance of Tsuen Wan's developmental trajectory was to influence change throughout the New Territories, including Yuen Long.

No other part of the New Territories had as large an industrial sector, or concentration of non-local investment. The Tsuen Wan village representative was a mediator between his constituency (his village or area) and a host of other forces, the dominant one of which was the government, but which also included immigrant businessmen who were not resident in Tsuen Wan, as well as those who resided locally. In other parts of the New Territories, village representatives were also mediators and the Hong Kong government was a critical influence. External investment and commercial activities were certainly key elements in such places as Yuen Long, Sheung Shui, Tai Po, and Sha Tin, but in the

---

11. Freedman, 'Shifts of Power in the Hong Kong New Territories', 11.
12. Elizabeth L. Johnson, *Recording a Rich Heritage: Research on Hong Kong's 'New Territories'* (Hong Kong: Leisure and Cultural Services Department, 2000) makes the point throughout her book.
13. Lee Ming Kwan, 'The Evolution of the Heung Yee Kuk as a Political Institution', in Faure, Hayes, and Birch, *From Village to City*, esp. 171–77 for a comprehensive analysis of a complex situation.

1960s the scale of those activities, and their novelty, could not compare to the developments in Tsuen Wan.

The constituency of the Rural Committee was small and unified, and it had one great resource: land. The major issue in the late 1960s was that land in the old centre of Tsuen Wan, and in the villages that lay within the core of the new town centre, was strategic to any development efforts, and it was controlled and owned by some of the constituency of the Tsuen Wan Rural Committee. Great tracts were indeed owned by members of the Rural Committee themselves and the lineages of which they were part. Freedman argued in the 1960s, at a time when the New Territories, Tsuen Wan aside, was still essentially the rural backdrop to the older urban area, that village representatives 'take their strength from their success in handling the administration and promoting the economic well-being on which all eyes seem to be fixed'.[14] This was true, except that it was the economic well-being of their constituencies that was uppermost in their efforts and their mandate as village representatives, and not any generalized well-being.

This is not a criticism of village representatives and the way that they perceived their leadership functions. It was a consequence of the structure of power and authority in Hong Kong. Hong Kong was a colony, and in many ways, the assumptions on which government was conducted had changed but little since 1898, despite a massive change in the nature of Hong Kong. There had been economic transformation, immense growth in its physical problems, and political complexities at global, regional, and local levels.

The New Territories, furthermore, were viewed and administered in an altogether different light from those parts of Hong Kong that were ceded to the British crown in 1841 and 1859. It was what Lockhart had called as early as 1898 'the great difference'.[15] For Tsuen Wan, the political structure that had existed before the occupation remained and was given formal sanction by the colonial authorities. Vast changes had taken place in Tsuen Wan since the days before the occupation, and indeed since 1947, when the political structure that was intact in the late 1960s was set up. A structure that had been developed for small country market towns and their hinterlands remained the dominant framework in formulating decisions. It impacted a population that, in Tsuen Wan, was 40 times larger, and infinitely more diverse than it had been 20 years previously and was now dominated by industrial production.

The leaders who made up the largely indigenous Tsuen Wan Rural Committee had had little active involvement in the process of industrialization, although their constituency, most of whom still lived in their formerly agricultural villages, gained considerable benefits from the process. Their knowledge of the problems and difficulties of the immigrant population was but modest, and in many respects, indigenous leaders were much less sophisticated than their immigrant counterparts. They were certainly not 'country bumpkins', but their breadth of experience was limited and a certain country village mentality did prevail. Again, this was not surprising. Not only were their educational achievements in general limited when compared to immigrant leaders, although there were exceptions, but less than a quarter had spent any time away from Tsuen Wan. Most village representatives had their roots in a tradition of village leadership. In all, 19 had been village representatives since the Rural Committee was first founded in 1947, and 10 had held office as village head since the Japanese occupation. Only eight village representatives had been preceded in office by a man who was not a close (blood) relation. During the occupation, seven village representatives had close relatives (father, paternal uncle, or brother) who were formal office holders. While only two village representatives had held office before 1941, 24 were closely related to the heads of pre-occupation days.[16] It is also worth

14. Freedman, 'Shifts of Power in the Hong Kong New Territories', 11.
15. See Hayes, *The Great Difference*, which has considerable information about Tsuen Wan and its distinctiveness, and its place in the New Territories.
16. Eleven village representatives said there were no village headmen before the Japanese occupation in their villages.

noting that with only five exceptions, the formal office of village representative was combined with the ritual office of lineage head.

Indigenous leadership was thus closely integrated with its constituency. Its organized expression, the Rural Committee, was highly favoured by the Hong Kong government, which provided formal channels of access to the citadels of governmental power. In an extremely short space of time, the older way of life of Tsuen Wan had been transformed by new forms of economic enterprise and new kinds of people. In the face of the threat to their existence and privileged status as original inhabitants, indigenous leaders saw the necessity both to protect their constituency and to allow their members to profit from the new forces. Indigenous leadership recognized that it had some grave weaknesses. Many were poor former farmers (although not all) who stood little chance of competing with the sophisticated business interests from Shanghai and elsewhere. Their constituency was also largely devoid of relevant skills and was quite unprepared to take advantage of the new situation in an active way, except by renting out their land and out-buildings and profiting from development via Letters of Exchange. Despite their apparent weaknesses in terms of numbers, skills, and sophistication, the indigenous population, through their leaders, and through the colonial system, maintained a decisive influence in local affairs into the late 1960s.

A Ferry Dispute

One example of indigenous leadership abilities will suffice to demonstrate this influence. In April 1969, a Hong Kong ferry company, which ran a ferry service from Central District to Tsuen Wan via Tsing Yi, changed its service. It reduced from four to three the number of boats operating on the run, cut out the Tsing Yi stop, and instituted a shuttle service between Tsing Yi Island and the mainland. At this time there was no bridge connection. The changes to the service were made without any local consultation, which created an uproar. The entire Tsing Yi Rural Committee resigned, which was not accepted by the district officer, and then began to mobilize support to pressure the ferry company to restore the Tsing Yi Island stop. The ferry company argued that passenger numbers did not warrant this. The Rural Committee rebutted their argument by stating that it was not the passengers but the pig feed from Hong Kong Island that was the critical element, and that the ferry company by its action had precipitated a rise in costs and compromised the business of raising pigs on Tsing Yi. The three rural committees in Tsuen Wan District began to mobilize support and within a short space of time had gained public pledges of support from 25 key organizations (the political associations, five economic associations, seven fellow-countrymen's organizations, four neighbourhood associations, and five leisure associations) encompassing virtually all the leaders in the district. A joint meeting was held in a rare example of solidarity, and a number of positions were publicly stated. Working through the Heung Yee Kuk, which set up a subcommittee to look into the matter, a bargaining position was made. Within a month, a settlement was reached. It is not entirely clear why the immigrant leadership agreed so speedily and with unusual unanimity to the native leadership's request for solidarity. The actions of the ferry company were seen to be arbitrary and there was no consultation with Tsuen Wan interests. The indigenous leaders were clearly persuasive, but the immigrant leadership probably also saw that there was an issue of high-handedness on the part of the ferry company, which had negative consequences for the place in which they and their members lived, and which they increasingly identified as their community.

The settlement was clearly to the advantage of the indigenous population, for it guaranteed some stops at Tsing Yi and a direct route for its pig feed. Yet the outcome was not a solution that benefitted the Tsuen Wan commuters who worked on Hong Kong Island. In the absence of a direct ferry, they were obliged to catch a minibus to Sham Shui Po or Jordan Road and then cross by ferry to

Central District, or to take the somewhat slower ferry. The interests of the indigenous population were predominant and the losers were neither the ferry company nor the natives but the immigrant commuters, who were not numerous at this time. The ferry dispute suggested that the indigenous leaders had the power to mobilize support during a crisis. The real keys in the ferry dispute were the degree of indigenous solidarity and the ability of indigenous leaders not merely to tap the support of immigrant leaders but to work through politically effective channels. A threat to the economic well-being of a segment of the indigenous population was seen, and indigenous leadership sought to meet that threat. It was able to take the issue through the Heung Yee Kuk and obtaining support from that organization on the issue was important to its speedy resolution.[17]

Immigrant solidarity was, in general, less well defined. It is hard to think of an issue that was significant enough in its effects on all immigrants to cause a similar mobilization. In the ferry dispute, all the political leg work was done by the indigenous leaders, although they did obtain crucial support from immigrant associations, persuading them that the issue had broad community-wide implications for Tsuen Wan residents. The most significant characteristic of immigrant leadership was its sectional nature. Until late in the 1960s, there was no single political organization which effectively crosscut the interests of immigrant leaders, nor were there any formal structures, such as a Rural Committee or the Heung Yee Kuk, which they could work through. For immigrant interests it was a question of haphazard parallel access to government at best. Immigrant leadership was obliged to work with a multiplicity of government departments, whose policy initiatives were often discrete, whereas the Rural Committee had formal access to one, the District Office, which had overarching responsibility for the wellbeing of Tsuen Wan.

Immigrant Concerns, No Clear Access to Solutions

With the growth of industry, population, resettlement estates, and squatters, such problems as transportation, sanitation, and water supply grew, and there was growth in the number of government departments established in the New Territories, and particularly in Tsuen Wan, to deal with them. Prior to the development of Tsuen Wan, the New Territories Administration had remained supreme in the New Territories. By the late 1960s, the extent of jurisdiction of the various departments was unclear. Whether the major government representative was the District Office, as of old, or some of the newer departments was no longer certain. For the indigenous leaders there were no problems. For immigrant leaders there were problems, and a lack of formal access was only one part of the solution. For a resettlement estate *kaifong* welfare association both the Resettlement Department and the District Office were crucial. Yet it was hard to know which one could, and should, take precedence. For a hawkers' association wanting to win fixed pitches in the area of a resettlement estate, such issues were particularly difficult to resolve neatly and fairly.[18]

One set of issues in the discussion of leadership dealt with the character of political structures. This turned on the legacy of history and the kinds of policy that had emerged in the 70 years of colonial rule in Tsuen Wan and the New Territories, based on the earlier half-century of policy developments in what had become the older urban areas of Hong Kong and Kowloon. Another set of issues derived from the nature of the immigrant population. Indigenous leadership was strong because the problems of its constituency were largely unambiguous. It was a highly solidary constituency. The same could

---

17. For full accounts on the dispute, see *Wah-kiu Yat-po* (Hong Kong) 20 April 1969; 22–23 April 1969; 24 April 1969 (Tsing Yi Rural Committee Press Conference); 3 May 1969 (Heung Yee Kuk Press Conference); and 11 May 1969 (The Agreement), all in the 'New Territories Section'.

18. Large numbers of people struggled to make a living as hawkers at that time, offering much-needed inexpensive food and services but creating massive problems of control in the town. Hayes, *Tsuen Wan*, 113–18. The prevailing corruption among police made hawkers' lives harder.

not be said for immigrant leadership. It was diverse in spoken language, culture, and experience. These were of importance for the conduct of leadership, and the achievement of its goals. One such leader stated, somewhat bitterly:

> Hong Kong is a British colony and the government is not interested in social welfare or those things that take money to achieve. Thus, welfare work is undertaken largely by associations. We must help ourselves.

This was echoed by another immigrant leader who said:

> I don't advise government much on questions about the development of Tsuen Wan or what would be the best policies for Tsuen Wan. I am much more concerned about the welfare of the members of our association and the difficulties that we have in the association. There are many things that the government doesn't help us with. The government may or may not have the ability; it certainly doesn't have the inclination.

More than the lack of political structures caused the immigrant leaders to turn inward.

The Paradox of Leadership

One of the great puzzles of Tsuen Wan's development, as we perceived it in the late 1960s, was that despite the massive changes that had occurred over the previous two decades, an older political structure had been preserved and actively strengthened. There were only a few ways for newcomers to penetrate the barriers that favoured indigenous leadership. Politically and socially, Tsuen Wan was a divided community. There was little that brought the factions together. In the laissez-faire colonial economy of the 1960s, induced change was sorely lacking. Associations were of critical importance in the development of Tsuen Wan. Leadership of the numerically preponderant immigrant portion of the population sprang from an associational base. If the population continued to grow, and assumptions of governance remained unaltered, the associational inventory would likely grow more diverse. The particular conditions of economic development in Tsuen Wan, the specifics of Chinese culture, and the peculiarity of British colonialism contributed to the emergence of particular kinds of associations and particular forms of leadership.

The nature of leadership, as it existed in Tsuen Wan in the 1960s, posed an apparent paradox. Men of only modest educational achievement, limited experience, poorer and less involved socially than their immigrant counterparts, maintained a dominant voice in local affairs in the face of dramatic economic transformation. This paradox is easily explained. Indigenous leadership was favoured by the politically dominant colonial authorities in an era of minimalist government. Newcomers could never hope to have the influence of indigenous leadership unless the assumptions of colonial governance were to be radically altered.

Perhaps one group could have challenged the indigenous leaders for access to influence and sustained that challenge, namely the owners of large business enterprises, but they did not. The group of men who invested in the major cotton spinning, dyeing, and other industrial enterprises that changed the face of Tsuen Wan and Hong Kong had little interest in Tsuen Wan as a community. Tsuen Wan was a place to conduct business, and socially it was alien to many of the entrepreneurs. Their social province was not Tsuen Wan but the elitist atmosphere of older urban Hong Kong. Immigrant leadership in Tsuen Wan in the late 1960s was dominated with only few exceptions by the middle echelons of economic power. They were an immigrant group not entirely accepted by the colonial authorities because there was no category into which they could be neatly fitted. Their power bases were the immigrant associations. They had responsibilities, first and foremost, to the membership of these associations. They represented a number of separate constituencies. Until the end of the 1960s, there was no political structure which could articulate their interests in the same sense that the Rural Committees could articulate indigenous interests. The interests of immigrants were not necessarily, and perhaps only rarely, coincident with the interests of the colonial government. The Federation of Societies in early 1970 was new and untried, and governmental initiatives to fundamentally shift administrative structures in the New Territories were not yet apparent.

Immigrant associations were of immense importance in Tsuen Wan in the 1950s and 1960s. In the drama of change that had characterized Tsuen Wan, they had a crucial role to play in the adaptation of largely rural migrants to an industrial way of life far away from their home regions. Equally, the leaders of these immigrant associations had a crucial role to play as interpreters of new ways of behaving. Yet these problems were met largely independently of formal (or even informal) political channels. The major problems of transition were solved internally. Immigrant leaders were not only unable to develop political channels of communication, but they also had few external political roles to play.

Migration, economic change, and population composition determined a particular associational profile. 'New Territories affairs for New Territories people' was a position taken by the indigenous leadership and government alike. In the absence of any political structures other than those agreed to by the colonial authorities a small, and increasingly smaller, proportion of Tsuen Wan's population had the greatest influence. As in many of the overseas Chinese communities, the nature of the colonial response was the dominant element in the structure of power and authority in the Chinese community of Hong Kong, of which Tsuen Wan was one part. When we left in 1970, it seemed impervious to change. This was not, however, to be the case.

8

Tsuen Wan's New Face

Transition to a Post-industrial City

The 1970s

By 1970, the Hong Kong economy had changed dramatically. The manufacturing sector, a critical component of which was located in Tsuen Wan, had created one of the most vibrant economies in the world, and had experienced a consistent annual growth of 7% since the mid-1950s. Hong Kong's economic success was a key element in the restructuring of the global economy in which East Asia occupied a strategic place. During the 1970s, Hong Kong became a major global financial centre. In the plans for infrastructural development, which was a major policy initiative of the Hong Kong government after 1970, the New Territories was no longer seen as a marginal rural appendage, but instead as part of a strategy for the overall improvement of the colony. Tsuen Wan's experience, its successes and failures, did much to inform the new direction of development in Hong Kong as a whole.

A crucial impetus for the new directions that Hong Kong was to take, with implications for Tsuen Wan's own trajectory, was the governorship of Sir Murray MacLehose, from 1971 to 1982. Sir Murray's decade in office, the longest of any colonial governor, was marked by major policy changes. It set the scene for a dramatic reordering of colonial rule, and ultimately, for the end of colonial rule itself. The process was incremental, but as the decade ended the changes were obvious and pointed to a very different future for Hong Kong and Tsuen Wan than could have been foreseen in 1970.

The choice of Sir Murray as governor was unusual. His career had been in the British Foreign Service. He was a Chinese-speaking diplomat who had begun his diplomatic service in China, but after the Japanese seizure of Xiamen [Amoy], where he was posted, he had helped train Chinese guerrillas behind Japanese lines, under the cover of a diplomatic posting in Fuzhou.[1] He had been political adviser to Sir Robert Black, Hong Kong governor from 1958 to 1964, and then to George Brown, foreign minister in the Labour government of Harold Wilson. Prior to assuming the governorship in Hong Kong, he had been British ambassador to Vietnam at the height of the Vietnam War.

When we left Hong Kong in 1970, there were a number of domestic issues that were in need of urgent attention. Many were the consequence of colonial policies, and colonial attitudes, which had barely moved with the times. Some had become painfully obvious during the political upheavals of 1967, and considerable soul-searching had occurred in government circles during our first sojourn in Hong Kong. Few significant policy changes had occurred, although there were some important beginnings. One was the City District Officer initiative, which introduced possibilities for change

---

1. Sir Murray began his career in Malaya and his first Chinese language was Hokkien. It was a path that was closely followed by Sir David Akers-Jones, who was a critical adviser during the MacLehose years, and beyond. See his *Feeling the Stones: Reminiscences by David Akers-Jones* (Hong Kong: Hong Kong University Press, 2004). Sir David was district officer Tsuen Wan for a brief but critical period in the late 1950s.

in governmental administration. There was little evidence of new initiatives in Tsuen Wan, which continued to grow, and remained economically vibrant, but was beset by problems that needed urgent resolution.

During the MacLehose governorship policy initiatives were launched which had a far-reaching impact. There was civil service reform, including by the early 1980s a policy of localization,[2] and changes in the structure of the central government. After 140 years of British rule, Chinese became an official language of a territory that was 98% Chinese. There was the establishment of a social assistance scheme, increases in social welfare provisions for the elderly, and the beginnings of recognition that disabled individuals required additional facilities to help them integrate into the broader community. Nine years of free and compulsory education was introduced, and the number of schools grew. There was an increase in subsidized senior secondary school places, and plans were made for the expansion and upgrading of tertiary education beyond the two existing universities. The health care system was upgraded, and publicly funded hospitals grew in size and number. There was a new Labour Ordinance, paid holidays were introduced, weekly rest days were mandated, and labour tribunals were formed.[3]

The issue of corruption, a blight in Hong Kong's social and political fabric and a burden for its people, was tackled head-on. In 1973, Peter Godber, a senior and decorated police officer, fled Hong Kong upon the discovery that he had accumulated substantial unexplained sums in local and foreign bank accounts. He was later extradited from Britain, found guilty of corruption, and sentenced to a period in prison. This raised the issue of corruption not only in the police but also in many other areas. It led, very quickly, and before Godber's trial, to the establishment of the Independent Commission Against Corruption (ICAC), a body independent of the civil service, appointed by the governor, and after 1997, by the Chinese central government on the recommendation of the chief executive. On a broad front, therefore, the government became much less 'minimalist'.

The 'New Town', the Town Manager, and the District Board

The New Territories was poised to become a critical element in a hoped-for resolution of Hong Kong's housing crisis through the creation of planned 'new towns' based on a British town planning model, many to be in the former market towns.[4] Some aspects of Tsuen Wan's experience during its development were crucial in the planning of Sha Tin, Tuen Mun, Yuen Long, Tai Po, and Fan Ling/Sheung Shui. Among these was the presence of the original inhabitants, whose ancestral rights to land had been a complicating factor in Tsuen Wan's development, and which were to remain so during new town growth in the 1970s. The central feature of the initiatives was that these new towns were to be planned. Tsuen Wan was clearly a new (and industrial) town, but despite efforts to rationalize its growth from 1960, it had been anything but planned.

To be successful, this policy had to reduce the alarming densities in the older urban areas and rehouse Hong Kong's still very large squatter population. It therefore required not merely a commitment of government resources to the provision of new housing but also an increasingly robust commitment by private sector interests to work with broader government objectives. It also required massive infrastructural improvements that would allow inhabitants of the new towns to move from their places of residence to their places of work, and for the new towns to be vibrant communities, with markets, schools, hospitals, and community centres to meet the needs of the new population. They had to be created from the ground up. They were, initially, all former rural market towns, and

---

2. This was a policy of emphasizing recruitment to the senior ranks of the civil service, and other publicly funded organizations such as schools and universities, from the Hong Kong population and relying less on the recruitment of expatriates.

3. See M. Castells, L. Goh, and R. Y.-W. Kwok, *The Shek Kip Mei Syndrome: Economic Development and Public Housing in Hong Kong and Singapore* (London: Pion, 1990), esp. 136–54.

4. See R. Bristow, *Hong Kong's New Towns: A Selective Review* (Hong Kong: Hong Kong University Press, 1989), 77–114.

with the possible exception of Sha Tin, remote from employment opportunities, and without extensive commercial, educational, or community facilities.

Tsuen Wan, as ever, was distinctive. It was certainly representative of the various policy issues at the forefront in the 1970s. Housing was a key element in the town's near future, although the district was growing massively as the Kwai Chung estates were populated. The infrastructure projects, which got underway in the 1960s, were having an impact, not least with the reclamation of Gin Drinkers Bay and the beginning of the container port as a response to the changing technological character of global shipping. This was to have a dramatic impact on the economy of the district, although in ways that could not have been foreseen in the late 1960s. Similarly, the construction of Kwai Chung Road, which was a second link to Kowloon, took pressure off Castle Peak Road, which for over 50 years had been Tsuen Wan's connection to Kowloon. The new corridor was crucial for the rapidly growing population of Kwai Chung, and provided access to industrial sites, which were an important source of employment for the residents of the new estates. In the 1970s, the population of Tsuen Wan District doubled, and was over 600,000 at the end of the decade. The Rambler Channel between Kwai Chung and Tsing Yi was bridged, opening Tsing Yi for housing and other developments, which was to transform this delightful rural backwater. This set the scene, eventually, for three new towns within the historic area of Tsuen Wan District: Tsuen Wan itself, Kwai Chung, and Tsing Yi.

The scale of development in Tsuen Wan had been impressive in the two decades before 1970. In the 1970s, the pace of development increased, along with attendant problems. It was hoped that planned development rather than the ad hoc growth that had occurred in Tsuen Wan could be avoided in the other new towns. Tsuen Wan still had tenements, and the conditions in some were as dire as some of those in Mong Kok. It still had a large squatter population on crown land, arrayed in an arc to the north of the town, but also scattered throughout the district. The overcrowded original villages still in situ were distinctive. They were as congested and, in many ways, more problematic than the older tenements in Kowloon or even in Tsuen Wan itself. Crammed with a wide variety of enterprises, industrial and otherwise, their local Hakka landowners lived in old village houses, with large numbers of tenants often housed in flimsy and inadequate structures. These villages occupied land that could be used for commercial and other amenities central to rational urban development. Squatters could be cleared, if not always easily, for their tenure to the land they occupied was illegal. Indigenous villagers, by contrast, had rights which could not be brushed aside.[5]

By the mid-1970s, plans for Hong Kong's transportation needs were part of the overall commitment to infrastructure change. Plans indicated that Tsuen Wan was to be the terminus for one line of the proposed mass transit railway system. Implementation of this plan was enormously disruptive. With no warning, it involved resiting four or five villages with millions of square feet of village land, as well as tens of thousands of people, and more than 1,000 factories.[6]

All aspects of planned urban development in central Tsuen Wan in the 1970s were much more complex than in other new towns such as Sha Tin, which had a relatively small market centre, at Tai Wai, and a series of non-industrialized agricultural villages, which were served by the railway. Tai Po, Sheung Shui, and Fan Ling were also primarily market towns with a railway connection to the older urban core. The new town of Tuen Mun, which replaced the old fishing settlement of Castle Peak, was relatively lightly populated, although its remote location presented some difficult planning issues.

---

5. See James W. Hayes, 'Government and Village: Reactions to Modern Development by Long-Settled Communities in the New Territories of Hong Kong', in *An Old State in New Settings: Studies in the Social Anthropology of China in Memory of Maurice Freedman*, ed. Hugh D. R. Baker and S. Feuchtwang (Oxford: JASO, 1991), 107–26.
6. See Hayes, *Tsuen Wan*, 80–85 for some first-hand details.

Town Manager

Tsuen Wan's complexity put enormous stress on local administration. The District Office had a relatively small staff, which was insufficient to deal with the many challenges that the district faced. The district officer reported to the New Territories Administration, while many decisions were taken by government departments that lay outside the formal reach of the district officer. He[7] was well equipped, although understaffed, to negotiate with indigenous interests.[8]

The recognition that Tsuen Wan, although within the New Territories, was not typical, resulted in two important changes in the nature of political administration in the leased areas. The first acknowledged that the changing character of the New Territories meant that it was to have new towns. The older assumptions that a district should be run as New Territories' districts had always been since their incorporation into Hong Kong were no longer appropriate. From 1975, therefore, the Tsuen Wan district officer became a 'town manager', a pattern that was to be followed by other new towns. It did not make the task of running such an agglomeration easy, but it broke down the lines of bureaucratic communication and allowed the enormous variety of tasks to be handled in a holistic fashion. A single office could coordinate town matters, which increasingly affected the outlying portions of the district which, like Tsing Yi and Ma Wan, had been somewhat insulated from the developments of the mainland portions of the district. From the 1970s, their development became intermingled.[9]

The second challenge was the establishment of regular and meaningful contact with the enormous population of the district, which was not included in the established principles of consultation that worked well for the indigenous residents. Associations of all kinds, as we have suggested, were crucial in the early stages of development by helping to meet the special needs of the newcomers. The complex needs of the town population required some formal mechanisms whereby grievances could be aired and solutions suggested. In 1976, the Tsuen Wan New Town Recreation and Amenities (Advisory) Board was created. As its name suggests, it focused upon recreational needs in a growing town with few public amenities. Its members were appointed from both the indigenous and immigrant segments of the population. In late 1977, it was supplanted by the Tsuen Wan District Advisory Board, which was created to be an experimental sounding board to deal with various issues, largely sporting and cultural. Its formation was important in creating solutions to some long-neglected problems and extending the principles of formal consultation beyond the time-honoured methods of dealing primarily with the population of original inhabitants.

In mid-1980, the government floated a proposal to extend the Tsuen Wan experiment to the entire territory,[10] and in early 1981 ushered in District Boards through the District Board Ordinance. The ordinance stated that the tasks of a District Board were: '(a) to advise the government (i) on matters affecting the well-being of the District of public facilities and services; (ii) on the provision and use of the public facilities and services within the District; (iii) on the adequacy and priorities of government programmes for the District; (iv) on the use of public funds allocated to the District for local works and community activities; and (b) where funds are made available for the purpose to undertake (i) environmental improvements in the District; and (ii) the promotion of recreational and cultural activities within the District'.

This fundamentally altered the nature of the government in Hong Kong.[11] In the short-term, it incorporated the majority of Tsuen Wan's population into formal mechanisms of consultation,

---

7. It was some years, and not until after 1997, that a woman occupied the senior administrative position in Tsuen Wan.
8. See Hayes, *Tsuen Wan*, esp. 129–35.
9. Hayes, *Tsuen Wan*, 108–11.
10. See also Hayes, *Tsuen Wan*, 136.
11. The discussion (Green) paper, 'A Pattern of District Administration in Hong Kong', was made public in June 1980. The text is available along with the (White) paper 'District Administration in Hong Kong' released in January 1981 and can be found in *A*

although their effective participation was to take some time to implement. This was to take place in a context in which Tsuen Wan was to change physically, administratively, economically, and socially as Hong Kong as a whole began a shift to a very different political form.

1979: A Year of Significance and Unexpected Consequences

The final year in the turbulent 1970s was a pivotal one in the history of Hong Kong, having consequences for Tsuen Wan which could not have been foreseen a decade earlier when we ended our first stay in the town. Infrastructural transformation, which became a central feature of Hong Kong outside the older urban core in the decades after 1965, had begun in Tsuen Wan. The Gin Drinkers Bay reclamation saw the end of a noisome and malodorous ship-breaking industry and the construction of the first of a series of container ship berths. This not only changed the handling of cargos in the harbour, but fundamentally changed the port of Hong Kong, as it became one of the three busiest ports in the world, rivalled only by Singapore and Rotterdam. Roads were built to service the port and the extensive new housing estates, largely public, that were built both on reclaimed land and on the upper portions of the Kwai Chung area. Tsing Yi was linked to the mainland, ultimately by six bridges, and housing development began to transform the island.

The population growth of the Kwai Chung portion of Tsuen Wan new town began to outpace that of central Tsuen Wan and its westward extension and was almost twice its size in 1981. The combined population in the 1981 census was 608,000. In 1982, a decision was made to administratively divide the district into two segments. The new boundary went along Castle Peak Road and down Texaco Road to the harbour. Tai Wo Hau, Tsuen Wan's first resettlement estate, became administratively part of the new Kwai Tsing District, although its village representative, and those from villages in the mainland portion of the new district, retained their seats on the Tsuen Wan Rural Committee.

Perhaps nothing was to facilitate massive redistribution of Hong Kong's population more than the building of the MTR and associated upgrading of the British-administered section of the railway link to Guangzhou which, as one of the first major infrastructure projects in the New Territories, had been completed only a decade after the lease in 1898. In 1979, direct passenger rail service was restored to Guangzhou after a 30-year hiatus. The improvement of the railway was important not only as a link to south China, but also to facilitate the development of new towns and population growth in the eastern segment of the New Territories.

The construction of an underground railway revolutionized transportation in the older and newer urban areas of Kowloon, linking them to Central District. Its later extension along the north shore of Hong Kong Island facilitated the development of the eastern end of the island as far as Chai Wan, which the picturesque, but slow, tramcars had never reached. The first stage emerged above ground at the Tsuen Wan boundary and a terminus was established in central Tsuen Wan, close to the old compound village of Sam Tung Uk and the central Tianhou temple, Tsuen Wan's historic ritual centre. The marshalling yards and repair facilities ran parallel to Castle Peak Road and were established in close proximity to Muk Min Ha village. Negotiations with villages in the path of, or close to, the new system were intense. They were concluded, and villages were relocated in agreed-upon sites, complete with their ancestral halls. Their residential tenants were rehoused in by now superior government housing, and the industrial tenants in new locations.[12] The Tianhou temple was restored

---

Documentary History of Hong Kong: Government and Politics, ed. Steve Tsang (Hong Kong: Hong Kong University Press, 1995). Eighteen boards were established throughout Hong Kong and from 1982 members, who were elected from constituencies within the geographical areas of the boards, increased in number, and greatly outnumbered appointed members, who typically were local government officials and included, in Tsuen Wan, the chairman of the Rural Committee. They continued after the end of the colonial period, although they become known as District Councils.

12. For a first-person account of the Mass Transit clearances, which were completed with great urgency, see Hayes, *Tsuen Wan*, 80–85.

and stood in an imposing compound in the middle of a private housing complex, Luk Yeung estate, surrounded by its high-rise buildings. The old village of Sam Tung Uk, with its distinctive historical Hakka village architecture, was preserved as a museum, serving as a reminder of a way of life that is gone. Exhibitions recreate village house interiors as they might have been,[13] when agriculture was the dominant occupation.

The completion of the MTR in 1979 had a major influence on Tsuen Wan's future. It provided speedy, efficient, and affordable access to much of Kowloon and Central District. It was possible to live in Tsuen Wan and work elsewhere. The privately built Luk Yeung estate provided attractive accommodation targeting a growing middle class that had generally prospered in the 1970s. Before the MTR shortened commuting time, such housing had barely existed. Part of the strategy for property development involved constructing housing complexes close to MTR stations. In Kwai Chung, middle-class housing complexes, anchored by what were later to be called 'shopping malls' (商場) could be found close to Kwai Hing, Kwai Fong, and Lai King stations. With completion of the MTR, major property development corporations began to develop sites of substantial proportions in Tsuen Wan, creating high-rise housing for the increasingly affluent and growing Hong Kong middle class. Some were on former industrial land, facilitated by changes in zoning regulations, and some on reclamation along the shoreline. It could not have been anticipated in 1979 how common such projects were to become in the very near future. Tsuen Wan, although still distinctive in 1979, became more firmly integrated with urban Hong Kong and began to reflect the contemporary character of the territory.

China: The Joker in the Pack

At the onset of the 1970s, China was an enigmatic presence, seemingly tolerating Hong Kong, despite its capitalist economic system and continued British colonial occupation of Chinese territory. Hong Kong did have its uses. Despite an official ideology of self-reliance in the People's Republic of China, Hong Kong was a window on the world, a source of foreign exchange from the sale of manufactured goods and agricultural produce, and remittances from Hong Kong and the wider Chinese diaspora. It was especially important for Guangdong province, the ancestral point of origin for the bulk of the Hong Kong population.

For many residents of Hong Kong before the 1970s, China was a place that they had left behind. The socialist transition had created a troublesome past in their native villages, as it had been mishandled by cadres and soldiers of the new China, who rarely appreciated the complexity of Guangdong's languages, landholdings, and culture. The food shortages of the Great Leap Forward, especially during 1959 to 1961, and the violence of the Cultural Revolution generated anxiety. The manifestation of the Cultural Revolution in Hong Kong itself was divisive. Hong Kong had its problems, but there was food and shelter, and even if the political realm was authoritarian, it was relatively secure and stable.

China had cut itself off from the world for much of the decade from 1966 to 1976. The upheavals of the late 1960s often made little sense in the general absence of reliable information. In late 1969, Canadian and Chinese diplomats in Stockholm announced a formula whereby the two countries could establish formal diplomatic relationships and exchange ambassadors. It was a breakthrough that saw most of the Western world accept the Canadian-inspired formula and establish diplomatic relations. In 1971, the People's Republic of China assumed the China seat on the United Nations Security Council. The Republic of China on Taiwan, which had held the seat since 1949, was obliged to relinquish it.

---

13. There was little material culture left from the past, and museum curators went over the border to the Hakka areas of eastern Shenzhen and Huizhou to acquire appropriate household items. The idea of preserving Sam Tung Uk owed much to the efforts of James Hayes, who was district officer and town manager from 1975 until 1982.

The enigmatic character of Chinese politics was not over. Lin Biao, a major figure during the early and most violent phases of the Cultural Revolution, fled China in 1971, died in an air crash in Mongolia, and was quickly declared a renegade. A group of four leftist leaders, later dubbed the 'Gang of Four', assumed leadership roles in the party structure. Zhou Enlai, the long-term premier, however, began to reconstruct the government. He brought Deng Xiaoping, well versed in political organization, back from political exile. Deng assembled a team that pressed for major reform in agriculture, industry, the educational system, and in the military.

In 1976, there was great tension. In January, Zhou Enlai died, generating an enormous display of public sympathy. Deng Xiaoping delivered the eulogy at Premier Zhou's funeral.[14] It was expected that he would follow as premier. He promptly disappeared and was labelled a 'revisionist', a strong epithet indicating that his influence should be expunged. At Qingming in April, vast numbers thronged Tian'anmen Square in Beijing, laying wreaths in Zhou's memory, and reading poems with a clear message of protest against party leadership. Deng Xiaoping was accused of masterminding the protests.

In early July, Zhu De, a major revolutionary hero, died. On 28 July, a massive earthquake destroyed Tangshan, an industrial city in Hebei, some 150 kilometres to the southeast of Beijing, killing perhaps 200,000 people. In September, Mao Zedong died. A generation of revolutionary leaders had passed on in a matter of months, and major natural disasters were the traditional portents of dynastic change. In early October, the Gang of Four was removed from office.

Deng once again returned from political exile and in December 1978, a party plenum introduced a wide-ranging policy of reform which was to fundamentally reshape China's highly centralized economic system, which had taken form in the early 1950s under Soviet tutelage. This policy would have global repercussions, and in a short period of time it reshaped the economy of Hong Kong. In 1979, Deng Xiaoping also raised the issue of the expiry of the New Territories lease in 1997. In March, Governor MacLehose made an official visit to Beijing and discussed this question with Deng in the Great Hall of the People.

Sir Murray's suggestion that Britain's lease over the New Territories could be extended was politely rejected. His visit to Beijing, however, suggested that the Chinese central government was willing to discuss the question of what might happen in 1997. Negotiations got underway, although the path was not always smooth or without tension.[15] Sir Edward Youde, Sir Murray's successor as governor, and like him a Chinese speaker, was deeply involved.[16]

In late 1984, Britain and China signed an agreement regarding the resumption of Chinese sovereignty.[17] After the signing of the agreement, the political character of Hong Kong changed, and some of its colonial features receded during the 13 years of transition to retrocession. Hong Kong's distinctive international character, built on its own variety of 'Chineseness', was only furthered.

The 1970s had begun with few expectations of the kinds of drama that were to unfold during the decade globally, regionally, and within Hong Kong itself. Tsuen Wan was to be dramatically changed by their ramifications.

---

14. The ceremony was broadcast live on Hong Kong television, which by 1976 was omnipresent. Hundreds of thousands had earlier queued to sign a book of remembrance in the Bank of China building

15. See David Akers-Jones, *Feeling the Stones*, 133–56 for a senior Hong Kong government official's memories of the period in which negotiations occurred.

16. Sir Edward died in Beijing. His successor, Sir David Wilson, also a Chinese speaker, completed the negotiations.

17. The original agreement is to be found in *A Draft Agreement between the Government of the United Kingdom of Britain and Northern Ireland and the Government of the People's Republic of China on the Future of Hong Kong* (Hong Kong: Government Printer, 1984). The Basic Law, which outlined the post-1997 constitutional framework for the Hong Kong Special Administrative Region [SAR], was approved by the National People's Congress in April 1990, in an atmosphere changed significantly by the traumatic events in China, and reaction to them in Hong Kong, during the spring of 1989.

The 1980s and After

After 1979, Hong Kong assumed new roles in China's economic future. Its social and cultural impact on China, and especially, but not restricted to, its immediate hinterland, was considerable. Such developments had consequences for the increasingly affluent residents of Hong Kong and had a major impact on the adjacent region of China, which underwent a major transformation that in many ways resembled that experienced by Tsuen Wan between 1950 and 1970. After 1980, a relatively homogeneous cultural and economic region, the Pearl River delta broadly defined, which had been disaggregated by colonialism on the one hand and a distinctive variant of state socialism on the other, became increasingly reintegrated in a new fashion in which Hong Kong, looking to a Chinese past and a globalised future, decidedly influenced the outcomes.

Hong Kong's fractured links with its Chinese hinterland in the period before 1979 had a pronounced effect on its own economic performance in a global context and had contributed to the industrial transformation of Tsuen Wan, especially as Guangdong had been forced to remain agricultural. The links to China changed significantly after economic reform began in China in 1979. These had major consequences for Tsuen Wan and affected the overall character of the territory as it moved towards becoming the Hong Kong SAR of the People's Republic of China on 1 July 1997.

Hong Kong economic interests were a major element in the transformation of the Pearl River delta. Structural changes took place as local production systems in parts of the Pearl River delta became incorporated into the global economy. Entrepreneurial activities with Hong Kong partners were key to this economic transformation, especially in the early phases of reform, and continued into the 1990s and beyond. One of the consequences, which was particularly significant for Tsuen Wan, was that the Hong Kong partners were often manufacturers. They saw in the new policy of openness a willingness to experiment with economic forms that had been proscribed for three decades. In this context, they could operate on culturally familiar ground, with incentives to relocate production facilities, cheap land, and an abundant supply of low-cost labour. These could not merely reduce the costs of production but, given the delta's proximity to Hong Kong and its expanding port facilities, also provide ready access to export markets. The movement of economic activities to China was to hasten the demise of certain kinds of labour-intensive manufacturing in Hong Kong, including textile production, and within a decade it brought to an end the economic activity that had been so typical of Tsuen Wan for 30 years. The Hong Kong economy had prospered in the 1970s, although there were structural shifts already apparent, because of a willingness to rapidly change economic activities if market conditions changed. After 1979, market possibilities changed dramatically. Guangdong was given enhanced privileges by the Central Government. Hong Kong was in an advantageous position to explore new possibilities, especially because of the intense kinship and locality ties that straddled the Guangdong-Hong Kong border.[18]

Consequences of Economic Transformation for Tsuen Wan

In the years immediately after the formation of the People's Republic of China, despite the economic difficulties that cessation of the China trade created, an efficient and prosperous manufacturing economy had been fashioned in Hong Kong. By 1980, Hong Kong had a per capita GNP on par with some southern European economies and was second only to Japan in Asia (with the exception of oil-rich Brunei).

---

18. See Graham E. Johnson, 'Changing Horizons for Regional Development: Continuity and Transformation in Hong Kong and Its Hinterland, 1950s–1990s', in *The Hong Kong–Guangdong Link: Partnership in Flux*, ed. R. Kwok and A. So (Armonk, NY: M. E. Sharpe, 1994), 64–86.

Up to the mid-1960s, textiles were dominant, both in terms of employment and as the major commodity for Hong Kong's domestic export performance. There was, however, a gradual shift from spinning and weaving textiles to the production of garments and accessories, beginning even in the mid-1960s. By the mid-1980s, Hong Kong was one of the major global producers of fashionable clothing. Other technological possibilities were also rapidly incorporated. Plastics made their appearance in the late 1960s, and in the late 1970s, electronics products (including digital clocks and watches) were added to an already substantial electrical goods industry. Thus, technological change and, after 1980, relocation of production facilities, led to changes in Tsuen Wan's industrial activities. Enamelware and silk weaving, for example, became less prominent, as they could not be readily and economically relocated in the new town, which took planning much more seriously than it had in the 1950s and 1960s.

Manufacturing was still a significant component of GDP and employment in Hong Kong. Its share, however, had been declining since the early 1970s. It comprised 40% of GDP in 1965, declined to 31% in 1971, was a little over 20% throughout the 1980s, and by 1997 was less than 6%. Its share of the labour force fell to 26% in 1991 and steadily declined thereafter. It was less than 14% in 1997. The labour force in manufacturing continued to shrink. In 2001, it had declined to 11% and by 2011, only 4% of the labour force was working in the manufacturing sector. In 1985, as the shift in manufacturing capacity from Hong Kong to China got underway, the manufacturing sector had employed 918,800. By 2011, it had declined by more than 84% and had fallen to 142,973.[19] The overall labour force had grown by almost 30% over the same period. The impact on Tsuen Wan was noticeable. The industrial working-class town which we left in 1970 was transformed in the space of two decades. The larger factories simply ended production. The smaller factories were closed as the old villages were relocated and the squatters removed from the hillsides. Tsuen Wan changed its economic character and adopted a new post-industrial face.

Hong Kong became a major financial centre in the 1970s. This was, in part, due to changes in the nature of the global economy, which saw the production of key manufactured goods shift away from Europe and North America to East and Southeast Asia. The tertiary sector in Hong Kong had assumed major proportions as early as 1970. Transport, storage and communications, finance, insurance, real estate, business services, and the growing tourist industry became increasingly important. Total employment in these areas grew from about 40% in 1970 to almost 50% in 1980. With reform in China, the sectors continued to expand and their employment share was over 70% at the end of the colonial period.

Trade has always been a key component for Hong Kong's economy but until the late 1970s the entrepôt trade with China was minuscule. After 1950, China remained an important source of Hong Kong's imports, but Hong Kong's domestic exports sought other markets and forged an international economic presence. Hong Kong's trade performance was good throughout the 1970s. After 1980, with China's 'open door' reform policies having a major impact in southern China, the entrepôt trade was reborn. The volume of Hong Kong's trade increased dramatically as the composition of Hong Kong's trading partners also changed. China became Hong Kong's largest trading partner, but equally, Hong Kong became China's largest trading partner. China's domestic export trade grew dramatically by the mid-1990s of which at least a quarter, likely double that, was conducted with Hong Kong. As one consequence, substantial investible funds were generated. Hong Kong entrepreneurs became global in their activities, and like other entrepreneurs in East Asia, began to have an impact on economies where they previously had only little or no involvement

The impact of the new economic relationships with China led to the demise of much of Tsuen Wan's industry. Hong Kong's role in the export of much of what China began to produce from the

---

19. Figures are from the *Hong Kong Annual Digest of Statistics* published by the Census and Statistics Department of the Hong Kong government.

1980s had a major impact on Tsuen Wan's economy and did much to offset the decline of industrial employment. The container port, under construction at the end of our first stay, expanded dramatically in the 1970s and into the 1990s as the technology of transoceanic shipping changed, and transformed both Kwai Chung and Tsing Yi. It became the outlet for a large proportion of China's foreign trade, in large measure because Hong Kong was the only deep-water port on the China coast for much of the first 25 years of the reform period.[20] The expansion of trade-related activities and the handling of cargo both were enormous. There is no rail link from the port, and the links between logistic centres in China and the Hong Kong container terminal are by road. Tsuen Wan and Kwai Tsing are replete with logistical enterprises and their roads are now clogged by container lorries, with major consequences for air quality and traffic congestion, presenting challenges for the quality of life in Tsuen Wan.

Social, Political, and Cultural Change

Less precise to document than the economic changes are the social, political, and cultural dimensions of change. Government intervention, especially through its housing policies, was crucial for Hong Kong's economic success from the mid-1950s. Low levels of taxation and the implicit subsidization of wage rates also contributed to increasing prosperity. Government revenue nonetheless was substantial and grew along with the economy. It stood at HK$1.8 billion in 1967 and reached HK$202.0 billion in 1996/97 fiscal year. Public expenditure grew in a similar fashion. In the 2013/14 fiscal year, government revenue was HK$455.7 billion and expenditure was HK$435.7 billion. Fiscal reserves were HK$755.7 billion. The government presently commits proportionately more to health, education, and social welfare, over 60% of government expenditure, than it did during our first stay in Hong Kong. Approximately 22% of recurrent spending is allocated to education at all levels, 18.4% to social welfare, and 16.8% to medical and health care.[21] Thus, in Tsuen Wan, poverty is much less in evidence than it was, although it still exists, especially among elderly women, who can be seen collecting materials which can be recycled. The health of the general population is much improved, because of ready access to clinics and hospitals. Universal and affordable education through Senior Secondary[22] has had significant effects.

The Hong Kong government has always committed substantial sums to physical infrastructure, although some major projects have been completed by the private sector. It is the increased volume of public expenditures that has been dramatic. Housing is an obvious example of government intervention, with welfare consequences. Both the stock and the quality of public housing have improved. Many first and second generation government housing projects have been demolished and replaced by larger and more comfortable structures than those that first appeared in the 1950s and into the 1960s. Tai Wo Hau has been dramatically upgraded, as have some of the estates in Kwai Chung, which were built in the 1970s to inadequate standards. In addition, there has been enormous growth in private sector housing.

New housing has gone hand in hand with infrastructural improvement. The new town development projects beginning in the 1970s had a major role not only in redefining the character of the New

---

20. This is no longer strictly true. Zhanjiang in southwestern Guangdong has two deep water ports, one of which is the home base for the Chinese fleet which patrols the South China Sea. The civilian port was, and remains, isolated. The port of Ningbo has been expanded, and Shanghai has built a deep water port in Hangzhou Bay, some 30 kilometres off shore. Port facilities in Shenzhen have grown appreciably. These have had consequences for Hong Kong's share of the China trade.
21. All figures, as noted, are from the Hong Kong Census and Statistics Department Annual Digest of Statistics.
22. Students typically attend six years of secondary education (three years of junior secondary and three years of senior secondary), although only junior secondary is fully subsidized and compulsory. On completion of Secondary 6, students take one public examination, the Hong Kong Diploma of Secondary Education Examination. Education beyond Secondary 6 is preparation for entry to university or other post-secondary educational institutions. The changes date from 2009, with the '3-3-4' system replacing the older (British-style) 'form system'.

Plate 43: Tai Wo Hau public housing estate after redevelopment was completed in 1993, as seen over the roofs of Kwan Mun Hau village.

Territories as a whole, including Tsuen Wan, but also areas of Hong Kong and Kowloon that once had been remote from the centres of commercial and industrial activity. There have been significant reductions of density in the older centres of population, while the formerly rural areas of the New Territories have undergone substantial urbanization, and the agricultural way of life that was still clearly discernible 50 years ago has disappeared.

Urban planning decisions went hand in hand with major infrastructural investment, especially in transportation. Until 1969, a single road ran around the New Territories. The journey from Tsuen Wan to Shau Kei Wan, at the eastern end of Hong Kong Island, required the better part of a frustrating day to make the round trip. One way can now be completed in 40 minutes. It is possible to commute from Tuen Mun, Sai Kung, or the Outlying Islands to Central District. In the 1960s, such undertakings involved uncomfortable (and sometimes terrifying) journeys by battered buses, and picturesque, but painfully slow, ferry rides. In the 1990s, transportation became speedy, cheap, efficient, clean, and, while crowded, reasonably comfortable. An impressive subway system, an upgraded railway, and a light rail system between Tuen Mun and Yuen Long move large numbers of commuters. Bus routes have increased in number, and the buses are air-conditioned. They are supplemented by privately owned minibuses, also air-conditioned, which ply well-defined routes. Taxis are omnipresent and readily available in Tsuen Wan, where they were found only rarely before 1980. There are designated taxis, coloured green, in the formerly rural areas of the New Territories, and blue taxis on Lantau Island. All but the taxis are linked to an electronic payment system, and seniors pay at most only HK$2. Thus, Hong Kong is a much easier place to move around than it once was.

Perhaps the most dramatic infrastructure project was the airport development. The need for a new airport to replace Kai Tak, which had been in operation since the 1930s, was urgent. Kai Tak's capacity had been reached, given the increases in air traffic during the 1980s and into the 1990s. The

decision to build a new airport at Chek Lap Kok on Lantau Island can also be seen as a boost to confidence in the months after the trauma of June 1989. It was an enormously expensive undertaking and
resulted in some spectacular disagreements with the government of China, which strongly questioned
the commitment of such a large sum on the eve of retrocession. The project involved the construction
of associated facilities, such as mass transit, roads, and bridges, to move people and freight to and
from the new airport. It was the outgrowth of a strategy for the comprehensive development of port
facilities, and road connections, the Port and Airport Development Strategy (PADS), which was first
presented in 1988. The strategy argued for a comprehensive approach to all forms of transportation,
including the movement of goods and people within Hong Kong, across the border into China, and
to the world as a whole. At its core, there was a well-formulated position that Hong Kong is not only
a global city with massive international connections, but also the dominant transportation hub in the
south China region, which China's resumption of sovereignty has not compromised.[23]

The consequences for the Tsuen Wan district were major. Shifting the airport from its urban location in Kowloon west to Lantau only furthered the physical integration of Tsuen Wan with urban
Hong Kong and gave it a strategic location in the expanded transport infrastructure. The Tung Chung
MTR line provided quicker access to Hong Kong Island via the interchange at Lai King. Tsing Yi's
transformation was furthered through a station on the rail link to the airport, including the inevitable
shopping mall and apartment complexes for the well-to-do. Ma Wan, over which the magnificent
Tsing Ma Bridge passes, was utterly transformed when an exclusive housing complex was built on this
formerly isolated segment of Tsuen Wan's historic area. Indeed, the coast from western Tsuen Wan
through Ting Kau, Tsing Lung Tau, and on past Sham Tseng has been developed as an upper-class
residential area.

The developments had consequences for the growth of the tourist industry in Tsuen Wan, now
only a short journey from the airport, as two new hotels were opened, supplementing a very large
hotel which had been completed in the mid-1980s. The older hotel is favoured by tourists from
China, whose presence has become more prominent on the streets of Tsuen Wan and on the MTR
into Kowloon and Hong Kong. Integration and the tourist trade have had a major impact upon the
commercial character of central Tsuen Wan where, in the past, shopping had been largely for daily
necessities and household needs.

Large-scale commercial properties began to be developed after completion of the MTR. The first,
and one of the largest, adjacent to Tsuen Wan station, was developed by a textile group that had begun
in Tsuen Wan in the early 1950s.[24] The first middle-class housing complex, Luk Yeung estate, was
developed at the same time. It was also adjacent to the station and included a shopping mall with many
brand-name shops and well-known restaurants. A walkway from the station connects to a residential-
commercial complex built on and adjacent to the old factory area. It was completed in the late 1990s.
In 2007, a two-towered commercial complex containing a five-star hotel, a convention centre, an
office tower, and two elegant shopping malls, was completed on reclaimed land that had expanded the
foreshore well beyond the limits of the central area as it had been in 1970, and the site of the old ferry
pier. The complex is linked by a walkway to the MTR station and to the Tsuen Wan West Rail station
which was completed in 2007 and connects Tsuen Wan to Yuen Long.

23. The PADS documents were complemented with *Metroplan*, a strategic land use and transport development plan for the metro-
politan area of Hong Kong. It followed on from PADS by assuming that Hong Kong's position as an international business and
financial centre, a centre for light manufacturing industry, and a major destination for international tourism should be augmented.
It argued for infrastructural developments to reflect Hong Kong's international character and its regional dominance, which the
planners saw had increased with the developments of the south China regional economy, and greater global linkages, in the 1980s.
Both PADS and *Metroplan* began with the territorial boundaries that had been created in 1898. They did not fully appreciate the
extent of future development within the Pearl River delta hinterland, or the need to integrate planning in Hong Kong with the
adjacent regions of China.
24. Foresightedly, it began to move into property development as early as 1965.

Plate 44: Former factory buildings, including Central Textiles, and modern office buildings in western Tsuen Wan, 2014.

Cultural Identity

The improvement in Hong Kong's physical space was a reflection of Hong Kong's increasing affluence, in which its former Third World characteristics largely disappeared. With it came a sense of Hong Kong cultural identity, which was not apparent until the 1980s.

By 1991, the census reported that almost 60% of the population was Hong Kong–born, while the proportion born in China stood at 35%, in great contrast to the situation 30 years earlier, when the majority of the population was China-born. This demographic shift is important. In the late 1960s, the people were still predominately immigrants. The trauma of relocation from China to Hong Kong in the late 1940s and 1950s was salient for much of the adult population. Hong Kong was a refuge and a place to remake lives disrupted by war and political transformation. It was not a place to which the bulk of the adult population was linked by close emotional bonds. Their sentiments likely were still attached to homeland locations, however compromised by the social and political changes of the 1950s and 1960s. It is for this reason that many associations in Tsuen Wan were grouped around locality and kin ties. Links with the homeland, however, became fractured and charged with ambivalence in the wake of radical policy changes. Until the late 1970s, there were only limited opportunities to return to ancestral points of origin, and reluctance on the part of many to return to scenes of flight.[25] The older generation was often silent as to the reasons for out-migration, and critical cultural knowledge about ancestral localities was not always transmitted. The links with ancestral homelands were re-established in the 1980s.

---

25. See Diana Lary, *China's Civil War: A Social History 1945–1949* (Cambridge: Cambridge University Press, 2015), esp. 217–38.

For the younger generation, however, the emotional impact was blunted by the unwillingness of the senior generations to be fully open about the past. The younger generation, which came to maturity in the 1970s and 1980s, did not carry the emotional baggage of the older generation. A sense of identity with Hong Kong was established by the Hong Kong–born population, which saw a growing cultural gulf between the experiences of coming of age in an increasingly affluent and largely apolitical Hong Kong, with its increasing links to the international system, and the China alternative.

There seems little doubt that China, and especially Guangdong Province, had exerted a dominant cultural influence over Hong Kong for most of its history. That cultural dominance receded after the establishment of the People's Republic of China. It was, in part, a consequence of the tight central control which was maintained over all of China's provinces after 1949, a control that was especially marked over the complicated provinces of the coastal southeast. Regional cultures in general were overwhelmed by an effort to create national cultural forms with a 'socialist' character. The expression of Cantonese culture, and the other local cultures of Guangdong, cuisine aside, was compromised. The hinterland was 'lost' in terms of its economic and cultural significance in the first 30 years after 1949. A distinctive version of a local culture, significantly independent of forces from China itself, emerged. This had a major effect for the younger generation and contributed to the development of a Hong Kong identity in which the older China-born population could not fully share.

The creation of cultural forms which the younger generation began to absorb occurred in a context of major changes in the technology of mass communications, especially television. As Hong Kong became increasingly integrated into the global economy and began to share in some potent internationalized cultural processes, it became culturally disassociated from China which from the middle 1960s had adopted a strident revolutionary cultural form. This had little appeal to increasingly affluent Hong Kong youth.

Despite the impact of Western popular music, and other influences, Hong Kong was, however, still culturally Chinese. It began to experiment with popular culture within the context of the Cantonese language. This was the lingua franca of the Hong Kong population as regional versions of Chinese began to attenuate, particularly under the impact of the educational system, film, and television. Therefore, from a variety of sources, some global, some local, and some broadly Chinese, Hong Kong began to create a distinctive identity.

Both the public and private sectors became involved in the creation of Hong Kong cultural expressions. Government involvement grew over time. Before 1970, Hong Kong's City Hall was virtually the only permanent public venue for the performing arts, which were not well represented and were poorly funded. Facilities expanded after the 1980s, as Hong Kong's affluence increased. A dedicated facility for the performing arts was created in Wan Chai, but the dispersal of the population to new towns, including Tsuen Wan, saw the creation of facilities in them for performances of all kinds. Orthodox high culture (with a bias towards Western cultural forms) is vigorous, and government-subsidized spaces have also become increasingly important for the performing arts whose traditions are Chinese (or non-Western). Cantonese opera, and other Chinese regional forms, have experienced growth, in part due to the availability of public performance space. The government built a Town Hall in Tsuen Wan in 1980, adjacent to the Magistracy and the old ferry pier, which became the heart of a vibrant commercial centre.

A development of great significance was the expansion of museums. Hong Kong now has a number of significant museum complexes and historic sites such as the Sam Tung Uk Museum in Tsuen Wan, and two buildings, one a house built by Yau Yuen-cheung, now surrounded by a much-appreciated park, where Lower Hoi Pa once stood.

In 1970, the government created Kowloon Park on the site of a former barracks. This marked the beginning of a process through which large tracts of land were set aside for public use. Many of the outlying areas of the territory were designated as country parks, now lush and green, which are fully utilized by hikers and campers on weekends and public holidays. The Tsuen Wan MTR station, especially on weekends in the cooler months, is full of hikers on their way to Tai Mo Shan Country Park, part of which is a forest preserve. Many climb up to Chuen Lung, where teahouses and locally grown watercress are enjoyed by visitors. There is also a park established around the Shing Mun Reservoir, which is readily accessible via the transportation services provided by Lo Wai village. Clearly, one of the changes that prompted expenditures on public facilities is the new-found leisure that is a corollary of affluence and the regulation of hours of work. There are, however, also implications for an emerging Hong Kong cultural identity.

The development of orthodox high culture reflects a process of embourgeoisement of the Hong Kong population, or a segment of it. Museums, and to a lesser degree country parks, attempt to foster heritage preservation. Hong Kong was created to meet commercial needs. A sense of heritage has been largely lacking. The commercial drive that it has exhibited over time has overwhelmed its sense of the past. Little of Hong Kong's architectural past remains with the exception of temples. The formerly rural New Territories, country parks and remote areas aside, have become thoroughly urban in form. The education system, driven by colonial interests until 1997, and conscious of the problematic nature of historical interpretation, has tended to de-emphasize history in the school curriculum. Somewhat late in the day, efforts were made to create awareness of the past.

The social, cultural, even political boundaries for the people of Tsuen Wan have changed dramatically, not merely since the late colonial period, but also in the two decades since retrocession. Much of the local Hakka population is resident in their villages, many of which are in new locations. Their political structure is largely intact, although now co-existing with larger political forms. Indigenous culture is becoming muted, as the following chapter will explain. Tsuen Wan has been fully open to the forces of cultural change in Hong Kong since 1980 and is now no longer as readily distinguishable from the rest of Hong Kong as it once was.

Political Culture

A relatively recent, and contentious, aspect of Hong Kong's emerging cultural identity relates to political values and their expression. It is contentious because it is new and has been driven by a number of factors, one of the more significant of which was the changed system of administration in the wake of retrocession, with ultimate authority resting in Beijing rather than London. Political behaviour, as with other forms of social behaviour, has been conditioned by the changes following a negotiated solution to the issue of the resumption of Chinese sovereignty.

Politics in Hong Kong, for much of its history after 1841, were constrained by the assumptions of colonial policy. Consultation processes occurred with selected members of the population who were incorporated into the political process. The majority of the population had no formal input into the work of the government. Only in the New Territories, in the post-war period, was a system of representative consultation developed for the indigenous population. In the 1970s, the colonial government recognized the importance of broadening the consultative base, and Tsuen Wan became an important point of initial experimentation. During the 1980s, the principle of directly electing representatives to sit on various bodies such as District Boards, the Regional Council, and the Legislative Council, or indirectly electing them through 'functional constituencies', was put into effect.

Elections to the Legislative Council, which had begun in 1985, reached a new beginning in September 1991 when 18 members were directly elected to the Council from geographical constituencies and a further 21 members were elected indirectly through functional constituencies. The increase in the number of seats that were directly elected was, in part, a response to the large and unprecedented demonstrations in Hong Kong in the spring of 1989. The significance of the 1991 elections was that, for the first time, a majority of the seats were no longer held by government appointees. Of equal significance is the fact that political parties contested the elections and those who won seats were, in the main, social activists who were either critical of government or had taken a major role in Hong Kong's public protests against the heavy-handed role of the Chinese central government during the political protests in China during the spring of 1989. Another effect was to give the budding politicians of Hong Kong, including those in Tsuen Wan, a forum to explore political possibilities in Hong Kong.

Political attitudes are volatile and complex. The essentially conservative (even Confucian) values of a substantial majority of the Hong Kong population appeared to reject a confrontational approach in dealing with representatives of the Chinese government, in efforts to cope with different interpretations of what form post-colonial Hong Kong, under Chinese rule, should appropriately take. Political behaviour was dramatically different in an era when British officials assumed ever fewer high level administrative roles in government, and in which Hong Kong Chinese businessmen took over an economic domination once reserved for the British elite. It also differed quite substantially with respect to age, education, and social class. As one consequence, the Chinese government had little compunction against formulating rules of its own choosing to select a chief executive, despite some opposition in Hong Kong, or dismissing representatives who had been elected in 1995 under circumstances which it found questionable, while overseeing the creation of a Provisional Legislature that took office on 1 July 1997. Equally, there were no challenges to the elections of 1998, which in many ways restored the status quo ante, including a vocal opposition to a majority that supported the post-colonial forms of governance. Hong Kong rules generally prevailed in Hong Kong after the establishment of the SAR, and the district councils had an important role to play.

Hong Kong, Guangdong, and the Pearl River Delta

The Pearl River delta region has been transformed since economic reform was initiated in China in 1979. Rapid economic growth in the region has been fuelled by industrial and tertiary sector growth in which outside investment, entrepreneurial skill, and management expertise have been extensively utilized. No region of China has developed as rapidly as has the delta—especially since the mid-1980s. The major stimulus for growth, initially, was Hong Kong. We draw attention to the Pearl River delta region and its transformation, in part because Hong Kong entrepreneurs had a critical role to play at the outset, and they continue to be significant, although no longer dominant. From our perspective, the process of change and development in the delta region closely parallels that which we observed in Tsuen Wan in the 1960s and 1970s. Furthermore, after 1980 much of Tsuen Wan's industry was relocated into the delta.

The Pearl River delta became one of the most attractive regions in China for labour migrants, as its rapid industrialization and commercialization created a huge demand for labour of all kinds. Surplus rural labour from China's agricultural interior, especially from Hunan, Guangxi, Henan, Sichuan, and the poorer regions of Guangdong, has been absorbed into the burgeoning, and often export-oriented enterprises, located in townships and villages, infrastructural projects, and other sectors. The 2011 census showed that the number of both inter- and intra-provincial migrants in Guangdong was over 30 million in 2000,[26] and a decade later approached 50 million.[27]

Delta residents are members of two categories: they have either a local household registration (*hukou* 戶口) or a temporary registration allowing them to live and work in the delta. The local (*dangdiren* 當地人) and the outsider (*waidiren* 外地人) designations constitute an economic and social

---

26. This statistic compares the permanent population at year end with the portion of the population holding local household registration.
27. State Statistical Bureau, *Guangdong Statistical Yearbook: 2008* (Statistical Bureau Press, 2009), compare table 4–5 and table 4–7.

divide which is as profound as the former distinctions between 'agricultural' and 'urban' *hukou*. They have become salient and crucial indicators of social status.

Labour migrants in the delta do not have access to the same welfare benefits as do the local inhabitants of the Pearl River delta many of whom, unlike most of the migrants, now have an urban *hukou*. Their settlements are designated as urban, despite their appearance. There are still some villages in the Pearl River delta that derive income from the agricultural sector and cultivate the fields, tend orchards, or raise fish. These have become fewer in number and the agricultural resources that exist are often contracted out to migrants. Throughout the delta, but especially in the Guangzhou suburbs and the eastern delta region, many of the former agricultural resources, the fields, orchards, fishponds, and former grazing lands, have been converted to industrial and commercial activities. Village land is, however, collectively owned, and the collective is defined in terms of local title. After land reform in the early 1950s, land was allocated to village households, whose claims were ancestral. While individual title was lost to the collective economy in the 1950s, it was re-established in the early reform period, as household production was resumed, only to be overwhelmed by the demands for a new industrial and commercial economy. Village lands are still owned collectively and have significant economic value. Land and/or industrial facilities are rented to entrepreneurs, many from Hong Kong, Taiwan, or from within China itself, providing local village administration with cash income, which is often substantial.

A new collective economy is in place in all the villages in the delta with which we are familiar. The details vary, but in all but the west delta region dominated by overseas Chinese dependents, and still primarily based on rice agriculture, the outcomes are similar. Local households receive dividends based upon their 'shares' in the economic corporation, organized on the basis of the production teams of the former communes, of which the villages were once part. The resemblance to the situation of the indigenous inhabitants of Tsuen Wan in its industrial development from the 1950s is substantial. There are of course differences, both in scale and in terms of rights in the place of residence. The migrants to Tsuen Wan had fled across a political boundary and had little immediate desire to return to their points of origin, and shortly after their arrival they had the legal right to remain in Hong Kong. Over time they became fully integrated into Tsuen Wan and Hong Kong, and their migrant origins became less important. In contrast, labour migrants in the delta region have no legal rights to settle in the place to which they have come to work. They are also denied certain critical citizenship rights such as education and health care, and have become sojourners, destined in the long term to return to their points of origin, unless fundamental legal changes affect their status.[28] In both Tsuen Wan and the Pearl River delta, however, residents with ancestral ties to land have not merely survived massive economic transformations but have become beneficiaries of its prosperity.

Conclusion

The final quarter of the twentieth century saw dramatic shifts globally, regionally, and within Hong Kong that fundamentally changed the character of Tsuen Wan. The colonial government became responsive to perceived needs, especially the challenge of housing. Increasing attention was paid to education at all levels, social welfare, and administrative change resulting in greater public participation in decision-making and consultation. The already substantial commitment to infrastructural improvements became even more dramatic, particularly in the final decade of British rule. Port development, roads, bridges, mass transit, and ultimately a new airport opened Tsuen Wan district as a

---

28. Graham E. Johnson and Zhang Feng, 'Partners, Neighbours, Outsiders: Understanding Labour Migrants in the Pearl River Delta', in *Guangdong: Challenges in Development and Crisis Management*, ed. Joseph Y. S. Cheng (Hong Kong: City University of Hong Kong, 2010), 363–95.

whole to the expansion of private housing projects, which, with the rapid decline in its industries, shifted the town away from its working-class character. Tsuen Wan increasingly resembled other parts of Hong Kong and on the surface appeared less distinctive than it had been for much of the twentieth century.

There was, however, one distinctive aspect that remained. Tsuen Wan had grown around a core indigenous population. The indigenous population had been favoured by colonial policies. That distinctiveness was crucial for Tsuen Wan's development and remained in the Basic Law, the negotiated constitutional framework of the Hong Kong SAR after 1997. The changes in the 30 years of industrial Tsuen Wan, and then those of its deindustrialization, were dramatic for the Tsuen Wan population as a whole. The indigenous population remains as a vibrant, if changed, part of the new post-industrial Tsuen Wan.

9

The Fading of Distinctiveness

Original People in a Sea of Newcomers

You could say we are more quiet, more humble, primarily because we are fading (淡化了) into the rest of the population. This has particularly happened in Tsuen Wan because it was the earliest place to become a city. In comparison, other groups of natives remain more concentrated.
—Ho Wing-kwong, 1996

By the 1990s and thereafter, many of Tsuen Wan's original people would have described their situation with this image, as it was clear that they were losing much of their distinctiveness.[1] When we observed ceremonies, men often commented that they had been simplified. We also discussed with them their perceptions of the strength of their language and culture at that time, their sense of their identity, and their relations with those who shared in it.

Their interactions with people of other backgrounds also formed part of our research. These relationships were present in many contexts, with their schoolmates and work mates, and with others in the broader community. On a community scale, such interactions were brought into sharp focus during a particular event, the annual Tianhou festival at the central temple.

We were also interested in their quality of life at this time, in post-industrial Tsuen Wan. In this phase of its development, both private and lineage trust properties were even more valuable, bringing steady incomes to those who were in positions to benefit from them. We also tried to ascertain how their quality of life might have improved with the changes in social welfare and amenities implemented by government.

By the 1990s, the population of Kwan Mun Hau reflected the playing out of the demographic transition. Families with large numbers of children were a thing of the past. The many older people generally enjoyed good health[2] and leisure activities. It was fascinating to explore with them their aspirations for their children, their attitudes towards the life choices of those who were grown, and their assessments of their own situations.

The political context of the time, just before Hong Kong's retrocession in 1997, was certainly salient. We were fortunate to be present on 1 July 1997 as witnesses to the acknowledgement of this momentous event by the people of Kwan Mun Hau.

---

1. Hayes uses the word 'diluted' to describe the weakening position of New Territories indigenous leaders from the 1980s, *Friends and Teachers*, 295.
2. Cancer was taking a marked toll among middle-aged people, however, a possible effect of the environmental pollution of earlier years.

Indigenous People and Newcomers in the 1990s

By this time, indigenous people constituted only a small proportion of the total, but they continued to enjoy the benefits to which they earlier had been entitled. They appreciated the fact that they had a home of their own (歸宿), a base or foundation (基礎) upon which they could depend, although the extent to which this offered security of housing depended upon various individual factors. Nonetheless, they enjoyed the tangible and intangible benefits of belonging to a defined place, Tsuen Wan with its long-established villages. Those who lived in the villages were surrounded by their own people, albeit intermixed with tenants, and even those who lived elsewhere could return to this base. In addition to this security, there was that conferred by the lineages upon their members, some of which offered material rewards as well. As one Chan lineage man said:

> In this present society, I think we have some advantages but these are not very different from those of some newcomers. Now society is very prosperous, so people should have their own welfare and rights. We Hakka native people can enjoy the benefits of our ancestors' hard work. We are fortunate, as we don't need to work so hard and can still benefit, but our ancestors really had to sacrifice.

Indigenous people continued to benefit from the work of the Rural Committee, which, through their village representatives, acted on their behalf to ensure that they received the benefits to which they were entitled. The chairman of the Rural Committee also had an appointed seat on the District Board (later District Council), giving natives additional input on government policy decisions. Village representatives served as a bridge between villagers and government, and one of their roles was to certify people as indigenous, if their status was challenged, or needed to be verified to secure benefits.

There were various situations in which indigenous people required intercession or advocacy, and individual petitions did not carry the weight of those from members of the representative body. Examples included putting up mat-sheds for events, temporarily obstructing traffic for special activities, repairing ancestral tombs, which required certification that the applicants were indigenous, and obtaining burial plots in their special cemeteries. As new burials were no longer permitted in the mountains, families had to apply for plots in the two cemeteries above Chuen Lung. One is for those whose ancestors had been present before 1898, and the other for long-term residents present before the occupation but not certified as original inhabitants.[3]

The Rural Committee also takes responsibility for mortuary urns (金塔) that have been found within the district, often during infrastructure development. As of 1995, they had created three repositories in which the urns are respectfully placed in covered rows. In the 1950s, the Wo Yee Hop Charitable Tomb was constructed, accommodating 500 to 600 urns. In the 1980s, this was relocated near Chuen Lung to make way for an electrical pylon and expanded so that it could hold more than 930 urns. Another repository for 100 urns had been constructed there in the 1960s.[4] In 1994, the Rural Committee learned that during road work near Ting Kau, 27 urns had been found that had to be moved. With the permission of the Ting Kau village representatives, the Rural Committee arranged to construct a repository for them in Heung Shek Cemetery, offering the indigenous residents the opportunity to place other urns there together with those that had been found. Applications were received for 199 urns. A geomancer was employed to determine the appropriate dates and orientation, and a repository for these remains was completed in December 1995. The repository has three plaques, the central one stating that it is the soul tablet for the urns of deceased members of Tsuen Wan district (鄉). The plaque on the left has a respectful quatrain written by the chairman of the Heung

---

3. In these cemeteries their mortuary practices have been simplified, as they no longer take up the bones for placement in funerary urns.

4. Summary of speech by Chan Lau-fong, chairman of the Tsuen Wan Rural Committee (荃灣鄉事委員會川龍響石金塔龕完山典禮　一九九五年二月七日).

Yee Kuk, while that on the right has a statement from the three responsible members of the Rural Committee describing the circumstances of the repository's creation. The prayer text that is included in their commemorative publication emphasizes the duty of the Rural Committee to look after the basic needs of the people, one of which is proper care after death. It notes the benevolence of the local people in building such a shrine and expresses the hope that the deceased may rest there and receive the offerings presented to them during ceremonies in the spring and autumn. The deceased include fishing people and immigrants as well as villagers.

Another ongoing challenge faced by Tsuen Wan's indigenous people, and by the Rural Committee on their behalf, has been the government's need for the removal of ancestral tombs in the hills to make way for further urban development and infrastructural improvements.[5] Such ancestral remains could be resited in the mountains once the appropriate permissions had been obtained, rather than in the cemetery, but the descendants have to find geomantically beneficial sites, build new tombs, and conduct the appropriate rituals, while meeting any costs not covered by the compensation offered.

One question of particular concern has been the political affiliation of lineages whose members are spread over several villages, as this affects their voting rights in elections and in village removals. The question of residence does not concern those who are renting elsewhere because of a shortage of housing, as they maintain legal residence in their ancestral villages, but instead affects those who have always lived in a village other than that which contains their ancestral hall, or who have bought houses in other villages. According to Ho Wing-kwong, the Rural Committee had discussed this question in depth in about 1990, because it was such a concern for Tsuen Wan people. He himself was originally from Hoi Pa and was elected to be a village representative, but he resided in Sai Lau Kok, where he owned a house. According to the Rural Committee's decision, a person may change residential affiliation after having moved for ten years, but in Tsuen Wan it is hard to designate people as being indigenous to particular villages, although this may be their family's self-identification. They are, instead, simply considered to be Tsuen Wan indigenous people (荃灣原居民).

The terms of village removals were also sources of concern and comparison. By this time, all of the central Tsuen Wan villages had been moved to the periphery, under terms that in many ways were seen to be increasingly beneficial, because those who moved later could negotiate on the basis of what those before them had gained. It was not possible for us to systematically survey the differences in the terms of the moves and people's satisfaction with them, but opinions offered by those we interviewed gave some insight. For example, even though the Chan of Sam Tung Uk had allegedly received better terms, a Kwan Mun Hau man of the same surname, and therefore related to them, argued that the geomantic prospect of their new site was bad, with the result that many residents had sold their houses and moved down into the city, or even emigrated. It certainly appeared to be bleak, with few shrines or plants in evidence, and it overlooks a major road. Their new ancestral hall is beautiful, however, and is surrounded by lush foliage. The value of their three-storey houses seems to be outweighed by the unattractive nature of the village and its prospect.

Muk Min Ha moved under pressure from the MTR construction schedule. Its new village is attractive, with an imposing double ancestral hall,[6] on a pleasant site, as are the nearby new villages of Chun Sham Yun and Sai Lau Kok. Hoi Pa, with its several sub-villages and numerous surnames, was divided into segments that moved to several sites at different times. Memories of the former central Tsuen Wan villages are preserved in street names in the downtown core, as well as in the preserved village of Sam Tung Uk and the Hoi Pa historic houses.

---

5. Another problem has been squatter structures impinging on hillside tombs. Hayes, *Tsuen Wan*, 105.
6. One hall commemorates their founding ancestor, and the other someone believed to have helped him. James Hayes, *South China Village Culture* (Hong Kong: Oxford University Press, 2001), Plate 10.

Some villages such as Yuen Tun and Tsing Fai Tong at the western end of the district moved down to the coast for reasons of convenience, and the surroundings of all of the western coastal villages have changed beyond recognition with the development of elegant villas and housing complexes. Other villages outside the city centre, such as Chuen Lung and Lo Wai, remain in situ, as does Wo Yee Hop. Sheung Kwai Chung is still a secluded preserve, with its large old trees.

Residents of Kwan Mun Hau knew that the terms of their resiting were less favourable than those who moved later, in that they received only two-storey village-style houses, with no provision for sons beyond the exchange value of property that some families had. They remembered that they had moved under duress, however, because of the flooding that had made the original village intolerable, and we met no one who did not agree that they had obtained a prime site, the 'king of sites' (地王), because of its location. Although initially it was considered to be less convenient to the centre of Tsuen Wan and the ferries to Hong Kong Island, by the 1990s its position just above the Tai Wo Hau MTR station and Castle Peak Road gave its inhabitants easy access to all of urban Hong Kong as well as to the new airport.

A number of men interviewed, both community leaders and residents of Kwan Mun Hau, stated that Tsuen Wan natives had less room for expansion than did those living elsewhere in the New Territories. There was almost no vacant land available to build new houses for grown sons. This was accepted as a fact of life, counterbalanced by the value of living in a 'new town' with its amenities and transportation links, as well as greatly increased property values. One man did argue that if the government had not resumed so much land in central Tsuen Wan at low rates of compensation, there would have been more available for additional housing for sons. He was one of a number of Kwan Mun Hau natives who believed that the government had profited greatly in its early land transactions with them. Given that much of their land was classified as agricultural, they had received low prices for it, but he believed that the government had then sold it at considerable profit for later industrial and commercial development, although the system of Letters of Exchange did give them some opportunities to strike their own bargains.

Relationships to the Central Temple: Original People and Immigrants

The construction of the Tsuen Wan line of the MTR was profoundly disruptive to the northern part of central Tsuen Wan, commencing in the autumn of 1978. The impact on the landscape was extreme and put the Tianhou temple at great risk. Furthermore, the Luk Yeung Estate was to be built in front of and beside the temple. In 1979, the Rural Committee called a meeting of all village representatives, together with government officials and engineers from the MTR, to discuss how they should handle this threat to the integrity of their temple. They had to decide whether or not it could be preserved and, if the former, how this should be done. They established the Tianhou Temple Restoration Committee to oversee the process, and worked under the guidance of an architect from Hong Kong University and a geomancer, other advisers, and village elders.[7] They decided to strive to preserve the temple's original structure, and to renovate it and enhance its surroundings.[8] The front was shored up with a retaining wall 40 feet deep, buttresses were put in place, and the attached structures were demolished. A temporary temple was built behind the old one for use by worshippers during construction. When the MTR line had been completed and the site prepared, the temple was renovated and new side chambers and exterior surrounds were completed. The costs were met by the government, as well as by donations from 20 individuals and families.

7. Chan Shui-cheung 陳瑞璋 (Compiler), *Special Publication on the Ceremony Commemorating the Restoration of the Tsuen Wan Tianhou Temple 12/12/1984* (荃灣天后宮重修開光典禮特刊一九八四年 (甲子) 十二月十二日).
8. The two temples on Tsing Yi were resited as development proceeded. Hayes, *Tsuen Wan*, 149.

Plate 45: Massive clearances for the MTR and the development of northern Tsuen Wan, 1979, photographed from the same place as was Plate 20. New housing in west Tsuen Wan is in the distance.

Plate 46: The precarious state of the central Tianhou temple in 1980, shored up as the excavations for the MTR and the construction of Luk Yeung estate are carried out around it.

Plate 47: The Tianhou Festival, 1969. On the right are chickens offered in the distinctive Hakka way, but the large fowl is a goose, likely offered by a Teochiu immigrant.

The result is a beautifully decorated temple with imposing walls and gates, despite its relatively small size. The surroundings are attractively landscaped, with trees, bamboo, gardens, sitting-out areas, and a pleasant park behind. The contrast between its present setting and that which we remembered from the 1960s is profound, as the temple then had been surrounded by vegetable fields and small enterprises, with drainage ditches that also served as open sewers. The grand reopening (開光) in late 1984 was a memorable occasion, and the Rural Committee engaged an opera troupe to perform for four days and five nights.[9] Government officials and the chairman of the Heung Yee Kuk attended, as did many villagers, who also sent unicorn dance teams. It is likely that other Tsuen Wan people were also present, as by this time residents of various origins were actively interested in the deity and her powers.

When we were first in Tsuen Wan, the people worshipping at the temple appeared primarily to be local Hakka women. Men also worshipped on special occasions such as weddings, as well as on the first days of the New Year. Aside from their dress, Hakka women could be identified by their characteristic pairs of offering baskets, with four-cornered bases and round lids on which the offerings were presented. The offerings were distinctive in that the papers to be burned were presented flat, fanned out, and if it was an important occasion or festival, the principal meat was a steamed chicken, its head angled back, and its intestines and a disc of its blood placed on its back.[10]

9. Barbara E. Ward explains the importance of opera on celebratory occasions, including deities' annual festivals, in 'Regional Operas and Their Audiences', in *Popular Culture in Late Imperial China*, ed. David Johnson, Andrew J. Nathan, and Evelyn S. Rawski (Berkeley: University of California Press, 1985), 161–87.

10. The exception is that ducks are offered on the fourteenth of the seventh lunar month.

By the mid-1990s, and later, few Hakka women were in evidence. The caretaker who receives donations of money for incense and oil is always a villager hired by the Rural Committee.[11] He said that not many indigenous women came, except at festivals. This may reflect the more distant locations of their removed villages, the general weakening of their traditional rituals, and the presence of many diversions in urban Tsuen Wan.

The temple, however, was hardly empty. It was busy every day, the courtyard thick with smoke from burning incense sticks and candles, including expensive incense coils suspended overhead. It was the only temple in central Tsuen Wan, and at New Year and other festivals it was full of worshippers. The monasteries and even Yuk Ha Kok, in altered form, survived on the periphery of the built-up area.

By 1996, there was another speech group prominently involved in the temple. This was a group of Teochiu women, devotees of the goddess, who could be seen there every day, cleaning the temple and even the image of the deity, chanting sutras in the side hall, and folding paper offerings into ingot shapes, as was their custom. Their offerings differed from those of the local Hakka people, not only in the care they took to prepare the papers, but also because they included diverse kinds of meat or fish, as well as vegetarian dishes.

The group of devotees carried out their own work for the goddess and her temple, but shared this with the Rural Committee, which had final responsibility for the management of the temple and the conduct of regular rites. We learned about this relationship from discussions and interviews with members of both groups as well as with the temple caretakers. We also had the good fortune to be present at the time of the 1996 Tianhou Festival, an occasion when the rites of the two groups, conducted in their distinctive ways, intersected.

According to one of the caretakers, many of Teochiu women had been resident in Tsuen Wan for about 30 years, and hence were considered to be 'half-native' (一半土人). Some had been committed to the temple for that long, and they supported it in many ways. The temple plaque acknowledging donors to the 1984 renovation included several Teochiu shop owners, for example. Members of their community were major donors and were said to contribute more than twice what the Rural Committee spent on the temple in any one year. The devotees were not necessarily personally wealthy, but they approached people in their community to solicit donations of funds and also gifts in kind: expensive robes for the deity, and furnishings, such as a new palanquin, that they learned were needed through communications with the deity. They also contributed their labour, despite the fact that the Rural Committee paid people to clean the temple. According to the caretaker, they took responsibility for changing Tianhou's robe, which in the past had been done by villagers. He said that the Rural Committee welcomed their contributions.

In contrast to the Rural Committee, they were an informal group. This was likened to the groups of village women who materialized on the occasion of a wedding or a death to do what was needed without direction. Their shared cultural background and familiarity with their rituals provided them with the knowledge that was needed.

In addition, they had the informal leadership of one of their members, a woman who believed that she had a special relationship with the goddess. She said that she had learned of the special power of the Tianhou in Tsuen Wan, and had come to petition her, saying that if her sons did well in school she would devote her life to her. Her sons had been successful, so she honoured her vow and moved to Tsuen Wan. She lived simply and devoted her time and resources to Tianhou from then on, chanting sutras with the other women, preparing offerings, and doing the menial work of cleaning. She said that her work was guided by direct contact with Tianhou in heaven,[12] where she learned from her what

---

11. This position rotates among the villages and surnames.
12. We would say that this was through visions or dreams, but she did not express the experience this way.

she needed. Whenever the need arose, she solicited donations from members of their community, and said that she could keep a record of them even though she was illiterate.

For example, during the MTR construction she perceived that Tianhou felt that she was falling over, and so she raised funds to purchase two generals for her, one to stand on each side. She also told us that sometimes Tianhou grew very tired and (speaking to us in a weak voice) needed a bed on which she could rest. After obtaining permission from the Rural Committee, they did arrange for the purchase of such a bed, and it now stands on the floor to one side of the altar. She said she told the goddess, however, that if people came in to worship her she would have to get up to return to her post.

The 1996 Tianhou Festival

The annual festival in honour of Tianhou was organized by the Rural Committee, whose Temple Committee remained responsible for the management of the temple, continuing to honour its responsibility to conduct various rites for the benefit of the people of the territory.[13] At the beginning of the year, they petitioned the goddess for blessings during the year, for which they thanked her on the first of the twelfth month. In the spring at Qingming and in the autumn at Chongyang they made offerings to the deceased of the district for whom they had taken responsibility, and at the same festivals they made offerings to the souls of the 17 martyrs who had died defending Tsuen Wan. In addition, the chairman of the Rural Committee worshipped at the temple on the first and fifteenth of each month.

The 1996 festival took place in and behind the temple itself. Early in the twentieth century, the festival had been held on the waterfront, and a villager active in the temple said that this was because fishing people, who were very devout, also participated. Furthermore, the rice fields around the temple were soft and would have been damaged by the mat-shed for the opera.[14] The festival apparently was not celebrated with opera around the middle of the twentieth century, perhaps because the Rural Committee head was Christian, and there also were times when puppet opera was offered rather than live performances. Even though the surroundings were simple and people had to stand to watch it, the opera had provided a meaningful annual event at that time. In the 1980s, the performances had been changed to full opera with human actors. Regardless of how it was performed, it had always been Cantonese opera, never Hakka. People who could not understand Cantonese[15] could follow the plots through the actors' gestures and their familiarity with the stories. Furthermore, Cantonese opera has what Barbara Ward has called 'multiple redundancy',[16] a rich symbolic vocabulary, sets of conventions of sound, colour, role types, and costumes meaningful to regular theatre-goers.

Series of opera performances are important to temple festivals because they are, as Ward has argued so well, not simply entertainment but also offerings. It is the organizers' responsibility to ensure that the deity can see the performances, either through the temple door, or if this is not possible, from a temporary shrine to which the deity's image or a tablet representing it is carried. The hope is that the performances are efficacious, bringing benefits because of the god's presence and through their inherent qualities of sound, colour, light, and movement, both of the actors and of the festive crowds who are attracted, as well as through the generally happy endings of the operas themselves, which include success, reconciliation, and reunion.[17]

---

13. According to Patrick Hase, a rural committee is most likely to have these religious duties if they are a continuation of an earlier body with these responsibilities, as in Tsuen Wan; otherwise another body takes charge. We were assured that the rites were for the benefit of all, not just the local Hakka people.
14. Plate 1 in Hayes, *Tsuen Wan*, shows the waterfront at Hoi Pa in about 1900, with an impressive mat-shed theatre in place.
15. Even Cantonese opera had been performed in 'official speech' (官話) until about the end of the nineteenth century.
16. Barbara E. Ward, 'Not Merely Players: Drama, Art, and Ritual in Traditional China', *Man (NS)* 14, no. 1 (1979): 34.
17. Ward, 'Not Merely Players', 24–30.

Plate 48: Chan Lau-fong, chairman of the Rural Committee, waits for the unicorn dancers' arrival, with Teochiu worshippers and the palanquin that will carry the deity to the festival site, 1996.

Plate 49: The deity in procession to her temporary shrine, her palanquin and regalia carried by members of the Rural Committee with the Teochiu women devotees, 1996.

In 1996, it was clear that the Rural Committee was taking very seriously its responsibility for organizing the festival, and for carrying out the rites. There were no other specialists present. They were led by their Temple Committee, with directions from its chairman as needed. The other groups present were nuns, perhaps from a local monastery, chanting sutras; and, even more in evidence, the Teochiu women devotees.

As there was no room in front of the temple door for the opera performances, it was necessary to move a tablet representing the deity.[18] On the morning of the first day, two members of the Rural Committee brought out the palanquin. Not long afterwards, we could hear a unicorn dance team approaching,[19] and a caretaker hit the temple bell and drum about 20 times—a haunting sound. There were not many people present, but a man asked that they stay back and not block the unicorn, which worshipped outside the enclosure and then inside the courtyard, where it was met by the chairman of the Rural Committee. A woman scattered pomelo leaf infusion during this time, continuing throughout the procession. The Rural Committee members worshipped inside the temple, the chairman asked that all should go well, and they bowed in unison. The unicorn continued through the temple, weaving around the pillars, and on into the Heroes' Hall, where the Rural Committee representatives also

18. Before the formation of the Rural Committee, this was done by young unmarried men of the district.
19. The unicorn dance team came from a Hakka boxing academy in Tsuen Wan whose members were from Huizhou. A Rural Committee official said that the nearby villages no longer had them, and it would have been 'too much trouble' to invite one from a more distant Tsuen Wan village.

worshipped. Then the chairman and vice-chairman carried out the tablet and incense pot and placed them carefully in the palanquin. When the procession was ready to set off, they lit a long string of firecrackers.[20] Until then it had been raining very hard, a violent thunderstorm, but at this point the storm suddenly stopped.

The dancing unicorn led the procession, followed by the palanquin, which was carried by workers and some women. The Rural Committee representatives walked on each side, and the Teochiu devotees, walking with them, carried Tianhou's ceremonial umbrella and fans. When they reached the temporary altar, the men carefully installed the tablet and incense pot, and when all was ready they bowed together, each with a stick of incense, which they placed in the incense pot, while the devotees came forward with offering papers.

At this moment, the downpour resumed. The timing of the events had been determined by a geomancer, and when the chairman spoke with us later, he emphasized the significance of the cessation of the storm, saying it showed that the goddess was efficacious (令). He asked that we bear witness to this remarkable event and said that he felt a deep affinity with her power.

The closing procession several days later was conducted in a similar way, but in reverse. After one of the women had sprinkled pomelo leaf infusion all around the area, the Rural Committee representatives and the women escorted the tablet to the temple, where the unicorn wove around the front pillars. The palanquin was carried into the temple and placed by the altar, and the representatives carefully carried the tablet to the front of the temple, while many of the women knelt and worshipped. The unicorn circled the palanquin and made biting motions: 'biting the breath of the palanquin' (咬車氣), a Rural Committee member said, while women made brushing motions through and over it towards themselves. The caretaker once again hit the bell and drum, completing the symmetry of the rites, and the unicorn worshipped, while the women put lucky money in its mouth. The Rural Committee members then went in to worship together, while the devotees who had been present lined up for a formal photograph.

On this important occasion in the ritual cycle, the two groups, one indigenous to Tsuen Wan, with a history there of nearly 300 years, and the other considered by some to be 'half-indigenous' because they had lived there for several decades, co-operated in carrying out crucial aspects of the rites in honour of the deity who was central to both. The natives worshipped her as the protector of their territory, which they helped to govern, and the devotees because of the special powers that they attributed to her. At critical points that began and ended the rites, they worked together to ensure that all went smoothly and in ways appropriate to her status.[21]

Between the processions that opened and closed the festival, the activities of the two groups diverged. The devotees chanted sutras, apparently in conjunction with a group of nuns, presented vegetarian offerings, and, on the third day, prepared vegetarian food to share with others. They also burned their many elaborate paper offerings sometime near the end of the festival.

The Rural Committee representatives, meanwhile, were responsible for the presentation of the opera. They had arranged for a mat-shed with a stage to be built facing the deity's temporary shrine, with seats for the audience. The operas began on the night after the procession and continued for three days and three more nights. Admission was free. The mat-shed was relatively small, suggesting that they did not expect a very large turnout, but by the last night it was full. The natives sat together in a block—as one woman said: 'You can find me with the Hakka people'—and most were older women. They gave the operas their rapt attention.

---

20. Firecrackers were illegal at that time, so the Rural Committee dared not buy them, but a caretaker said that he had bought them using his own money as well as donations from others, and if someone had to go to prison for this act he would do so.
21. An insightful native woman described them as conducting parallel activities, saying that such behaviour was typically Chinese.

At midday on the third day the Rural Committee representatives were present, well-dressed for the occasion and some wearing ties with the committee crest. They gathered in front of the shrine and worshipped together with offerings of a roast pig and incense, while another string of firecrackers was set off to punctuate their rites. Afterwards they presented banners of appreciation to various people, including one of the nuns. Meanwhile, the operas reached a climax with a much higher calibre of performers. They performed, in succession, three auspicious ritual acts rich in symbolic content that are staged only on special occasions upon request but are typical of festivals in honour of deities.[22] These were followed by a comic opera about a woman and her love affairs, which was much appreciated by the audience. The evening's opera attracted the maximum attendance, with all the seats taken and people standing around the perimeter. During the intermission, an announcement was made inviting everyone to come at two o'clock the next day 'to hear our Hakka mountain songs'. These had been an occasional feature of the festival in recent years.

This event attracted a large and cheerful crowd which nearly filled the mat-shed. Most, but not all, were older women speaking Hakka. A group of men, including some from the Rural Committee, appeared on stage and more banners were presented. One made a speech, as follows:

> Now is the time for the Rural Committee's annual ceremony to thank the goddess for her benevolence towards us. The ceremony includes many kinds of celebrations, of which this is the last. Here is the King of Songs in the New Territories, Mr Ho San, with the best singers, who have come here without compensation. Asia Television Channel is recording this performance, for which we thank them.
>
> As for the Hakka mountain songs, 95% of the people in the New Territories are Hakka,[23] but many of the mountain songs are disappearing and are no longer popular. In the past the rural villagers liked to sing them, but now that we are a satellite city they are gradually being forgotten. So, we hope that we can have the Hakka mountain songs once a year to continue the custom.
>
> I represent the Tsuen Wan Rural Committee in wishing everyone good health and success in everything.

One of the singers introduced the group, and then sang a song in which he thanked Tsuen Wan and the government. About eight people sang in all, men and women, some very strongly and expressively. At least some of the songs were improvised, as was appropriate. The audience loved the performance and clapped and laughed. One middle-aged local man said he could understand only about 40%, and thought some performers were perhaps from Meixian, but the older women seemed to have no trouble. Such songs, which when they were young had been embedded in daily life, now were heard only as performance.

The Teochiu devotees were not present at this time, and there was a pile of ashes where their paper offerings had been. They reappeared the next morning for the concluding procession. There were various indications that their contributions, while welcomed, were subject to certain limits. A notice said that sutra-chanting should be carried out only with the permission of the Rural Committee, for example. We asked the chairman whether they would allow another type of dancing in the procession, the animal favoured by Teochiu people called a *peihyau* (貔貅), and he said that this would not be allowed, as the unicorn is typical of Hakka people. Furthermore, when we asked whether they would permit Teochiu opera, he said that this, too, would be denied. It was clear that although activities that supported the temple and the festival were permitted, there were limits to the diversity that the Rural Committee would tolerate in the temple that had long been the centre of their territory. These guidelines took priority over the value that additional kinds of offerings might have brought to the festival. Even the palanquin that the women had donated was inscribed with the name of the chairman of the Rural Committee.

---

22. Ward, 'Not Merely Players', 29–30.
23. This may be a mistranslation.

Photographs in the 1995 biennial report of the Tsuen Wan Rural Committee depict various aspects of festival offerings that year. They show the Rural Committee representatives worshipping at the temporary shrine to ask for 'favourable winds, bountiful rain, and peace for the households and people'; welcoming the unicorn dance team in front of the palanquin; and standing in front of the shrine to welcome the opera performers. The troupe members, shown on the stage, are 'worshipping the god with hopes for peace', according to the caption, while another photograph shows a group of women seated in a mat-shed, identified as 'various believers reciting sutras to create good fortune'.[24]

With regard to the rites in honour of Tianhou, it is worth making a comparison with those analysed by Watson in Ha Tsuen and San Tin, which are large Punti single-lineage village complexes[25] in the northwest New Territories. His work reminds us, once again, of the socio-cultural division proposed by Hayes and others between this form of social organization and the attitudes embedded in it, and those of communities of small multi-lineage villages. A short summary does not do justice to Watson's complex arguments, but in brief, he argues that 'Tian Hou is generally perceived by land people in rural Hong Kong as a jealous goddess who reigns over an exclusive territory. In many areas, she has become a symbol of lineage hegemony and participation in her cult is enforced by coercive means'.[26] We did not encounter such attitudes or behaviour regarding the deity or her territory, either remembered or in the present.[27] In his arguments he also proposes a complementary perspective, however, saying that temple cults may be perceived as bringing together for a common purpose people with diverse identities within a community, thus helping to create and maintain the cohesion of the social system. He states that this perspective may be applicable to multi-surname communities without powerful lineages,[28] which would make it appropriate to Tsuen Wan.

Indigenous People's Roots and Sense of Identity

In our discussions with representatives of the Rural Committee, and in their public statements, they expressed their identity as Tsuen Wan Hakka people clearly, even as they acknowledged that overt expressions of this identity were fading in the contemporary context. One goal of our interviews with other men was to ascertain their ideas, and so we asked a small group of middle-aged Kwan Mun Hau men how they would answer a question about what kind of person they are, a question that seemed to be meaningful to them. One said that it would depend on the context, and who was asking. If he was abroad, he would say that he was Chinese, and that he was a Hong Kong person. If the person asking was Chinese, he would say that he was Hakka, and he agreed that if he met another Hakka person he would feel a special affinity with him:

> I would speak some Hakka. It is like two dogs, one coming from the east and one from the west. When they meet they will play a little. This is based on a feeling of common identity.

---

24. In Tsuen Wan the festival had little of the transformative effect upon its surroundings like that which was described by Ward in Kau Sai or could be seen in other rural settings. Its scale in relation to the surrounding high-rise buildings of Luk Yeung Estate and the city beyond was modest, although the experience of the festival itself was intense within the temple precincts. It was not possible that it could dominate Tsuen Wan, or the lives of its many inhabitants, in the late twentieth century. Barbara E. Ward, 'Regional Operas and Their Audiences: Evidence from Hong Kong', 161–87, 184–85.

25. James L. Watson, 'Standardizing the Gods: The Promotion of Tian Hou ("Empress of Heaven") along the South China Coast, 960–1960', in Watson and Watson, *Village Life in Hong Kong*, 269–310; James L. Watson, 'Fighting with Operas: Processionals, Politics, and the Specter of Violence in Rural Hong Kong', *Village Life in Hong Kong*, 311–24.

26. Watson, 'Standardizing the Gods', 293.

27. Watson says, however, that conceptions of the deity held by women and fishermen were entirely different from those held by men of the dominant lineages, 'Standardizing the Gods', 300.

28. Watson, 'Fighting with Operas', 316.

Two men said that if someone asked them where they were from, they would say they were Hakka, one giving the example of meeting other Chinese people when he was visiting his son in Canada. They agreed that they, too, would feel an affinity with another Hakka person whom they met, and would talk more with that person. They said that most people their age were not concerned to conceal their Hakka identity, but that they had met younger people who were, as they were afraid of being thought old-fashioned and without culture. They themselves did not share this concern and had never been ridiculed because they were Hakka. Another man, temporarily returned from Canada, said he would tell a Hong Kong person that he was Bao'an Hakka, but that their situation now is different, as they do not all live in the same village, so he would not tell people of his origin there. Their numbers are increasing, he said, and they are spreading out like the branches of the tree in front of his father's house. They are being integrated into the mainstream. Unlike some other indigenous people further out in the New Territories such as the Tang, he added, they are not arrogant in relation to others.

By the mid-1990s, the occasions on which we heard Hakka being spontaneously spoken in Kwan Mun Hau were becoming rare. Ancestors are addressed in Hakka when there is someone available who can speak it even now, in 2017. Older people, especially women, sometimes spoke it with their grown children, and many of the former said that they were more comfortable speaking Hakka than Cantonese, but their children often said that they themselves did not speak it well. Almost all had no hopes or expectations that the younger generations would carry on the language, as they recognized that in Hong Kong it was overwhelmed by Cantonese, although some knew that it was continuing elsewhere. The language of the Rural Committee was not Hakka, as some of its members, such as the fishing people's representative and some of the younger members, did not speak it. When asked, most people acknowledged that despite their preference that their language should continue, it would not. One middle-aged man summarized their situation as follows:

> This must be faced by contemporary people ... This is the new environment. When you meet friends or work in your company, you must speak Cantonese. In the past, in the village we could speak Hakka together, but when we move outside the village and the language there is mainly Cantonese, we are immersed in it. Gradually, it will fade away and be forgotten. This is beyond our control.

Another explained the situation further:

> As time goes by, the next generation won't speak it. They seldom have the chance. I myself can speak some, simple. In the past the community was small. A high percent spoke Hakka. Now lots of other people have flooded in. The schools are not in Hakka. It is not the common language. Hakka people are a small community here, compared with the Shanghai or Teochiu people ... I seldom speak Hakka to the children. They speak English and Cantonese. Why bother?

As for the continuation of Hakka customs, these would not have been readily apparent to anyone who did not know what to ask or where to look. Their clothing and ornaments were now like those of other Hong Kong people, and showed universal Western influence. Women's ability and need to do heavy labour, mentioned by some people as being distinctively Hakka, were virtually gone, and only a handful of women still collected firewood. Older men and women referred enthusiastically to particular Hakka foods, the several often-cited dishes, and some continued to make them for special occasions. *Chahgwo* of the types specific to the various festivals were still being made by middle-aged and older Hakka women who had married into the village, but few now had the large wood-burning stoves needed to steam them in quantity, and older people acknowledged that festival foods were now less popular. Many considered the pork dishes to be unhealthy and said that younger people did not enjoy the *chahgwo* as they themselves had in the past. Furthermore, people agreed that with their greatly improved economic situation, these foods and the festivals with which they were associated held less appeal than they had in the past:

When I was small, we were really enthusiastic about festivals. We had nothing to play with. We were very poor. We had no money to buy soda. Then at Chongyang you could have as much as you wished. . . . So we were very keen about this occasion. We longed for it. We counted the days. Like at New Year: when we worshipped, we got lucky money. There were firecrackers *bing bom*. The children looked forward so much to these occasions. . . . During these twenty years, because the economic situation is better, or perhaps because I am older and my thinking and my financial situation have changed, I no longer long for them. The meal really attracted people in the past, but not now. Even though we go to the ancestral hall, the feeling is not the same as when we were young. It is just like a routine matter. Now people have grown up and are moving out and our financial situations have improved, so a meal is less appealing.

Likewise, a woman who was about 60 years of age gave her perspective:

In the past, New Year was very festive, as was the lantern-raising. On the last day of the old year, the women would all get up early to kill a chicken as an offering. We would arrive by noon and place the chickens on the altar to see whose was the biggest. Now people don't want to get up so early. Everything is simplified. We used to raise pigs. When a sow had ten piglets, we could sell them and save the money for special occasions. Then festivals were very important, as people could eat special foods. Now we can eat chicken every day.

Lineage and Village Relations and Rituals

Although festivals may not be as enticing as they once were, significant unifying events in Kwan Mun Hau continued to be carried out in the context of the lineages, and occasionally in the village as a whole.

The halls of both lineages were well maintained. In 1993, the Chan hall was extensively renovated, with a green tile roof added. Its caretaker lit incense daily and opened it on the first and fifteenth of the month. They no longer held regular annual meetings as they previously had done. They had three managers who looked after the accounts, and lineage members met according to need. They did not have a regular distribution of profits from their property but they used the income for the annual Chongyang worship, and had a substantial amount in a bank account. The income was drawn on for New Year lucky money, which was given to all members, male and female. A senior man said that lineage men and women used to worship together on the first day of the New Year, but that they now did so individually and simply, and received lucky money whether or not they worshipped. Their hall was open, with firecrackers exploding and people worshipping, on both the last night of the year and the first day of the New Year in 1996, and men were playing gongs and cymbals, as they were at the Yau hall. Their ties with the Chan lineage of Sam Tung Uk remained strong, and both had reinstated the practice of holding a banquet to celebrate the birth of new sons, with a joint banquet at their ancestral halls, alternating years between them. Many stated, however, that in comparison the Yau ceremonies were more festive and impressive, and their members more united.

Representatives of the Yau lineage continued to hold regular quarterly meetings, which gave them opportunities to discuss matters of common interest beyond their finances.[29] The Tsuen Wan Yau lineage, and others in Hong Kong, had developed ties with lineages in China through the China Qiu [Yau] Clansmen's General Association (華丘 (邱) 氏宗親聯誼總會). This association had plans to build a hall dedicated to their legendary founding ancestor, where the Tsuen Wan lineage could pay to have a tablet dedicated to their own founder. A photograph of hundreds of members meeting to discuss the establishment of a museum hangs in the Tsuen Wan ancestral hall. Painted ancestral

---

29. According to the accountant, they had about 200 members in 1969 and in 2011 had 430, of whom 30 lived abroad.

portraits, in Qing officials' robes, continue to hang in the hall, the founder and his wife on one wall and his second son and his wife opposite.

At New Year in 1996, the Yau hall had impressive floral displays, and many men came at midnight to worship the ancestors and to talk. When they came to worship in the morning, each member, including unmarried daughters, received $100 lucky money. Those over 60 years of age received double. In 2004, we participated in their lantern-raising ceremony, which was held as it had been in earlier years. The family of the baby hosted a catered *puhnchoi* (盤菜)[30] banquet of 11 tables, followed by the procession to the shrines and hall, where the lanterns were raised. Afterwards, there was a banquet of five tables in and around the hall, consisting of good Cantonese food cooked on site, apparently by a restaurant. Young men played gongs and cymbals to the appropriate rhythms, and many young people attended, friends of the family. They held their ceremony on the fourteenth of the lunar month, while the Chan held theirs on the fifteenth so that they could attend each other's banquets.

The Yau lineage continued their Chongyang rites as they had done in previous years, with several busloads of men, women, and children going to the tombs of the senior ancestors.[31] The offerings had been somewhat simplified, in that they no longer offered a whole roast pig, as we had seen in 1969, but only a slice of pork, as the branch principle of division had meant that some people had received almost no pork. A festive dinner at the ancestral hall followed. The Chan lineage also continued their rites, although they no longer cooked a meal at one of the ancestral tombs as they had done in the recent past, and their banquets were held in restaurants.[32]

Some people could be seen worshipping in the halls at festivals. We were told that fewer went than in the past, however, with the exception of New Year, and that even the Winter Solstice was acknowledged less than it had been. As hall worship had been done primarily by women in previous decades, this raised the question of how it would be done now that the younger daughters-in-law had not been raised in their traditions and, furthermore, were likely to be employed.

Despite the increasing outside influences on the two lineages, Christianity was not at all important. One Chan family had been Christian for some years, the father having converted because of the priest's kindness during his illness, but once he had died, his wife resumed her care of the gods and ancestors, albeit without shrines. Their son said that although he was Christian, he himself was not rigid, unlike some of his friends, and that he had decided to worship with incense in the hall and at the ancestral tombs, not in the hope of obtaining benefits, but in order to show his respect for his ancestors.

Aspects of other ceremonies relating to major life changes still took place in the ancestral halls. Most wedding ceremonies, although considerably simplified, were said to include the presentation of the couple to the ancestor in the hall, and their worship there, unless the family lived far away or decided to do otherwise. For those living in or near the village, the family might hold a banquet there, followed by a gathering of village people, primarily women, to make red *tongyuhn*. The groom would then worship the ancestors in the hall for the ceremonies of *seuhng tauh* and the initial audience with the ancestors, now conducted without the hat with gold ornaments, the rice measure, and the basketry tray. On the morning of the wedding, he might worship Tianhou in her temple before going to meet his bride at her home with his lineage brothers playing gongs and cymbals. After their

---

30. *Sihk puhn* (食盤) means 'to eat from the common pot' and refers to a celebratory meal of various ingredients cooked separately and then combined in pots and seasoned before being eaten. Small groups share common pots. It is typical of Cantonese people in the Yuen Long region, although a Hakka variant was said to have existed in Tsuen Wan. It has become a convenient banquet food in Hong Kong. James L. Watson, 'From the Common Pot: Feasting with Equals in Chinese Society', in Watson and Watson, *Village Life in Hong Kong*, 105–23.

31. We last participated in 2011, when women also joined in offering incense. In earlier years, men had worshipped in order of seniority, with elders first, but this had ended by the late 1960s. Likewise, only elders had eaten in the hall.

32. Individual families have also continued their Qingming worship at the graves and tombs of their own more recently deceased ancestors.

Plate 50: The presentation of a groom and his bride to the Yau ancestors in their hall. A senior member of the lineage officiates, 1981.

ceremonial entry to the village, the couple would worship the Baak Gung and the ancestors. *Gaau jih*, the principal ceremony in the hall, has been considerably shortened. The *sung chah* visit from the bride's family takes place on the same day as the wedding, not three days later as was done in the past. For those families who now live elsewhere, the lineage marriage ceremonies might be reduced to the first, with the major ceremony, the presentation of the couple to the ancestors, held in their home if the family wished.[33]

Other changes have included the occurrence of divorce, and a loss of the previous relationships with lineages from which brides had come, as they are now more likely to have come from kin groups fragmented by migration. Marriages with women from other Hakka lineages have become a thing of the past.

Funerals are rarely held in the village, and the procedures are considerably abbreviated. This is because of the demands of people's employment, but it also reflects the fact that they take place in funeral homes, where the specialists profess to being able to conform to the practices of the various speech groups. People expressed mistrust of this, however, and also wondered how the needs of a soul could be met through ceremonies that are so much shorter. These used to last entire nights, but now end at 11:00 p.m. Since mortuary rites involving the care and burial of the body are now carried out entirely by paid professionals, village people no longer have the opportunity to learn from others how they are done, and the funeral homes offer all-inclusive packages in which they provide everything that is needed, down to the last detail. People worried because those priests did not know them personally

33. This detailed information was provided by Paul Siu-kwong Yau, 2015. We lack specific information for the Chan lineage, but were told that hall worship is still part of the ceremony.

and would not take ritual precautions to protect vulnerable people, such as pregnant women. They also expressed great concern that a soul might not find its way home,[34] given that death generally took place in a hospital and the body reposed in a funeral parlour before being taken directly to its place of burial in the natives' cemetery, sometimes with a stop on the road by the village so that the people could pay their respects.

Care of the soul after the immediate funeral rites are over has remained the responsibility of the family and lineage. The belief continues that once the soul has been installed in the ancestral hall,[35] it will be at peace, and will enjoy the offerings and the company of the other ancestors. As a man of the Yau lineage stated:

> Then when her son comes to give her offerings, she will tell the others of the eight branches: 'My son is coming to give me wine and food.' She can be proud to sit there.

The Fan family whose members we interviewed kept a tablet[36] at home to memorialize those who had died, but not, we were told, in the expectation of any benefits or protection. Mr Fan, who was 73 years old at that time, said that they, and the other Fan families, had simplified their rituals but still held them. They raised lanterns for new sons, for example, but hung them in their homes, and invited related families. They rarely went to the temple and shrines, and he himself had never gone, not even to the Baak Gung, until the 30 June 1997 ceremony, in which he participated. He did, however, take care of their ancestors' remains, although he did not believe in geomancy. They had been dispersed in various locations, and he arranged for them all, more than 50 mortuary urns, to be moved to one location in Chuen Lung so that by being together it would be easier to care for them. One of his daughters had the means to help meet the costs, $80,000 in all, some of which they received in compensation. He went there only at Chongyang as the weather was good then.

Kwan Mun Hau in the 1990s and Afterwards

We witnessed two occasions when the continuing unity of the village was emphasized. In 1996, people told us that a unicorn dance team would come on the second day of the New Year, as they had done for the previous three years. The importance of this event was apparent in the sense of anticipation that built up as the day approached, and the number of people present that morning despite the cold rain. They encouraged us to attend and take photographs to show to people in Canada. The unicorn dance team was from the related Yau lineage in Nam Wai, Sai Kung, and its members were referred to as 'brothers' (兄弟).[37]

A reception group of senior Yau lineage men, including one of the two village representatives, waited at the parking lot to welcome the unicorn dance team when it arrived. The dancers then went directly to the shrines, where the unicorn first worshipped Hungshenggong and then the Kau Wai Kung. After this they danced to the Yau hall, where the unicorn, after nibbling some of the New Year flowers by the door, worshipped in front of the offering table and then danced behind it to worship the tablet directly. From there, it danced up to the Chan ancestral hall, where it was received by their welcoming committee, including the village representative of that surname, and danced in the same way, punctuated by another string of firecrackers. Afterwards it danced along some of the lanes in the

34. Families take great care to ensure that members' souls do not become separated either from their remains in their graves or from their soul tablets, leading them with burning incense if the location of either is changed, and informing them through spirit mediums. 'It is important that they know where they are'.
35. This may now happen on the day of the burial 'as people have to work'.
36. Mr Fan said that the souls had to be installed in this tablet with the intercession of traditional priests, just like those who conducted the rites for the installation of souls in the ancestral halls of lineages.
37. The two lineages participated in each other's special celebrations.

Plate 51: The unicorn from the Yau lineage village of Nam Wai, Sai Kung, pays its respects to the ancestors in the Yau hall, where elders receive it with reverence, 1996.

Plate 52: After being received by Chan elders in their hall, the unicorn pays its respects to their ancestors, dancing behind the altar table to worship the tablet.

village, stopping to pay respects at all the native households, even those living on upper floors, whose members lit firecrackers and gave red packets of lucky money.

When they reached the Country Village Store they had a brief rest and were given food. The older people spoke Hakka together, but the younger did not. After their rest, they went to the remaining native homes in the village, including those of the unrelated Chan family. The unicorn then danced at the village gate, rubbing sinuously around all its surfaces, and returned to worship once more at the Yau ancestral hall. The team then was invited to a banquet in Tsuen Wan, after which they went to Hoi Pa to continue dancing.

A second, and even more important, event took place on 30 June 1997, the day before Hong Kong was returned to Chinese jurisdiction. The village erected a celebratory *huapai*, as did many, if not all, native villages. On the morning of this momentous occasion, elders of the native surnames gathered at the Baak Gung for a formal ceremony of worship to inform them of the change in government and to ask for their continued protection. In the afternoon, a banquet was held in and around the parking lot, taking place in two sittings because of the large numbers of villagers and guests who were present. There were speeches, and elderly villagers who had been supporters of the communist East River Guerrillas sang some revolutionary songs. This did not, of course, mean that all Kwan Mun Hau natives shared their enthusiasm for the new government, but they did at least have the reassurance of the fact that their continued rights as New Territories people were included in the Basic Law of the new Special Administrative Region.

Kwan Mun Hau remained a distinctive place within the changing urban surroundings of Tsuen Wan, retaining the environment of a village because of the architecture of its houses and the terraces between them. These were now lush with plants, and some people took great pleasure in the flowers they grew there. A few elderly women still grew small quantities of vegetables, tending them lovingly and discussing them with others. The chickens were gone, however, as was most of the firewood. The clutter of raw materials and finished products from the workshops that had existed was also gone, and the areas where they had been the densest were much cleaner as a result.[38]

The social environment had also changed considerably from that which had existed when we first arrived. Television and air conditioning continued to have an impact, and few people sat outdoors, except for those who were very elderly, and a small number of apparently underemployed or retired men. Most of the younger people were employed elsewhere, often at quite sophisticated jobs that they obtained because of the high level of education so many had achieved. There were fewer children playing together outdoors, reflecting the much smaller numbers being born, and the pressures of the school system that kept them busy with homework. Those older native women who were not working could be seen going out in the morning to buy food in the market in central Tsuen Wan. They often went to a teahouse first, a major change in lifestyle for them. Men went as well, and some even went as couples. Women could no longer be seen sitting outdoors and talking, however, and one said that she missed the more intense physical and social environment of the old village, where they regularly saw each other and knew what they were doing. Now, she said, she only saw neighbours if they happened to meet while emptying their rubbish. Men also said that relations were less close, and wealth differences greater because of differential property holdings.

Despite the fact that some people regretted the loss of regular social contact that had existed in the past, they acknowledged that others would give help when it was needed, on the occasion of a wedding, for example. It was also enjoyable to hear native men and women continue to refer to each other by the nicknames that seemed to stick with them for their entire lives.

---

38. One reason for the loss of village workshops may be that the government reduced the electric power to that suitable only for domestic use.

Plate 53: Kwan Mun Hau displays a *huapai* and pennants with the bauhinia flag for the celebrations of 1 July 1997.

Plate 54: On the morning before retrocession, village elders worship the Baak Gung to inform them of the change in government and ask for their continued protection.

Plate 55: The terraces of Kwan Mun Hau have changed over time from being stark and cluttered with workshop materials to being lush with the villagers' trees and plants.

One man, who had to live elsewhere, said that he much preferred the village environment, where there were people to talk with, because in high-rise buildings the doors were always shut. In Kwan Mun Hau, those native men who had free time gathered at the Country Village Store to talk, drink, and play mah-jong. At that time, there was also a second mah-jong parlour run by some younger native men, which was very noisy, especially during horse races. When we interviewed village men, we asked whether it would be desirable to have a village hall where people could gather to talk and hold meetings, and many agreed. Some lamented the diminution of contact among native men as compared with the situation in the old village. The village hall that had existed in the late 1960s was not centrally located, and after a short period of use had been rented out as housing. Rent from this building had been used to refurbish the shrines dedicated to the Baak Gung, and they were well-maintained and impressive. Each now has a red terrazzo table in front for the placement of offerings because, as one man explained, these should not simply be placed in their mouths. A sign is posted asking that the honourable worshippers keep the area clean and stating that football should not be played there.

The major village-based events, such as the New Year unicorn dance celebration and the acknowledgement of the transfer from British to Chinese sovereignty, were held despite the fact that many middle-aged and younger people were living and working elsewhere by this time. Two men said that it had become harder for them to act in a unified way because in the past they had lived together and worked at farming, whereas now this was no longer the case. One person acting alone could not maintain important customs, one said. Some men had moved out because of the limitations on village housing, whereas others did so voluntarily, seeking the perceived advantages of living elsewhere in Hong Kong, or abroad.

As we have explained, many of those families who had large numbers of children born and surviving in the post-war period did not have sufficient housing for their grown sons. The expansion of houses to three stories was under discussion in 1996 but had not yet happened. Some housing for sons had been built and allocated, and notices had just been posted concerning a second group, but they were quite far away, in Yau Kom Tau, to the west of central Tsuen Wan.[39] Wealthier families who had more houses could stop renting them out and give them to their sons as they married, but the property they had been allocated or obtained through Letters of Exchange at the time of the village removal was not necessarily within the village; it could be in central Tsuen Wan or in other villages.

This meant that over time former Kwan Mun Hau, Hoi Pa, and Ham Tin families were becoming more dispersed. One woman said that all of her eight children except the unmarried youngest daughter now lived elsewhere in Hong Kong, although she saw them frequently. There was no mass international emigration comparable to that which had taken part in much of the rest of the New Territories, although some men had moved overseas long-term, just as there were daughters who had emigrated with their husbands to many parts of the world: Europe, New Zealand, Canada, and England. Some men who had gone abroad for university educations and even for employment returned, however, and others returned temporarily to visit the village and to worship ancestors. Their village, with its lineages and ancestral halls, has remained the focus of their life in common. As long as they maintain contact, they are acknowledged to be lineage members. Some younger men sold the property they had inherited in order to purchase property abroad, and it could be sold to non-natives. Others, who were older, stated firmly that they would never sell their inherited houses, as they were not the products of their own labour but rather that of their ancestors.

---

39. These houses were allocated to sons of families of Kwan Mun Hau, Ho Pui, and Yeung Uk by drawing lots, with recommendations from village representatives. Those eligible to receive them had five or more family members and no housing of their own.

Changes in Families

An impressive phenomenon, and a major generational difference within many families, is the extent to which the children of Kwan Mun Hau natives of all three surnames have studied in universities. This has been facilitated by the compulsory and affordable primary and lower secondary education and the increase in subsidized senior secondary school places made available to their generation by changed government policies. Some had been admitted to the various universities that by 1996 were available in Hong Kong, and many went abroad, primarily to Canada, but also to England and the United States. In the late 1960s, there had been few secondary school graduates and only two or three university students, but by the 1990s we knew of more than 20 men and women who had studied in universities, seven at the prestigious Hong Kong University, with its high standards. Doubtless, there were more. By this time, parents appeared to support the higher education of daughters as well as sons. They often expressed satisfaction and even pride in their children's and their sons' wives' achievements. One man, father of many children, greeted us in 2014 by saying: 'My daughter studied in university!' In 1996, another man said:

> My financial situation was not good. My wife came when she was in her teens and worked for a long time. We had children, three sons and two daughters. My sons are very good; all three studied in universities. One studied at Hong Kong University, and teaches at Ho Chuen Yiu Memorial Secondary School. One earned an MA from a Canadian university. He studied there for eight years; I don't know where. Now he has been a secondary school teacher for more than 10 years. The third studied at Chinese University. . . . I didn't help them. I had no ability, but they studied.

He agreed that there were many university graduates in the village:

> Yes, there are a lot, including girls. For example, three daughters of [a relative] studied in universities. His two sons studied in American universities. He has two sons and five daughters. His financial situation is better than mine, and he could support his sons' studies. His younger brother also has five daughters, and no sons. Three of that man's daughters also studied.

These greatly increased educational advantages made a big difference in the opportunities available to younger people. As so many disparate influences affected them, their experiences and worldviews diversified significantly. These brought benefits to their parents and other family members, but also contributed to the dispersal of better-educated people, as they took advantage of the opportunities that then presented themselves.

Through their education, employment, and social lives, young men met potential wives and although these almost never were Hakka, most of the parents whom we asked were generally open-minded in this regard. Several men said that it would be better to have Hakka daughters-in-law; the others said that they had no opinions about this, and some said that even a Western woman might be all right, as was happening elsewhere in the New Territories.[40] The daughters-in-law we knew were of diverse origins, an important factor in the loss of the Hakka language within families.

There were some indications of increased closeness in older couples' relationships. By 1996, many families also had close relations with their married daughters; evidence of this was common. Some lived in the village and quite a few exchanged help with their parents. They also came back with their families for special occasions. In addition, there were several middle-aged women, filial daughters, who had never married and devoted themselves, instead, to helping their elderly parents.[41]

---

40. During our various visits to Tsuen Wan, however, we saw almost no Western people, despite the fact that there were more expatriates in Hong Kong than in previous years.
41. The mother of one said that her husband loved their daughter very much, and that she loved him.

Children were no longer expected to give much help to the family before they were grown. Two middle-aged men analysed this change in detail, saying that in the past life had been very simple, whereas now it was advanced and modern, and conditions were much better. In the past, all children had to help, especially the girls, and fathers were both strict and distant with their children. In their generation, however, parents were committed to giving their children guidance and emotional support, a reason for not having so many. Parents also were able to provide a much higher standard of nutrition and care, and children looked healthy, without the skin problems that had plagued those of earlier generations, and well-dressed, with toys to play with. Once children were grown and employed, it remained the norm that they should give financial support to their parents, and those who did not were a serious disappointment.

In some families, grandparents found pleasure in caring for their grandchildren, whether those of sons or daughters, thus helping the parents so that they could work. Mr Fan told us how much he enjoyed children, and how his daughters' five children came to his house for care. He helped them with their homework, and they kept him from being lonely. Many families now had domestic helpers from the Philippines to care for their children, however, although grandparents might be present.

An area of significant change has been the care of seriously ill family members. By the 1990s, most deaths took place in hospitals. Good and timely hospital care was generally very costly, and one woman praised her husband, saying that he had sold two floors of buildings in Tsuen Wan to pay for her heart surgery.

Quality of Life

By the 1990s, it had become common for elderly people to be cared for by domestic helpers,[42] and even those who did not need care generally had them to do household tasks. Those with complex problems sometimes had to be placed in care homes. Younger families had helpers as well, freeing up women and men of working age for employment. The helpers hired were women from the Philippines,[43] and, more recently, from Indonesia. The cost was not particularly high; one elderly woman said in 1996 that their married daughters paid HK$3,200 per month for a maid to help them. Families who had been of very ordinary means in the past now often had helpers. Their presence has led to new kinds of interactions within people's homes and increased the exposure of family members to people from other cultures. The language differences could pose problems, especially if the maids were caring for elderly people or others who did not know English or who had special needs.

Villagers' increased leisure time as a result of household help and better conditions of employment has resulted in a significant change in lifestyle. Older men and women gather to play cards and mah-jong, especially in the afternoons, and younger people have entertainment such as karaoke, as well as enjoying the shopping malls now available. There also are many government-sponsored sports and cultural events, and the country parks, established in 1976, provide opportunities for young people and families to go hiking and camping. By the 1990s it was quite possible for villagers to go to teahouses every day, and it appeared that most did. The government pensions that elderly people received gave them pocket money for pleasures like this that previously had been unheard-of luxuries, impossible because of the unceasing demands of work. One man said that going to a teahouse became a real addiction, like smoking, and his wife said that she felt quite unwell if she did not go. The social aspect of this was and is also important, of course, and teahouses as well as the elegant restaurants now available are important meeting places for business and political discussions as well as pleasant

---

42. Unlike many contemporary Hong Kong people, they have space for them to live in.

43. For a detailed study of this complex intercultural phenomenon, see Nicole Constable, *Maid to Order in Hong Kong: Stories of Migrant Workers* (Ithaca, NY: Cornell University Press, 2007).

interactions with relatives, friends, and colleagues. One elderly woman said that she went to teahouses with friends from elsewhere, those she had met when travelling, for example. In the past these wider social relationships had not been possible.

The amount of travel that people did was impressive, even in the 1990s. Some men went with village- and lineage-mates around the New Territories, and people signed up for excursions organized by the Rural Committee to destinations such as Sai Kung. They were all-inclusive, with a meal, and the prices were low. What was truly astounding was the amount of international travel they did, usually on organized tours unless they were visiting emigrant relatives. One woman, for example, had gone on numerous tours in China organized by her union, and had visited relatives in Canada and Germany. Many others, even those from relatively poor families, had gone on organized tours to Japan, Taiwan, Southeast Asia, Australia, New Zealand, and Europe. Older people were generally accompanied by an adult child, who probably also covered the costs. Such travel led not only to experiences of novelty and broadened worldviews, but also to new social contacts.

It is extraordinary to realize that within the space of less than two generations, it had become common that Tsuen Wan natives, women included, had gained the opportunity to extend their experience from the confines of their homes, their former fields, and local wage labour sites to the world. Furthermore, they had this experience, not as emigrant workers like many New Territories people, or Tsuen Wan men in the past, but instead as travellers expanding their horizons in the company of others.

Conclusions: The Distinctiveness That Remains

The original people of Tsuen Wan almost certainly would have dispersed, and lost their unique identity, had it not been for the rights guaranteed to them, first by the colonial government and then by the Basic Law of the Special Administrative Region. These enabled them to maintain their lineage and family property, a solid foundation for those who chose to retain it, providing the funds to support the rituals that bound them together, those in this life and those in the next.

In February 2004, we participated in an impressive event that demonstrated the cohesion sometimes expressed by Tsuen Wan natives. The occasion was an outdoor *puhnchoi* banquet to celebrate the inauguration of the new Tsuen Wan Rural Committee, held on a central sports ground and attended by 6,000 people, indigenous people as well as their guests such as ourselves. We sat with a group of Kwan Mun Hau men, who had cause for special pride because Yau Kam-ping (邱錦平), a son of the former lineage and civic leader Yau Po-sang, had been elected vice-chairman.

Despite such occasions, it was clear that there were many forces at work contributing to the dilution and even loss of many aspects of their distinctiveness. We heard the word 'simplified' many times, as people described their inevitable responses to the complexities of life in contemporary Hong Kong and the world beyond. At the same time, no one we knew would have exchanged their present quality of life for that of the past. They acknowledged the great changes that had occurred, but in general believed that what they had gained was worthwhile and counteracted the losses, accepting the inevitability and value of the changes while still acknowledging and even regretting that certain aspects of their distinctiveness were gone forever.

10

An Unexpected Opportunity

Kwan Mun Hau Celebrates 50 Years

In the summer of 2014, we received an invitation to witness a special event: the people of Kwan Mun Hau were planning a celebration of the 50th anniversary of their move to their present site. This was an occasion that we could not miss: an opportunity to see old friends, to share in their happiness, and to learn as much as we could about Tsuen Wan and Kwan Mun Hau as they are now. We made arrangements to stay for one month, and arrived a few days in advance of 9 November, the date chosen because it was an auspicious day and the weather was likely to be good.

When we visited Kwan Mun Hau a few days before the celebration, the village was bright and festive, with preparations well underway and a palpable sense of anticipation. A villager was busy painting the offering burners by the Baak Gung, which were surrounded by new paving and decorated with red and gold papers, ribbons, and rosettes as though they were being prepared for New Year. There were strings of multi-coloured pennants throughout the village, and big yellow triangular flags presented by unicorn dance teams. Red lanterns adorned the village gate, and three large congratulatory *huapai* faced the road for passers-by to see.[1] Four others faced the celebration site, presented by each of the resident lineages: the Yau, Chan, Fan, and the other long-resident Chan families with roots in the New Territories, who now had an ancestral hall in one of their houses.

The Country Village Store still sold drinks and functioned as a mah-jong parlour, but, more importantly, it now also served as the village office or hall. The sign reading 'Country Village' remained at the back. It was a popular gathering place—one man called it his 'clubhouse'—and the men sitting inside and around it greeted us warmly.

The celebration had been proposed by Yau Kam-ping, vice-chairman of the Tsuen Wan Rural Committee and one of village representatives. He had called a meeting of representatives of every household and gained their enthusiastic support. He and Chan Yuk-kwong, a retired headmaster of the Tsuen Wan Government School, had then worked for ten months with the planning committee. The representatives had considered holding the celebration in a nearby hotel but decided that this would not be meaningful and that it should be held in the village, with a *puhnchoi* banquet. Mr Yau said that this was possible because they are fortunate enough to have sufficient space and manpower.[2] In fact, about 2,000 villagers and guests participated in the actual event, and he said that many New Territories office-holders were upset with him because they had wanted to participate, but they literally did not have enough space to invite all of them. As it was, the parking lot and lanes of the village were filled with tables on the day of the event.

---

1. These had been presented by the Tsuen Wan Rural Committee and two organizations, a Tsuen Wan boxing academy and the Tseng Lan Shue [Sai Kung] Village Youth Club, that were sending unicorn dance teams. Both were headed by men surnamed Yau.
2. Funding for the event came from the property of the Baak Gung, the four lineages, the Tsuen Wan and Ma Wan Rural Committees, and sponsors.

Plate 56: Congratulatory *huapai* presented on the occasion of the 50th anniversary of Kwan Mun Hau's move to its new site, with unicorn dance teams' flags, 2014.

On 9 November the weather was clear, as predicted. Once we had done our best to finalize the speech we had been asked to deliver, with the very welcome help of one of our close friends, and had eaten delicious savoury *chahgwo* prepared by one of his neighbours, we joined the crowds of villagers and guests who were assembling, receiving impressive commemorative books with historical photographs, a history of the village, and messages of congratulations. The calligraphy from both sides of the village gate graced the front and back covers. Villagers who were volunteering their help wore special pink T-shirts, and we were given them for ourselves and our sons. More than 20 large congratulatory flower baskets arrived, sent by Tsuen Wan villages, associations, companies, and individuals, and were placed around the area.

A unicorn dance team arrived at noon, the first of five sent by various villages and a Tsuen Wan Hakka association. The unicorn and its small companion animal danced around the village gate, rubbing it, and then up the stairs, photographed, it seemed, by virtually everyone who was there, using cameras or the now-omnipresent mobile phones. After worshipping the Baak Gung it danced to the Chan hall, then went frisking along the lanes to the Yau hall and the newly established Chan hall, and then back to the Baak Gung, where it performed extraordinary acrobatics before noticing and devouring vegetables set out with a red packet of 'lucky money'.

The assembled people then queued to receive incense so that they could worship at the Baak Gung, and receive a share of the ritual pork. Soon afterwards, the next unicorn dance team appeared, and the afternoon passed in this festive way, with Yau Kam-ping extremely busy, and others helping with preparations to ensure that all went well. Dignitaries arrived, including the district officer, Jenny Yip, and the chairman of the District Council, Chan Iu Seng, and were seated on the stage. At 6:00

Plate 57: The first of the five unicorn dance teams that arrived, paying their respects to the Baak Gung.

Plate 58: This unicorn dances along a village terrace, worshipping at villagers' homes and the new ancestral hall that had been established in one of the houses.

Plate 59: Offerings made during the afternoon to the Kau Wai Kung.

Plate 60: The shrine to Hongshenggong late in the evening, incense and candles still burning.

p.m., each gave speeches of congratulations, including ourselves, the 'foreign friends'. The invited officials all gave eloquent speeches, with Chan Iu Seng summarizing the recent history of Kwan Mun Hau, including the conditions that had precipitated their decision to move. The district officer and other officials then awarded village scholarships to the five students who were entering universities that year, and an official presented banners to the unicorn dance teams.

The speeches were followed by the *puhnchoi* dinner, and people lingered in the warm evening to sit and talk with their relatives and neighbours at their tables in the parking lot or in front of their houses. Guests at our table included the first female village representative in Tsuen Wan, a woman from Lo Wai village with a degree in commerce from Canada. After the dinner, there was loud and festive Cantonese popular music, and a performance by a group of village women. When we left, incense and candles still burned at the Baak Gung, where offerings remained.

Kwan Mun Hau in 2014

The village appeared to be prospering,[3] although a few of the original houses were in need of repair. Eleven houses had been rebuilt to three storeys with flat roofs,[4] and more were planned. If rented out, these new flats might bring in rents nearly twice those of flats in the older houses. The housing for sons in Yau Kom Tau now totalled 48 floors, and we learned of four cases in which floors of village houses had been bought by or for married daughters or other matrilateral relatives, as well as others rented to them. Houses can be sold to non-natives, and since 2006 there has been a fourth village representative for such people resident in the village (居民代表), as with other villages in Tsuen Wan.[5]

The surroundings of the village have changed dramatically. In the 1960s it had been surrounded by a stark landscape, the result of the Japanese occupation, fuel-cutting, and site terracing, but this has softened and become green as the trees have grown. The surrounding built environment has also been transformed. Looking east towards Kwai Chung, there are large commercial buildings, and a new high-rise residential complex looms on the horizon. To the south, Tai Wo Hau's new multi-storey buildings have replaced the early generation resettlement structures, and the view from the village to the town is obscured by a massive fortified police station. Nearby, to the west, overlooking what had once been a dense mixture of small industries and scattered fields, there is now a large and lush park, anchored by the Shing Mun Valley recreation complex with a swimming pool.[6] Beyond this are the towers of middle class residential developments, beginning with the Luk Yeung complex, beyond which, in the former factory area, are more large private residential complexes. To the north, the Shek Wai Kok Resettlement Estate can be seen.

The general air of prosperity in the village is reflected in the figures we were given for the income of the principal Yau ancestral trust, which indicate that it had increased 129 times since 1964, when there had been no dividends or other financial benefits, but just enough to pay for the worship of ancestors and for ritual pork. Dividends are paid on a branch basis three out of every four quarters. The fourth-quarter dividends are used for the Chongyang ancestral worship. The lineage is governed under a clear set of rules by 15 office-holders: the chairman, vice-chairman, rental manager, accountant/rental manager, secretary, auditor, administrative assistant, and representatives of the eight branches.[7] It offers benefits that include lucky money at New Year and Chongyang ('in lieu of pork'), financial assistance for marriages, costs for families raising lanterns for new sons, and a substantial benefit (帛金) for funeral expenses.

We were not given information on the finances of the Chan lineage, but its hall is well-maintained and was open on the day of the celebration. It continues its Chongyang worship, although the members no longer cook and eat by the tombs. The man who described this said that he worries about what may happen with future generations, because some, like his family, live elsewhere and may study abroad, and no longer spend time together, as children did in his generation.[8] Other families, unlike his, are poor, with many sons, and some are forced by lack of housing to live elsewhere. The Chan families in Ham Tin moved in 1978 to their new village further along Kwok Shui Road. He stressed

3. A Yau man told us with great enthusiasm that it is so prosperous because, as they were told by their grandfathers' grandfathers, the Kau Wai Kung have protected them.
4. The flat roofs of these houses are clearly visible in the aerial view of Kwan Mun Hau Tsuen that is available on Google Maps, most easily found by searching initially for the Tai Wo Hau MTR station, and then moving north.
5. A member of the Fan lineage is now (in 2016) one of the three indigenous village representatives.
6. One woman born in Kwan Mun Hau offered the insight that these facilities offer companionship to the elderly as their fellow villagers pass away. They go there to enjoy sports such as ping pong (table tennis) and swimming, and to take courses in computers and other subjects.
7. All receive nominal stipends.
8. He is a wealthy businessman, and likes the amenities provided by his condominium in Kowloon, such as a clubhouse and parking. He plans, however, to retire to the village, and to update their genealogy, adding sons and daughters who have been born.

that there are very few Kwan Mun Hau people overseas, in contrast to members of Chan higher-order lineage branches from such New Territories villages as Luk Keng and Tap Mun, although he himself studied and worked in England for some years. Still, he said, many live elsewhere and may lose contact in the next generation.

He added that although those from other New Territories villages living overseas still speak Hakka, it is being lost in Kwan Mun Hau.[9] The Yau quarterly meetings are still held in Hakka, and the prayers to the ancestors are read in Hakka by a senior lineage member, 'even if it is not clear'. None was used in the anniversary celebration, and it would not have been understood by the great majority of the guests.

In 2014, the village had rental income from the property of the Baak Gung, the house that had once been the village hall. This is used for the benefit of village residents. They have annual excursions, give a financial contribution upon the death of an indigenous resident age 60 and over, and award scholarships of HK$2,000 to village students, male and female, who are accepted into universities. Such income also helped to make the anniversary celebration possible.

Contemporary Tsuen Wan and Its Governance

The Kwan Mun Hau celebration gave us the perfect opportunity to meet current Tsuen Wan officials, and through our speech, to inform them of our work. We immediately contacted them in the hope of making appointments, and found them to be receptive, generous with their time, and helpful. The district officer organized an informative luncheon that included herself, her assistant, Chan Iu Seng, the chairman of the Tsuen Wan District Council; and Philip Sai-kwong Chan, vice chairman of the New Territories Commercial & General Association and chairman of its Tsuen Wan Branch, and active in many other Tsuen Wan associations. He was, we discovered, the son of Chan Wing-fat, a Kwan Mun Hau village representative in the 1960s.

Tsuen Wan now has a population of 300,000[10] and Kwai Tsing has 600,000. The two districts vary considerably in their characteristics. Tsuen Wan now has very little public housing, but a substantial amount of private housing, ranging from the old shop house buildings, with their nearby markets, in the centre[11] to luxurious estates along the shore. It includes the majority of the native villages in the two districts. Public housing predominates in Kwai Tsing, which includes the Tai Wo Hau Estate. North Lantau is part of the district, but its people live in flats in Tsuen Wan.

According to the district officer, education is important in Tsuen Wan, as exemplified by the Kwan Mun Hau scholarship awards, and there are band one schools in the district. It also includes many amenities: two Country Parks, the Sam Tung Uk Museum, a football field, two swimming pools, and many beaches. She added that people like the convenience of the MTR and the West Rail, that the MTR is important in bringing people together, and that Tsuen Wan, with its markets and malls, is a popular shopping destination on Sundays. Philip Chan also stressed the importance of the MTR, saying that Kwan Mun Hau had prospered because of it. Other government officials said Tsuen Wan's proximity to urban Hong Kong and its convenient rapid transit mean that it has been spared the youth problems that prevail in some other areas of the New Territories, where parents must commute long distances to work, leaving their older children unsupervised.

Tsuen Wan is one of Hong Kong's 18 districts under the District Council system. The majority of the 21 representatives are elected, and they are important in the administration of the district.

---

9. A Yau man in his sixties recently said that theirs is the last generation to speak it.
10. The population has been stable for ten years, according to another official. The district officer said that a new waterfront housing development was expected to bring in about 20,000 more people.
11. We learned from the district officer that the old town centre is unlikely to be redeveloped because this would not be worth the expense.

Likewise, the Rural Committees and Heung Yee Kuk still exist, and, as the district officer said, the rights of the indigenous people are protected and the government listens to them. We met separately with Yau Kam-ping, who said that the Rural Committee now has more than 90 members, as compared to approximately 60 that it had in the past. They continue to manage the Heung Shek Cemetery, and to gather together the remains of the unknown dead of the district, making offerings to them.[12] Rural Committee members who are Christian do not burn incense, but stand respectfully, as they do during the annual Tianhou Festival, which the Rural Committee still sponsors. As was the case earlier, the Rural Committee office site belongs to the Tianhou temple. The District Office continues to provide improvements to the villages, such as Kwan Mun Hau's new playground and the paving around the Baak Gung.

We were extremely fortunate that a meeting of the Tsuen Wan District Council was held while we were there. Anyone is welcome to attend, and simultaneous translation is provided into English, *putonghua*, and Cantonese, according to need. We benefited from excellent translation into English. The district officer provided us with the agenda in advance, and we found the meeting to be an impressive experience, ably and firmly chaired by Chan Iu Seng, and an example of participatory government in contemporary Hong Kong. The agenda items included environmental concerns,[13] support for people with mental health problems, and a variety of transportation issues, including transport noise barriers and aircraft noise. The need for a direct light-rail link between Tsuen Wan and Tuen Mun has been an outstanding concern for some time. Senior officials from the Transport and Housing Bureau and the Highways Department outlined a transportation strategy for Hong Kong, which presently does not include a Tsuen Wan–Tuen Mun rail link. Their broad policy discussion was abruptly terminated by the chair, who asked that senior officials from the Board and Department return to the Council once they had a firm proposal in hand. There followed a 'crime report' by the district commissioner of police, who stated that security and public safety in Tsuen Wan, as in much of Hong Kong, rank high in world terms. Tsuen Wan's problems, such as they were, focused largely on street prostitution and street gambling. The Occupy Central movement, then in its second month, had an effect of draining personnel, and some 200 officers, a third of the complement, had been drafted to address the problems, although they did not affect Tsuen Wan. This had not led to an increase in crime but had hampered the detection rate.

The District Councils invite relevant government officials, as well as those from non-governmental organizations, to make presentations and respond to questions. The presenters typically are high-ranking officials and most of their presentations were comprehensive and relevant. Their presentations may be followed by searching questions from District Council members.

We learned from the assistant district officer that associations in Tsuen Wan continue to exist and grow, despite the fact that most of the residents are no longer impoverished immigrants. Associations are still part of the social fabric, although they appear to have different roles to play than they did a half century ago. The associations of factory owners and the weaving trades are no longer present, nor are most trade unions, although trade and commercial associations, including the venerable Chamber of Commerce, with a changed name, are numerous. Also notable are associations that offer support to vulnerable segments of the population such as the elderly, youth, women, and immigrants. There are large numbers of sports, cultural, and leisure organizations. Religious organizations are overwhelmingly represented by large Hong Kong–wide groups, and the folk religious activities of the past seem less prominent. There are still large numbers of fraternal and fellow-countrymen's associations, including many of long standing. Major additions to the associational inventory are the political party

---

12. He added that all districts have such a place and obligation.
13. This presentation included not only the physical environment and concerns with such matters as waste disposal and recycling, but also air pollution, sea-water odours, heat reflected from glass, and roadside pollution from fumes.

organizations that now exist throughout Hong Kong and make for lively political discourse at the level of the Legislative Council and within the District Council. Another development is the growth of neighbourhood organizations. Some are related to long-standing *kaifong* associations in the old town centre, associations of residents in former squatter areas, or in resettlement estates. Others include residents' associations in the many new housing complexes that have grown up, especially in west Tsuen Wan and along the waterfront. They have become very important in the selection of candidates who stand for election to the District Council. The degree of political participation in the day-to-day affairs of Tsuen Wan is one of the more dramatic changes in daily life when compared to that of the 1960s.

Two memories stand out from our last few days in Tsuen Wan. Late one afternoon, we were walking through a series of malls when a student about 12 years of age spoke with us in excellent English and politely opened doors for us, saying that he could see that we are old. Yes, we thought, this is now true. A day or two later we were talking with Kwan Mun Hau friends over a restaurant lunch and Yau Kam-ping, who was meeting with other leaders at a nearby table, came over and talked with us, ending by saying that we are *jihgeiyahn* (自己人): 'our own people', a spontaneous statement of acceptance that we found to be very moving.

From all that we have learned over the years, it seems that the people of Kwan Mun Hau did have much to celebrate on 9 November 2014. Despite the struggles and privations of earlier times, they have benefited greatly in the past 50 years from their location in the New Territories' first 'new town' and from their agreement to move, as an entire village, to a new site within it. They have insisted on and received security of tenure with regard to their ancestral property, and have maintained this to their great advantage, given their favourable location and openness to having their tenants live among them. Various levels of government have been supportive of the maintenance of their traditions. They can enjoy the many amenities and recreational facilities available in the nearby urban environment. They had good governance from James Hayes, who is still fondly remembered and respected for his work to make Tsuen Wan a better place during very difficult times, and, at the highest level, from Murray MacLehose, in particular, who did so much to make Hong Kong a fairer and more enjoyable home for all of its residents, both pre- and post-1997. They also had and continue to have dedicated leaders at the village level, and their loyalty to them was apparent in their commitment to making the anniversary celebration a success.

We ourselves have benefited greatly from the knowledge that so many Tsuen Wan people, men and women, shared with us. We are grateful for their trust, as foreigners in their midst. They have enriched our lives, and those of our sons. We hope that we have succeeded in recording what we were privileged to learn, 'so that it will not be lost'.[14]

---

14. Paul Siu-kwong Yau, November 2014.

Conclusions

Tsuen Wan in Retrospect

Almost a half century ago, when we first lived in Tsuen Wan and began our investigations, it met our expectations that it would be an appropriate place to explore the complexities of rapid social and economic change. Although we imagined that after our two-year period of research we would in all likelihood never return, we were fortunate that the professions we entered supported and encouraged further research, and that improved, and cheaper, air travel made this possible. We were therefore able to return many times, expanding our knowledge of Tsuen Wan and the depth of our relationships. As a result, we have been able to recount its continued development, as seen from our perspective.

In retrospect, we realize what special opportunities we have had to learn about social relations in Tsuen Wan, past and present. Our perspective extends over more than a century, given that local people shared their memories with us as well as knowledge that they had gained from their elders. They also gave us copies of their historical documents.

Out of all that we learned, certain insights stand out, and we will present them here. These findings are especially valuable for making comparisons not only within Tsuen Wan, but also with other Chinese contexts. When we began our research, the 'Chinese phase' in anthropology and sociology, as well as local historical research, had only just begun. There were very few studies published. Since then, there has been an outpouring of studies, focussed initially on Hong Kong, Taiwan, and the Chinese overseas. From the 1980s, the People's Republic of China became accessible to foreign scholars, and social science there was reborn. Initially, there was little local or comparative information available to us, but it has expanded dramatically since then. We have therefore attempted to place our findings in a wider context.

At first, we focused on the twin forces of industrialization and urbanization that had transformed a largely rural economy. The colonial government was only minimally involved until change was well underway and conditions required urgent attention. Resolution of a number of rapidly worsening problems involved the descendants of the original inhabitants, whose land rights had been acknowledged since Tsuen Wan became part of the British colony. They were key to efforts to achieve a rational and negotiated outcome. Resolution also involved the immigrants, who greatly outnumbered the local Hakka population and, given then-prevalent government assumptions, had very few rights. The nature of colonial governance, the past and continuing indigenous presence, and immigrants' adaptation to drastic change were not issues that we had contemplated before we immersed ourselves in our research, but they quickly became central, and have remained important.

Urbanization in a Chinese historical context was well documented, but industrialization was not. Ours was one of the first attempts to analyse an urban and industrial revolution in both a Chinese and a colonial context. The process was significant for both the local Hakka and the immigrant populations, but in different ways. There was little to guide us regarding its impact on the population of original inhabitants, and only a little more for the immigrants.[1] The significance of voluntary associations, and their links to the Chinese cultural past, was both understandable and astonishing. From the broad literature on industrial and urban change, it was clear that immigrant workers in new contexts created associations to cope with the culturally and socially disruptive forces of migration and industrial employment. When Chinese people moved to cities, in China or abroad, they had a history of forming associations for mutual support. The significance and extent of associations in Tsuen Wan in the 1950s and the 1960s were beyond expectations, but newcomers could not have coped without them.

Colonial governance initially did not seem significant to us, and the literature was generally silent on the topic, remaining so for some time.[2] It quickly became obvious to us that development policy in Tsuen Wan was sensitive to the local Hakka population, but slow to formulate policies concerning immigrant needs and interests. In the late 1960s there were few mechanisms for consultation with the vast majority of the population about matters that concerned them and their well-being. Part of the problem was that Tsuen Wan was in the New Territories, and the system of government had changed very little since its incorporation in 1898. The 1971 census revealed that Tsuen Wan was not only the most populous district in the New Territories, with 41% of the population; it was also the most industrial and the most urban, and contributed disproportionately to Hong Kong's economic advancement. Furthermore, only 4.9% of its population had been born in Hong Kong. The remainder had only fragmentary access to decision-making, and the administration of the district was not dramatically different in nature and scale from when it had been an area of farmers and fishing people, despite the dramatic shifts in its economic character and the composition of its population.

Our initial research was conducted at the end of an era, although in 1970 this was not apparent. The colonial system of governance began to change for a number of reasons,[3] some relating to policy shifts in Britain, others to developments in Hong Kong, and worldwide, in the two decades following the formation of the People's Republic of China. Administrative reform was underway, but was sidetracked by unrest during the summer of 1967, which generated a sense of crisis in the government, a temporary loss of economic confidence, and a stock market collapse. During the early stages of recovery from the economic downturn, the City District Officer scheme was introduced into the urban areas of Hong Kong and Kowloon, in the hope of creating greater public participation in policy formulation.

The period of change under Governor MacLehose was lengthy, comprehensive, and dramatic. The Tsuen Wan experience became a major factor in transforming the role of the New Territories in Hong Kong, and brought a decentralized system of consultation and administration, in the form of District Boards (now District Councils), to all of Hong Kong. Change included advances in education policy and major commitments to new infrastructure, including mass transit and roads. Of long-lasting significance was the fact that the colonial government, in response to policy changes in China, also began to address the issue of the New Territories lease.

In the 35 years after 1980, changes in China's economic policies led to the economic transformation of Tsuen Wan, a transformation as momentous as the three decades of its development after 1950. With one important exception, post-industrial Tsuen Wan is now much like the rest of urban Hong Kong, and closely resembles the rest of the wealthy and globalized territory that has become a Special Administrative Region of China. The exception is the muted presence of the indigenous population which, although now only a tiny proportion, nonetheless remains, as it has elsewhere in the New Territories.

---

1. See, for example, N. J. Smelser, *Social Change in the Industrial Revolution: An Application of Theory to the British Cotton Industry, 1770–1840* (London: Routledge and Kegan Paul, 1959).
2. Likewise, anthropological studies on Taiwan tended to minimize its complex political history.
3. David Faure, *Colonialism and the Hong Kong Mentality* (Hong Kong: Centre of Asian Studies, University of Hong Kong, 2003).

Tsuen Wan has been distinguished by its local people's openness to immigrants, a characteristic that helped to keep it harmonious as it began to experience profound change in the mid-twentieth century. This has proven beneficial to both original inhabitants and to newcomers as they became progressively more interdependent. They have increasingly interacted in education and employment, and, inevitably, local Hakka men have married women of non-Hakka origins. As time has passed, all have been absorbed into the dominant Cantonese language and culture of Hong Kong. In the 1990s we heard a new image used to describe the relationship between them: that the distinctive identity of the original inhabitants was diminishing and fading. They remain an identifiable group within the overall Hong Kong population, because their special rights as original inhabitants are still protected under the Basic Law. This identity becomes visible on those occasions when it is relevant and they choose to make it known, as well as through the presence of their villages, but they otherwise blend into the general population.

Within the local Hakka community, despite the enormity of change taking place in the 1960s and the 1970s, two of the lineages, the Yau of Kwan Mun Hau and Hoi Pa, and the Chan of Kwan Mun Hau and Ham Tin, made the commitment to update, expand, and print their genealogies. They somehow found the time and resources to do so at a time when challenging decisions had to be made concerning their livelihood, their property, and even the location of their villages. These commitments demonstrated loyalty to their lineages, and concern to maintain their identity, as well as the presence of dedicated leaders. It is significant that the lineages of Kwan Mun Hau and its related villages continue to this day, caring for their ancestors through traditional ceremonies, albeit with some simplifications due to the demands and distractions of contemporary life. Their valuable urban trust properties play an important role in this. Other Tsuen Wan lineages also remain, although the Yau and Chan are reputed to be the wealthiest, and the most committed to their traditions. The lineages of Lo Wai are the most distinctive in their adaptation to contemporary change.

Committed local leaders also have been present at the village and district level, helping to guide the original inhabitants through the profound challenges presented by Tsuen Wan's rapid development. Now, in much more prosperous times, such leaders continue to be chosen. In the characteristics of its historic cultural and social system, Tsuen Wan continues to resemble other multi-lineage communities, distinguished by relatively egalitarian and peaceful relations, cooperation, and considerable self-governance by respected leaders. Such communities contrast fundamentally with the powerful and highly competitive single-lineage villages of the New Territories, a fundamental insight first articulated in 1977 by James Hayes in his important comparative model of local political systems.[4]

Among our unanticipated discoveries were those that gave us awareness of types of social relations very different from those now prevailing: relations with, through, and among women. People remembered their existence, or had experienced them in the past, and they are important for comparison with the types of relationships that existed elsewhere. For example, the prevalence of various forms of marriage was a revelation to us, not only marriages made with small daughters-in-law, but also the 'replacement marriage' of a woman with a widowed man, resulting in kinship relations between her and the family of his first wife, with whom she was 'grafted'. The extent of polygyny despite the prevailing poverty, and the possibility of other forms of marriage with more than one woman, living, or in the form of a soul tablet, was also surprising, as were the relationships between bride-giving and bride-receiving lineages expressed by polite forms of address. The importance to young married women of their relationships with their natal families was reinforced in this context. These were expressed by exchanges of special foods that they carried between their natal families and those into which they married, and by their husbands' families hosting theirs for meals.

4. Hayes, *The Hong Kong Region*, 194–201.

We also learned about the strength of the relationships among women, the groups of 'sisters' who, despite the absence of maiden houses, supported each other while working and in the days before marriage. Women continued to create such groups after marriage, while working together outdoors. They shared a tradition of mountain songs and laments that allowed them creative outlets, and the opportunity to express their personal sorrows and grievances. Daughters' laments were also essential in settling the soul of the deceased, to the extent that they were adopted to fill this role if necessary. This tradition was just coming to an end when we first arrived, and we were fortunate to learn of it.

Some of these types of relationships were specifically Hakka, although we have to be careful about making generalizations, as boundaries were not absolute. The inclusiveness of souls' rights to be seated in the ancestral hall is one specific characteristic, through the rites that incorporate the souls of men and women into the single tablet, where they receive offerings and sit contented, and at peace.

Shortly before our initial sojourn in Tsuen Wan, Peter Laslett wrote an important book on the 'lost world' of pre-industrial England, in which he explored the family composition, community structure, and social class relations of that time.[5] In the process he destroyed some myths and brought a past era alive. Likewise, we initially tried to convey something of a world that is now lost, the chaotic industrial working-class town of Tsuen Wan. As we studied the character of the emerging town, and carried the story of its growth and development on to its post-industrial form, we also became increasingly aware of the world that had preceded it. This was the rural Hakka world of pre-industrial Tsuen Wan, with its own distinctive history and social forms, which was to be increasingly subsumed under complex economic, cultural, and social forces. We were privileged to learn of the past, and are conscious of how important it is to preserve these memories, so that present and future generations, who are caught up in very different lifestyles, can be aware of and cherish the contributions of those who preceded them, as we appreciate the contributions of those people who remembered, researched, recorded, preserved, and shared with us their history and their cultural knowledge.

---

5. Peter Laslett, *The World We Have Lost* (London: Methuen, 1965).

Bibliography

A Draft Agreement between the Government of the United Kingdom of Britain and Northern Ireland and the Government of the People's Republic of China on the Future of Hong Kong (Hong Kong: Government Printer, 1984).

Aijmer, Goran, ed. *Leadership on the China Coast*. London: Curzon Press, 1984.

Akers-Jones, David. *Feeling the Stones: Reminiscences by David Akers-Jones*. Hong Kong: Hong Kong University Press, 2004.

Baker, Hugh D. R. *Chinese Family and Kinship*. New York: Columbia University Press, 1979.

Baker, Hugh D. R. *A Chinese Lineage Village: Sheung Shui*. London: Frank Cass Press, 1968.

Baker, Hugh D. R. 'The Five Great Clans of the New Territories'. *Journal of the Hong Kong Branch Royal Asiatic Society* 6 (1966): 25–48.

Baker, Hugh D. R., and S. Feuchtwang, eds. *An Old State in New Settings: Studies in the Social Anthropology of China in Memory of Maurice Freedman*. Oxford: JASO, 1991.

Banton, M. ed. *The Relevance of Models for Social Anthropology*. London: Tavistock, 1965.

Berkowitz, Morris L. 'Plover Cove Village to Taipo Market: A Study in Forced Migration'. *Journal of the Hong Kong Branch Royal Asiatic Society* 8 (1968): 96–108.

Blake, C. Fred. 'Death and Abuse in Marriage Laments: The Curse of Chinese Brides'. *Asian Folklore Studies* 37, no. 1 (1978): 13–33.

Blake, C. Fred. *Ethnic Groups and Social Change in a Chinese Market Town*. Honolulu: University of Hawai'i Press, 1981.

Boxer, Baruch. 'Space, Change, and Fung-Shui in Tsuen Wan's Urbanization'. *Journal of Asian and African Studies* 3, no. 3/4 (July–October 1968): 226–40.

Bristow, Roger. *Hong Kong's New Towns: A Selective Review*. Hong Kong: Oxford University Press, 1989.

Burgess, J. S. *The Guilds of Peking*. New York: Columbia University Press, 1928.

Caldwell, J. C. 'Toward a Restatement of Demographic Transition Theory'. *Population and Development Review* 2, no. 3/4 (September–December 1976): 321–66.

Castells, M., L. Goh, and R. Y.-W. Kwok. *The Shek Kip Mei Syndrome: Economic Development and Public Housing in Hong Kong and Singapore*. London: Pion, 1990.

Census and Statistics Department. *Hong Kong Annual Digest of Statistics* (various years). Hong Kong Government Publications.

Chan, Margaret. *Ritual Is Theatre, Theatre Is Ritual: Tang-ki Chinese Spirit Medium Worship*. Singapore: Singapore Management University Wee Kim Wee Centre, 2006.

Chan, Shui-cheung 陳瑞璋 (compiler). *Special Publication on the Ceremony Commemorating the Restoration of the Tsuen Wan Tianhou Temple 12/12/1984* (荃灣天后宮重修開光典禮特刊一九八四年 (甲子) 十二月十二日).

Chen, Ta. *Emigrant Communities in South China: A Study of Overseas Chinese Migration and Its Influence on Standards of Living and Social Change*. English Version Edited by Bruno Lasker. New York: Secretariat, Institute of Pacific Relations, 1940.

Cheng, Joseph Y. S., ed. *Guangdong: Challenges in Development and Crisis Management*. Hong Kong: City University of Hong Kong Press, 2010.

Cheung, Gary Ka-wai. *Hong Kong's Watershed: The 1967 Riots*. Hong Kong: Hong Kong University Press, 2009.

Chun, Allen. *Unstructuring Chinese Society: The Fictions of Colonial Practice and the Changing Realities of 'Land' in the New Territories of Hong Kong*. Amsterdam: Harwood Academic Publishers, 2000.

Cohen, Myron. *House United, House Divided: The Chinese Family in Taiwan*. New York: Columbia University Press, 1976.

Colonial Secretariat. *A Gazetteer of Place Names in Hong Kong, Kowloon and the New Territories*. Hong Kong: Government Printer, 1960.

Cooper, J. *Colony in Conflict: The Hong Kong Disturbances May 1967–January 1968*. Hong Kong: Swindon Book Company, 1970.

Committee of Hong Kong Kowloon China Compatriots of All Circles for the Struggle against Persecution by the British Authorities in Hong Kong. *The May Uprising*. Hong Kong: n.p., 1967.

Committee of Hong Kong Kowloon China Compatriots of All Circles for the Struggle against Persecution by the British Authorities in Hong Kong. *We Shall Win! British Imperialism Will Be Defeated*. Hong Kong: n.p., 1967.

Constable, Nicole. *Christian Souls and Chinese Spirits: A Hakka Community in Hong Kong*. Berkeley: University of California Press, 1994.

Constable, Nicole, ed. *Guest People: Hakka Identity in China and Abroad*. Seattle: University of Washington Press, 1996.

Constable, Nicole. *Maid to Order in Hong Kong: Stories of Migrant Workers*. Ithaca, NY: Cornell University Press, 2007.

Crissman, L. W. 'The Segmentary Structure of Urban Overseas Chinese Communities'. *Man (NS)* 2, no. 2 (June 1967): 185–204.

de Rome, F. J., N. Evans, and E. C. Thomas. *Notes on the New Territories of Hong Kong*. Hong Kong: Ye Olde Printerie, 1937.

Dwyer, D. J., and Lai Chuen-yan. *The Small Industrial Unit in Hong Kong: Patterns and Policies*. Hull: University of Hull Press, 1967.

Faure, David. *Colonialism and the Hong Kong Mentality*. Hong Kong: Centre of Asian Studies, University of Hong Kong, 2003.

Faure, David, James Hayes, and Alan Birch, eds. *From Village to City: Studies in the Traditional Roots of Hong Kong Society*. Hong Kong: Centre of Asian Studies, University of Hong Kong, 1984.

Faure, David. 'Notes on the History of Tsuen Wan'. *Journal of the Hong Kong Branch Royal Asiatic Society* 24 (1984): 46–104.

Faure, David. *The Structure of Chinese Rural Society: Lineage and Village in the Eastern New Territories, Hong Kong*. Hong Kong: Oxford University Press, 1986.

Freedman, Maurice. *Chinese Lineage and Society: Fukien and Kwangtung*. London: Athlone Press, 1965.

Freedman, Maurice. 'A Chinese Phase in Social Anthropology'. *The British Journal of Sociology* 14, no. 1 (March 1963): 1–19.

Freedman, Maurice, ed. *Family and Kinship in Chinese Society*. Stanford: Stanford University Press, 1970.

Freedman, Maurice. 'Immigrants and Associations: Chinese in Nineteenth-Century Singapore'. *Comparative Studies in Society and History* 3, no. 1 (1960): 25–48.

Freedman, Maurice. *Lineage Organization in Southeastern China*. London: Athlone Press, 1958.

Freedman, Maurice. 'A Report on Social Research in the New Territories' (mimeo, 1963). Republished in the *Journal of the Hong Kong Branch Royal Asiatic Society* 16 (1976): 191–261.

Freedman, Maurice. 'Shifts of Power in the Hong Kong New Territories'. *Journal of Asian and African Studies* 1, no. 1 (1966): 3–12.

Hayes, James. *Friends and Teachers: Hong Kong and Its People 1953–87*. Hong Kong: Hong Kong University Press, 1996.

Hayes, James. *The Great Difference: Hong Kong's New Territories and Its People 1898–2004*. Hong Kong: Hong Kong University Press, 2006.

Hayes, James. *The Hong Kong Region 1850–1911: Institutions and Leadership in Town and Countryside*. Hamden, CT: Archon Books, The Shoestring Press, 1977.

Hayes, James. *The Hong Kong Region 1850–1911: Institutions and Leadership in Town and Countryside with a new introduction*. Hong Kong: Hong Kong University Press, 2012.

Hayes, James. 'A Mixed Community of Cantonese and Hakka on Lantau Island', *Aspects of Social Organization in the New Territories, Royal Asiatic Society Hong Kong Branch Weekend Symposium*, 9–10 May 1964: 21–26.

Hayes, James. 'The Old Popular Culture of China and Its Contribution to Stability in Tsuen Wan'. *Journal of the Hong Kong Branch Royal Asiatic Society* 30 (1990): 1–25.

Hayes, James. 'The Pattern of Life in the New Territories in 1898'. *Journal of the Hong Kong Branch Royal Asiatic Society* 2 (1962): 75–102.

Hayes, James. *The Rural Communities of Hong Kong: Studies and Themes*. Hong Kong: Oxford University Press, 1983.

Hayes, James 'Sandalwood Mills at Tsuen Wan', *Journal of the Hong Kong Branch Royal Asiatic Society* 16 (1976): 282–83.

Hayes, James. *South China Village Culture*. Hong Kong: Oxford University Press, 2001.

Hayes, James. *Tsuen Wan: Growth of a New Town and Its People*. Hong Kong: Oxford University Press, 1993.

Hayes, James. 'A Village War'. *Journal of the Hong Kong Branch Royal Asiatic Society* 17 (1977): 185–98.

Ho, Chuen-yiu 何傳耀. Quanwan Fazhan Shilu 荃灣發展實錄 [An Outline History of the Development of Tsuen Wan], Wah-kiu Yat-po 華僑日報 (Hong Kong, 7–9 July, 1969).

Ho, Ping-ti 何炳棣. *Zhongguo Huiguan Shilun* 中國會館史論 [Historical materials on Chinese Landsmannschaften]. Taipei: Taiwan Xuesheng Shuju 台灣學生書局, 1966.

Hong Kong Government. *Commissioner of Labour Annual Report 1948/49*. Hong Kong Government Publications, 1949.

Hong Kong Government. *Hong Kong Government Annual Report 1947*. Hong Kong: Ye Olde Printerie, 1948.

Hong Kong Government. *Hong Kong Government Annual Report* (various years). Hong Kong: Government Publications.

Hong Kong Government. *Hong Kong Government Report of the Riots in Kowloon and Tsuen Wan, October 10th to October 12th 1956*. Hong Kong: Government Publications, 1956.

Hong Kong Government. *Hong Kong Government Report of the Working Party on Local Administration*. Hong Kong: Government Publications, 1967.

Hong Kong Government. *New Territories Administration, Annual Report* (various years). Hong Kong: Government Publications.

Hopkins, Keith, ed. *Hong Kong: The Industrial Colony: A Political, Social, and Economic Survey*. Hong Kong: Oxford University Press, 1971.

Jarvie, Ian, and Joseph Agassi, eds. *Hong Kong: A Society in Transition*. London: Routledge, 1969.

Jaschok, Maria, and Suzanne Miers, eds. *Women and Chinese Patriarchy: Submission, Servitude, and Escape*. Hong Kong: Hong Kong University Press, 1994.

Johnson, David, Andrew J. Nathan, and Evelyn S. Rawski, eds. *Popular Culture in Late Imperial China*. Berkeley: University of California Press, 1985.

Johnson, Elizabeth L. '"Patterned Bands" in the New Territories of Hong Kong'. *Journal of the Hong Kong Branch Royal Asiatic Society* 16 (1976): 81–91.

Johnson, Elizabeth L. *Recording a Rich Heritage: Research on Hong Kong's 'New Territories'*. Hong Kong: Leisure and Cultural Services Department, 2000.

Johnson, Graham E. 'Leaders and Leadership in an Expanding New Territories Town'. *The China Quarterly* (March 1977): 109–25.

Johnson, Graham E. 'Voluntary Associations and Social Change: Some Theoretical Issues'. *International Journal of Comparative Sociology* 16, no. 1–2 (March–June 1975): 51–63.

King, Ambrose Y. C., and Rance P. L. Lee. *Social Life and Development in Hong Kong*. Hong Kong: Chinese University Press, 1984.

Kwok, R., and A. So, eds. *The Hong Kong–Guangdong Link: Partnership in Flux*. Armonk, NY: M. E. Sharpe, 1994.

Lai, Chun-yan. 'Some Geographical Aspects of the Industrial Development in Hong Kong'. Unpublished MA thesis, University of Hong Kong, 1963.

Lary, Diana. *China's Civil War: A Social History 1945–1949*. Cambridge: Cambridge University Press, 2015.

Laslett, Peter. *The World We Have Lost*. London: Methuen, 1965.

Lethbridge, H. J. 'A Chinese Voluntary Association in Hong Kong: The Po Leung Kuk'. *Journal of Oriental Studies* 10, no. 1 (January 1972): 32–50.

Li, Chen-hua 李振華. *Jindai Bimi Shehui Shilu* 近代秘密社會實錄 [True narrative of contemporary secret societies]. Taipei: Wenhai chubanshe 文海出版社, 1965.

Lin, Yueh-hua. *The Golden Wing: A Study of Chinese Familism*. New York: Oxford University Press, 1947.

Moore, Gerald, ed. *Tsuen Wan Township: Study Group Report on its Development*. Hong Kong: Hong Kong University Press, 1959.

Morgan, J. P. *Triad Societies in Hong Kong*. Hong Kong: Government Press, 1960.

Morse, Hosea B. *The Gilds of China: With an Account of the Gild Merchant or Co-Hong of Canton*. New York: Longmans Green, 1909.

Nissim, Roger. *Land Administration and Practice in Hong Kong*. 3rd ed. Hong Kong: Hong Kong University Press, 2012.

Palmer, Michael J. E. 'The Surface-Subsoil Form of Divided Ownership in Later Imperial China: Some Examples from the New Territories of Hong Kong'. *Modern Asian Studies* 21, no. 1 (1987): 1–119.

Potter, Jack M. *Capitalism and the Chinese Peasant: Social and Economic Changes in a Hong Kong Village*. Berkeley and Los Angeles: University of California Press, 1968.

Pratt, Jean. 'Emigration and Unilineal Descent Groups: A Study of Marriage in a Hakka Village in the New Territories of Hong Kong'. *The Eastern Anthropologist* 13, no. 4 (1960): 147–58.

Salaff, Janet W. *Working Daughters of Hong Kong: Filial Piety or Power in the Family?* New York: Cambridge University Press, 1981.

Schlegel, G. *Thian Ti Hwui: The Hung League or Heaven and Earth League*. Batavia: Lange & Co., 1866.

Scott, Ian. *Political Change and the Crisis of Legitimacy in Hong Kong*. Honolulu: University of Hawai'i Press, 1989.

Sinn, Elizabeth. *Power and Charity: A Chinese Merchant Elite in Hong Kong (with a New Preface)*. Hong Kong: Hong Kong University Press, 2003.

Skinner, G. William. *Leadership and Power in the Chinese Community of Thailand*. Ithaca, NY: Cornell University Press, 1958.

Smelser, Neil J. *Social Change in the Industrial Revolution: An Application of Theory to the British Cotton Industry*. London: Routledge and Kegan Paul, 1959.

Snow, Philip. *The Fall of Hong Kong: Britain, China and the Japanese Occupation*. New Haven: Yale University Press, 2003.

Sparks, D. W. 'Interethnic Interaction—A Matter of Definition: Ethnicity in a Housing Estate in Hong Kong'. *Journal of the Hong Kong Branch Royal Asiatic Society* 16 (1976): 57–80.

Sparks, D. W. 'The Teochiu Ethnicity in Urban Hong Kong'. *Journal of the Hong Kong Branch Royal Asiatic Society* 16 (1976): 25–56.

State Statistical Bureau. *Guangdong Statistical Yearbook, 2008*. Beijing Statistical Bureau Press, 2009.

Stafford, Charles, ed. *Living with Separation in China: Anthropological Accounts*. London: RoutledgeCurzon, 2003.

Stone, Linda. *Kinship and Gender: An Introduction*. Boulder, CO: Westview Press, 2014.

Strauch, Judith. 'Community and Kinship in Southeastern China: The View from the Multilineage Communities of Hong Kong'. *Journal of Asian Studies* 43, no. 1 (November 1983): 21–50.

Sung, Hok-p'ang. 'Tsin-Fuk (being an account of how part of the coast of South China was cleared of inhabitants from the 1st year of Hong Hei [Kangxi] until the 8th year of Hong Hei)'. *Hong Kong Naturalist* 9, no. 1–2 (1938): 37–42.

Topley, Marjorie. 'The Emergence and Social Function of Chinese Religious Associations in Singapore'. *Comparative Studies in Society and History* 3, no. 3 (1961): 289–314.

Topley, Marjorie, ed. *Hong Kong: The Interaction of Tradition and Life in the Towns*. Hong Kong: Royal Asiatic Society Hong Kong Branch, 1975.

Topley, Marjorie, ed. *Some Traditional Ideas and Conceptions in Hong Kong Social Life Today*. Hong Kong: Royal Asiatic Society Hong Kong Branch, 1966.

Tsang, Steve, ed. *A Documentary History of Hong Kong: Government and Politics*. Hong Kong: Hong Kong University Press, 1995.

Vogel, Ezra. *One Step Ahead in China: Guangdong Under Reform*. Cambridge, MA: Harvard University Press, 1989.

Ward, Barbara E. 'Not Merely Players: Drama, Art, and Ritual in Traditional China'. *Man (NS)* 14, no. 1 (1979): 18–39.

Ward, Barbara E. *Through Other Eyes: Essays in Understanding 'Conscious Models'*. Hong Kong: Chinese University Press, 1985.

Ward, J. S. M., and H. G. Stirling. *The Hung Society or the Society of Heaven and Earth*. London: Baskerville Press, 1925.

Watson, James L. *Emigration and the Chinese Lineage: The Mans in Hong Kong and London*. Berkeley: University of California Press, 1975.

Watson, James L., and Evelyn S. Rawski, eds. *Death Ritual in Late Imperial and Modern China*. Berkeley: University of California Press, 1988.

Watson, James L., and Rubie S. Watson. *Village Life in Hong Kong*. Hong Kong: Chinese University Press, 2004.

Willmott, Donald E. *The Chinese of Semarang: A Changing Minority Community in Indonesia*. Ithaca, NY: Cornell University Press, 1960.

Willmott, William E. 'Congregations and Associations: The Political Structure of the Chinese Community in Phnom-Penh, Cambodia'. *Comparative Studies in Society and History* 11, no. 3 (1969): 282–301.

Willmott, William E., ed. *Economic Organization in Chinese Society*. Stanford: Stanford University Press, 1972.

Wolf, Arthur P., and Chieh-shan Hwang. *Marriage and Adoption in China, 1845–1945*. Stanford: Stanford University Press, 1980.

Wolf, Arthur P., ed. *Religion and Ritual in Chinese Society*. Stanford: Stanford University Press, 1974.

Xie, Li Tao 謝李陶, ed. *Jinri Quanwan* 今日荃灣 [Modern Tsuen Wan]. Kowloon: Xinjie wenhua fuwu chubanshe 新界文化服務出版社, 1965.

Yang, Ching-kun. *Religion in Chinese Society*. Berkeley: University of California Press, 1959.

Index

Heung Yee Kuk, 12, 127, 135, 147, 149, 149n13, 151, 152, 152n17, 178, 203

Ho Chuen-yiu, 20n13, 135

Hoi Pa village, *23 map 2*, 81

Hongshenggong, 24, 33n52, 47, *200 plate 60*

Ho Pui village, *23 map 2*, 24, 31, 34, 35, 84, 87n6, 106, 193n39

household division, 15, 101–2

household size, 100–101

housing policy: 3, 5, 76, 78, 79–80, 79n4, 86–88, 102, 123, 127, 156, 159–60, 164, *165 plate 43*, 171; housing for sons, 176, 193, 193n39, 201, 202

Ho Wing-kwong, 19, 23, 24n25, 29, 31, 31n47, 38n72, 173, 175

huapai, *140 plate 41*, 142, 142n1, *143 plate 42*, 191, *192 plate 53*, 197, *198 plate 56*

immigrants: before 1941, 19, 21, 31–32, 47, 98n35, 114n6, 140n31; after 1945, 4, 9, 11–13, 15, 76, 78, 82–83, 88, 107, 109, 110–14, 120–21, 125, 127–29, 134–35, 137, 141, 144–46, 148–49, 151–54, 158, 167, 175–76, 178–184, *178 plate 47*, 203, 205–7

incense: mills 19, 20, *23 map 2*, 41, 42; production, 77, *77 plate 15*

indigenous people. *See* original inhabitants

industrial development: 1930s, 20–21; 1950s–1980s, 3–5, 11, 14, 75–83, 85, 116, 145, 149–50, 162–64, 171, 205

infrastructural development, 11, 155–57, 159, 164–66, 166n23, 171, 174–75, 206

Japanese occupation, 18, 25–26, 29, 43, 72–74

Jarvie, Ian, 14n16

jouh seh, 33, 40

Jubilee reservoir. *See* Shing Min reservoir

Justices of the Peace, 147

Kau Wai Kung, 19n21, 24, 47, 84n1, 189, *200 plate 59*, 201n3

Kau Wa Keng village, 10, *23 map 2*

Kau Wa New Village, 10, 134

Kwai Chung, 10, 26, 32, *54 plate 14*, 60, 66, 69, 71, 82, 106, 134n27, 157, 159–60, 164, 176, 201

Kwai Chung container terminal, 157, 159, 164

Kwai Chung road, 157

Kwai Tsing District, 159, 164, 202

Kwan Mun Hau village, 10–18, 20, 22–23, 23 *map 2*, 24, *28 plate 9*, 31, 33, 42, 44, 46–47, 52, 72, 84–110, *85 plates 21–22*, *90 plate 23*, *99 plates 24–25*, *104 plate 24*, *105 plates 29–31*, *165 plate 43*, 173, 176, 184–96, *188 plate 50*, *190 plates 51–52*, *192 plates 53–55*, 197–202, *198 plate 56*, *199 plates 57–58*, *200 plates 59–60*

Kwok Yung-hing, 16, 36, 64

Kwun Tong, 80, 82, 82n30

lantern-raising, 37–38, 48–49, 54, 92, 104–6, *104 plate 28*, *105 plate 29–31*, 186–87, 189, 201

leaders and leadership, 11, 15, 46, 106, 110, 118, 121, 127, 134–35, 142–54, *143 plate 42*, 174–76, 179, 196, 204, 207

leisure, 21, 89, 90–91, 122, 126–27, 169, 191, 195–96, 201n6, 202

Lethbridge, Henry J., 148n9

lineages, 14–16, 23–24, 27, 29, 34–38, 40–49, 53, 57, 60, 63–64, 64n36, 69–71, 73, 84, 87–88, 93, 95, 97, 100, 102–10, *103 plates 26–27*, *104 plate 28*, *105 plates 29–31*, 125, 146, 150–51, 174–75, 184, 186–89, *188 plate 50*, *190 plates 51–52*, 193, 196, 198, 201–2, 207

Longgang (Bao'an), 36, 140n35

Lo Wai village, 9, 22, *23 map 2*, 32, 41, 46, 106, 124–25, 127n20, 169, 176, 200

MacLehose, Sir Murray, 148, 155–56, 155n1, 161, 204, 206

Manufacturers' Association, 119–20, 144, 203

markets: 7–8, *7 plate 3*, 9, 19n2, 20–21, 23–24, 26–27, 31–32, 31n47, 47, 89, 125, 156, 191, 201–2; daily coastal market, 20, 20n8, 22; marketing 112

marriage: age at, 5; area, 36; arrangements, 55–56, 58, 63, 207; blind, 55, 58; changes after Japanese occupation, 58, 98, 118; dowry, 25, 99, *100 plate 24*; forms, 20, 36, 55–61, 207; laments, 18, 53, 53n14, 56–57, 56n20, 60, 66, 98, 207; polygynous, 60, 207; relationships through, 35–36, 45, 99, 102, 207; replacement, 31, 36, 58, 63, 207; rites, 38, 46, 56–57, 59, 94, 98–100, *98 plates 24–25*, 187–88, *188 plate 50*; small daughter-in-law (*sanpouhjai*) 58, 58n27, 59, 59n29, 60, 66, 207; teasing of bride, 57–58; terminology, 55; uxorilocal, 29–30, 30n43; welfare benefits after, 112, 116, 116n10, 122, 201; with non-Hakka women, 30, 98

martial arts. *See* boxing associations

martyrs. *See* conflict

Mass Transit Railway (MTR): 44, 85 *plate 22*, 157, 201n4; associated property development, 166, *167 plate 44*; benefits of, 159–60, 166, 169, 176, 202; clearances, 157, 159, 159n12, 175–76, *177 plates 45–46*, 180